Listening to the Future

The Series in Contemporary Music

Volume 2

By the same author:

Matrix and line:
   Derrida and the possibilities of postmodern social theory

Humanism and its aftermath:
   The shared fate of deconstruction and politics

Politics in the impasse:
   Explorations in postsecular social theory

music of Yes:
   structure and vision in progressive rock

Listening to the Future

The time of progressive rock, 1968–1978

Bill Martin

Open Court
Chicago and La Salle, Illinois

Photo of Robert Fripp courtesy S. Morley/Redferns.
Photo of Jethro Tull courtesy David Redfern/Redferns.

Copyright © 1998 by Carus Publishing Company

First printing 1998

Printed and bound in the United States of America.

Library of Congress Cataloging-in-Publication Data

Martin, Bill, 1956-
    Listening to the future: the time of progressive rock, 1968-1978
/Bill Martin.
        p.   cm.—(Feedback: v. 2)
    Includes discography, bibliographical references,
and index.
    ISBN 0-8126-9368-X (pbk.: alk. paper)
    1. Progressive rock music—History and criticism.   I. Title.
II. Series: Feedback (Chicago, Ill.); v. 2.
ML3534.M412 1998
781.66—dc21   97-36495
                                                              CIP
                                                              MN

For my mother and father,
Eve and Gene Martin

The past carries with it a temporal index by which it is referred to redemption. There is a secret agreement between past generations and the present one. Our coming was expected on earth. Like every generation that preceeded us, we have been endowed with a *weak* Messianic power, a power to which the past has a claim. That claim cannot be settled cheaply.

A chronicler who recites events without distinguishing between major and minor ones acts in accordance with the following truth: nothing that has ever happened should be regarded as lost for history. To be sure, only a redeemed humankind receives the fullness of its past—which is to say, only for a redeemed humankind has its past become citable in all its moments. Each moment it has lived becomes a *citation à l'ordre du jour*—and that day is Judgment Day.

The soothsayers who found out from time what it had in store certainly did not experience time as either homogenous or empty. Anyone who keeps this in mind will perhaps get an idea of how past times were experienced in remembrance—namely, just in the same way. We know that the Israelites were prohibited from investigating the future. The Torah and the prayers instruct them in remembrance, however. This stripped the future of its magic, to which all those succumb who turn to the soothsayers for enlightenment. This does not imply, however, that for the Israelites the future turned into homogenous, empty time. For every second of time was the strait gate through which the Messiah might enter.

Walter Benjamin, from "Theses on the Philosophy of History"

Contents

Acknowledgments   ix

Preface: Future anterior   xi

Chapter one: Introduction: Seize again the day   1

Chapter two: The prehistory of progressive rock:
Generosity and synthesis   21

Chapter three: The time of progressive rock: Toward a
theory   55

Chapter four: Sent through the rhythm: A guided
discography   150

Emergence, 1968–1969   162

1968   162
1969   171

Apogee, 1970–1974   177

1970   177
1971   190
1972   205
1973   215
1974   227

Trials and transformations, 1975–1978   233

1975   234
1976   239
1977   241
1978   243

Sixty-two essential albums   245

Chapter five: After the time of progressive rock,
1977–1997   247

Afterword: Zeitgeist: Sea change or heart murmur?   299

Appendix: Resources   307

Notes   311

Additional discography   330

Bibliography   332

Index   337

Acknowledgments

As with my earlier *music of Yes*, *Listening to the future* was also written as a labor of love. I want to offer heartfelt thanks to everyone who helped with this project. This includes a rather long list of friends both old and new, who shared with me their ideas about music—sometimes without knowing it: Jim Abraham, Alison Brown, Kevin Condatore, Al Cinelli, Billy Chapman, John Covach, Andrew Cutrofello, John Collinge, Glen Di Crocco, Jim DeRogatis, Martin Donougho, David Detmer, Sarah Dowless, Zane Edge, Lydia Eloff, Nina Frankel, Aaron Fichtelburg, Henry Frame, Miller Francis, Diana Fuss, Stephen Gardner, Mark Giordano, Tom Greif, Brett Gover, Lewis Gordon, Peter Gunther, Stephen Houlgate, Patricia Huntington, Craig Hanks, Christine Holz, Joanie Jurysta James, Leslie Jones, Tony Kirven, Nick Kokoshis, Dana Lawrence, Michael Lind, Raymond Lotta, Chris Mitchell, Tina McRee, Brad Merriman, Edward Macan, Brenda MacDonald, Lisa Mikita, Innes Mitchell, Sam Martin, John Martin, Lynne Margolies, Thomas and Coral Mosbo, Clay Morgan, Todd May, Martin Matustik, Kate Murphy, David Orsini, Jeff Rice, Garry Rindfuss, Jane Scarpontoni, Dale Smoak, Chelsea Snelgrove, Gary Shapiro, Catrina Thundercloud, George Trey, Jerry Wallulis, Cynthia Willett, Deena Weinstein, and Robert Young.

For their friendship and encouragement, I would like to thank my colleagues in the philosophy department at DePaul University: Ken Alpern, Peg Birmingham, Cindy Kaffen, Daryl Koehn, David Krell, Niklaus Largier, Mary Jeanne Larrabee, Will McNeil, Darrell Moore, Michael Naas, Angelica Nuzzo, David Pellauer, and Katherine Rudolph.

Thanks to the people at Open Court Publishing for their support of this project, especially my ever-patient editor, Kerri Mommer.

I have the great fortune to be married to the African Japanese queen of Kansas, Bascenji. Thanks, my Yoko and SdB, my dear Kathleen, standing by your vinegar boy and guttersnipe even under conditions of dark existentialism.

Finally, for giving me life and for giving me much in life, this book is dedicated to my parents, Eve and Gene Martin.

Preface: Future anterior

A funny thing happened on the way to the forum. About a year-and-a-half ago, I felt sure that I was coming to the end of writing the first book-length study of the music of Yes. Then it came to my attention that a fellow Yesologist named Thomas Mosbo had just published a book on the group, *Yes, but what does it all mean?* Still, finishing *music of Yes* in the late spring of 1996 (the book came out in October of that year), and turning to the writing of the book you are reading now, I gave in once more to a feeling of certainty, namely to the idea that I was writing the first intellectually oriented study of the larger field of progressive rock.

Foiled again! Indeed, at a bookstore party for the release of *music of Yes*, my graduate assistant, Aaron Fichtelberg, came up to me and said, "Hey, have you seen this?" He was holding Edward Macan's *Rocking the Classics*. As many readers will know, the book features a concert photograph of Yes on its cover. Zeit-geist or what? As a matter of fact, I fervently hope so.

About six months later, as I was entering into the final stages of writing this book, I happen to see an advertisement in *The Wire*. (This is an English magazine, by the way, that often attacks progressive rock in terms that, by now, are all too well known to readers. Well, *The Wire* and other nemeses of progressive receive some well-deserved lashings in what follows.) I purchased that particular issue of the magazine to read an interview with Chris Cutler, percussionist and composer with Henry Cow—one of the greats, in my view. (The interview is discussed in chapter 3.) Then what should I come across but an advert for yet another book on progressive rock, Paul Stump's *The Music's All That Matters*. Having the advantage of intense insomnia, and therefore almost always being awake in the middle of the night, I called over to London to order the book. It arrived perhaps ten days later (as it turned out, the book was released on the day I called), and, on first glance, the book looks pretty doggone good.

So, not the first book on Yes, but the second; and not the first book on progressive rock, but perhaps the third—depending on what happens between now and October.

I engage with Edward Macan's book throughout, but especially in my third chapter. For the sake of deadlines and continuities, I could tell that it would be fatal to try to read Paul Stump's book as I was completing this one. Still, as a scholar and theorist, I am committed to taking account of and building on the work of others, and giving credit where it's due; in addition, at least my place in the order of publication gives me the opportunity to address what I think is an important question anyway, namely the Zeitgeist. Therefore, I come back to these issues in the afterword.

I am happy to see that others are taking up the cause of progressive rock in a systematic way, and I don't see any need to inject any element of competition into this field. Progressive rock is important enough to me, and I daresay to my fellow authors Macan and Stump, and to those who have sympathetically followed the music in these past decades, that three or five or ten books does not exhaust the field. Indeed, with this book and the books by Macan and Stump, there is finally the start of a basis for a much better discussion of what progressive rock is all about, and one can only hope that *this* discussion will be extended further. Clearly, too, there is a need for more work on the oeuvres of particular groups and artists, and I hope that, both as a theorist and as the series editor of "Feedback: The Series in Contemporary Music," I can play a part in helping such work come to fruition.

There are, however, some important differences between the books by Macan, Stump, and myself. Perhaps the reader will find it useful, here at the outset, if I lay out the basic differences in approach and say what mine is. (The books also differ in *perspective*, but this is best dealt with in the larger body of the text.)

Quite simply, Edward Macan is a musicologist by academic training and profession, Paul Stump is a music journalist whose aim is to tell the history of progressive rock (as his subtitle has it), while I am a philosopher and social theorist. What we have in common, among other things, is an interest in situating the music in terms of history, society, and culture (and even, what Macan has so brilliantly placed in the center of debate, counterculture). The kind of musicology practiced by Macan is not of the purely formal sort practiced by some, but instead a dynamic intertwining of study of musical form and cultural analysis and critique. Stump is also interested in form, but perhaps more in culture and history.

On one level, my approach is similar to Macan's. In my book on the music of Yes, I attempted to bring the discussion of musical structure and philosophical vision into a unity or synthesis. However, reading *Rocking the Classics* during the early stages of writing *Listening to the future* helped me to further sharpen my sense of what I'm trying to do.

I'm not a musicologist. When it comes to that specialized field and its language, I pick up as much as I can on the fly, as it were. On some level, I'm even quite willing to admit that, as far as analysis of musical structure goes, I'm "faking it." That is, when it seems necessary to use some bit of technical language for something that is happening in the music, I just dig out one of the technical books I have on the subject and look it up. On the whole, however, I do not find the use of such language to be a very fruitful way to communicate either my own intellectual interest in music or with others who are interested in progressive rock. (I'm not saying that this language isn't fruitful for other purposes.) In other words, I could try to supply terms such as "retrograde inversion" (and sometimes I do), but then I would be addressing another audience than the one I am interested in. In fact, I wrote *music of Yes* and *Listening to the future* hoping to break out of the purely academic scene.

On the other hand, I think that it is appropriate to attempt to stretch what is meant by "analysis of musical form," and to not allow this to be only the domain of academic musicology. It is true that, when I discuss the formal qualities of a piece of music, I tend to appeal to analogies, images, and narrative frameworks. (There was a line in *music of Yes* about "the persistent afterglow of several tenor saxophones spreading in different directions like the opening of a flower that has petals the size and consistency of elephant's ears." That's stretching things a bit, I know, but I also could say, "you had to be there"—namely at the end of "Then" from *Time and a Word*—and then it all makes perfect sense.) That is, I am interested in the many experiences (including nonmusical) that the piece is drawing from, and in what picture is painted, what story is told. I'm also interested in how the sounds and silences combine and unfold. In my view, this approach has both its strengths and its limitations, but that is also why it is good that the discussion around progressive rock is finally taking off and that books are being published from a number of perspectives. The music certainly seems big enough, to me, to warrant a diversity of studies and perspectives.

I also try to bring to this book the perspective of a musician who has performed in various rock, jazz, and avant-garde contexts for twenty-five years. I am not a "schooled" musician, but, on some level I "know" what I'm doing—and I think I have some sense of what other musicians are doing as well.

The analogies and other ways of getting at the form of the music serve an instrumental function in my work. My larger aim is to develop the philosophy and social theory of progressive rock. As far as philosophy goes, then, I am interested in what might be called "musical ideas." Progressive rock is a fertile territory for such exploration—indeed, progressive rock is most likely rock music's first real "music of ideas." The very idea of "musical ideas" works on several levels, from the more purely formal to those places where it is difficult to distinguish "music" from "philosophy" (or "thought," "theory," etc.). If we were to ask what Beethoven's "idea" was in the Ninth Symphony, we might give an answer in terms of the Western musical canon and the possibilities of an expansion of the harmonic universe, or we might answer in terms of the Enlightenment, ethical and political universalism, and brotherhood. I'm interested in how it all comes together. These notions are explored further in the third chapter.

In social theory, my aim is perhaps different than what the reader might at first expect. Of course I am interested in understanding the "role of music in society," and therefore I offer an extended historical and cultural perspective on progressive rock, especially in the second and third chapters. But, even more, I am interested in the way that the "aesthetic" is a crucial and essential dimension of human life—and not just as entertainment, but as "world disclosure" and as dream of another world. Great art engages in "poiesis," the creation of worlds. It seems clear to me that progressive rock aspires to this and, at least in the best work, contributes to such creation. This is where the division between "politics" and "art" breaks down, for it is obviously a "political" act to imagine a world—even if that world contains little of, or even seems to negate, what counts as "politics" in our world. These themes are explored in the first chapter.

This is, then, a book of arguments. I would be happy if it could be placed alongside books such as Macan's *Rocking the Classics* and Theodore Gracyk's *Rhythm and Noise* (which I take up in the second and third chapters), books that attempt to deal with rock music in a systematic way, dealing with the music and its ideas and culture, rather than primarily with personalities and biographies. Go to your local bookstore and look at the section on rock music, and you will find that such books are few and far between. It may be that most rock music cannot really sustain such argumentation (and I am not saying that there is something necessarily wrong with rock biographies); but some rock music clearly can, and progressive rock is in that category.

The arguments found here are sometimes a tangled weave, often quite polemical, sometimes defensive, often presented with the idea of going on the offensive. (Certainly the latter is seen well enough in the title of the first chapter.) Indeed, the arguments here are often sprawling and sometimes seem to go far afield of the subject of progressive rock. The tangle and sprawl might even be seen as mimicking much progressive rock. My aim is not to excuse flabby argumentation or thinking that is too diffuse; however, I hope that the reader will see that it is a strength of progressive rock that it can be part of a wide-ranging discussion of philosophy, culture, and society. In our present period of fragmentation and overspecialization, it is difficult to find much that could really be called a "culture"—which is why one trend in recent political thought is geared toward a revival of "tradition" (not only in art, but in "family values," etc.). As far as the West is concerned, it seems to me a fact of great significance that the last "culture" we have seen where ideas freely circulated between art, politics, and theory, was the sixties counterculture—and progressive rock was a part of that scene. Since then, unless one goes in for neotraditionalism (the political basis of which is highly suspect), it has been a difficult uphill battle to find a way to keep trends in art, politics, and philosophy from simply carving out their own little niches and staying there.

Perhaps another way of stating this theme, and of showing readers my larger perspective, is to say that my largest interest in this music and its associated ideas and politics is indeed emancipatory and utopian. In other words, my interest and perspective is of a piece with the countercultural politics of the sixties. Although there are certain aspects of the more academic discussions that are useful in understanding progressive rock (or the sixties counterculture, for that matter), a *purely* academic discussion seems quite pointless to me.

There was a great deal of discussion between my editor, Kerri Mommer, and myself regarding the title of this book. In fact, this is the first of my books to have a title that I did not come up with entirely on my own. My original proposal, speaking of academic perspectives, had been what is now the book's subtitle. I think that what we ultimately chose for the title captures very well what progressive rock has tried to do; yet the title also provides a different, perhaps complementary, perspective to Edward Macan's main title, *Rocking the Classics*. The question arises, however, whether the future that progressive rock musicians were listening to is in any sense still "the future"? In a BBC special on the music of Yes that was aired around 1971 (around the time that *Fragile* was released), Jon Anderson spoke somewhat dramatically to the possibilities that were being opened up by progressive rock. He said something to the effect that, as much as the music might seem advanced and adventurous, he was looking forward to seeing (hearing) how much further along music would be in another ten or twenty years. Quite clearly, Anderson was listening to the future. But it would be difficult to argue that the future he was listening to, or perhaps "for," has come to pass.

Indeed, I would invite the reader to take a look, at the outset, at pages 245 and 246. These pages contain a partial list of the progressive rock albums dealt with here (primarily in chapter four) and also other important rock (and a few jazz) albums that were released in the years 1968 to 1978. This is just a list, really, but looking at it can convey the sense of a certain rhythm and a certain movement (to use one of Jon Anderson's favorite words). "Listening to the future," the *idea*, not the book title, has to do with following out a certain rhythm and movement—but it seems that these have led somewhere else, to another "time."

In other words, the world that progressive rock portended is not the world that we live in now. And this has important implications for how we listen to the music in this world, this world that the music was *not* listening to. I attempt to proceed in terms of both of these worlds, the world that I think the music was listening to, and the world that we have. This book hopes to be a bridge between the two.

Chicago, June 1, 1997

1

Introduction: Seize again the day

For a brief, shining moment, there was a time when the trend in music known as "progressive rock" captured the imaginations of millions of listeners. Although this book defines the "time" of progressive rock in terms of the years 1968 to 1978, the shining moment was a somewhat shorter period, perhaps from about 1971 to 1975. Writing on the eve of the fin-de-millennium, this brief period seems as though it was an eternity ago. And yet, no matter how brief the moment, and no matter how long ago it might seem now (and, from another perspective, 1972 was just yesterday), this was a significant period for music.

Indeed, the period of the late sixties and the years immediately following were significant for many reasons, not least of all for the fact that the world was being turned upside down by widespread, and global, social upheaval. This was a time of both protest and possibility, and even revolution—and some great music was inspired by what seemed to be the retreat, at least on the ideological front, of systems of exploitation and domination, and the emergence of a new world, or, at least, a new understanding.

This music took many forms, both within rock music and beyond. Indeed, there was a general opening of genres and a letting down of barriers. To a great extent, these barriers have yet to

1

be fully erected again in their previous form, which is one of the lasting legacies of the sixties. (When I use the term, "the sixties," I mean this more politically and culturally than in a strict chronological sense.) This was a time of both raw and harsh music of protest, and of visionary experimentation. (In some rare cases, there was even a combination of the two, for example in the "fire music" of Archie Shepp; another interesting example, from rock music, was the *Blows Against the Empire* album by Paul Kantner and Jefferson Starship.) These musics of both radical negation and radical affirmation were certainly linked at the time—it was perfectly obvious to everyone that both came out of a more generally experimental social milieu. Progressive rock, to the extent that it is seen at all, is rarely seen in this context. This is not only a mistake made within the field of music history (a mistake that has been made, for example, in the Public Broadcasting System's documentary series, *Rock & Roll*); even more, this is a mistake in cultural and even political history that has large cultural and political ramifications.

In its time, progressive rock represented something unique in the entire history of art: a "popular avant-garde." For most aestheticians and social theoreticians, the very idea is oxymoronic. Supposedly, an avant-garde can only be appreciated by an elite; supposedly, this elite appreciation is part of the very definition of the concept of avant-garde. But we might take a page from Marx, and argue that "once the inner connections are grasped, theory becomes a material force." Not to be obtuse or cute, the point is that the motive forces of society are grasped when a significant part of society is compelled to expand its understanding of these forces. Then this understanding becomes a real force in the lives of many people. As the late sixties gave way to the seventies, many people were prepared by their social experience to be open to experimental, visionary, and utopian music that was brilliantly crafted and performed.

Perhaps the key preparation for this possibility was made starting about ten years earlier, by John Coltrane. He and a number of other post-boppers expanded the frontiers of jazz; they were popular, at least among a significant and international public, and their music had to be understood against the background of both the oppression and struggle of Black people, the Civil Rights Movement, and the emergence of Black Power. (This is not to say that I advocate any kind of crude reduction of this music to particular aspects of social movements or upheavals. More on this general question in a moment.) John Coltrane, certainly one of the greatest visionary and virtuoso musicians of any time period or genre, was always pushing the limits. Indeed, as any avant-garde composer or musician must do, he placed into question the very nature and possibility of music itself—for which some critics called his music "anti-jazz" or "nihilistic."

There came a moment, perhaps best captured by the *Concert in Japan* album, when Coltrane seemed to take a leap into the stratosphere, and many of his admirers had great difficulty following him. Perhaps as long as only two of the basic elements of music were stretched to the limit, or perhaps somewhat beyond the limit, and the other four elements were relatively restrained, then Coltrane was able to take many people along on the journey. (I'm taking the "basic elements" to be melody, harmony, rhythm or meter, timbre, duration, and dynamics.) But, as soon as the figure no longer seemed to have a ground, there was a sense of complete suspension and fragmentation, and fewer people were ready for it. The jazz that continued to go down this road (or up into this space), for instance that of Ornette Coleman, Cecil Taylor, or Anthony Braxton, no longer had a mass following. From this time, serious jazz increasingly became the province of intellectuals (many of them white, male, and middle class); this Black music became separated from the masses of Black people.

An instructive counterexample is provided by the late-sixties music of Miles Davis. This is the Miles who had heard Jimi Hendrix, Sly and the Family Stone, and the Byrds—and his music from this time, *Bitches Brew*, *Jack Johnson*, *Miles Davis at Fillmore* (where Miles and group opened for the Byrds, in fact), was a part of the general crossing of musical and social barriers of this time. Whereas the time was not entirely ripe for a popular avant-garde just a few years earlier (John Coltrane died in 1967 at the age of forty-one), by the time Miles Davis played the Fillmore East, in June 1970, dramatic changes had taken place. Not that the critics necessarily liked these changes; for instance, in *The*

Illustrated Encyclopedia of Jazz for 1978, authors Brian Case and Stan Britt argue that, prior to *Bitches Brew*, "Miles cut what, from the jazz fan's viewpoint, was to be his last album (*In a Silent Way*)" (p. 59). "Although labels are arbitrary, Miles Davis' subsequent output is of little interest to the jazz record collector" (p. 59). So much the worse, then, for the "jazz record collector"—but what of those who saw that music was taking an adventurous turn along with culture and politics more generally? An account by Morgan Ames, from the liner notes to *Fillmore*, is instructive:

> I went to see Miles at the Hollywood Bowl recently, in concert opposite The Band. At least half the audience was young rock fans. There were also jazz people of all categories—middling executives with their tolerant wives, boppers, suede-covered mods who like both rock and jazz. There was black pride, in vivid African shirts and robes. And young girls with young children. There were celebrities, particularly from the music world. Most had come to see what Miles was up to now. The night was warm and the air was laced with waiting: Miles Davis and The Band? What does that mean?
>
> Miles opened the show. He and his group played for about 45 minutes without pause. The critics wiped him out in the paper the following morning. But the audience loved him. In amphitheaters as large as the Hollywood Bowl, a roaring ovation can sound like a polite coming-together-of-hands, unless you listen closely and look around you. I did. Hippies were on one side of us, non-descripts were behind, a black couple was on the other side. Front-to-back it was a happily received evening. People liked what Miles was about, even if they couldn't grasp the free-form display. They felt his honest effort, his adventure, his openness, and they took him in without asking why. For Miles Davis has the hunger and the ability to entertain through exploration.

Of course, another thing that had changed in the years 1967–1970 is that, by the latter year, electricity permeated everything. Arguably, this was not the best thing for jazz in the long run, and perhaps not for anything. At the time, however, there was certainly a feeling of "electric freedom" (as in "Sound Chaser" by Yes) that crossed all boundaries and was perhaps a necessary component of a culture and politics where "the whole world's watching."

Throughout the short history of rock music up to that point, there had been, along with more commercial and mainstream efforts, an adventurous trend—going right back to Chuck Berry and Little Richard and, someone I've come to appreciate more and more in this respect, Bo Diddley. Into the 1960s we see harmonic and timbral innovation, especially on the part of the Beach Boys and the Beatles. With the latter, we see an increasing drive toward a global synthesis of music. Rock music begins to develop an avant-garde, and a subgeneration of musicians emerge who have tremendous instrumental, lyrical, and compositional skills. And millions of people are into it.

My aim in this book is to explore this very uncommon period. I hope, in the case of those of us who were around during the time of progressive rock, to recapture the feeling that what happened in music in that period was *important, significant*. I want to provide the philosophical, aesthetic, and social theoretical terms that would allow us to see that this period not only *was* significant but, indeed, still is and should be. For those of us who are new to this period (either we weren't around then, or we didn't pick up on what was happening at the time), I want to provide some access. We live in a time when it is very hard for anything to be significant or important, a time of an immense cultural machinery of pure distraction. Between 1968 and now, there lies an effort, which might especially be associated with the administrations of Ronald Reagan and Margaret Thatcher, to blame the sixties for all sorts of things, and to attempt to make sure that, apart from superficial aspects of fashion, something like that doesn't happen again. Progressive rock might seem to be a relatively minor part of the truly major social and cultural upheavals of that time. After all, 1968 saw the largest general strike to ever occur in a Western, industrialized country (the "events of May," in France), and mass strikes in Mexico City, Chicago, Prague, Shanghai (there with the actual encouragement of a revolutionary government), and many other places. So, yes, it is the case that, from one valid perspective, the progressive rock chapter of this immense volume called "the sixties" would be relatively short. But there is something in that chapter that should not be lost, something that we need today, and it is toward the possibility of seizing again this moment that I write.

The reader will more than likely have figured out that I am writing not only from a perspective that is sympathetic to the sixties, but indeed from a perspective that is radical and, yes, somewhat Marxist. I feel that I need to say some things about this, "up front," as it were.

Of course, this is not my first extended foray into these questions. I have written other books that explore various dimensions of radical social theory, as well as a book that readers of the present text may be familiar with, *music of Yes: structure and vision in progressive rock*. This book, about the music of what I regard as one of the essential *pillars* of progressive rock, argues not that the music of Yes is "Marxist," in any sense, but that it instead partakes of the radical spirit of the sixties and carries this forward in a utopian and radically affirmative way. One thing that can be said about Yes is that there is not a trace of cynicism in their music—and this is an extraordinarily rare thing, even in progressive rock. Indeed, the music of Yes is something of an antidote for cynicism, and therefore is especially despised by "critics" who believe that a cynical attitude is the height of hip.

Edward Macan ends his interesting and important book on English progressive rock, *Rocking the Classics*, with the following:

> Above all, progressive rock, like the period which gave rise to it, was optimistic. The whole underlying goal of progressive rock—to draw together rock, classical, jazz, folk, and avant-garde styles into a new metastyle that would supersede them all—is inherently optimistic. So too is the attempt to bridge the gulf between high and low culture, which I consider progressive rock's worthiest ambition: by creating a style of music that combined technical innovation and sophistication with mass appeal, progressive rock musicians achieved a goal that avant-garde composers could only dream of. The heroic scale on which so much progressive rock unfolds suggests an abiding optimism; as do the epic conflicts and the grapplings with the Infinite and otherworldly which dominate so much progressive rock. It is also possible to see in the "uncommercial" nature of progressive rock a reminder of a time when the music industry was more tolerant of experimentation and individual expression, and less concerned with standardization and compartmentalization.
>
> At its best, progressive rock engaged its listeners in a quest for spiritual authenticity. Sometimes its earnestness could lapse into a rather sophomoric naivete. However, even at its most naive it was never wide-eyed or saccharine, while even at its bleakest, it never gave way to bitterness, cynicism, or self-pity. In short, I suspect that progressive rock has retained its attraction for many of its older fol-

lowers—and has even drawn some younger ones—because it encapsulates an optimism, a confidence, and perhaps even an innocence that is a refreshing antidote to the cynicism and pessimism of more recent times. (p. 222)

Although I might have approached one or more of the aspects of the question with a different emphasis than Professor Macan's, I think what he says here is insightful and essentially right. (I will discuss *Rocking the Classics* in detail in my third chapter.) But what is the connection to larger political and cultural questions? Although this connection may be perfectly obvious to many readers, let's try to set it out systematically—my view is that doing this will help us see why progressive rock is historically important in the realms of music, culture, and politics in a broad sense.

Let's begin with a question: What is "the cynicism and pessimism of more recent times," and what is the basis of this? Another way to come at this is, What is the sense in which optimism and cynicism are opposites, and what is the sense in which this opposition is materially grounded?

In the largest frame, pessimism is the view that either the human project can come to no good end, or that there really is no human project—or even prospect, in any collective sense—in the first place. I think that if there is a human project, it is the sort of thing argued for by Aristotle: the bringing about of *eudaimonia*, *flourishing*, which involves an intertwining of the good person, the good life, and the good society. If the question is, What might humanity *hope* for and *strive* for, I don't see any other answer. Now, of course, neither "flourishing" nor "good" in these formulations is self-defining, and there is the question of what might truly be possible in any given historical period. Marx's contribution to all of this was to give material grounding to the immense possibilities that exist in our time. Pessimism and cynicism, however, regard the prospect of all of this as either undesirable or highly unlikely. Of course, as Marx demonstrated, this pessimism is also materially grounded, in that it is in the interest of some social classes that a collective human project of mutual flourishing not emerge. In other words, some classes depend on the majority of humankind being held in conditions of subjugation and exploitation—and these oppressing classes promote the view that, because of "human nature," the "permanence of greed," or some such cliché, nothing else is possible.

Radically affirmative or utopian strivings emanate from the felt experience that society does not have to be based on exploitation and domination, and that something else is indeed possible. The pessimism and cynicism of our time are especially driven by the fact that, in the twentieth century, movements and ideologies working for an alternative to capitalism have been defeated, derailed, or have rotted from within by the very tendencies that need to be overcome. In the wealthier countries, and among the wealthier classes, this cynicism has been accompanied by a certain euphoria, one that aims at a "partial utopia" mainly through the acquisition of lots of toys (often of the high-tech variety) and accommodations and plots of land cut off from the general condition of humankind. Although one shouldn't become too concerned for the welfare of these "rich kids" in a world where, through the new processes of globalization, whole continents are being written off (namely, Africa), the fact is that even this little bit of "utopia" is not and could not be "true flourishing." Perhaps the pleasures of "cybersex," real enough on *some* level, but certainly limited and really quite thin, are a good demonstration, by way of negative example, of the idea that true flourishing has to be mutual and ever open to its extension to others. (Indeed, in the music of Yes, there is clearly the sense that mutuality has to extend beyond humanity itself, to nature, the world, and the cosmos more generally.) Or simply think of the idea of feasting at a small banquet that is surrounded by thousands and even millions of starving people, especially starving children, and inquire into the nature of the "happiness" that might be achieved in such a feast.[1]

Here's yet another way of coming at this question in terms of hopes, dreams, and aspirations—imagine someone saying something like this: "I dream of a world where people are divided into classes, and where what they might accomplish in the world is heavily conditioned by this division; I dream of a world where people are divided by gender and ethnicity, and where there is an advantage to being one gender or ethnicity rather than another; I dream of a world where a few have much, and where many have little or nothing; and I dream that, in this world, I am one of a small minority that occupies the top part of this hierarchy, and that reaps the benefits from the collective labor, strife, and suffering of the immensely larger bottom part." Such a "dream" could only be the product of a sick mind—or a sick social system.

Certainly, and this is the contribution of Marx to this discussion, what will first of all bring down the system of anti-mutuality is not its failure to achieve true happiness, but rather the fact that the oppressed and excluded cannot hold body and soul together. As their numbers and immiseration increase—and this *must* happen, according to Marx, because of the fundamentally exploitive nature of the capitalist *system* (one of Marx's greatest insights is that the cause of exploitation is not first of all that there are bad, oppressive people running things, but instead that there is a social system based on exploitation)—so does the possibility of an explosion of protest, rebellion, and even revolution against this system. Such movements must aim, ultimately, to achieve a global community of mutual flourishing (this is what I mean by "communism," with a small "c", or what I sometimes also call "radical communitarianism.") Such movements must *not* aim to simply replace those who are at present the beneficiaries of the machinery of exploitation.

In its best moments, this immense collective transformation is what the sixties and its cultural expressions were all about. What is overwhelmingly obvious is that such a transformation did not occur—though, significantly, many of the expressions of the possibility of such a transformation have been extraordinarily difficult for the system to bury, despite an equally extraordinary effort to do this. What has worked best for the system is to *recuperate* elements of the sixties as mere fashion (though even this strategy of cynicism has its dangers—I would identify the whole area of sex and gender as especially rich with possibilities). Likewise, progressive rock, at its best, is also an expression of this utopian, radical, and transformative spirit—even if not in a straightforward "political" way, at least as that term is often understood (or misunderstood). In fact, this is all to the good, because therein lies progressive rock's potential staying power and relevance to a time of pervasive cynicism.

But why get into these questions here, in a book about progressive rock—or even in a book about any kind of music or art? I do reject purely "political" readings of artists and works, of the sort one gets from critics of a more sociological bent (such as they are—and they are a motley group, from the boorish to the insightful, from Lester Bangs to Greil Marcus or Dick Hebdige). If music is simply a matter of the "political statement" it makes, what is the point of it *as music*? In other words, why not just cut to the chase and put out the pamphlet or flyer? "Political statement" music, by the way, is sometimes called "agit-prop" ("agitation and propaganda") art, and it is certainly the case that a good deal of this has been generated under the heading of one or another formulation of "Marxism," or under the heading of a "worker's movement" or even "power to the people." My view is that, if any of this agit-prop music turns out to be "good," it is primarily good for what it primarily is, namely agitation and propaganda. (Incidentally, I would not put some of the better punk music under this heading, as some who reject the sociological reading of music tend to do.)

On the other hand, I also reject purely formalistic analyses of art, which attempt (though they can never succeed, in my view) to see works as not being grounded in any historical, social, cultural, or political context. If a work of art has any significance (indeed, if *anything* has any significance), it must be in terms of some context (or set of contexts) and its relation to this context.

My guess is that the basic issue here is one that is close to the hearts of people who love progressive rock music: What *is* music (or art more generally), fundamentally? It seems to me that there are two basic possibilities: *either* music is fundamentally entertainment, *or* music is something capable (at its best) of speaking to the human spirit and the human condition. I'll wager that folks who love progressive rock music are attracted to it because it speaks to the soul and to deep and significant human possibilities.

This is not to say that progressive rock cannot be entertaining as well, even if perhaps on a quite different level than what we expect from most "entertainment music." Perhaps one way to put it is that there are kinds of entertainment that can be fulfilling and that can generate the deeper happiness that I mentioned earlier. There are other kinds of entertainment that are the equivalent of junk food or perhaps a mildly pleasant sensation or even a more intense giddiness, but one that has no lasting value. Indeed, it is because progressive rock is not readily consumable in the terms of our giddy junk-food society that the rock music establishment has largely rejected it.

Great music is able to speak to the soul, I think, because it offers (or perhaps "conjures," in a truly magical way) the possibility of a different world. When this is done with intensity and vision and skill, as it is in the best of progressive rock music, the gesture is a profound one, a radical affirmation of human possibility. Such a gesture is more deeply "political" than much of what ordinarily goes under this heading—which, again, is not to say that there is any kind of straightforward "swap" possible (or desirable) between art that has this utopian dimension and the other things needed to deal with reshaping our world, e.g., political theories, movements, activism. (There is also an art of radical negation, which I think is also necessary for social transformation. In my book about Yes, I deal with this under the heading of what I call "the YesPistols question," pp. 185–90.)

I hope that it is clear that I am a rather unorthodox Marxist. Although I believe that there is a great deal to be learned from Marx and others more properly identified as Marxist revolutionaries (Lenin, Mao) and Marxist philosophers (though here I have a *very* diverse canon—Adorno, Sartre, Jameson, many others), there are many others who are helpful in the critique of capitalism and the imagination of a radically different world who do not fit well into the Marxist canon (some examples would be Jacques Derrida, Wendell Berry, Ursula LeGuin, Octavia Butler, and Orson Scott Card). I am happy to learn from any of these and many other sources—including, obviously, progressive rock, almost none of which fits under the heading of Marxism (the exceptions would be Henry Cow and Robert Wyatt). I won't belabor this point much further here, but I hope that readers who encounter the Marxist side of my perspective will avoid cold-war clichés. Certainly there have been social systems and movements and theories that have called themselves "Marxist" or "Communist" that have nothing to do with real liberation and the creation of a global community of mutual flourishing. Of course I reject these systems, movements, and theories. Certain ideas and possibilities have been dragged through the mud. Marxism isn't the only thing this has happened to—I could see many of my arguments being made from a certain kind of radical religious perspective, and religion has certainly been dragged in the mud by some of its adherents and many of its supposed leaders. There are tremendous difficulties to be overcome; but none of this makes capitalism any less grotesque or the need to transform society any less real.

Some of these thoughts were first formulated (as regards progressive rock music, that is) in response to a critique of my book on Yes.[2] The author of this critique, while overwhelmingly positive and generous regarding *music of Yes*, began by saying that he was annoyed and distracted by my "Marxist/Communist views." He then repeated a few of the standard clichés. But, having thus vented, he went on to say that, "It is probably the first time I have ever read intelligent, convincing interpretations of Jon Anderson's lyrics that actually SOUND RIGHT!" (emphasis in original), and that "[i]n general, I agreed with Mr. Martin's analyses and opinions (on purely musical issues, that is . . .)" (ellipses in original). These comments raise (at least) three very important issues.

First, and not to be self-aggrandizing about it, if my interpretations of what everyone agrees is very difficult music and lyrics "sound right," then might that not be a point in favor of the perspective out of which these interpretations have been generated?

Second, it is quite significant that, in the face of a politics that one has difficulty with, there is a standard move toward formalism—in this case, one concerning "purely musical issues." Such issues do not, in my view, exist—which is not to say that formal analysis of musical structures is either impossible or unimportant. But form itself has content, and this content is historically, politically, socially, and culturally informed.

Third and finally, it may be the case that the radical perspective on these issues is well and good, but isn't it distracting, as my critic claims, to go on at length about this perspective in a book on music? Or, again, Why not stick more closely to the "purely musical issues"? As a matter of fact, beyond this introduction, I do intend to focus primarily on musical forms and their context(s). But if we also want a way to say that progressive rock is significant and important music, there has to be a perspective from which to make this claim.

Of course, others are most welcome to develop their own perspectives. In my book on Yes, I'm sure I got it wrong here or there, or went overboard, and I know that I didn't engage with some contexts that are also important for understanding the music of Yes or progressive rock more generally (for instance, I didn't go deeply into the influence of non-Western belief systems on Jon Anderson or Steve Howe, in part because it is beyond my competence to discuss these things). I certainly hope that readers will correct me or extend the discussion where needed—and I will certainly be happy if one major outcome of this book will have been to provoke such discussion. Like any great art, progressive rock music works on many levels and inspires many interpretations. But I will stick to my claim that there is something fundamentally liberatory and utopian about progressive rock, and I imagine that readers, whatever they might have heard about some things called "Marxism" or "Communism," will for the most part agree with this.

Incidentally, if such a thesis can be fleshed out, this will help to show not only how social theory and philosophy have something to contribute to the understanding of music, but also how an exploration of music can contribute to social theory and philosophy. The approach I take, then, has the virtue of avoiding both purely sociological or purely formalist perspectives, even while availing itself of the best insights of either. I think this approach fits progressive rock pretty well, and it also helps to flesh out the better possibilities of the radical communitarian perspective.

So, I would argue that following out such a perspective is not a distraction *if* there are important reasons for taking up such a perspective—*but it can be rough going*, undoubtedly. In this respect, I would like to quote my friendly critic one more time, because I feel that he has understood something important.

I did find myself occasionally skimming through the philosophical sections, just to get to the musical "meat." However, in retrospect, all of the writing is significant, and it short-changes the book to read it merely to get the "warm fuzzies" from experiencing someone else's praise for something that one already admires (although this DOES unmistakably feel good). (p. 4)

This is very generous and much appreciated. Naturally, I don't want to prevent anyone from getting a warm feeling from revisiting the glory days of progressive rock—on the contrary, I want to help us seize again those days and the great energy and inspiration of them.

Edward Macan situates progressive rock in terms of a broad sixties *counterculture*. Progressive rock is no longer a part of this counterculture—which itself now only exists in the form of embattled or recuperated fragments. But if there was ever a "culture" (if such it is) that needed to be countered, the one we live in is it. In two important books, *Postmodernism* and *The Seeds of Time*, Fredric Jameson has spoken to the way that meaning and history are flattened and consigned to stasis and oblivion in this period of postmodern capitalism. In the latter book, he describes this in terms that are brutally stark:

> Parmenidean stasis [changeless Being in itself, to which Jameson is comparing the postmodern resistance to history] . . . to be sure knows at least one irrevocable event, namely death and the passage of the generations. . . . But death itself . . . is inescapable and [has been rendered] meaningless, since any historical framework that would serve to interpret and position individual deaths (at least for their survivors) has been destroyed. A kind of absolute violence, then, the abstraction of violent death, is something like the dialectical correlative to this world without time or history. (p. 19)

When I argue that we should seize again the day, and take up again the idea that music, and a certain music in particular, was and is important, it is ultimately this absolute violence to which this argument and this proposed raid is opposed.

As Macan argues, progressive rock has gone from being part of a more general counterculture to being simply what sociologists call a "taste public." This means, as Macan explains, that whereas there was something like a world view associated with being an afficionado of progressive rock at a time when this kind of music was part of a larger counterculture, after the heyday of progressive rock it is more likely that afficionados only share an interest in the music, and do not necessarily share any larger set of values (see especially pp. 72–83). There is a good argument to be made that the degeneration of a counterculture into a mere taste public fits in all too nicely with a more general "culture" of consumerism and with the idea that there is nothing more at stake than individual "tastes." Furthermore, and returning once again to the question of formalism and my friendly critic's attempt to isolate "purely musical issues" from "political" questions, the move from counterculture to taste public is surely a monumental defeat, in that the move is an acceptance of the idea that music is not really that important in terms of this larger thing called "life."

So, again, What *is* music? If it is only capable of being entertainment, something to occupy us in our leisure time, but of no greater importance, then perhaps some of the components of the sixties counterculture really were invested with a significance all out of proportion to their actual worth.

The response to this charge, I think, is seen first of all not in one of my more theoretical discussions, but instead in the fact that people who are into progressive rock seem to *love* this music, seem to think that it is important, seem to feel that it speaks to them on the level of the soul and not just as passing entertainment; there is a deep feeling that this music can be *engaged* with. Why, then, retreat into a sterile formalism when the larger issues begin to get rough and where one is challenged to examine where one's commitments lie? My aim, instead, is to show why we need to go in the opposite direction.

Another way to put this is that, if I dealt with this music only from the standpoint of history or musicology done from a purely academic perspective, or as a mere nostalgia trip—"warm fuzzies" and nothing more—then there wouldn't be much point, as far as I'm concerned, in attempting to deepen our *understanding* of this music. Instead, I'd just put on *Thick as a Brick* or *Larks' Tongues in Aspic*, and sit around with my friends and say, "Man, that is really something, that is really cool!" Of course, it is really something, it is really cool (in the pre-jaded sense of "cool," that is), and it is good to just sit back and listen from time to time, without too much of an agenda as to what one will *make* of the experience. But my perspective is that there are two central issues here that are deeply linked. First, there is something about progressive rock that is not only to be enjoyed on the surface, but also to be understood and appreciated in depth. This depth appreciation is not unassociated with enjoyment, but here we would be interested in moving beyond surface pleasures and more into the realm of what speaks to the possibilities of human flourishing. Second, I would argue that, if we break with formalism (which, again, doesn't mean absolving ourselves of the need for analysis of musical structure), then our perspective on the aforementioned understanding, appreciation, and enjoyment must be an *engaged* perspective. That is, we accept that, although "music" (or art more generally) and "life" do not at every point describe the same thing or activity, neither is there a way to strictly separate the two. This would go even more for the kinds of music that one could get very seriously involved in, "wrap one's life around"—and, of course, I hold that progressive rock is one such kind of music. (In this connection, I can't help but think about the title of Valerie Wilmer's book on four major jazz innovators, including Cecil Taylor: *As Serious As Your Life*.) *Therefore*, a commitment to the importance of a kind of music that goes beyond surface enjoyment, toward that which speaks to the human spirit and the possibilities of human flourishing (and even a cosmic co-flourishing), must be understood, on reflection, to also entail a commitment to working those changes in the world that will enable this flourishing.

This is to ask a great deal of music and of any one kind of music. And yet, I imagine that the kinds of people who are deeply interested in progressive rock will be able, *upon reflection*, to follow out these claims and to grapple with them. After all, we are interested in progressive rock because it is a *thoughtful* music.

Alright—I realize that I am asking a great deal of you, dear reader; I hope that you will take this in the same spirit as progressive rock itself, which also asks a great deal (and therefore isn't something that thoughtless rock music "criticism" has any time for). Just to be clear, I am not arguing that there is any single progressive rock "ideology" or political "agenda," or something on that order, but rather that there is a fundamental connection between thoughtfulness and care in art and an engagement with the possibilities of human flourishing.

Now let us turn to a brief tour of the rest of this book.

Chapter 2 will deal with what I call the "prehistory of progressive rock." Here we will discuss the history of rock music from the founders (including, for instance, Ray Charles and Chuck Berry), up through the Beatles, as well as other more experimental forms of rock that prepared the way for the emergence of progressive rock. This will necessarily be a skewed and slanted history; I do not believe that the only *raison d'être* of other kinds of rock music than progressive rock was to prepare the way for the latter, but in chapter 2 I will proceed as though this were the case. In addition to those already mentioned, I will discuss the Beach Boys, Hendrix, Cream, the psychedelic movement, and then four groups that are very important for being close to the edge (to coin a phrase!) of progressive rock: The Who, Led Zeppelin, the Moody Blues, and Pink Floyd. Obviously, I will need to explain why I do not place the Floyd, especially, in the category of progressive rock, and this will require the construction of definitions. Some of this work will be done in the second chapter, some in the third. Finally, I will discuss a group that was truly transitional to progressive rock, namely The Nice.

In taking up this somewhat channeled history, I will foreground the experimental tendencies that have been around since the beginnings of rock music in order to show what larger cultural and social forces shaped these tendencies, and, ultimately, how these tendencies underwent, in the late sixties, a transformation of quantity to quality such that a distinct trend in rock music, progressive rock, emerged. I will argue, in a dialectical but I hope not a too-overdetermined way, that the seeds of progressive rock were always already present in the music of the "founders," especially Ray Charles, Chuck Berry, Little Richard, Jerry Lee Lewis, and Bo Diddley. (When I say that I hope to avoid overdetermination, I mean that there was no absolute dialectical necessity that these seeds blossomed—which is again where there is a need to go beyond merely formalistic analysis.)

In chapter 3, "The time of progressive rock," I will discuss the definition and the conditions of emergence of the phenomenon itself. I originally took up some of these questions in a section in *music of Yes* (pp. 37–45); here I will rearticulate these themes and

expand on them. Definitions can be dangerous, they can be con-
fining ("by definition," this is what definitions are all about)—and
this is especially a problem where such an expansive phenomenon as progressive rock is concerned. My aim will be to generate
a definition that is enabling, that helps rather than hinders understanding. To this end, in the second chapter I will also take up a
rather large group of bands that are not ordinarily grouped under
the heading "progressive rock"—as that term is understood or, in
fact, badly understood, today—yet were clearly a part of the
expansion of rock music's possibilities in the early seventies. This
is a large set of groups—I'm thinking of such exciting and innovative artists as Traffic, Chicago, Steely Dan, Santana (to name
some of the famous ones). My aim will not be to say anything
definitive about these groups (though they are all deserving of
extended treatment), but more to deal with the expansion and
contraction of the phenomenon and definition of progressive rock
itself.

In the third chapter I will also deal with the fact that, although
not all progressive rock bands are from England, by any stretch,
there is something about the progressive trend that is very centered in England.

Finally, in chapter 4, I will turn to the bands and their music.
As the subtitle indicates, chapter 4 is meant as a kind of anno-
tated discography. Even though the chapter is quite long, my aim
was to create something that the reader could move through at a
fairly quick pace, mainly in order to get a sense of the rhythms
and dimensions of the larger progressive movement. In my final
chapter, I will take up developments in progressive rock beyond
its "time." In the main, however, I limit more extensive discussion
to groups that made important albums in the years 1968 to 1978.
(Admittedly, even this choice of years is somewhat conditioned by
the desire to present a nice, even decade.) I will deal with both
the famous and the obscure—making it plain that, just because
some groups such as Yes or Emerson, Lake, and Palmer became
quite famous does not mean that they were necessarily more
"commercial" or "watered down" (I don't know who could call
Tales from Topographic Oceans "commercial" or "Karn Evil Nine,
2nd Impression" "watered down"). There's a tendency to punish

some of these groups for their fame, when, in fact, they were also making better music than *some* of the more obscure groups. At the same time, some other groups were undeservedly obscure and were certainly as creative as the more famous groups. In other words, I focus on quality, not quantity of albums or concert seats sold.

In what, I am sure, will be a controversial move, I divide the discussion of groups in chapter 4 into three categories. First, I make a distinction between what I see as the "first-line" and the "second-line" groups. The first line consists in what I will argue are the most consistently innovative contributors to the genre. Of this list of thirteen groups, about five or six of these would be in the category of less famous, while the others are fairly well known (of course, most of them will be familiar to long-time followers of the genre). In alphabetical order, these are the "first-line" groups of progressive rock: Caravan, Emerson, Lake, and Palmer, Genesis, Gentle Giant, Gong, Henry Cow, Jethro Tull, King Crimson, Magma, Mahavishnu Orchestra, PFM, Soft Machine, and Yes.

My second category will also be controversial. Within the category of "first line," I will identify two groups in particular as the *pillars* of progressive rock, namely King Crimson and Yes. This does not mean that these groups were or are absolutely the best of the lot—though, in my opinion, they are. Instead, the idea is that these two groups, taken together, give us something like an "archetype" for the genre.

A smaller, but still significant, part of the fourth chapter will be devoted to a much longer list of groups, approximately fifty of them, that are both less well known and are among the less "heavy hitters" and are more peripheral to the progressive trend. They constitute, in other words, the "second line." This category includes groups such as Curved Air, Greenslade, Egg, Nektar, Jonesy—to name a few. Here I will not attempt to be exhaustive, but I will try to give readers/listeners access to this easily forgotten chapter in rock music (and even a forgotten chapter of progressive rock music). In the resources section, I will also give some sources where listeners can obtain albums by these groups. In every case, these groups have made at least one important album and therefore a real contribution to progressive rock.

In making the "first-line"/"second-line" distinction, I will undoubtedly rankle a few readers. My hope is not only to make some judgments of quality, but also to provoke further discussion. If a disgruntled reader wants to launch a campaign to demonstrate that, in fact, Grobschnitt should have been considered within the first line, then let's debate it out in the newsletters, journals, and other forums. I should say, as well, and by way of preparation, that just because I think some of these bands are more important does not mean that I wish to diminish the contributions of the others. On the contrary, I hope to show that progressive rock in the seventies was a very diverse and vibrant trend. At the very end of chapter 4 I present a list of fifty-nine of the most noteworthy albums, which would form a solid basis for a progressive rock album collection.

Finally, in chapter 5, I will discuss the fate and possibilities of progressive rock after its "time," that is, after 1978. I will consider the factors that led to the close of the progressive rock era as a major musical trend, as well as the more recent trajectories of some of the principal groups as they navigate the post-progressive period. Some attention will be given to punk, new wave, and recent music that might be called "postmodern." I will also discuss the music and thoughts of Brian Eno as a figure who bridges the progressive era and postmodern music. Finally, considering Yes's recent *Keys to Ascension*, I will ask whether progressive rock has a chance of once again becoming a force in the world.

In the afterword I will share a few thoughts on Paul Stump's recent book, *The Music's All That Matters*, especially concerning the distinction he makes between "alternative" and "mainstream" progressive rock. I will also discuss alternative approaches to the genre that might prove fruitful for future research.

Is there hope for the future? I see this book as an attempt to gather a few, mostly overlooked, seeds of redemption, and I look forward to a larger discussion with readers regarding the possibility of the sort of society that could enable good music, and the sort of music that might encourage us to work toward mutual human flourishing in a good society.

2

The prehistory of progressive rock: Generosity and synthesis

Above all, rock music is two things: it is *synthetic*, and it is *generous*. Taken together, these elements ensure that, at least in some significant sense, there *always* has been a progressive trend in rock music. One can only hope that the ongoing corporate commodification of everything will not lead to a day when the possibility of a progressive trend no longer exists. This more ominous thought properly belongs to the final chapter of this investigation, however: here, let's focus on a much happier subject, the way that rock music became the first truly global music of immense possibility.

My aim in this chapter is to present a somewhat potted history of rock music—or, at least, a series of reflections upon that history—from the standpoint of progressive rock. Admittedly, this is something of a perverse project in that we will be pretending that progressive rock was the *destination* of rock music from its origins. The reality is otherwise, of course: rock music is a very big tree, with many diverse branches. (It is significant, though, how often the branches—or at least twigs here and there—intertwine. This can be seen most graphically in Pete Frame's rock family trees.) I'm not of the opinion that progressive rock, or even what I would more broadly call "experimental rock," is the only musically valid branch of the tree. An analogy might be made to Western classical music. Was it a valid creative approach for composers such as Leonard Bernstein or Benjamin Britten to write works more in the mainstream of the classical style, when avant-garde composers such as John Cage or Elliot Carter were working far outside of the classical forms? Closer to home, was it valid for artists more in the mainstream of rock music to continue to create songs grounded in blues progressions when the Beatles, and especially *Sergeant Pepper's*, had opened up fundamentally new territory?

This is perhaps a weird way to broach the subject of musical avant-gardes, since the legitimacy of radical innovators is what has most often been called into question—even more so in rock music than in jazz and classical music. It seems that the prevalent point of view has been that rock is not supposed to become avant-garde. My standard response to this now well-established dogma is, "Blame it on the Beatles." But what I hope to show here is that, in fact, the roots of progressive rock are intertwined with the roots of rock music more generally.

When I claim that "generosity" is one of the fundamental elements of rock music, one of the things I mean is this: "rock music" is an exceedingly large category, under which many, many kinds of music can flourish. However, we might identify two kinds of rock music that do not always get along so well. The first might be called the "real rock 'n' roll" camp, which is mainly defined by statements about what is *not* (or what *ain't*) "real" rock 'n' roll. There is also the camp of simply rock 'n' roll, which is more able to define itself by what it likes as opposed to what it is willing to excommunicate—the point being that "rock music" is now the broader category, which includes rock 'n' roll. The "real rock 'n' roll" camp is dismissive of anything that departs from basic blues-chord structure or beat, so I sometimes call this camp the "blues orthodoxy."[1] The music that especially departs from this orthodoxy is, of course, progressive rock.

Generosity in rock music also refers not only to the breadth of the form, but also its tendency to be ever open, ever growing, and ever willing to engage in experiments with redefinition. The irony is that, especially as regards the critical establishment around rock music, blues orthodoxy has been the dominant trend since the late seventies, even while this trend is, demonstrably, the least generous. Or, at least, it seems that the blues orthodoxy has come down heaviest on progressive rock, because the latter has taken rock music where it is presumably not supposed to go.

Perhaps rock music tends to be generous in whatever present it finds itself because it was synthetic in its origins. Rock music represents a flowing together of diverse music cultures: most especially musics of the African American experience, from Black church music to blues, jazz, and rhythm-and-blues, but also elements of country music, folk music, and the tradition of American popular song associated with such figures as Cole Porter and the Gershwin brothers. Arguably, rock music provided the first forum for what has more lately been called "multiculturalism." Perhaps we would find, upon further study, that those who today warn us of the dangers of the latter were yesterday those who warned us about the former. Indeed, there was never a time when the social and the musical experimentation of rock music was not intertwined, as both the music and its larger culture presented the sedate, post-war, 1950s "era of good feeling" with its first truly dangerous example of "race mixing." Today it may be the fashion in Lubbock, Texas, to pretend as though dear, departed Buddy Holly has always been the local hero, but in his day all he heard was condemnation from the older white generation for playing "nigger music." Meanwhile, when Buddy and the Crickets showed up to play the Apollo Theater in Harlem, they turned out to be a good deal more pale of complexion than expected.

At the same time, class and gender also asserted themselves as central issues. This new music was made, for the most part, by both Blacks and whites who were from the wrong side of the tracks. Indeed, one of the frightening things about the music, from an establishment point of view, was that it had the potential to transcend racial barriers and prejudices by showing poor whites and poor Blacks that they had a great deal in common. In the United States, of course, there is not and never has been a question of class that can be isolated in a pristine way from the legacy of slavery, anti-Black oppression, and racism.[2] (Similarly, in England, there is no pure question of class that can be

completely separated from English imperialism, colonialism, and
the ideology of "rule Britainnia.")[3] However, the fact that the kids
were dancing together and digging some of the same music—
what was, significantly, originally called "race music"—was a
good start; could the specter of "miscegenation" be far behind?

Here, too, the question of gender—and the more recently
named question of "sexuality"—is already intertwined with race
and class. Even as the cultural, political, and economic establish-
ments hoped for a "well-ordered" and "smoothly functioning"
society, where ideology had come to an end and the appropriate
roles and behaviors for well-adjusted individuals at all levels of
the social hierarchy seemed rock solid, there began a kind of
groundswell on the cultural front, a rebellion against the little
boxes all made of ticky-tacky.

What brought these diverse musical and cultural elements
together and allowed them to congeal into something called "rock
music"? Arguably, the musical streams that flowed into the music
could not have given rise to a new musical form without one key
element: *electricity*. Rock music is the first music to be entirely
formed in the age of electricity. It is also, therefore, the first music
to emerge in the time of the maturing of the mass media—and to
some extent as an expression of mass media. This is perhaps what
most of all links rock music with other artistic genres that are not
even possible without mass media, especially film and video.
Indeed, in recent years it seems that rock music—and "popular
music" (a term that will require further interrogation) more generally—has been increasingly absorbed into the Hollywood/Los
Angeles entertainment machine, with the movie business at the
heart of this complex.

Therefore the question has to be asked: Does the corporate
serpent wend its way over *all* forms of rock music, including progressive rock? Taking the "nontechnological" elements that went
into rock music, there is a solid core of rebellion. But make these
elements dependent upon electricity (and advanced technology
more generally), and it appears that there is always a ready recipe
for cooptation. In the case of the industry-promoted "rebels,"
such as Madonna, Bruce Springsteen, or Prince (or some of the
younger generation, for example the "angry" or "bitter" music of

an Alanis Morrisette), antiestablishment postures cannot help but be somewhat contrived, even while certain social conventions seem to be contravened. For sure, the "rebellious" aspect of certain rock superstars *is* simply posture. Yet, I am not convinced that this is entirely the case with any of the first three artists—or "artists formerly known as"—whom I named; there I think the motives are more of a mixed bag, that there are some honest motivations mixed in with an attempt to negotiate a very difficult cultural and economic arena. The point remains, however, that there is something problematic about saying that some rock music has "sold out" or "gone commercial," when the connection with commercial imperatives is so built into the emergence and development of the very form.

Without being reductivistic or deterministic about it, there remains a great deal to be said for the claim that every form of culture bears a significant relationship to the social formation in which it arises, and to the mode of production that is at the heart of any given formation. Rock music could not have existed in the time before advanced industrial economy and global social relations. These relations are unequal and for the most part predatory, even though they are also part of a single, global, competitive mode of production—the stage of capitalism that Lenin called imperialism. One hundred or more years into this development, we now have systems of media that are productive of consciousness on a level unimagined in previous centuries. It might be said that imperialism plus MTV/CNN/etc. equals "postmodern capitalism." Rock music, then, is the form of music that has arisen in this time and against this background.

Furthermore, and to reiterate, rock music is unthinkable without electric amplification, electronic sound modification, and advanced recording technology. The electric guitar (and perhaps in a lesser, though also related, way, the electric bass guitar) is at the center of rock music. "Acoustic" sounds in rock music play the role of "relief" or dynamic contrast, and, for the most part, are not *really* acoustic anyway (as anyone who has watched an edition of "MTV Unplugged" can see). Theodore Gracyk, in *Rhythm and Noise: An Aesthetics of Rock*, goes so far as to argue that rock music is so thoroughly mediated by technology that, in

fact, its technology *is* its art. In his book on English progressive
rock, Edward Macan identifies sampling technology as one of the
innovations that led to the downfall of progressive rock—if a person can, by pushing a button (or a single key on a keyboard), activate a sample and thereby play a passage that even the most brilliant virtuoso could not play, this would seem to make a rather
large dent in the attractions of virtuoso rock music (see p. 191).
I'm pretty sure that Gracyk has little use for progressive rock anyway, so Macan's argument would, from Gracyk's perspective, provide a fitting capstone to his overall argument—that, with rock
music, technology is what it's really all about.

But let's back up a minute. Gracyk's arguments concerning the
way that technology, especially recording technology, affects rock
music, right down to its very "ontology" (as he puts it), are
insightful, but wouldn't this argument have to have as its destination a music that is mainly produced with, as Beck Hansen says,
"two turntables and a microphone"? In thinking about this, perhaps I am starting to have some sympathy for the "real rock 'n'
roll" types who, among other things, are skeptical of progressive
rock for its displacement of the electric guitar from center stage
(an issue that I will return to). One doesn't have to be a Luddite or
to think there is no room in rock music for some of the new technical innovations, such as sampling or MIDI (or, earlier, electronic
keyboards and synthesizers), to think that there's a problem when
the music, increasingly, is no longer being played by people whom
you would ordinarily call "musicians" (though talented *technicians* they may be).[4] Perhaps I am simply expressing a prejudice
of the pre-postmodern sensibility however. As Fredric Jameson
argues, the thing that allowed for the cult of the "modern artist"
(the great genius who could aspire to be the "world's greatest
painter"—"a Picasso" or some such) was the charm of the fact
that, in an age of mass production, the artist practiced an older,
perhaps even outmoded, craft (see *Postmodernism*, pp. 305–311).

This is not simply a prejudice, however; it is a considered
worry concerning what might happen when, even in the realm of
music, people become "mere appendages of the machine" (as
Marx put it). In terms of rock music's deal with the technological
devil, however, one might say, "in for a dime, in for a dollar."

When it comes to understanding society and culture in the large, there is a great deal to be said for a *structural* approach:[5] social structures (which include, as Freud demonstrated, structures of the mind) shape what people, whatever their intentions, will be able to do. Social structures set the terms for human intentions and achievements. (This is not to imply that these terms are set univocally or through an absolute determinism.) The originators of rock music—at least, the musicians, as opposed to the technicians and the record company people—brought a sense of rebellion on many levels. But perhaps the commercial and technological terms of global, imperialist, and even postmodern capitalism meant that, despite this intention, what they would create instead was just a new form of distraction, always already coopted by the entertainment industry. After all, these new rock musicians already had at least a few toes in this door (and some jumped in with both feet).

In recent years, it has become especially easy to reach the same conclusions concerning "popular" music that Theodor Adorno reached in the immediate postwar period, namely that this kind of music is simply a product of an emerging "culture industry," a product designed to distract people from the real conditions of life in global capitalist society. This is music as palliative, salve, drug, distraction, and mere amusement. To the extent that there seems to be a "rebellious element" in this music, it may be that it is no more than what Paul Piccone, extending Adorno's analysis, called "false negativity." Piccone's argument is that the culture industry, as well as the larger capitalist society of which it is a part, actually needs some elements that appear to be rebellious or not simply affirmative of the status quo, for two reasons. First, there has to be some form of entertainment for those who have some inkling that something might be wrong with the way things are. The idea is to channel this feeling into a purely existential realm—such as listening to your records by yourself or with a few similarly alienated friends, thereby, at most, only becoming part of a "taste public" that never gets beyond the minimal social consciousness of there being a few others out there who like some of the same things. Second, the system itself needs to allow some creativity at the margins, in order to regenerate itself—given that it mainly depends on dull, administrative apparatuses (whether these be bureaucracies of the state or corporations) composed of "well-adjusted" individuals who are not supposed to think in any critical or creative way. The system itself needs a new idea from time to time, so it allows a little "free" or "wild" space, though this is carefully controlled and also carefully channeled.

We should note that, for Adorno, most Western classical music is in the same fix—it also tends to be "affirmative," in the sense of affirming the way things already are. But rock music, especially, is so rigged in advance to be affirmative in this way that Adorno does not see any way out. Now, in Adorno's scheme, there are only two kinds of music, really: Western classical music, which is compromised most of the time, and "popular music," which seems fundamentally compromised. There is by now, as the reader might imagine, a great deal of literature dissecting Adorno's views on this subject.[6] My aim here, however, is not to rehearse every one of these issues, but instead to show that the possibility of rock music being something truly important—as opposed to simply being something like the music of our adolescence, whenever that was—does face some real difficulties. And these difficulties do not just come from Adorno, for whom there are at least three shortcomings in his approach to the questions that are relevant here.

First, Adorno undoubtedly was simply too "European," too steeped in the idea of "high culture," to have appreciated any music outside of the Western classical canon. In other words, he had a human failing and prejudice here; part of his reaction to jazz, blues, and rock music was merely visceral, and it is unfortunate that he elevated this reaction to the level of a system.

Second, the category of "popular" music is too sweeping, especially when it comes to the role played by the culture industry. Here is where there remains a fundamental difference between the Hollywood film industry, which is at the core of the culture industry, and the making of music: to be a part of the former, one has to move in very big money circles and through a system of "connections" (this is just the tip of the iceberg); to make music, on the other hand, it is still possible to "find yourself an electric guitar, and take some time, and learn how to play." Undoubtedly, at the "star performer" level, the interconnections between music and the Hollywood core become more concentrated, and this has certainly been driven even further in recent years by the formation of massive entertainment conglomerates and distribution networks. Still, despite the fact that the distinction cannot be made hard and fast, and despite the way that monopoly capital in the entertainment industry continues to erode the distinction, we might all the same make a distinction between "mass culture" and "popular culture." "Mass culture" has its point of origin and initiation in the culture industry itself—the Hollywood film would be the prime example. "Popular culture" at least begins somewhere closer to the streets—rap and hip-hop would be examples, but so would early rock and roll. (More on this in a moment.)

Third, and relatedly, Adorno seemingly had blinders on when it came to actual outbreaks of protest and rebellion, and he didn't see the possibility of experimental music linking up with a real assault on the existing system. Therefore, the idea of a "popular avant-garde" would never have occurred to him.

Again, most of these arguments (and many more) have been made by others—but not this last argument. Allow me to reconnect with my opening claim, from the introduction to this book: this brief, shining moment, where there was the possibility, completely unprecedented, of a "popular avant-garde," simply came and went so quickly, and with so many forces arrayed against it, that we simply have not taken stock of its significance to this day.

There is an interesting dynamic that shapes this failure to see this particular possibility. I agree with Adorno that there are many factors that make it very, very unlikely that expressions of rock music will transcend what seem to be basic limitations and compromises. In fairness to Adorno, and against some of his interpreters, he never argues that this transcendence is simply impossible. But there is a larger historical issue. Every kind of music emerges and develops against the background of a larger history, society, and culture, and every music stands in some relation ("affirmative," "negative," or, more likely, some very complex mixture of these attitudes) to these things. With the development of capitalism into imperialist and postmodern forms, however, the argument might be made that the "background" assumes an

especially resilient character, and that those genres of art (for
example, rock music) that are especially tied in with the economic and technological structures of this very background face
tremendous and unprecedented difficulties when it comes to
inspiring critical consciousness. When I said, earlier, that in more
recent years it has become even easier to agree with Adorno, I
assume the reader knows the sort of thing I have in mind: the
contemporary prevalence of rock artists and "music" that, from
the veritable get-go, are thoroughly shaped by commercial imperatives, where the making of music is fundamentally a corporate
process, where there are no real musical decisions but instead
business decisions, and where the planned outcome is marketable
and interchangeable product.

Anyone who cares about the possibility of important music
has already thought and worried about this state of things end-
lessly, so I won't go a great deal further into the issue here. What I
want to highlight, instead, is the fact that the mainstream of rock
music "criticism" is complicit in this affair by its disavowal of the
episode of progressive rock. So, by way of reconnecting with the
more specifically musical developments in rock music, I want to
argue that, whereas it is admittedly a one-sided approach to the
history of rock music to understand it as precursor to progressive
rock, the cancellation of the period of progressive rock is also an
assault on the idea of rock music having any greater significance
than as simply entertainment for adolescents (or preadolescents
or those remembering adolescence). In other words, progressive
rock presents a challenge, but this is a challenge implicit in the
history of rock music up through the late sixties. In order to show
the possibilities that progressive rock music (or any other rock
music during or after the time of progressive rock) might have for
either a radical negativity or a radically utopian stance, it is necessary to show that the form (rock music) has always carried
within it the seeds of these capacities and that these seeds have
not been snuffed out by the overwhelming force of the culture
industry and postmodern capitalism.

∎   ∎   ∎

At the origins of rock music we find a minimal adherence to
song form, distilled through a lot of energy, banging, and noise.

Rock music has roots in folk and country music, but especially in rhythm and blues. This latter itself has roots in jazz, gospel, blues, the tradition of American popular song that we associate with such greats as Cole Porter, the Gershwin brothers, and Tin Pan Alley, and, of course, more generally in that untotalizable wellspring known as the African American Experience. It is not inappropriate to see a single individual, namely Ray Charles, as the "midwife" of rock and roll. Charles especially forms a link between jazz and rock, in the form of rhythm and blues. When one thinks of his piano style, both energetic and yet tightly controlled, then one also sees the influence of honky-tonk and boogie-woogie music in the process by which a new synthesis emerged. (Of the progressive musicians, Keith Emerson is almost alone in occasionally putting this style in the forefront of the mix.) Another tendril reaches out to ragtime music. Another key transitional figure was Louis Jordan, singer and alto saxophonist whose use of horns along with a raw, rocking sound formed a transition between swing-era big-band music and rock.

What's most interesting, then, is the way that this complex set of ingredients led to, at first, what seemed to be a rather simple style. Put this way, however, perhaps we should acknowledge that early rock was not as simple and straightforward as it first appeared to be. My own preference, in terms of the early rockers, is for a well-known triumvirate, namely Chuck Berry (b. 1926), Little Richard (b. 1932), and Jerry Lee Lewis (b. 1939). It boggles the mind to think that Chuck Berry, the oldest of the three, is now over seventy years old! This triumvirate represents an interesting mix: two black, one white—specifically "white trash"; one from the industrial north (well, St. Louis at any rate), the other two from the Deep South. At least two of them had serious church backgrounds, and have spent parts of their lives on fire with religion. All three have had skirmishes with the law, on and off. All three represent the synthesis of simplicity and complexity, on musical as well as more general social or cultural levels, that made for early rock. Indeed, and not to run this word into the ground, what gives their music such power is the way that it *distills* complex musical and social experience into a very direct and raw form.

The best music of each is entirely expressible with just three instruments: either piano or electric guitar, and a rhythm section of bass and drums. And perhaps another key moment occurred when the piano was displaced from center stage by the electric guitar—"Move over rover, let Jimi take over!" Although it is difficult to displace talents with the intensity of Little Richard or Jerry Lee Lewis ("they don't call me 'the killer' for nothin'"), in a sense the transition from piano to electric guitar is emblematic of a larger cultural shift. With the electric guitar at its core, rock music consolidated itself as just as much African as European, but also just as much American as African (I can't help but recall that Lenin saw "American electrification" as one of the elements of the future society). The synthesis that emerged is part of what country-rocker Webb Wilder insightfully called "Afro-Celtic" culture. The formulation needs both expansion and narrowing. On the one hand, what Wilder is after is the synthesis of the story-telling traditions and tunefulness of the British Isles (England, Ireland, Scotland, Wales) with the story-telling traditions and rhythms of African and African American peoples. On the other hand, the influence of the Isles has been rewoven and distilled by its transplantation to a particular swath of the American South, namely Appalachia. So, perhaps we should speak of both rock music and many other distinctively American contributions to culture as having its basis in "Afro-Appalachian" culture. It turns out that what emerged from this cultural cauldron has been remarkably and improbably generous and synthetic—out of this mixture has emerged the first true "world music."

In rock music from Chuck Berry to now, from roots rock to world music, the bass and drums have provided an anchor. In much rock music, this occurs in a somewhat formulaic way: the bass is there to "lay down the bottom," while the drums are there to "keep the beat." Perhaps another way of coming at this is that rock music begins as *dance* music. "If its got a backbeat you can't lose it"; but what if it doesn't have a backbeat? Not to get too far ahead of ourselves, we can still take this moment to mark out three distinct differences between rock and roll and progressive rock; setting these differences out will help us see the developments that unfolded between the fifties and the late sixties. First, in progressive rock, the bass and drums are often *not* playing the traditional roles. In particular, progressive rock is generally not "dance music," and the "rhythm section" is often just as much in the forefront as any of the other instruments. Second, the electric guitar is no longer at the center of things; it continues to play an important role (except, of course, in those bands that do not use the instrument), but this is in a situation of relative parity with keyboards, wind instruments, violins, and what have you— including the occasional sackbut or crumhorn (Gryphon) or space whisper (Gong)—as well as acoustic steel-string and classical guitars. Third, there is a shifting of the cultural balance back toward Europe, as well as an expansion outwards toward Asia and (to a lesser extent until more recent years) Latin America. At any rate, it can certainly be argued that progressive rock is less "Black" than most of the rest of rock music (with the possible exception of heavy metal).

Whether this necessarily makes it more "white," however, is a question I will leave for further exploration. What I will insist on, regardless of the answer to this question, is that the development of rock music *up through* progressive rock, and not merely around it, is what gives us the rich possibilities of rock music today. (Leave aside, for the moment, the commercial and technological forces that presently stand in the way of these possibilities.) In the fifties, composer and educator Gunther Schuller (president for many years of the New England Conservatory of Music) theorized the possibility of "Third Stream" music, which he saw as emanating especially from a synthesis of European classical music and jazz. In some sense, this Third Stream was already fully present in works such as George Gershwin's *Rhapsody in Blue*, Scott Joplin's opera *Treemonisha*, and Duke Ellington's various "suites" and other large-scale, symphonic works (e.g., *Black, Brown, and Beige* from the 1943 *Carnegie Hall Concert*). As full-blown synthesis, however, I would argue that we do not see the real emergence of the Third Stream until the development of progressive rock—because it was at this point that rock emerged as the first true "world music." And this is why, in more recent years, we have seen the development of the genre that is called by this name.

Indeed, if Third Stream music represents the synthesis of European harmony and counterpoint with non-Western rhythms, timbres, and tonalities, then perhaps experimental and progressive rock brings us to the "fourth stream" by incorporating the electric and electronic timbres and recording possibilities of the post-WWII period.

♫   ♫   ♫

What might be the essence of, shall we say, "protoprogressive rock," that is, the trend that led to the emergence of progressive rock in the late sixties? I would identify two elements in particular.

First, there is a continuation, or perhaps a continual restatement, of what might be considered to be the "underground" element in rock music. This might be contrasted to the "pop" element, even if both aspects are sometimes found in one and the same song. A very good example of this combination is Little Richard's brilliant "Tutti-Frutti" (1956). Obviously there is a pop side to this song, which was isolated to sickeningly sweet perfection in Pat Boone's lily-white version. In a "pop" world, our ears become accustomed to hearing only this bleached and starched aspect of the song, even when we are listening to Little Richard. Turn your head a little bit, however, and this song becomes quite weird and even a little scary. As with many of Little Richard's creations (and indeed his whole persona),[7] "Tutti-Frutti" drips with both the charismatic Black church (especially as a Southern institution) and a raw, polymorphous eroticism. My thinking on this question, incidentally, is rather at odds with Professor James F. Harris's in *Philosophy at 33 1/3 rpm*. Harris uses "Tutti-Frutti," and in particular the memorable "word," "Awopbopaloobopalop-bamboom," as examples of a period in rock music when, "[f]or the most part, the lyrics were irrelevant."

> These memorable lines are memorable just because they are so completely insignificant. The lyrics are, at best, superficial and shallow, and, at worst, silly and meaningless. It is the beat which is important, and you can substitute almost any words or sounds for the original lyrics without losing very much. (pp. 3–4)

Harris is interested in the "themes of classic rock music," as he puts it, mainly from the sixties. His notion of a "theme" has exclusively to do with the lyrics, whereas I am more interested in understanding the intermotivations of sounds and lyrics. With its manic religious eroticism, "Tutti-Frutti" may push the envelope of meaning, of "sense," but this "nonsense" is hardly insignificant.

The most important thing is that Little Richard has chosen to speak a "secret language" here. In order to get a glimmer of the significance of this language, we have to place "Tutti-Frutti" in at least three overlapping contexts: those of race, sexuality, and spirituality. I will not presume, here, to give an ordering to the relative importance of each of these contexts; however, in each case there is something like a language of resistance at work. It perhaps goes without saying that a Black person who finds him- or herself in the midst of an "American century" where everything the least bit weird is suspect[8] and where the attack on rock music is openly conducted as an attack on "race-mixing" (and where the specter of miscegenation is continually invoked), might be interested in speaking a language that is both unknown to the dominant white culture and in fact quite unsettling to it.[9] Indeed, everything that still unsettles defenders of the King's English (never mind for the moment that most of these defenders would be hard put to speak it themselves), that is, attackers of the various forms of Black English, is present in "Tutti-Frutti"—and not just in its "words," but in its raucous tone and manic beat. In like fashion, the song conjures images of unchained, polymorphous sexuality. There is a fluid, to say nothing of completely queer, set of identities at work here, the sort of thing that drives those with a fascist and racist cast of mind completely nuts—this is what Judith Butler calls "gender trouble." The "authoritarian personality" (as Adorno put it) demands stability of identity (and, if your identity is not stable, you'd better at least pretend that it is). The worst danger is that of "mongrelization," the contaminating element that disrupts racial and sexual "hygiene" (the Nazi term). The suspicion is that "Tutti-Frutti" is rubbing mongrelization right in the faces of those who fear identity disruption—and getting some of the youngsters, white and Black, to dance along with it.

Perhaps it goes without saying that there is also a playful rebelliousness to lyrics that, to the extent that they can be recontextualized into "standard English," seem to be saying that it is "all righty" ("all-a-rootie") to be "all fruity."

Finally, in a paradoxical twist, there is the obvious connection of "Tutti-Frutti" with the charismatic practice of glossolalia, also known as speaking in tongues. Although it would be stretching things a bit to see "Tutti-Frutti" as "sacred" music, it's not entirely "secular" either—this is, in fact, another way in which the song trangresses boundaries that some would prefer to remain fixed. Especially with the signature "awopbopaloobopalopbamboom" (which is perhaps the antidote to "supercalifragilisticexpialado-cious"—or is it the other way around?), there is clearly the sense of something "coming through" from some "other side," some-thing welling up from unknown depths.

The genius of the song is that all three of these secret lan-guages are inextricably intertwined—and the underground code that is thereby generated is, I would argue, a thread that stretches from the early days of rock and roll to the time of progressive rock. "Tutti-Frutti" is not in the least superficial or shallow, but is instead an invitation to an intense engagement with love (and sex) and mortality. Certainly it is a feast for Freudian analysis and analysis in the terms of contemporary cultural theory—and the fact that the song is also fun to listen and dance to does not negate its significance in the least.

Perhaps, too, out of this complex intertwining, one can map two basic possibilities for rock music, one more "sensual" (or out-right sexual), the other more "spiritual." But even in the case where progressive rock (especially at its most "undanceable"—though I would argue that the critics who focus primarily on danceability simply lack imagination, as both critics and dancers) seems to go almost entirely in the latter direction, as perhaps most outstandingly in the music of Yes, there always remains the element of eros—of the embrace.

Little wonder that this underground, threatening movement has always been countered, at every step, with a "normalizing" movement—the queer Little Richard countered by Pat Boone and the famous (p)Elvis that ultimately shook itself into the U.S. Army and then Las Vegas.

The other key element of the protoprogressive trend—also connected to an underground sensibility as well as countered by "pop" normalizations—was the idea that the music should "go somewhere." In other words, even in the beginnings of rock music, or before the beginning with Ray Charles and Louis Jor-dan, there was the idea that this music, which already trans-gressed boundaries of race, gender, and class, should also reflect new possibilities in its form.

Again the triumvirate of Chuck Berry, Little Richard, and Jerry Lee Lewis is important, but I especially want to highlight the innovations of Mr. Bo Diddley (Ellas McDaniel, b. 1928). Of the early synthesists of rock, Diddley was, in my view, the most visionary. This is true even when, as was often the case, his music was harmonically simple. Famously, Jerry Lee Lewis said of Diddley, "[i]f he ever gets outta the chord of E he might get dangerous."[10] (The context makes it clear that Lewis said this affectionately.) For that matter, Diddley is even better known for his chugging, "shave and a haircut" rhythm (think of the song, "Bo Diddley," or "Who Do You Love?" or "Not Fade Away"). Obviously, the lines that one initially expects to extrapolate from Bo Diddley's music seem to lead more directly to hip-hop than to progressive rock—just as Little Richard's music and performance approach leads more directly to Prince or Michael Jackson. However, and this is important, both Little Richard and Bo Diddley influence this more recent music by way of the psychedelic blues that were an integral part of the milieu—especially in England—out of which progressive rock developed in the late sixties.

In any case, it is certainly true that Diddley built his innovations on the terra firma of roots rock—but, on top of these roots, Diddley had all sorts of interesting things going on, and the roots themselves seemed to run deeper, toward Africa via the Deep South (specifically, McComb, Mississippi) and New Orleans. If Jerry Lee Lewis and Little Richard came out of Southern charismatic churches where the religion is intensely physical, Diddley seemed to connect with something else, something, there as well, hidden in the charismatic Christianity of warmer climes (that Southern thing again)—something in the vicinity of the old religions of the Earth, something "pagan," animistic, akin to voodoo, and haunting.

It is worth noting that the intertwining of Christianity and the old nature religions will also be found in progressive rock. Perhaps the most important examples are Yes's *Close to the Edge* and *Tales from Topographic Oceans* (e.g., "a dew drop can exalt us like the music of the sun").[11] Admittedly, the intertwining found in this music is probably rooted in more specifically European and British Isles forms of hermeticism, but the link of affinity still has significance. At the very least, it is a question of a "force" that "comes through" (spoken to again quite recently in Yes's "That, That Is," as well as in Robert Fripp's notion that King Crimson forms when there is King Crimson music to be played). I think that every musician who hopes to "go somewhere" with the music understands this subterranean welling-up.

In Diddley's case, the welling up is also a redemptive force, as his seemingly simple one-note or one-chord meditations also call to mind the field hollers of slaves and poor sharecroppers. Listening to Diddley's music in preparation for this all-too-brief discussion of it, I was also struck by an interesting parallel. An omnipresent force in this music is the maraca playing of Jerome Green. The maraca is an instrument that goes back to Africa—it is basically a gourd filled with dried seeds or beans. There is something basically unpredictable in the use of maracas, something like a quantum effect at work—regardless of how much rhythmic sense the maraca player has, there's a limit to how much control can be effected over the falling of those seeds. Not to head too far into the territory of theoretical physics, the point is that the maracas fit well into Diddley's music because they represent the essence of that music—simplicity and steadiness combined with complexity and unpredictability. A parallel I am thinking of concerns the way that the great African (Nigerian) musician Fela Kuti always has the afuche (a gourd covered with strings of beads, which the player moves by hand over the surface of the gourd) at the center of his music. Fela has a rather large group (twelve or more instrumentalists, seven or eight singers, and seven or eight dancers), but the afuche is always in the front of the stage, in some sense leading the band—or perhaps serving as its soul. In either case—Diddley's maracas or Fela's afuche—there is an idea at work, and it is both simple and deep.

Incidentally, the maracas and the afuche are among those "simple" percussion instruments, like the tambourine, that everyone assumes they could easily play—but it ain't necessarily so.

Diddley also expanded the sonic range on top, with the use of violin and often very angular guitar (visually represented by Diddley's famous rectangular-shaped instruments, which also evoke another part of the Southern culture of poor people, namely the cigar-box fiddle).

It should be mentioned, too, that Diddley was probably the only early rocker to feature women instrumentalists in his groups (the best known of whom was a guitarist called "The Duchess").

The underground and innovative ("going somewhere") aspects of early rock music gave rise to a trend that was both developmental—"progressive"—and outside of the mainstream. Despite claims, from Theodore Gracyk and others (see, e.g., Gracyk, pp. 180–85, on the question of "selling out"), that most of rock music's "rebelliousness" is just a pose for selling records, certainly there is a sense in which the more developmental and underground aspects of rock music (perhaps even quite apart from what specific musicians thought they were doing) were set *against* the mainstream. The interesting rock music, whether from the fifties, or the time of progressive rock, or today, is set against pop formulas and pop sensibilities. In some of the early rock music, such as that of Little Richard or Bo Diddley, there is an expansiveness that is both sonic and social. It is quite possible to trace the lines of development, from the early and middle fifties, to the late sixties, that led to quantum leaps in the sophistication of rock music.

Many groups and musicians played important roles in this developmental process, but none more than the Beach Boys and the Beatles. A slogan that I will appeal to more than once in the course of this book is the following: "If you don't like progressive rock, blame it on the Beatles." I only mention the one group in my slogan for sake of brevity and for shock value (hardly anyone *wants* not to like the Beatles), but the same blame could be laid at the foot of the Beach Boys. Consider the "danceability" question. I admit, for what it's worth, that the issue of what happens to a music that is based in dance (or is originally meant to be primarily music for dancing to) when it is no longer danceable is a valid question. But, the fact is, the same reasons why much progressive rock is difficult to dance to apply just as much to "Good Vibrations" and "A Day in the Life" (where's that backbeat?!).

On top of the firm foundation laid by Ray Charles, Chuck Berry, Little Richard, Jerry Lee Lewis, and Bo Diddley, the Beach

Boys and the Beatles brought expansions in harmony, instrumentation (and therefore timbre), duration, rhythm, and the use of recording technology. Of these elements, the first and the last were the most important in clearing a pathway toward the development of progressive rock. Although this is an oversimplification, it might be said that progressive rock grew out of the combination of African rhythms and European harmonies that passed through the southeastern United States and then went out to the world as rock and roll. (This is the "Afro-Celtic" idea again, which has lately made a reappearance by way of hip-hop.) Certainly, by the time we reach the turning point represented by the Beach Boys' *Pet Sounds* (1966) and the Beatles' *Sergeant Pepper's Lonely Hearts' Club Band* (1967), it seems that Bo Diddley, Little Richard, Mississippi, New Orleans, and Africa are a long way away. Then again, when we trace the evolution of, say, Peter Gabriel, from Genesis to *Secret World*, it seems that things have come full circle—or perhaps "full spiral" would be a more apt description. (In the video of the *Secret World* concert, Gabriel closes with what to my mind is a fantastic song, "In Your Eyes." As the song and concert come to the finale, most of the large group of musicians is dancing around the edge of the circular stage, a wonderful—and utopian—image of this spiral.)

Framed once again in these terms, the line that leads from the originators, through the Beach Boys and Beatles, and ultimately to progressive rock, is clear. Look somewhere in the middle of this line, to King Crimson's *Larks' Tongues in Aspic* or the third part of Yes's *Tales from Topographic Oceans* ("The Ancient: Giants Under the Sun") or the Mahavishnu Orchestra's *Inner Mounting Flame*, and you find a solid core of adventurous rhythms, very much traceable to African music, and innovative harmonies, building on the tradition of nineteenth- and twentieth-century European classical music. A music historian might say, "So what? Isn't this combination already in place with Stravinsky's *Rite of Spring*?" Admittedly, there is a large component of Stravinsky in much of progressive rock—along with smaller doses of Debussy, Bartók, Sibelius, Orff, Messiaen, Cage, Stockhausen (and, though rarely, Schönberg and Webern)—but where the African European combination appears in Stravinsky as exoticism and dramatic juxtaposition (and even as colonialism and exploitation), in progressive rock there is an integration into a new kind of music. The Peter Gabriel example is apt, because the works by King Crimson, Yes, and the Mahavishnu Orchestra mentioned just now are already full-blown examples of "world music."

This generous synthesis is already well along with the Beatles' *Rubber Soul* (1965). This album represents a turning point in another regard: at this moment, for rock musicians who were pursuing the underground and developmental possibilities of the music, the *album* rather than the song became the basic unit of artistic production.

In discussions of progressive rock, the idea of the "concept album" is mentioned frequently. If this term refers to albums that have thematic unity and development throughout, then in reality there are probably fewer concept albums than one might at first think. *Pet Sounds* and *Sergeant Pepper's* do not qualify according to this criterion; of the major albums of progressive rock that will be discussed in chapter 4, only a relative handful can truly be considered concept albums in the thematic sense. (One example is *Thick as a Brick*—though, as readers undoubtedly know, it's more than a little difficult to figure out exactly what the "concept" is in this case.) However, if instead we stretch the definition a bit, to where the album *is* the concept, then it is clear that progressive rock is entirely a music of concept albums—and this flows rather directly out of *Rubber Soul* (December 1965) and then *Revolver* (1966), *Pet Sounds*, and *Sergeant Pepper's*.

Without getting too ahead of our story, we might note at this point that, in the wake of these albums, many rock musicians took up the "complete album approach." One magnificent example is Stevie Wonder's trilogy: *Talking Book* (1972), *Innervisions* (1973), and *Songs in the Key of Life* (1976). (There are a few weak moments on the last of these, but then, there are a few weak moments on the *White Album*, too.) Another great example is War's *All Day Music* (1971). These albums might belong to their own category: call it "progressive soul"—but, since they are coming out of rock music no less than *Sergeant Pepper's*, why separate them from progressive rock? I will develop this question in the next chapter, but I want to make it clear at this point that the categories I will attempt to delineate are not meant as valorizations in and of themselves. Certainly the presence of these complete albums in the early and middle seventies demonstrates a very broad progressive approach that many rock musicians were taking up—these musicians were trying to say important things, working the terms of the culture in a critical way and with an adventurous musical style.[12] What I am going to call "progressive rock" was just one segment of this larger trend—though one that has been much undervalued since its heyday. Going a bit further, it might also be argued that progressive rock was the core of this trend; I offer as "exhibit A" in this case the fact that, after the time of progressive rock, the tendency was for "albums" to once again be simply loose collections of songs.

Significantly, what this shows us is that progressive rock represented a concentration and heightening of all the trends in rock music that were set against the merely "pop" sensibility: the underground and developmental aspects, the complete album approach, generosity and synthesis. After the time of progressive rock, the dynamic that extended from the originators, through the Beatles, and to the broad progressive trend, was broken. How that happened will be explored in the final chapter of this book; for present purposes, however, the fact of this break demonstrates, in retrospect, that there really is such a thing as the prehistory of progressive rock.

Let us turn now to an altogether too-quick look at the further steps that led to the emergence of "full-blown" progressive rock. It is useful to keep in mind that everything that will be discussed in these next few pages happened in the space of about two or three years. Because there is *so much* to say about these years, roughly from 1966 to 1969—or from *Pet Sounds* and *Sergeant Pepper's* to *In the Court of the Crimson King*—I am in fact not going to say much at all. Indeed, it pains me to even mention, with almost nothing in way of thematic development, the next set of groups whose music will simply be used as a stepping stone. The point is simply to show, in broad terms, the creative milieu that made it possible for progressive rock to become the next logical step—even if this step also represented a qualitative leap. In concluding this chapter, let us set the stage for progressive rock;

some of the themes introduced here will be developed extensively in the next chapter.

◼ ◼ ◼

Insomuch as any attempt to expunge progressive rock from music history must ultimately come to terms with the later Beatles, let us remind ourselves of the many attempts on the part of other bands to make their own *Sergeant Pepper's*. Among these albums found under the long shadow of the Sergeant we find such disparate works as the Grateful Dead's *Anthem of the Sun* and Simon and Garfunkel's *Bookends* (both 1968)—and, for that matter, *In the Court of the Crimson King* (1969), on which much more will be said in the chapters to come. Let's take a moment to consider what might be thought of as the "dark side" of *Sergeant Pepper's*, namely the Rolling Stone's brilliant *Their Satanic Majesties Request*. If any album is a direct response to *Sergeant Pepper's*, it is this one.

Significantly, *Satanic Majesties* so obviously belongs to the set of "transitions to progressive rock" that many hardcore Stones fans do not like the album at all. In fact, in *Rock: The Rough Guide*, a publication written by fans, Peter Shapiro writes:

> Brian Jones was fascinated with Moroccan music and obsessed with keeping up with the Beatles, of which there is ample evidence on "Paint It Black." This reached its peak with The Stones' response to *Sgt. Pepper*, the appalling *Their Satanic Majesties Request* (1967) which trawled the depths of 60s drug culture with its awful sci-fi concept and misguided space music. (p. 738)

To this, allow me to say that I like the album very much; in fact, on most days I would rather listen to it than *Sergeant Pepper's*, because of the darkness of it. I'm not myself a fan of the drug culture of any period; however, one gets the sense from this reviewer that the problem isn't so much the drugs, but instead which drugs; that is, the sort of Stones fan who dislikes progressive rock (I'd like to think that one could appreciate both for what they are) most likely prefers that Mick, Keith, and company stay with the drunk or strung-out variety of mind-altering substances rather than the sort that gets you onto Trans-Love Airways ("gets you there on time"—Donovan) or some other "sci-fi" excursion.

*   *   *

Now we have two further elements for consideration, psychedelia and science fiction. Both play important roles in progressive rock, each especially in their more visionary and utopian aspects. Of the many songs that could be mentioned in this connection, two from the late sixties that especially capture the visionary-psychedelic mood are "Journey to the Center of the Mind," by Ted Nugent and the Amboy Dukes, and "Crystal Blue Persuasion," by Tommy James and the Shondells. Shortly thereafter we hear the even dreamier works of Hendrix, Cream, and then two groups that overlap significantly with progressive rock "proper," the Moody Blues and Pink Floyd. In *Rocking the Classics*, Edward Macan especially sees psychedelic music's tendency toward time dilation and warping—i.e., playing long, trippy jams—as important in the transition to progressive rock (see pp. 18–23). All of this music came out in a very brief period, so similarities here are one part influence and one part *Zeitgeist*. The relationship between psychedelic and progressive rock will be explored in greater detail in the next chapter.

*   *   *

The Jimi Hendrix Experience and Cream also represent an interesting recapitulation of the blues roots of rock music, combined with extension, vision, and virtuosity. One argument that I will make in the next chapter is that a key element of progressive rock is virtuoso musicianship. Many of the musicians in groups such as the Beach Boys and the Beatles are underrated. However, with the arrival of Jack Bruce, Ginger Baker, Eric Clapton, Jimi Hendrix, Mitch Mitchell, John Entwistle, Jimmy Page, and others on the scene, we have entered the time of really excellent *musicians* who happen to play rock.

Of course, one might also say that the stage was well set at this point for everything to go completely overboard—and that progressive rock is exactly what you get when extended demonstrations of rock musicianship are ratcheted up that final notch.

Well, it's true that progressive rock, to say nothing of Clapton or Hendrix, sometimes went overboard. The other much-used term that comes up in this context is "pretentious." My argument will be that the best works of progressive rock (or Cream or Hendrix, for that matter) justify the risks or overextensions that were required—such risks are part of music that aims to develop.

◼ ◼ ◼

We cannot leave the realm of the late-sixties rock adventure without touching on two more bands, namely The Who and Led Zeppelin. They are another pair who reach back to the roots of rock and forward to sonic and intellectual explorations. Led Zeppelin did not form until 1968—the same year that Yes formed, as every reader of Chris Welch's liner notes from the first Yes album is reminded—and their career is contemporaneous with the time of progressive rock. In addition to psychedelia, the group brought an interest in magic and what has come to be called "fantasy." For our purposes they are not a progressive rock group, but instead a progressive blues-rock group that hovers at the edge of progressive rock. This distinction may seem an exercise in hair-splitting. Another way to put it is that Led Zeppelin show the ultimate difficulty in framing definitions and categories, because, as we shall see, they do meet the criteria for what I will call progressive rock. And yet, my guess is that most readers, even if they like or love Led Zeppelin's music (I like some of it), will recognize that they are somehow quite different from groups that we would more readily associate with progressive rock. Categories can break down, but this doesn't mean that they aren't useful; in fact, one way that categories can be useful is when we put them to the test and see somewhat precisely what their limitations are.

The Who is one of my all-time favorite groups. They are one of the groups that I feel especially pained to pass by so quickly.[13] As a "pure" rock singer, there's no one better than Roger Daltrey, at least in my humble opinion. Keith Moon's drumming was simply unbelievable—in the sense that no one could figure out what he was doing (perhaps least of all him), and yet it seemed to work in a bizarre, orchestral way. John Entwistle is one of the best bass guitar players, period, and he has influenced many other bassists, including several, such as Chris Squire, who have played an integral role in progressive rock. And now, here's a ridiculous comment: Pete Townshend is *not* a great guitar player. This is the singular and somewhat silly reason that I do not consider The Who to be a part of the progressive rock trend. Townshend is, of course, a good guitar player; more important, he is a visionary and brilliant composer of extended forms that are based in a very solid foundation of rock and roll. Townshend can do more with just a few chords than just about anyone. Among those albums that set the stage for the extended works of progressive rock, we have to include *Tommy* (1969)—even if, for one thing, its appearance is cotemporaneous with the first progressive rock albums, and, for another, Townshend himself would most likely be unhappy to think that he contributed to the emergence of progressive rock (this is a person who once referred to "the unspeakable horror that is Led Zeppelin"). *Quadrophenia* (1973) went even further—indeed, Dave Marsh, who is no friend of progressive rock, compared the album to the "art rock" efforts of Genesis and King Crimson (p. 493). Among my "rock intellectual" colleagues, the great *Tommy* versus *Quadrophenia* debate rages on!

◼ ◼ ◼

Now, for a moment, let us take what might seem a strange turn. Four of the groups mentioned in the last few pages feature excellent bass guitarists, musicians who opened new possibilities for what many people still think of, even now, as an instrument that should remain in the background. I've already mentioned John Entwistle, whose weaving, slithery lines started a revolution in bass playing. Jack Bruce and John Paul Jones, though more bottom-heavy in their approaches, all the same broadened the role of the instrument.

Then there is the great overlooked one: Paul McCartney. Of course McCartney has never lacked for attention as a member of the Beatles and as a singer and songwriter (nor can we say that he hasn't been adequately compensated in the financial department!). But one thing that is easy to forget about the Beatles— and our present visual-media-saturated society (that is, with movies and television as the main carriers of the society of the spectacle) has made it no less easy—is that, at the end of the day, they were first and foremost a *band*, a group of people who played musical instruments and sang songs. Given that the bass guitar is often overlooked anyway, and that many people couldn't even tell you who is playing the bass in the Beatles, perhaps it is to be expected that Paul McCartney's contribution on the instrument hasn't received its complete due. Listen to a song such as "Rain," which owes everything to the subtlety and melodicism of the bass-guitar part. (This song was released in 1966 as the B-side of a single, for which the A-side was "Paperback Writer"—in between the release of *Rubber Soul* and that of *Revolver*—all of which says a great deal about the enormous flow of creativity working in the world at that time.) In his very good book, *The Beatles*, Allan Kozinn writes,

> McCartney's bass, placed in front of the mix, is an ingenious counterpoint that takes him all over the fretboard. Yet even when it does comparatively little, it can be the most interesting element of the performance. At the chorus, for example, while Lennon and McCartney harmonize in fourths on a melody with a slightly Middle Eastern tinge, McCartney first points up the song's droning character by hammering on a high G (approached with a quick slide from the F natural just below it), playing it steadily on the beat for twenty successive beats. The next time the chorus comes around, though, he plays something entirely different, a slightly syncopated descending three-note pattern that almost seems to evoke the falling rain. (p. 143)

McCartney's bass lines are subtle, thoughtful, and virtuosic; from *Rubber Soul* forward, every Beatles album and almost every single provides an excellent school for bass-guitar playing, with *Abbey Road* demonstrating a very mature style.

Again there is a Beach Boys connection. Even more ignored as a bass guitarist than McCartney is Brian Wilson. His lines are not only melodic and integral to the compositions, they are also the product of some interesting studio technology—courtesy of Phil Spector (later infamous for his overproduction of the Beatles' *Let It Be*). Spector would sometimes record as many as eight different versions of a song's bass line, using different instruments and settings on the mixing board, and then piece together the final bass part from this conglomeration. Bass players used to go nuts trying to imitate what came out on the record!

And all of this also goes back to the Motown connection, which had such a great impact on English rock groups, both before and after the appearance of the Beatles. The bass lines of James Jamerson, Carol Kaye, and others had a melodic drive that simply took the music to a new place. And this is one part of the point I am aiming toward here: the expanded role of the bass guitar brought about a transformation in the music.

As a musician, my own main instrument is the bass guitar, so the reader might suspect that I am giving special attention to a personal interest of mine. Perhaps. However, there is still an interesting point to be made here, or perhaps a few connected points. First, all of the bass players I mentioned are well known and highly regarded, and none of them does what bass players are stereotypically thought or expected to do. Second, this instrument, which is supposed to be at the back or at the bottom of the music, played a leading role in the transformation of the music I have been discussing. In other words, "Rain," for instance, is the song that it is because of what is going on with the bass guitar. Put another way, in all of the cases I mentioned, from Motown to the Beatles to The Who, the innovations in the music can be seen in microcosm in the innovations of the bass lines. Third, the greater role for the bass in this music is symbolic of the way that, in the development of the underground and visionary trends that emerged in the late sixties, groups took a more "symphonic" approach to musical arrangement. In other words, the part for each instrument was carefully crafted as a contribution to a larger whole, and compositions emphasized the possibilities of diverse timbres. Instruments that had been "last" became, if not "first," then at least equal players in the band. And the contrapuntal contributions of McCartney and Entwistle, especially, encouraged a new level of synergy. This synergy flowered in the playing of Chris Squire, John Wetton, Glenn Cornick, Hugh Hopper, and the other major bass guitarists of progressive rock—and the music of their bands was qualitatively enriched because of this.

🎵   🎵   🎵

As we shall see, some groups were "born" as progressive rock groups, while others grew into this. Among the major groups,

Jethro Tull (f. 1967) and Yes (f. 1968) started out as perhaps not quite progressive, in the specialized sense in which I will use the term. In either case, each group began writing and playing "full-blown" progressive rock somewhere in the vicinity of their third or fourth albums: *Benefit* and *Aqualung* for Tull, *The Yes Album* and *Fragile* for Yes—in other words, around 1970–71. (Incidentally, *Benefit* and *The Yes Album* make a nice pair in my view, from their album covers to the individual songs.) Among the groups that played progressive rock from their inception are King Crimson (f. 1968) and Emerson, Lake, and Palmer (f. 1970). In both cases there was a predecessor group. King Crimson was preceeded by Giles, Giles, and Fripp, whose "cheerful insanity" (1968) is only of specialty interest today (though I still feel sorry for little Rodney thirty years later). However, Emerson, Lake, and Palmer was preceded by The Nice, and we should take a moment to mark the significance of this group for the development of progressive rock.[14]

Originally a foursome (the first two versions of the group included guitarists Davy O'List and Gordon Longstaff), The Nice became most interesting, in my view, with their third album, where they pared down to a keyboard-led trio. This assemblage, consisting in Keith Emerson, keyboards (mainly piano and Hammond B-3 organ), Lee Jackson on bass guitar and vocals, and Brian Davison on drums, was in many ways a streamlined paradigm for the progressive groups that formed around them. Starting with the first of the three albums recorded by this trio, *The Nice* (1969), Keith Emerson showed that it was possible to bring together a very large range of influences, including European classical music, jazz, ragtime, Broadway, boogie-woogie, psychedelic, and Bob Dylan. Emerson's classical influences at that point ran from Bach to Sibelius, while his jazz chops seemed especially indebted to Oscar Peterson.

The Nice's fourth album, *Five Bridges* (1970), was recorded live with a full orchestra. This was not the first major symphonic outing for a rock group—the Moody Blues had already pioneered this idea three years before, with *Days of Future Passed* (1967), which is certainly the superior album as well. However, as with the other sides of *Sergeant Pepper's* that we hear in such albums as the Stones' *Satanic Majesties*, there is something to be said for the second time something happens. In the case of The Nice, another blow was struck for an expanded range for rock music. The actual "Five Bridges Suite," which fills side one of the original LP, moves from a more baroque classical style to, ultimately, a mini-concerto for jazz reeds and brass, featuring some of the major figures from the English scene (including Alan Skidmore, Kenny Wheeler, and Chris Pyne). Keith Emerson's liner notes for the album capture nicely—if not altogether coherently (but that's part of the trip!)—the experimental mood of the times:

> On a journey from the almost Utopian freedom of our music to the established orthodox music school I met Joseph Eger [who conducted the Sinfonia of London in this project] who was travelling in the opposite direction.
>
> Since that meeting we have on various occasions been catalysts in combining together the music from our different backgrounds forming sometimes a fusion, and other times a healthy conflict between the orchestra, representing possibly the establishment, and the trio, representing the non-establishment; ourselves having complete trust in a rebellious spirit and highly developed, broad minded music brain whose reformed ideas in direction have been frowned upon, almost spat upon by some so-called music critics. That being Joseph Eger, the fighter.
>
> [The "Suite"] uses bridges as a musical symbol. I worked on building a musical bridge combining early baroque forms to more contemporary ideas. . . .
>
> In conclusion to all this The Nice and Joseph Eger have been trying to build bridges to those musical shores which seem determined to remain apart from that which is a whole.

It was easy then and it is easy now to be cynical about this sort of thing.[15] And so, a contrast opens up around Emerson's sentiments that continues to permeate the discussion regarding progressive rock: a contrast between a visionary idealism—albeit sometimes a naive one—concerning both purely musical and social aims, and a cynicism that regards striving for "utopian freedom" and similar goals as deluded.

Incidentally, *Five Bridges* features an album cover by Hipgnosis, who would design many important covers in the seventies (the best known of which is Pink Floyd's *Dark Side of the Moon*).

As protoprogressive rock, Keith Emerson and The Nice represented the best and the worst. At their best, The Nice could come
up with compositions and performances that were both subtle
and innovative. "Azrael," the lead-off piece from *The Nice*, is a fine
example of these qualities. At their worst, the group—and especially Emerson—resorted to bombastic histrionics, of a sort that
later became associated with progressive rock in general. (I've
seen Emerson abuse his organ a couple times with ELP, once in
the seventies and once in the nineties; at the expense of sounding
like a stick in the mud, I still have to say that I find the whole
exercise tedious, pointless, and unamusing—even if a large segment of the average rock concert audience gets off on it.)

Finally, something ought to be said about the absence of guitar on these albums. As the reader is undoubtedly aware, most
progressive rock groups have guitar players. Furthermore, it is
best, in my view, to resist the overidentification of progressive
rock with keyboard wizardry. (After all, one of the pillars of progressive rock, King Crimson, never featured multiple keyboard
work.) Still, we might consider The Nice, in its trio form, as presenting exemplary protoprogressive rock in that the guitar is not
the center or dominating force in the music. Obviously, there are
many other examples of this displacement, going back to Little
Richard and Jerry Lee Lewis, and coming forward to the later
music of the Beatles. The key issue here is not the guitar itself,
but instead what would be the dominating presence in rock
music—would music come through the guitar or the guitar
through the music?[16] Indeed, from *Rubber Soul* onward, a demar-
cation opens up between rock music that will remain more
closely tied to the blues form *and* to the electric guitar, and rock
music that explores other possibilities. Again, my term for the
insistence that only the former is "real" or "authentic" rock music
is "blues orthodoxy." To be sure, there is much music, including
music from the later Beatles, that straddles this line.

᭥   ᭥   ᭥

Looked at this way, we might also consider that progressive
rock straddles various lines as well, with one foot in the kind of

rock music that rejects blues orthodoxy, and the other foot perhaps out of rock music altogether. From the perspective of blues orthodoxy, this kind of music really isn't rock music at all. We will explore this issue further in the next chapter (and also ask why this matters in any case), but it still seems to me that the fundamental crossing of lines was accomplished by the Beatles. The Beatles made rock music with a developmental perspective; the question then becomes, Where do you draw the line, how much development is too much? But I would also like to ask, *Why* do we want to draw the line? What forces are at work in making us think that a line needs to be drawn?

The "forces at work" are not simply folks who want some "old time rock 'n' roll"—instead, this is a question of social and cultural shifts. But first we will need to explore the cultural currents that actually demanded some "new time" rock music.

Rock music, up to a point, developed through qualitative leaps that were not entirely or even primarily driven by the commercial imperative to deliver salable product. Instead, the driving force was a synthesis of social and musical experimentalism.

To conclude this strange and rather tendentious romp through the history of rock music, let's bring the connections forward one more time. Allan Kozinn discusses the way that John Lennon would often borrow a tune or a hook from some earlier song, and use it as the launching pad for his own composition.

> Not that Lennon worked this way all the time. Many of his best songs are entirely without precedent or model. Still, using an earlier piece of music as either a source of ideas or as the foundation for a new work is a time-honoured practice. In the fifteenth and sixteenth centuries, church composers like Guillaume Dufay and Josquin Despres routinely based their Masses on popular melodies, tunes that any listener of the time would have known. But these composers did not have copyright lawyers looking over their shoulders. Lennon knew that if he were going to use existing works as models, he had to disguise them, but occasionally he let a clue slip through. In 1969 he patterned "Come Together" after Chuck Berry's "You Can't Catch Me." (p. 24)[17]

Progressive rock represents a qualitative development in one of the core ideas of rock music: the generous synthesis, carried forward in an open and developmental way. The key issue, at least up through the time of progressive rock, was how to make that next musical step. Kozinn's excellent analysis demonstrates what the middle and late sixties scene was all about; as he explains, in the shaping of the *Sergeant Pepper's* album as a complete, integrated work,

> McCartney had a model of sorts in the Beach Boys' *Pet Sounds*, the album on which Brian Wilson, the group's principal composer, distanced the band from its surf music image. Its lyrics, for the most part, had the emotional depth that the Beatles had been working toward, and its quirkily-structured songs boasted colourful instrumentation and sound effects, to say nothing of the Beach Boys' magnificent vocal harmonies, which rivalled the Beatles' own. When McCartney heard the album at the time of its release in 1966, his reaction was, "how are we going to top this?"
>
> As it turned out, Wilson later said that he was inspired to make *Pet Sounds* after hearing the Beatles' *Rubber Soul*. But *Sgt. Pepper* brought this creative give-and-take to an end. Wilson's plan was to respond with *Smile*, a collection of material lyrically and musically more complex than *Pet Sounds*, and meant to be as daring as *Sgt. Pepper*. But Wilson's excessive drug use (among other personal problems) caught up with him during the sessions, which ground to a halt when he had a nervous breakdown.[18] Nevertheless, for as long as it lasted, the competitive interaction between the Beatles, the Beach Boys, the Byrds, Bob Dylan, and a handful of other rock musicians unquestionably helped transform the best pop music of this time from teenage ephemera into durable art. (p. 154)

A little while—two years, but two very long years—after the hullabaloo around *Sergeant Pepper's* had faded away, the Beatles released what was in fact the last album they made together as a group, *Abbey Road* (1969). (*Let It Be* was made earlier but not released until 1970.) This is a record of great maturity, and it is difficult not to look back on it and feel a certain wistfulness—for all kinds of reasons. By this time, the innocence of the summer of love had long ended—quite definitively, in the summer of 1968 in the streets of Chicago—but *Abbey Road* seemed really to signal a certain kind of end.

I would like to quote some lyrics here but, frankly, and keeping in mind John Lennon's legal difficulties over "Come Together," I would prefer not to give any money to Michael Jackson. My motives are not entirely selfish—indeed, they are a bit paternalistic, because, let's face it, What good has more money ever done for the King of Pop? This point is actually not as extraneous as it might at first sound, because the opening to the possibility of progressive rock, as well as the closing of this time, has everything to do with questions of money, forms of property, and structures of legality.

For this brief moment, however, let us contemplate the Beatles' final great achievement, where something came to an end, and yet where it was still the case that something was supposed to happen next. And in the same moment, let us also remember that 1969 was the year marked by the emergence of the Crimson King.

3

The time of progressive rock: Toward a theory

What is progressive rock? At least when it comes to forms of art, to attempt to form solid or stable categories is a dangerous thing. There always comes the moment when these categories do more harm than good, when they get in the way of creativity because they have become mere formulas. This is one of the themes of Immanuel Kant's *Critique of Judgment*. Kant argues that society cannot produce artists in the same way that it can produce scientists, because there is something in the work of the former that goes beyond education and training. Although Kant probably underestimated the role of creativity in scientific endeavors, surely there is something to his idea that there is an intangible and irreducibly nonformulaic element involved in the emergence of art.

One difference I have with Kant on this is that he calls this element "genius," whereas I do not see it in quite these—individualistic, it seems—terms. On the other hand, I do see something peculiar about the human organism, namely that its conscious actions and chains of reasoning are, on some level, unpredictable, in finding expression in creativity.[1] But organism here must be understood on the social level as well as the biological. We are the sort of creatures who engage in poiesis, or what Martin Heidegger called "world disclosure." Karl Marx has an interesting way of putting it: bees, he notes, are extraordinary architects; the structures they create are wonders to behold. The difference between human beings and bees is not in the level of sophistication or beauty of these structures (on some levels the bees clearly have us beat). Instead, Marx argues, the difference is that the human being builds the structure in his or her mind before building it materially. In our creative acts, we are shaping and building worlds—indeed, Nelson Goodman refers to "ways of worldmaking."[2]

In allying this activity with the work of the poet, Heidegger demonstrated a close connection between creativity, language, and what it means to be human. One reason for not viewing creativity as purely a matter of individual "genius" is that, for creatures such as ourselves, there is an irreducibly social element in our coming-to-be-in-the-world (what Heidegger calls "Dasein," literally "being-there"). A simple, if perhaps crude, way of putting this is that every little "genius" had a mother and other people who introduced him or her to the world, enabling his or her particular talents to shine forth. (Arguments that depend on an overly individualistic notion of genius invariably have as a key component an erasure of the mother from the creative process— even if they sometimes take over some of the vocabulary of mothering.) In coming into language—which is not the "product" of any individual—we come into the world. As Donald Davidson puts it, "There is no difference between knowing your way around a language and knowing your way around a world."[3]

Rock music, even with all of the commercial imperatives that surrounded it and even, to a large extent, defined it as a musical form, still inspired the imaginations of people who were inclined toward poiesis. I doubt that I have to convince readers of this book that there is creativity in rock music, but we also know that there are and have been forces arrayed against that creativity, and that most rock music—as "pop music"—is produced according to formulas. The worry is that these formulas are, as Adorno argued, "predigested"—surely we have to admit that this worry does apply to most rock music (and, I would say, to all "pop" music, *by definition*—which does not mean that there is no creativity in pop music).

In a powerful argument, Theodore Gracyk allows us to see the interarticulation of these themes. The immediate context for his argument concerns the way that some rock groups create for themselves a "signature" sound, then find themselves trapped within that "code." Gracyk quotes sociologist and theorist of heavy metal music Deena Weinstein: "On one level, the signature sound [of a successful band] is like the blue beads or the green flakes put into detergents to set off one brand from its all-but-equivalent competitors" (p. 153). Gracyk admits that this is *half* of the story (as does Weinstein for that matter), but he is critical of Weinstein's view that, even if "commercial considerations are not the whole story," still "each band's signature sound is inevitably a *'compromise'* [my emphasis] between self-expression and the predigested sonic, visual, and symbolic dimensions that distinguish metal from other types of rock" (p. 153). Gracyk's argument is that, if one takes seriously a level of analysis that is different from the purely commercial, the picture is transformed.

> The other level is, of course, aesthetic. Rather than a compromise which prevents rock bands from fully achieving self-expression, the "code" for success might be understood as *initial requirements* for meaningfulness. Self-expression cannot be the spontaneous outpouring of sensitive genius. If it were, it would be an inarticulate outpouring. As Ernst Gombrich and Richard Wollheim remind us, meaningful self-expression requires creation "within a set of alternatives that could, to a greater or lesser degree of completeness, be enumerated." Alternatives that are common to a community are a general style. Ones directly associated with an individual (in rock, often a band) are the individual's style, which may be adopted by others so as to become part of the general style. . . . Rather than *just* a commercial compromise limiting the individual, the process of generating a signature sound within a broader nexus of established alternatives is essential to self-expression. Calling it a compromise is like calling my children's adoption of English as their native language a career move. I call it a necessary step in their enculturation. Prior to that, their prattle and babble in the playpen was inarticulate. Music without identifiable stylistic features is equally inarticulate. (pp. 153–54)

Looked at in these terms, we can rethink the "compromise." We cannot think, speak, write, listen, or hear without categories, nor can we participate in world disclosure. On the other hand, neither is there any space for creativity if we only repeat what has already been predigested. Thus we find ourselves in the peculiarly human situation of between-ness: we need categories, but we also need to think at the limits of categories, sometimes pressing categories to the point where they break. At these limits, of course, there is the danger of sounding inarticulate—and this is in fact what happens with avant-garde music, whether this music is launched from the Western classical tradition, jazz, or rock music.

Now think about all of this in a context where the underground and visionary trends in rock music, those trends that, though working through categories and conventions, pressed forward with the project of creativity, were now challenged to answer a *call*: a call that was at the same time both aesthetic and social. A call issued in a time of breaking with received ideas.

■   ■   ■

1968 seems both like a million years ago and just like yesterday—even to people who weren't born at the time, but who know on some level that every contemporary fashion or style is marked by that period of tremendous upheaval. Grappling with the elements that made up "the sixties," and gauging the relevance of these elements to our present period (whatever that is) is a difficult task. Even for people who were "around" at the time (whether as a participant in "events," or as a spectator), it is hard, from this distance, to get a purchase on what seems, now, to have been the last gasp of something we used to call "history."

The aim here is not simply excessive irony—though, if historical recovery is possible, this will undoubtedly occur in an ironic mode. As a historical period, the sixties certainly stretched on into the middle seventies, at least until the time that final U.S. helicopter left Saigon (at which point it wasn't Saigon anymore) and the resignation of Richard Nixon some time after that. This all has to do with placing progressive rock in its time. But, on a happier note, progressive rock was able to partake of a certain *energy*, that of the late sixties, and to propel itself into the middle and even later seventies. At least until the time of punk rock (that is, around 1976 or '77), progressive rock was the carrier of a utopian, visionary, and critical *trace* of the sixties—and progressive rock carried this trace in a certain direction: *forward*. Just as, however, the recovery of 1968 as a historical juncture that was lived and felt is difficult from our present vantage point—and I am reminded of Fredric Jameson's claim that "history is what hurts"—it is also difficult now to recover that sense of forward-looking, of listening to the future, that we hear in progressive rock. But let us try!

1968 was above all a year of rebellion. To recover the sense of this is difficult in a time when, at least in the "first world" (basically, the U.S. and Canada, Western Europe, Japan), prepackaged "rebellion" outfits can be bought off the shelf at the Gap. Meanwhile, figures such as Madonna or (The Artist Formerly Known as) Prince engage in carefully calculated "outrages," and "alternative" has become just another marketing category. This last point has significance for our discussion here, given that, on the one hand, the progressive rock groups of the late sixties and early seventies were originally a part of a *real* alternative musical and cultural scene, and, on the other hand, today's so-called rock "critics" either deny or ignore this fact. But then, yesterday's alternative rock included the idea of going somewhere, whereas the predominant ethos in today's "alternative" music is that there's nowhere to go. Presented in the mode of radical negation, as we see in the music of the Sex Pistols ("I don't know what I want, but I know how to get it; I wanna destroy. . .") or Nirvana ("The finest day that I've ever had, was when I learned to cry on command"), *this* "nowhere music" retains a critical edge, and therefore presents (or evokes the necessity of, at any rate), an alternative. But without this edge, this negative power, the music of nowhere degenerates into mere cynicism. (I'm leaving aside mainstream pop music, which is the "affirmative" mirror image of this cynicism.)

These themes might seem more properly to belong to the final chapter of this book; for the most part, this is the case. An understanding of where we are now, however, might allow us some dialectical insight into the time of progressive rock. This is especially the case if "now" seems to be a time of an ever-present homogenization that is going nowhere and refuses all sense of vision or what used to be called "progress"; perhaps we can get a sense of what progressive rock was all about by moving through a kind of negation of this present.

One place to begin is with the way that the present homogenization renders music insignificant—in the sense that it becomes harder and harder to make music that *is* significant. Although progressive rock was not the most significant aspect of its time, this music did emerge in a period in which it seemed important to do significant things, and to make significant art. In taking account of everything that might be associated with the year 1968, it is not likely that social and cultural theorists will even notice that, for example, this was the year that King Crimson and Yes formed, to say nothing of Caravan or Henry Cow, or that the first Soft Machine and Jethro Tull albums came out. Such theorists, to the extent that they take account of what was happening with music, may note other music of the period, whether it is Jefferson Airplane's *Volunteers* (1969) or Marvin Gaye's *What's Goin' On?* (1971)—as well they should, as these are undoubtedly very good albums and significant cultural barometers.

What does it take for a piece of music to be or become a cultural barometer, a "representative work" of its time or some significant trend in its time? The question takes us back to Hegel, who argued that "philosophy is its time, congealed in thought." Even philosophy, in other words, is a cultural artifact (and is therefore not some reflection of an eternal mind rationally taking account of some ahistorical reality). Works of art, such as musical works, are even more likely to be reflections of particular cultures and historical periods (or, again, significant trends within cultures and societies). Historians or other theorists of the sixties, however, seem resistant to the possibility that works such as *In the Court of the Crimson King* or *The Yes Album* are representative of their time. Ironically, one reason for this is that these works are less *directly* caught up in their time than, say, the albums by the Airplane or Marvin Gaye mentioned previously. Although what I am about to say is something of a sweeping generalization, I think the point can be defended: the best works of a time of upheaval and social transformation are ones that both connect with this time and, to some extent, transcend the particular time and say something more general about the human project. On one level, it is difficult to think of progressive rock as "sixties music." But, on another level, the best of progressive rock is also some of the best music *of that time*. Undoubtedly the reader has picked up on the fact that I think the sixties, as a politically defined period from about 1965 to about 1975, was a great time— the last great concentrated period of alternative vision. Something similar might be said about progressive rock—not that it was the last movement in music that might be said to be great or to be visionary, but that it was the last great music that is visionary. Progressive rock was idealistic and innovative music for an idealistic and innovative time.

Progressive rock music is music with a *project*. In light of 1968, this term has to be understood with all of its Sartrean implications.[4] In Jean-Paul Sartre's terms, an essential aspect of the idea of a human project is an orientation to the future—and this is where we might begin to understand the political implications of *progressive* rock. When I discuss my interest in this music with people who are not familiar with it (for example, many of my colleagues in academia), I am often asked if "progressive rock" has to do with music that is politically progressive. In the most straightforward terms, this question would have to be answered in the negative. If one looks at the explicit politics presented in progressive rock music, one finds a mixed bag—not only in terms of different bands, but even in one and the same band. But, if we focus on the fact that the guiding impulse in all experimental rock music (including progressive rock—I will explain the distinction in a moment) is to develop, to find new ways of being creative, to "go somewhere," to have a project—and that this impulse is not just a matter of blue crystals and product differentiation—then we can understand that progressive rock has radical political implications. Of course this cannot and should not be understood in a programmatic sense (please recall my discussion of these issues from the first chapter); indeed, and here I am following Adorno, the question mainly concerns the way that formal innovations in art remind us and inspire us to imagine and work toward social innovation. Before moving into these formal issues, allow me to say two more things about the sixties and progressive rock.

First, one of the ways that we can understand progressive rock as an expression of the optimistic and utopian spirit of the sixties is in the way that most of another "decade" (again, defined more politically than chronologically, which means that a "decade" might last for more or less than ten years), namely the eighties, was dedicated to the erasure of this spirit. The eighties saw the dedication of an array of empowered ideological apparatuses to the negation of the sixties, indeed to the creation of an antisixties. (These empowered apparatuses included not only the elements of the state, but also media networks, think tanks, and religious institutions.) Obviously, this has continued into the "nineties." (In fact, there are antisixties campaigns that Bill Clinton can get away with that Ronald Reagan couldn't have, precisely because the former can lay some claim to being a "sixties person"—and all the good liberals and left-liberals follow right along, taking "lesser-evil"-ism to absurd lengths.) Even so, and even given that the early eighties (now in the chronological sense) were not very long ago, the whole period still seems completely bizarre—featuring as it did, for example, a president who would "joke" on the radio that, "We have just signed legislation that makes Russia illegal, and we begin bombing in five minutes," and a country with the largest military forces and most powerful destructive arsenal pumping itself up by making war on a country that was hardly larger than a golf course (Grenada).

Undoubtedly, a politics so bizarre and cruel demanded the sort of radical negativity that punk provided at its best; but we might also wonder why the rock-music critical establishment so quickly fell in line with the idea that support for the music that was responding to the antisixties required condemnation or denial of the music that best embodied sixties utopianism. Further exploration of this question will be left for the final chapter, but the point that we should take account of here is that the antisixties and anti-utopian ideology of the eighties found its correlate in the antiprogressive rock ideology of many rock critics and other appendages of the culture industry. Another way to put this is that capitalist social systems are such that, if they cannot win people over to outright jingoism, they will settle for cynicism (which soon enough becomes complacency).[5]

Just as the virulent and cruel strain of the antisixties ideology represented by the Reagan administration and its "conservative" cronies (what did they want to "conserve"?—after all, Reagan's Secretary of the Interior, James Watt, was famous for saying that, "If you've seen one redwood tree, you've seen them all") also demonstrates, at least through the lens of a negative dialectic, an obsession with the sixties, so perhaps does the cynical denial of progressive rock harbor the desire for the very elements of innovation most concentrated in the form. Again, I find the fact that critics of progressive rock will not extend their condemnation to the Beatles significant.[6]

Allow me to take this argument one more step. *Mojo* magazine recently ran an article on singer/songwriter Shawn Colvin. The article's headline makes the point that Colvin is "not in bed with Madonna"; further, "No Alanis [Morissette] or Sheryl [Crow], Shawn Colvin may not be one of the girls but she's all the better for it." The article concludes,

> Divorce, procreation, maturity, death—meaty themes in an entertainment field that is youth-obsessed to the point of blindness about the fact that life goes on after 30. The truth is that artists like Colvin really aren't welcome at the pop table any more: unlike Jewel and Poe and Tracy Bonham, they remind too many of the emotional retards in the music industry of their own mortality. Perhaps pop is merely the self-celebration of yoof; perhaps greying gals and balding blokes should stop trying to "keep up" with rock 'n' roll. But it would be a pity if music as penetrating as Colvin's no longer found an audience. As Bishop Berkeley said of the tree falling in the forest: if nobody out there heard it, would it exist?[7]

Well, this is interesting, and I have to wonder if this is an expression of wanting to have your cake and to eat it too. (Incidentally, I also have to wonder, when in my classes I quote lines from songs by Cream and The Who and my students think they're by the Spin Doctors or some such, who exactly has a problem with "keeping up"?) In other words, the reviewer here seems to want more depth, more sophistication, more maturity, and more engagement with difficult subjects from music, and to be able to throw in a little George Berkeley besides. The reviewer, Barney Hoskyns, wants music that goes beyond what passes for "youth culture"—which has little to do with the vibrancy and openness of youth, but instead with a Coca-Cola commercial conception of a life spent on the beach playing volleyball, with some dancing and necking thrown in for good measure.

My question is, Where should it stop? This may seem like a weird question, and yet, isn't the idea that, at least as far as rock music is concerned, depth, sophistication, and maturity *should* stop somewhere? Isn't the idea that, beyond this point, the music is simply pretentious? Is rock music simply not a medium for "heavy" subjects or difficult musical material? By definition? If this is the case, where is the line drawn—and *how* do we know where to draw it? In fairness to the reviewer here, it may be that he would agree with my line of reasoning. After all, he referred to the "pop table," wondering what is and isn't welcome at it. But this is where we might draw a useful distinction: some rock is "pop," and some isn't—and, for that matter, some jazz and classical music is pop, and some isn't, though the percentages might differ from genre to genre.

The alternative is to maintain that rock music should be preserved as a "youth" form, and then we will be stuck with whatever conception of "yoof" that the culture industry gives us. I agree with Hoskyns that it will most likely be an emotionally retarded conception, though I don't know if this is because the artists and repertoire and other media conglomerate executives fear a confrontation with mortality. That is giving them a bit too much credit, for who doesn't fear aging and mortality? No, I'm afraid the motivations are a good deal more banal: rock music should not progress, develop, or be visionary, because, in a marketing framework that depends on predigested formulas, quick turnover of "new" product, and shortened attention spans . . . well, you get the picture. Moreover, the framework that has now become entrenched is "generational," in the sense that each generation of rock music listeners should simply have its music, and each generation or other subdivision of rock music listener will simply be marketed to as a niche. Therefore, it doesn't matter if I have an appreciation for The Who's "I'm Free," while you're familiar with the song as performed by the Spin Doctors—in fact, none of it much matters, and those old guys, who've perhaps gotten a bit paunchy and grey, and who thought that they were going to make rock music that mattered, were kidding themselves.

My point here is not to argue for the sanctity of the "original" performance (which, with art in the age of mechanical reproduction and studio technology, is meaningless anyway). On the contrary, I am all for the idea of interpretation and think it would be great to have a good deal more of it in rock music, especially in the case of the production of new *versions* as opposed to simply "covers." (For instance, I'm quite enthusiastic about the idea of Phish's live performances of the complete *White Album* and *Quadrophenia*.) But, to return to Gracyk's point about "a broader nexus of established alternatives," what makes real interpretations interesting is the way that they play off of the "original." Niche marketing has nothing to do with this. In fact, in niche marketing, not only is "alternative" just one of the niches, so is "progressive," as long as this is understood as nostalgia for what one was interested in back when these albums were popular. To the reader who wants to have a deeper appreciation of progressive rock, I present this challenge: grapple with the music as visionary and developmental, not simply as a trip down memory lane.

Second, please allow me one final characterization of the sixties. At least in the first world, we might think of the sixties, and indeed the time from the sixties until now, as a tale of two texts. In 1964, two books appeared that are quite emblematic of the sixties: Herbert Marcuse's *One-Dimensional Man* and Marshall McLuhan's *Understanding Media: The Extensions of Man*. (Obviously, one way in which these texts are emblematic is that, it seems, everything had to do with "man" back then.)

Marcuse, unlike Adorno, was openly sympathetic to the popular uprisings of the sixties (as far as philosophers and social theorists went, Marcuse and Sartre were clearly the favorites among young people in the U.S. and Europe). Marcuse saw these uprisings as revolts against one-dimensionality. No one who has read the first sentence of the first chapter of *One-Dimensional Man* will forget it: "A comfortable, smooth, reasonable, democratic unfreedom prevails in advanced industrial civilization, a token of technical progress." This idea of a new and different form of alienation, one that works through rationality and democracy and even happiness and "affirmative culture," was one of the major legacies of a group of thinkers known collectively as the Frankfurt School, of which Marcuse was a key member. You might say that Marcuse's view is that human consciousness is increasingly shaped into a "preshrunk" form, so that it finds itself happy, more or less, in a one-dimensional society. Whereas some theorists now look back upon the sixties rebellions as a momentary preoccupation of middle-class students who depended on their parents for financial support (Alasdair MacIntyre is a proponent of this—fundamentally cynical, to my mind—view), Marcuse was heartened by the idea of members of the affluent society rejecting one-dimensionality. This rejection became not only a political issue, but also an ethical one: after all, what possible purely material reason could young people have for opposing the imperialism of the United States and other Western countries?[8] So, it was a time of ideals—of going beyond merely material interest—and challenges to one-dimensionality. Again, progressive rock does not stand out as the foremost representative of this time. And yet, as a powerful trace of this culture, a trace that we can still listen to and take inspiration from today, progressive rock is an important phenomenon. If we take the "pop" strain, at least at its most insipid and banal, at its most integrated into the *business* of selling musical product, as an exemplar of one-dimensionality, of calculation and predigestion, and of mere pecuniary motivation, then we can see that progressive rock represented the very opposite of these things and therefore was of a piece with the idealism and utopianism of the sixties.

Although McLuhan's politics, to the extent that they are understood, would seem at odds with Marcuse's, still there are many arguments in *Understanding Media* that help in understanding the dynamic history of rock music. One of McLuhan's famous distinctions is that between "hot" and "cool" media. McLuhan argues that hot media are those that invite greater engagement and participation, whereas cool media tend to encourage the spectator to chill out, so to speak. Radio is a hot medium, in McLuhan's view, and television and film are cool media. Media that do not primarily depend on visual stimulation require people to use their imaginations more. In this light—or absence of light, as it were, remembering that McLuhan uses the light bulb as the example of "pure media"—we can see a connection between a time when music seemed important—and a time not yet absolutely dominated by visual media. No one would argue that the sixties and seventies were not yet a time of television and movies, but certainly they were the last time before society became completely permeated by these media. We will take a larger measure of this shift in the final chapter, but let us take note at this juncture that we can see yet another reason for thinking of the sixties and its aftermath as a special time for important music, and perhaps the last great time that we know of.

Before leaving this subject, let us also note that there is a question of attention spans here. I find it curious and troubling that it is a common thing for rock critics to gripe about the fact that some of the progressive rock masterworks of the seventies went on for twenty minutes or more. Does this mean that the same person would not watch television or a film for more than twenty minutes? That would be a problem, because I hear that some films actually last an hour or longer! Instead of impugning the mental capacities of critics who are dismissive of progressive rock, as I am tempted to do, the more crucial point from the standpoint of cultural and social theory has to do with art in a time of social engagement, as opposed to art in a time when, it seems, the film aesthetic has become dominant—or, at a time when people go on about "great" films but, it seems, never read any books. My claim is not that these people are themselves morons (only a few of them), but that there is something about the time, namely that it is not a time for books or long, difficult pieces of music. Which means, or at least this is my Hegelian thesis, that the time of progressive rock *was* such a time.

◧ ◧ ◧

It is notoriously difficult, or perhaps too easy, to link forms of art, and genres, to their time in any substantial way. On the one hand one ends up saying a great deal about the character of the time, and then making a general statement to the effect that, for example, "idealistic times give rise to idealistic music." This is what I have done thus far in this chapter. But this tells us next to nothing about the form of this music, and why the formal qualities of this music should interest us *as music*. On the other hand, there are analyses that attempt to either treat these formal qualities as existing only in a pure world of music, or perhaps even mathematics or logic (Plato recommended that children study music in order to prepare their minds for the study of mathematics), or attempt to present a historicized analysis of particular musical works that is so detailed as to be utterly reductivistic. The former model, pure formalism, can present us with some interesting material for integration into more synthetic analyses. And the latter model, which might be called a pure "representationalism," can certainly generate an insight or two. But neither of these models really gives us the kind of specificity that is tenable, the kind of formal analysis that can take us beyond and yet also remain integrated into the broad historical analysis that we have discussed in this chapter to this point.

Catching the "vibe" of progressive rock is certainly a neat thing, but we are today in the position of theologians who must explain the time of miracles to a largely secularized audience in a decidedly unmiraculous time.

In the case of pure formalism, we seem to be interested in music that could not have been made by any actual human beings that you or I could truly know, but instead music of timeless gods who live in no earthly culture. Yes, it is interesting to focus, for this or that moment, on why the chord shifted from a major seventh to an augmented fourth. Most music, apart from oddities such as John Cage's "4 minutes 33 seconds", will consist in a series of such shifts. What is the basic level of formal analysis? There is a good argument to be made that the basic level will be the work as a whole, but then, the work has to be built up of its elements. Within rock music, at least, progressive rock represents a dramatic leap in the number and complexity of these elements, and we should spell out these elements for what they are. But just as no sound or mark has a meaning in and of itself, but only in the *context* of a system of signs—and it turns out that systems of signs are themselves *necessarily* open-ended—so also is it the case that musical elements, either at the level of the individual element or the whole work, only have significance in a larger context, a context that turns out to be historical and social. Of course, there is no such thing as an "individual" or "particular" musical element, except perhaps in a purely hypothetical or heuristic sense, but instead only elements in relation. In other words, if one tries to isolate a "single" musical element, for example some "note," one will find that there are always other elements that are inextricably attached: the note is played for some duration, sung or played on some instrument that has a particular timbre. Or, even if the note is just a mark on a musical staff, it still has an intrinsic relation to a system of musical notation, to modern Western standard tonality, to some key that it is either in or not in.

It would seem that, just as it is impossible to fix the level of formal analysis at the smallest level, so also is this true at the largest. Where does the "note" begin, and where does the "work" end?[9] These are questions that have difficult ontological and philosophical implications, which some readers might pursue fruitfully. But, strangely enough, this discussion also tells us a thing or two about progressive rock. For one thing, it tells us that we have to understand progressive rock not only in terms of the larger culture from which it emerged, but also in terms of the "canon" of rock music. John Lennon's "Come Together" came out of, directly and indirectly, Chuck Berry. The sounds that were developed, extended, and transmogrified into progressive rock came from a certain musical context or set of contexts. This goes for anything and everything that we might call a "purely musical element." Indeed, context is the reason why we can identify a group or piece of music as an exponent or artifact of "progressive rock." So, there is something about the form and there is something about the context. We have said a great deal about the historical context in this chapter, and even something about the musical context in the previous chapter. What remains is to show how the musical and historical contexts of the late sixties combined to give rise to a new form, progressive rock.

Let us turn, then, to the musical streams that flowed into the making of progressive rock. Following this discussion we will

turn, in concluding this chapter, to Edward Macan's book on progressive rock, *Rocking the Classics*.[10]

Where to begin? I argued in the second chapter that there has
always been an underground, visionary, and alternative trend in
rock music. I also argued that this trend sometimes sits side by
side with the more "pop" trend in one and the same artist or even
one and the same piece of music. Now I would like to make a further distinction. As the late sixties approached, and as the time of
Revolver, *Pet Sounds*, and *Sergeant Pepper's* came near, there
emerged a broad trend in rock music that I would like to call
"experimental rock." Although, as I argued at the beginning of
this chapter, the kinds of distinctions or categories we will find
ourselves working with here could never be absolute or hard and
fast, they can still be useful as guides to a certain musical terrain.
Right now we are within the territory of rock music, and the proposal is that, during a certain period, in the middle to late sixties,
a process of *divergence* opened up. Before this time, even going
back to the originators, there were certainly aspects of the music
that could be called experimental (I tried to show that even a pop-
rock classic such as "Tutti-Frutti" contained some very weird
stuff). By a certain time (I don't know if anyone can say for sure
when the exact moment occurred, though certainly by 1968, with
the appearance of albums such as Frank Zappa's *Lumpy Gravy*),
the experimental trend diverged from the evolutionary tree of
rock music and became its own species.

In fact, the divergence also represented a certain *convergence*:
on the one side, rock music developed according to its own stylistic logic, but to the point where it began to strain against all of its
entrenched conventions; on the other side, the middle sixties also
saw the emergence of what might be called a "general avant-
garde." This latter development represented the breakdown of
another set of entrenched conventions, whereby the making of art
required a certain pedigree. Of course there have always been
challenges to this system, and certainly there are important historical precedents for such challenges in the United States, from
Charles Ives to John Cage, and from Scott Joplin to Charlie

Parker and beyond. But the sixties was a time when all of the barriers seemed to come down. The point that I am driving toward is
that the experimental rock of the middle to later sixties had one
foot in rock music "proper," and the other in this general avant-
garde and experimental milieu.

Furthermore, the convergence was made possible by the fact
that rock music developed its own avant-garde. Returning to earlier themes, we can see here that rock music was becoming, by
the middle and later sixties, a very broad genre. This category
outgrew the earlier appelation, "rock 'n' roll," even absorbing the
earlier category into the larger genre of rock, where it now existed
as simply one division within the music, alongside others. That
all of the "divisions" did not sit comfortably together goes without
saying. Further, we can perhaps understand the old saw about
"that ain't rock 'n' roll" in a different light at this point. If we were
to take the defining features of "rock 'n' roll" and ask how many
of them are present in the experimental rock of the late sixties, we
might find many instances where none of these features are present. And yet, significantly, the music in question might still
remain recognizable as rock music. For example, "A Day in the
Life" is not a song that one would ordinarily think of for dancing
purposes; it doesn't "rock steady" with a continuous backbeat,
neither is it backseat smooching music. The music is not meant
to encourage feelings of comfort and security; quite to the contrary, there is a morbid, existential feeling to "A Day." There are
some memorable melodies, but these are neither of the pleasant
hummable sort, nor are they the totality of the song. Indeed, in
some sense, "A Day in the Life" isn't exactly a "song" at all, but
instead an orchestral suite that incorporates aspects of song
form. Despite all of this, however, would we say that "A Day in the
Life" is not rock music? I think most people would say that the
"song" *comes from* or *out of* the lineage of rock music and therefore still belongs to this lineage in some sense.

Rock 'n' roll purists may dispute this line of thinking to some
extent, but only at the peril of, first, having to blame the Beatles
for diverging from "real" rock and roll, and, second, denying or
not recognizing that it is of the "essence" of rock music to continually reconfigure its essence. Rock music is a hybrid, "mongrel"

music from the get, and proud of it. The emergence of experimental trends within rock music is simply a qualitative leap, which occurred under certain historical and social conditions, of the generous synthesis.

One of the primary aspects of this leap, and a place where we can see the proverbial transformation from quantity to quality, has simply to do with what we might call "stretching out." This simple concept, we shall see, has quite far-reaching implications. This phenomenon took a number of forms and worked on a number of levels.

Again, let's stay with the period from about 1965 to 1967, from the time of *Rubber Soul* to *Sgt. Pepper's*. One very direct way to identify the divergence of an experimental trend is to look at the way that some groups began writing *longer* songs, and songs with *more parts*. In the middle sixties, the standard pop-rock song lasted two-and-a-half minutes, and consisted of two to four verses, a chorus, and perhaps a short instrumental break (which often recapitulated the vocal line from either the verse or the chorus). Chord progressions were relatively simple—as were the chords themselves. Actually, the Beatles were among the first to use more sophisticated chords, which might also have reflected the fact that Lennon, Harrison, and McCartney were self-taught guitar players. (This doesn't mean that they weren't real good, by the way—I have said it before and I'll say it again, all of the Beatles are underrated as musicians.) What happens is that chord progressions (which are just different ways of putting one's fingers on the guitar neck, after all) are found on the guitar and shown to one's mates—and only later does some schooled musician write it down as Gsus4 or Ebmaj7 or some such. (Incidentally, the same thing is going on with Kurt Cobain's songs, where the chords do not turn out to be as easy to sort out as one might expect.) But, of course, these "new" chords are also the result of a creative mind's desire to find new sounds, sounds that do not simply repeat what has come before.

We can all appreciate early rock 'n' roll without being the sorts of purists who are akin to fundamentalists who believe we only need one book—the funny thing being that no one *really* believes that we only need one book or one way to make rock music. Take stock of this, mix in the appropriate social conditions, and experimental trends will emerge.

To say that an important part of the emergence of these trends was a period when it became possible to write rock songs with more than two or three parts or longer than three minutes is neither to automatically attribute any value to such music nor to denigrate songs that are "simple" or brief. Take a song such as "Ferry Cross the Mersey," by Gerry and the Pacemakers (another Liverpool group). The song is perfect the way that it is, and no amount of "complexifying" would improve it—on the contrary; its simplicity is an integral part of its perfection. Furthermore, the formal simplicity of the song is not indicative of music that is unsophisticated. There is a certain bleakness to both the music and the lyrics that, for me at any rate, conjures many levels and mixtures of feelings. (Here, too, is another demonstration of the limitations of pure formalism, and not just as regards feelings. How one understands this song—or one's ability to understand it at all—will certainly depend on social and historical factors.) Some pieces of music are both "simple" and sophisticated. It might be said that *all* complex pieces of music are "sophisticated," but perhaps some of these are merely sophistical, merely show-offy and pretentious—and this is often said, of course, of progressive rock music.

There was a time, then, when rock music became more sophisticated, complex, and, to introduce another term, "difficult." Again—and this really cannot be emphasized enough—the presence of sophistication, complexity, or difficulty (all relative terms, in fact) in a piece of music does not in itself make a piece of music *good*. And, let's face it, if in the final analysis a piece of music is not good, who cares (except perhaps from a purely sociological perspective) what else is going on with it? (In a moment, we will add another term to this list, namely "virtuosity," but the same caveat will apply.) What greater sophistication and complexity do bring to rock music is a greater range of possibilities. Then the question becomes one of what is made of these possibilities.

Another way to put this is that it is in the nature of experiments that they can either succeed or fail. One of the driving impulses in the post-*Rubber Soul* and, especially, post-*Sgt. Pepper's* period was to risk failure. One other level on which the "stretching out" approach was operative, then, concerned the possibility of going beyond formulas and conventions. For most of the history of rock music, approaching music in terms of tried-and-true formulas has been the name of the game. For most of this history, Adorno's arguments about small innovations being attempts at mere product differentiation (those "blue crystals" in the detergent) apply. As we approach the late sixties, however, we see the emergence of an experimental trend that had different aims. Variation in music as product differentiation does not risk failure *as music*, but instead only in terms of perhaps not receiving the market share that investors expected. There were big record companies (which all the same were nothing compared to the media comglomerates that exist now) who hoped to make a great deal of money, millions of dollars, off of the next album by the Beatles, Bob Dylan, or the Byrds. But the artists themselves increasingly flouted those desires. I will come back to this question of different kinds of risk, commercial and artistic.

In more purely musical terms, stretching out occurs in two basic ways. Here we will see how our simple concept has far-reaching implications that lead to experimental and progressive forms of rock music. In a nutshell, one form of stretching out is akin to jazz, while the other is more akin to Western classical music. One might think of the way that King Crimson, for example, has definite affinities with avant-garde jazz, while Yes has affinities with twentieth-century classical music. (This characterization oversimplifies, to be sure, and is only used here to make a basic point.) With either group, the divergence from formulas led into experimental territory where there was a convergence with the avant-gardes of jazz, European classical music, and the more general avant-garde that was then developing. In the case of King Crimson, what I am calling an affinity with "jazz" has especially to do with the presence of extended improvisation in both. In the case of Yes, the affinity with classical music has to do with the presence of many and diverse composed parts in any given piece.

For groups that wanted to stretch out, the most obvious path would seem to be extended improvisation—after all, why not "jam" your way into a far-out, extended composition? The case may be that most of the music that was made under that rubric during the experimental trend's initial period has been, thankfully, forgotten. Certainly, those of us old enough to have danced to "In-a-Gadda-Da-Vida" at some sock hop lo these many years ago know there were some pretty wretched, endless guitar solos back around 1968 or '69. We now know, from the many bootlegs that have surfaced, that even Jimi Hendrix had days when he wasn't exactly brilliant (though in some circles it remains sacrilege to say this). By and large, however, this was not the main trend. Taking the Beatles again as a paradigm case, it seems to me that the initial form of stretching out had more to do with the composition of more and different parts, in what amounted to the extension of song form into musical suites. George Harrison was certainly smart enough, and aware enough of the larger musical scene, to know that playing long guitar solos was not his forte. Later, *some* rock musicians developed ability with extended improvisation—and these players, from Hendrix to McLaughlin to Traffic to The Allman Brothers Band to Santana to King Crimson (especially in their *Larks' Tongues* period) played experimental rock music that converged with experimental jazz. (In my view, Carlos Santana is the outstanding example, virtually without peer in this respect, of a rock musician who can follow the logic of the "long line"; in this, he comes closer than anyone else in rock music to John Coltrane.) As for the other jammers, some are good but not necessarily experimental, some are perhaps experimental but not necessarily good, and some are neither experimental nor good.

◤ ◤ ◤

Still, stretching out by way of the extended jam was certainly part of the experimental music scene in the late sixties and, as Edward Macan argues, it was associated with other developments that were integral to the emergence of progressive rock. In particular, Macan argues that we need to look at psychedelic rock, hippies, and the effect that mind-altering substances had on the perception of time. Both Macan and Jim DeRogatis, author of *Kaleidoscope Eyes*, make a compelling case for seeing psychedelic rock and its audience and chemical accoutrements as the most direct predecessors and closest neighbors to progressive rock. In other words, evolutionarily speaking, psychedelic rock was one of the experimental trends that developed in the middle to late sixties, and, at the decade's close, progressive rock diverged from it.

If I may make a somewhat personal admission here, I would like to comment on the fact that I avoided this question almost entirely in my earlier book on the music of Yes. This seems strange, no doubt, given that three members of Yes had previously been members of psychedelic groups of some significance in the London scene, namely The Syn (Chris Squire and Peter Banks) and Tomorrow (Steve Howe).[11] Indeed, DeRogatis uses the title of one of Tomorrow's best-known songs, "My White Bicycle," as the title of his introductory chapter. Unquestionably, there is a great deal of psychedelic rock influence to be heard in Yes's music, from the first album straight through to *Going for the One*. I should add, too, that I do like a good bit of the psychedelic rock from the middle and late sixties. Furthermore, I have nothing against hippies, and I basically approve of spiritual quests and attempts at consciousness expansion (with the exception, that is, of when these become mere covers for escapism). What I did not want to get into, and I realize now that I avoided this without even really thinking about it, was the question of drugs. The books by Macan and DeRogatis were not out when I was writing *music of Yes* (in fact, all three of our books came out at about the same time— mere coincidence, or fact of cosmic significance? You decide), so I was blissfully unaware of their rather undeniable arguments.

I do have lots of problems with placing too much emphasis on the use of marijuana, LSD, and other psychoactive substances, as far as the development of creative trends in music are concerned. In discussing the transition away from American soul and R&B that Steve Howe went through in his various mid- to late-sixties bands—the Syndicats, the In Crowd, and Tomorrow— DeRogatis writes,

> by 1966, things were starting to change. "We were starting to 'psyche-delic' things up," Howe recalled. "It came from the Byrds, really. We were looking at more obscure music than the Beatles, but of course, they were in there, too." The change was partly due to the London social scene—the exchange of ideas as musicians gathered in the clubs—but LSD also played a role. (p. 81)

Following this last bit, DeRogatis immediately quotes Howe again at length. Given DeRogatis's premise, one might expect something here about Howe's experience—or lack thereof—with acid. Instead, Howe discusses his feelings regarding the fact that "[h]umanity had gone through two world wars" and the "incredibly irresistible . . . idea that you could go beyond normality" (p. 81).[12] Perhaps there is something implied or implicit here about the value of psychedelic drugs in all of this, but I don't see it. Indeed, within a few lines the discussion turns to the fact that many groups "copied psychedelic rock as a style without ever having had a psychedelic experience" (p. 82).

Admittedly, this may have been the exception more than the rule. And, please don't get me wrong: *Kaleidoscope Eyes* is an interesting and important study and documentation of a genre that has not, until now, received the attention it deserves. However, I get worried when it seems necessary to continually insert, into the middle of a discussion ostensibly about music, that the acid was flowing, the bongwater was spilling, and so on. I don't doubt that some people have used drugs for liberatory experiences, and I certainly appreciated DeRogatis's discussion of such experiments as the League for Spiritual Discovery (get it?), which included Timothy Leary and Allen Ginsburg. (It turns out that I am writing this only a few days after the passing of one of the best minds of his generation.) Psychoactive substances may play a role in the opening of "doors of perception" (as in the title of Aldous Huxley's memoir of a drug-assisted journey to "the white light," from which the Doors took their name and the Velvet Underground a song and album title), though I doubt very much that it is a necessary or essential role. My own experience, perhaps as someone born just a few years too late to be a true "sixties person," was only to see the destructive side of drug use, at the point where experimentation and consciousness expansion gave way to simply being messed up and strung out, and this basically had the effect of making me not want to have much to do with that scene (though, having long hair, it was often assumed that I was part of it). Of course, it could certainly be argued that, as someone who is into progressive rock music and many other kinds of rock and jazz besides, to say nothing of beat poetry, I've had plenty to do with that scene.

But, beyond these perhaps more personal concerns, I do think there are two valid issues that need to be raised.

First, even while acknowledging the role of psychedelic music in inspiring progressive rock, we might also grapple with the qualitative shift that occurred. In my view, the people who were really concerned with both the liberatory dimensions of drug experiences and the expanded possibilities of rock music found, on the whole, that they really didn't need drugs beyond a certain point. I suppose this might go to the old "Was Hendrix a visionary musician because of acid or despite it?" question, and I am certainly on the "despite" side. Perhaps this is a merely tendentious thing to say, but it occurs to me that an overemphasis on drugs here has something to do with the idea that what music is primarily about is a partying scene. The people who think this is what rock music is primarily about tend, as DeRogatis does, to dislike the turn from psychedelic to progressive.[13] Significantly, this dislike has been couched, in more recent years, with a denunciation of progressive rock's supposed pretentions—that is, it is somehow wrong and anti-rock for progressive musicians to be serious about music rather than to simply valorize partying.

The form of stretching out that progressive rock aims for at its best (and of course there are many embarrassing counterexamples of the far less than best—no one would deny that), is not the sort of thing that most musicians could do in a stoned condition. Whether it sounds as good or better or a lot worse if one is listening in this condition I could not say. Obviously, there is, or was, a very well known band whose music, when it doesn't sound so great, is often vindicated in terms such as, "You have to drop acid to really get into it." This band was certainly known for stretching out. Once in a great while this band would hit upon, at least to my unstoned ears, a great rendition of "Dark Star." Thankfully, we have recording technology to capture these renditions. However, it seems to me that, ninety percent of the time, this group sounded like a not very good garage band, a bunch of guys jamming and drinking too much beer. But hey, despite my judgmental tone here, I want to be quick to add that perhaps there is some other value and validity to the communal Dead experience, stoners swaying and swirling together like whirling dervishes (though, of course, American-style, eschewing any cumbersome commitments such as spiritual discipline). I'm sure it all fits very nicely into Harold Bloom's arguments about the "American religion."[14]

Progressive rock, on the other hand, went on with the music. Admittedly, it wasn't always much of a party. There may be a few exceptions, but it just is not very likely that one will become a musician of the caliber of a Bill Bruford or John McLaughlin if one is stoned and partying all the time.

Second, I want to raise the issue of the *content* of the vision and consciousness that psychedelic experimenters and those who took up (what DeRogatis rightly calls) their "ethos" were concerned to explore. Often, in more recent discussions of drug-induced mind expansion, from Samuel Taylor Coleridge to Aldous Huxley to Alan Watts to Jimi Hendrix, it seems as though substances such as LSD are somehow ends in themselves. My sense is that such characterizations reflect more recent cynicism and aimlessness.[15] In *Kaleidoscope Eyes* there is often, in my view, too much of this emphasis, as when, for example, DeRogatis says on the first page of his introduction, "In the beginning were the drugs" (p. xi). I would argue that, instead, the "beginning" is better expressed by the lines from Steve Howe that were quoted previously. The beginning of exploration has to do with what is wrong with this world, and the possibility of some other world, "beyond normality." In other words, it seems to me to make more sense to look at the radical and utopian impulse (and, to return to our earlier discussion, impulses of radical negativity and radical affirmation), and then to study the various ways that people have attempted to follow this impulse, including psychedelic drugs, but also including everything from bed-ins, maharishis, science-fiction stories, attempts to join music with protest and rebellion, and lyrical and formal visions of new possibilities.

What is most interesting is that such examples abound in *Kaleidoscope Eyes*, if perhaps in the margins. DeRogatis opens his book with the story of Albert Hofmann, the Swiss chemist who, in 1938, synthesized lysergic acid diethylamide (a.k.a., LSD-25). Apparently, the pharmaceutical company that Hofmann worked for, Sandoz, didn't see anything special in the drug, and decided not to pursue further research on it.

Five years later, Hofmann had an odd premonition that Sandoz staffers had overlooked something unique about LSD-25. . . . On April 16, 1943, he synthesized a new batch of LSD-25. As he finished his work, he began to feel dizzy. Thinking he had a touch of the flu, he closed his lab for the weekend and went home, and there he embarked on the first acid trip. "I perceived an uninterrupted stream of fantastic pictures, extraordinary shapes with intense, kaleidoscopic play of colors," he wrote. (p. 4)

As DeRogatis reports, Hofmann speculated that these hallucinations "had been caused by the drug, which he had handled without wearing gloves." Hofmann tested this theory a few days later, ingesting a small dose of LSD in his lab.

After forty minutes, he began to feel dizzy and anxious. He hopped on his beaten-up bicycle—the only form of transportation available in wartime Switzerland—and started the four-mile trip home. He felt as if he was barely moving, but the assistant who followed him on another bicycle reported that they pedaled at a furious pace. (pp. 4–5)

The account is completed with the obligatory exploding kaleidoscopic shapes and colors, but what interests me is DeRogatis's next paragraph:

Hofmann's bike ride would be commemorated (consciously or not) in several early psychedelic-rock songs, including "I Just Wasn't Made for These Times" by the Beach Boys, "Bike" by Pink Floyd, and "My White Bicycle" by Tomorrow. But it took two decades for his surprising discovery to make its way from the laboratory to the recording studio. (p. 5)

As soon as I read this, my first reaction was to think that "My White Bicycle" doesn't have anything to do with this scenario, except perhaps in a very strained sense of "not consciously." This reaction had me pulling out my rather worn and scratched copy of *Pet Sounds*. Unless I missed something underneath all of the pops and crackles, there is neither a bicycle nor anything explicitly relating to psychoactive drugs in "I Just Wasn't Made for These Times." The song I listened to had to do with feeling depressed and out of place. In *The Nearest Faraway Place*, Timothy White writes that "I Just Wasn't Made" was another song written with Tony Asher that features early use on a pop record of the theremin, the electronic fluctuant-pitch instrument devised by Russian inventor Leon Theremin and utilized as eerie punctuation in the Bernard Herrmann score of the 1951 science fiction classic *The Day the Earth Stood Still*. Not unlike the peace-seeking alien in the movie, Brian sang that he was looking for a place where he could fit in and speak his mind. (p. 253)

Besides having been a fan of *The Day the Earth Stood Still* for the last thirty-five years or so, I also think the allusion is appropriate, not necessarily because there is some direct or even "not conscious" connection between the song and film, but because the spirit of the film has much more to do with the song than do psychedelic bike trips. In other words, this is the same sort of transposed message of warning and message of hope that Steve Howe spoke to earlier; the content of this is primarily social, and only secondarily, at most, something that had to do with drugs.

As DeRogatis allows, "My White Bicycle" is in fact "about the Provos, a sect of anarchist hippies in Holland who shared communal bicycles" (p. 79). With this incomplete and tendentious characterization (in what sense was this group a "sect"—were they sectarian in their activities?), DeRogatis immediately gets back to his *Leitmotiv*, that this is really all about drugs. Well, alright, Tomorrow was a psychedelic band, and I'm sure there were some drugs around—but isn't there anything to be said for the express content of the song, as opposed to the content that the group was "not conscious" of? My understanding was that the Provos embarked on an experiment to place white bicycles around Amsterdam, to be used by whomever needed a bike at the moment. When the rider got to his or her destination, they simply left the bike for the next person who needed transportation.[16] Now, I see all of this as having something to do with capitalism and property, and especially with the idea of getting beyond private property. Sure, the whole bike experiment was a bit trippy, and, in my view, the main form of private property that needs to be socialized has more to do with the means of production and basic necessities of life (though, arguably, bicycles as an ecologically sound form of transportation are quite pertinent to these issues, and the anarchists therefore chose well in making their

point). The basic trippiness and coolness of the experiment was
what Tomorrow picked up on. Perhaps I should mention, though
DeRogatis doesn't, that another of Tomorrow's songs was called
"Revolution." The band also did a version of "Strawberry Fields
Forever," a song which, to my mind, brings together nicely psy-
chedelic and utopian themes.

In all of these cases, however, it seems to me that the expression of utopian themes is the aim of the music, and even what
might be called the "content," while psychedelic experience is
more the conduit. As DeRogatis notes, some time before Jim
Morrison and company, Aldous Huxley had himself lifted his reference to the doors of perception from William Blake: "If the
doors of perception were cleansed, everything would appear to
man as it is—infinite." That old radical and visionary, along with
some of his fellow romantics, had a good deal of influence on
progressive rock; for him, this hoped-for infinite vision was inextricably bound up with the redemption of the world. Even for
someone from the psychedelic scene who was, at least for a few
years, much more into LSD, this vision remained paramount. I
mean Jimi Hendrix, undeniably one of the most talented and
visionary musicians of the late sixties. This is one of the important examples from the margins that tells against DeRogatis's
overemphasis on the role drugs played in the music of this
period. DeRogatis writes:

> Unlike the songs of many of his peers, Hendrix's didn't directly
> address political issues. But as [Hendrix biographer Charles Shaar]
> Murray and others pointed out, Hendrix's whole public life was a
> political act—a challenge to conformity among both whites and
> blacks—and he did have a political vision, albeit a utopian one. Hen-
> drix was fascinated with science fiction (the exploration of outer
> space) and psychedelic drugs (the exploration of inner space), not
> because he wanted to escape but because he wanted to create an
> ideal world. He had a dream, and he called it the Electric or Sky
> Church. Murray described it as "a context for participatory worship,
> learning and communion without regard for denomination or
> demeanor." (p. 96)

To conclude this perhaps overlengthy sermon, which has
undoubtedly tried the reader's patience, my point is not at all to

contribute to establishment antidrug rhetoric. (Indeed, in my view, this rhetoric is little more than a cover for police invasions of Black and Latino communities in the U.S., and military interventions into the Third World.) Instead, my aim has been to raise the question, What is the most important aspect of the psychedelic experience, and what aspect of this experience and music most carried over to progressive rock? The way that one answers this question will most likely have to do with what one thinks is important in the world. It seems to me that, if one answers that the drugs themselves are the main thing, then one can't help but contribute to the path of escape (which will, at best, only be the temporary escape that is mostly available to the middle class). Perhaps it is worth noting that Hendrix himself tried to get away from drugs in the last couple years of his life, while at the same time he moved in the direction of more up-front radical politics (the film *Hendrix Plays Berkeley* gives a good sense of this). (As with Charlie Parker, Billie Holiday, and others, people who had an interest in controlling Hendrix kept pushing drugs in his direction.) In gauging the influence of psychedelic rock on progressive rock, my view is that the latter mainly took the utopian ethos and the stretched-out sense of time from the former, while mostly leaving behind the drugs themselves.

Before leaving the realm of psychedelic rock, let us take a moment to give long-overdue salutations to what is perhaps the most influential group that most people, especially in North America, have never heard of. The Fleur de Lys (who also recorded under the name *Les* Fleur de Lys) were formed in Southampton in 1964 and remained active, through many line-up changes, until 1969. They were essentially a singles band, and did not produce a complete album; only in 1997 has a compilation CD appeared, with the title *Reflections*, which contains twenty-four tracks. Almost all of these are not only fantastic but even revelatory. A great many of the sounds that fully flowered in the late sixties and early seventies, in both psychedelic and progressive rock, are here in well-developed form. This includes some outstanding work with a much-distorted Stratocaster that presages some of Hendrix's best soloing, as well as vocal and instrumental arrangements that foreshadow Procul Harum and the Moody

Blues, among others. As with Steve Howe's membership in Tomorrow and then later in Yes, the continuity between the Fleur de Lys and progressive rock is also demonstrated by the presence of Gordon Haskell as the bass guitarist for a significant part of the group's history. Haskell would later play bass and sing with King Crimson.

◪   ◪   ◪

Whether the extension of rock music followed improvisational or compositional pathways ("jazz" or "classical"), there were certain common elements. First, the newer possibilities that were becoming full-blown progressive rock pushed song form to its limits, sometimes fracturing the form altogether. For most groups, something like a "song" remained foundational (there are numerous ways of reading the line from Yes's *Tales from Topographic Oceans*, "What happened to this song, we once knew so well?"). Of the groups that I place in the "front line" of the progressive movement, this could be said of Caravan, ELP, Genesis, perhaps a little less of Gentle Giant, Jethro Tull, PFM, and Yes. However, "song foundationalism" is less present in the work of Gong, King Crimson, Henry Cow, Magma, the Mahavishnu Orchestra, and Soft Machine (at least beyond the first two albums). Even with the first set of groups, however, the relation to song, especially in the sense of "popular song," becomes tenuous; it becomes very difficult, for example, to simply think of *Thick as a Brick* or "Close to the Edge" as just very long songs.

Second, the dance aspect of rock music was also pushed to the breaking point. With most works of progressive rock, just as one gets into a steady dance groove—in the works where this is possible at all, that is—there is some sort of dramatic shift: starts and stops, difficult tempo changes, sections that do not have the sort of beat a dance step could hook onto, etc. In other words, in the trajectory from "A Day in the Life" to, say, "21st Century Schizoid Man," a form of rock music has developed that is no longer dance music.

Instead, and third, this new kind of rock music seems to be "music for listening." Whether or not this music lives up to the possibilities of being "serious" music, "art," and "avant-garde" is in some sense an issue that has to be discussed separately. Certainly, what I have just called "possibilities" were instead called "pretentions" by the mainstream of rock-music criticism; the "serious" idea continues to be dismissed by many, and the focus has instead been on the idea that this music has simply failed *to* rock and to *be* rock. The charge is that the new music neither lives up to the criteria of good rock music, nor makes it as avant-garde music either. Part of the discussion here, however, is to sort out these criteria—and to show how conceptually confused most dismissals of progressive rock are. Let us take up two examples for purposes of a brief demonstration.

The first of these again comes from Jim DeRogatis. A little less than a third of the way into his study of psychedelic rock, he takes up the issue of the "Art-rock nightmare." In his view, progressive rock represents a cul-de-sac in the trajectory of psychedelic rock, which later recovers its bearings with the music of such diverse groups as Parliament/Funkadelic and Hawkwind. (Please keep in mind that, although my framework for understanding this scene is quite different from DeRogatis's, my intention is not to be dismissive of these groups. Again, it has to do with where one places the greatest emphasis: DeRogatis's emphasis is on "keeping the faith" with LSD, while mine is on aesthetic-social experimentation.) DeRogatis laments the "move from psychedelia to art rock":

> As the name for a genre of music, "art rock" is misleading. Great rock is art, but there isn't much great art rock. What art rock, or "progressive rock," really signifies is music that self-consciously tries to elevate rock 'n' roll to high culture by embracing high culture values such as technical virtuosity and conceptual density. Many musicians in the first wave of British psychedelia were upper-middle-class kids who discovered rock, drugs, and the London nightlife and dropped out of college or art school. *Sgt. Pepper's* convinced them that they could make music that was just as serious as the art they'd been studying before they tuned in, turned on, and dropped out—and maybe it could even be respectable enough to please Mum and Dad.

Quoting John Rockwell (rock music critic for the *New York Times* and another despiser of progressive rock), DeRogatis goes on to argue that there was a special fixation among British rock musicians with the idea of "dignifying" their music, in part through

incorporating elements of European art music into it, in order "to
make it acceptable for upper-class approbation" (p. 84).

A similar line of argument is typified in one of the regular and
seemingly obligatory slurs against progressive rock in the English
magazine *The Wire*. Significantly, the slur comes in the middle of
an article on Chris Cutler, who played drums and composed
music with Henry Cow. There is an interesting phenomenon
among some critics of progressive rock, whereby the critic in fact
has one or two progressive groups that he likes, groups that must
be, therefore, somehow distanced from the larger movement.
Thus the following from Mike Barnes:

> With rock musicians struggling to be taken seriously in the mid-70s,
> an increasing number of groups, raised on psychedelia and R&B,
> looked toward classical forms for spurious credibility, to buy into the
> emergent notion of "Progressive rock". . . .
>
> Henry Cow were also a rock group who wanted to be taken seri-
> ously, but they were immersed in the music of Sun Ra, Ornette Cole-
> man, Syd Barrett's Pink Floyd and early Mothers of Invention. Most
> progressive rock groups drew upon the baroque or the 19th century
> Romantic era to fuel their particular form of bombast. Henry Cow
> were sifting through different areas. "Because we were rock musicians
> there was no academy and there were no rules: we could lift anything
> from anywhere we wanted," Cutler explains. So Henry Cow took their
> inspiration from the more astringent legacy of Bartok, Schoenberg,
> and Stravinsky. The "rock chamber ensemble" feel that they evoked . . .
> was quite intentional. (pp. 49–50)

The basic incoherence of all this tempts one to just think the critics here are not very bright. The prime reason for thinking this is
that, if we flush the basic premises out of these arguments from
DeRogatis and Barnes, I think that we would find a set of claims
that the critics themselves would not want to own up to. In fact, it
seems to me that something else is going on—but let us begin
with the aforementioned premises.

First, it seems abundantly clear that the music we have come
to call progressive rock developed out of 'the internal logic of
musical and social developments of the late sixties, and not out of
any self-conscious desire to initiate something called "art rock."
The term, in any case, was concocted by detractors of the music.

Second, what is it exactly about "technical virtuosity" that is a problem? Why is it a bad thing, necessarily, to attempt to become a better musician? If I am, say, a bass-guitar player, should I not attempt to become a *better* bass player, at least to a certain point?

Third, the same question goes for "conceptual density." Is the idea that this sort of thing just has no place in rock music? How much conceptual density is *too much*, and how much is just right?

Fourth, the class question needs to be dealt with in the context of the times. All kinds of borders were transgressed in the late sixties, especially those along the lines of class, gender, and ethnicity. The "establishment" (as we used to say, and I still think it is a useful term) and its definitions of class were exactly the sort of thing that young people were trying to drop out of. At the expense of perhaps unfairly mixing Barnes's and DeRogatis's arguments, it might be pointed out that, it was the members of Henry Cow who were rich kids, who met at Cambridge, while Jon Anderson was a poor kid from a mill town in the north, and Chris Squire's father was a cab driver. For that matter, Stravinsky was also a drop-out (his father wanted him to be a lawyer) who may have struggled with the questions of whether his music was important (or possibly even "respectable enough to please Mum and Dad").

Fifth, *so what* if progressive rock musicians incorporated bits of non–rock music that they picked up in college or art school or listening to the Beeb? That is one of the things rock music has always done, synthesized material from whatever source—and, of course, it is one of the things that both Mike Barnes and Chris Cutler valorize. Incidentally, the bit about art-school dropouts who use some of the material they picked up while they were there applies no less to a rather large group of English rock musicians, from the Beatles to the Gang of Four and beyond, as Simon Frith and Howard Horne demonstrated in *Art into Pop*.

Turn this idea on its head and you get the major premise in all of this that no rock critic, no matter how much they dislike progressive rock, could really accept: namely the idea that rock music is not supposed to grow or learn anything from outside of itself. No one really believes this. In fact, no one with more than two neurons to rub together *could* believe this, because rock music is *the* example of a kind of music where *all* of it comes from the outside. That's one of the things, the generous synthesis, that makes it capable of greatness. This is also one of the things that makes rock music suspect in the eyes of music purists; the remarkable thing is that this purism replicates itself within rock music itself.

Sixth, I doubt very seriously that, any more than any other rock musicians of the day, progressive rock musicians were much worried with making "respectable" music for their parents.

Seventh, is Barnes saying that, on the face of it, there is something better about drawing from Sun Ra than from nineteenth-century romantic classical music? What's the argument for this? Barnes then goes on to quote Cutler giving a virtual credo for progressive rock—the bit about "no rules: we could lift anything from anywhere we wanted." Barnes just seems to like the sources of Henry Cow's borrowings more than he does those of other progressive rock groups. That's o.k., I suppose, but why accept this idea of borrowing in the first place? After all, if one wants to listen to Sun Ra or Schönberg, well, there is plenty of their own music to listen to. Progressive rock groups borrowed and synthesized music from pretty much everywhere in the musical universe, from every continent and region and style. Is it simply that, in the view of a critic such as Barnes, Henry Cow hit on exactly the right things to borrow? Of course the idea is preposterous.

Eighth and finally—and this is the kicker—the thing that really gets me about Barnes's two-paragraph trashing of progressive rock is that one could write a vindication of most any progressive group using his very terms. To demonstrate this point, consider the following paraphrastic exercise:

> Yes were also a rock group who wanted to be taken seriously, but they were immersed in the music of Wes Montgomery, Chet Atkins, Art Blakey and the Jazz Messengers, Elvin Jones, the later Beatles, the Byrds, and John Entwistle's Who. Most Progressive rock groups drew on the baroque or the nineteenth-century Romantic era to fuel their particular form of bombast. Yes were sifting through different areas. "Because we were rock musicians there was no academy and there were no rules: we could lift anything from anywhere we wanted," Jon Anderson explains.
>
> So Yes took their inspiration from the more astringent legacy of Stravinsky, Sibelius, and Prokofiev. The "rock chamber ensemble" feel that they evinced . . . was quite intentional.

Alright, having undertaken this exercise, we can see some important differences between Yes and Henry Cow. The sources of
Henry Cow's synthesis were more "astringent," as Barnes puts
it, and the sharp edge is what I especially admire in their music.
And it is probably true, as Barnes claims, that many progressive
groups took more inspiration from romantic and baroque music;
it might also be added that there was a dimension of "medievalism" in some progressive rock, a topic that will be explored further. At the same time, it might be argued that there were other
sources in, for example, the music of Yes, that deserve valoriza-
tion in their own right. Perhaps the paraphrase experiment would
work even better if the example was King Crimson or Magma. (At
a slightly later point in Barnes's article, Cutler makes this very
point, saying that, "[I]f Carl Orff had had Magma at his disposal
he would have been in seventh heaven, because the effects he
often tries to create with several grand pianos hammering on the
low notes, for example, Magma could easily achieve with the
application of technology and amplification" [p. 50]). But all this
simply serves to show that Henry Cow, Yes, King Crimson,
Magma, and the rest were part of a significant *movement* in musical experimentation; you can *attempt* to reject the movement *tout
court* while making exceptions for particular groups, I suppose,
but then you land in the kinds of incoherency that I have just
enumerated.

Obviously, all of this makes me *angry*—I take it personally
when someone cynically and nonchalantly dismisses what seems
to me to have been a very important and *good* development in the
world. What's more, most of the music that is covered by *The Wire*
and similar *hip* music magazines wouldn't even exist without progressive rock as the force that consolidated the possibility of
avant-garde experimentation in rock music. The musicians know
this and are almost always generous with their recognition of it;
indeed, because I respect Chris Cutler tremendously, and because
his theory comes out of his practice as a musician, I will turn to
some of his other comments on progressive rock in a moment.

So, what else is going on with the "critics"? Perhaps this is a
low blow of sorts, but I want to assert a little authority on this
question as a writer who is also a musician. When I dealt with the
question of "technical virtuosity" above, I had to wonder if the

idea is that a musician who is in danger of developing too much
of a musical vocabulary (which is really all that virtuosity is
about) should take steps to insure that this does not happen. Or
perhaps someone on the verge of "conceptual density" should just
stop thinking so much. After all, our society is in great danger
from too much thoughtfulness!

In my view, the critics are dealing with a double-edged sword.
On the one hand, they have embraced the absurd notion that rock
music should only develop so far, and no further. Most of them do
not have any sense of the internal logic of music, or what it takes
to play an instrument well, so they are not troubled by these
issues. On the other hand, even where some of the more sophisticated music publications are concerned, there is a certain com-
pulsion toward assimilating music, not allowing it to get out of
hand. In other words, most music writing is a part of the larger
music industry. (Would it simply be disingenuous to suggest that
these writers also want to show their articles, from "respectable"
glossy magazines, to their Mums and Dads, in the hopes that they
will be pleased?) This does not mean that there is not some room
for discussing more experimental music; otherwise there certainly would not be room for articles about Chris Cutler. But
notice, we are discussing Henry Cow twenty years after their heyday, and furthermore, we are discussing them in a context where
the idea of linear progression in music has been almost entirely
suppressed. Progressive rock is developmental music; its basis is
an increase in musical vocabulary, often propelled by a high level
of instrumental skill and the dreaded "conceptual density." Some
of the music that developed out of the materials of progressive
rock in the past twenty years depends more on "verticality." Much
of this music can rightly be called "postmodern pastiche." In publications such as *The Wire*, occasional raids are made on the progressive rock legacy, to recover materials for incorporation into
this postmodern music of vertical stacking (in which, incidentally,
few of the "musicians" play actual instruments—praising Henry
Cow for its borrowings from Sun Ra, who was nothing if not a
romantic, fits in nicely with music writing where the "composer"
receives praise for choosing well with his or her samples). The
new vertical aesthetic fits this age of film rather than the age of

radio. The resulting music is also a music for listening, but in a trance or ecstatic rave mode rather than an intellectually challenging, conceptually dense mode. Some of this music is interesting and innovative, to be sure. But it also has the virtue, in our postmodern consumer society, of being more readily packageable than progressive rock would prove to be in the long run. For one thing, the duration of one's listening does not seem to matter— simply slice off as big or little a piece as you have time to hear. And significantly, this pastiche music—including techno, house, jungle, industrial, and electronica—seems more suited to production by individuals than by groups. I will return to these themes in the final chapter.

◪   ◪   ◪

As I just mentioned, stretching out in progressive rock, whether through extended composition or extended improvisation, or some combination of the two, generally takes a linear form. In other words, there is a developmental logic to progressive rock works. This logic has played out against the background of, and, to a large extent, recapitulated, the developmental trajectories of Western classical music and jazz. As this logic gave rise to the more extended and difficult forms of progressive rock, the song and dance forms that have been the origin of all "art" musics were stretched into qualitatively new domains.

Perhaps the term that encompasses this logic, in the largest sense, is "counterpoint." Typically, when mentioned in European classical music circles, counterpoint has to do with the intermotivation of melodies: two or more melodic lines play off of one another, exchanging position or parts of each other against the background of harmony, rhythm, and timbre. In some sense, the history of Western classical music is the history of the complexification of both melodic counterpoint and the level of interaction of the other basic components of music. The tendency in classical music, up through the late romantic period (the archetypal composers here would be Wagner, Brahms, Mahler, and Bruckner), was toward greater complexity and density. Around the last decades of the nineteenth century and for the first few decades of the twentieth century, three trends emerged in reaction to late romanticism. There was what might be called the "neo" movement, consisting in neoromanticism and neoclassicism, which sought to employ the harmonic resources of late romanticism, but with an economy more typical of Haydn or Mozart. There were movements rooted in the national cultures of countries outside of the core of European "great powers," especially the countries of Scandanavia, Central and Eastern Europe, and the Mediterranean. Finally, there were composers who looked beyond Europe for new rhythms, timbres, and scales.

Many important composers fell into more than one of these categories. Stravinsky, for example, could be said to have been an exponent of all three, though perhaps not simultaneously. The same might be said of Shostakovich.

Left out of this scheme, seemingly, is the music of the "second Vienna school," Arnold Schönberg and his pupils, Anton von Webern and Alban Berg. In the wake of Wagner and Mahler, Schönberg seemed to bring *system* to the increasingly hyperchromatic world of late romanticism. Schönberg's "twelve-note system" could be seen as a reinvention of counterpoint and harmony at a point when chromaticism seemed strained to the breaking point—that is, when the idea of having a piece of music that is in a recognizeable "key," or where the chords in some sense "resolve," has been exhausted. Without wanting to diminish the achievements of Schönberg, Webern, and Berg in any way, I would still like to advance the (debatable, to be sure) proposition that the second Vienna school still fits within the first category described above, with the special proviso that this school developed a set of "procedures" or a "system" for creating an economical neoromanticism. (On some level it is tempting to compare the transition from Wagner to Mahler to Schönberg with the development of German idealist philosophy from Kant to Hegel to Marx.) But this system also led from late romanticism, through the "three trends," into the post-WWII period, when increasing harmonic density has given way to fragmentation. In other words, following out its own premises, the system deconstructed itself.

Although in a more compressed time frame, encompassing most of the twentieth century, jazz followed a similar trajectory.

The history is somewhat complicated by the fact that dialectics of simplification and complexification have occurred in ten- to twenty-year cycles, such that the collective improvisations of New Orleans jazz groups from the 1920s and the Art Ensemble of Chicago and Ornette Coleman's harmolodic groups from the 1960s to the 1980s seem to have more in common than the latter groups have with, say, early bebop or the "cool" jazz of the late fifties. Jazz, of course, brings musical and other resources from outside of the European tradition. In the case of jazz's greatest exponents, however, there has always been an awareness of the European tradition, and a willingness to interact with it or react against it.

Furthermore, by the sixties, both had begun to flow into what I have called the "general avant-garde." Rock music is a late-comer to this process. Rock purists would prefer, I suppose, that there not actually be a "process," in the sense of a developmental logic of rock music that allowed it to interact with music other than blues or perhaps American popular song. Be that as it may, an experimental trend developed out of the materials, including the specific instruments such as electric guitar, bass guitar, and trap drums, and this trend began to both attempt to take account of the developmental logics of jazz and European classical music, and to make contributions of its own to the general avant-garde.[20]

This experimental rock music, an umbrella term that includes progressive rock, had one foot in the field of rock music, and one foot in this general avant-garde. As with all hybrids, experimental rock garnered its share of skeptics—it was criticized, as one might expect, from both sides. The purists on the rock side forgot that all rock music is hybrid in nature. Some of the skeptics on the avant-garde side held to a Eurocentric or otherwise elitist conception of "high culture," a conception that took a great fall in the late sixties and has yet to be put back together again by all the king's horses or men (except perhaps in the thoroughly isolated minds of a handful of academic musicologists). What the skeptics of today, especially those who affirm more experimental trends in music ("adventures," as the *Wire* masthead has it), fail to appreciate, is that all of the more recent experimental trends come through and are enabled by the activity of the late sixties and early to middle seventies.

*** * * * ***

The late sixties, a time of ideological retreat for oppressive social systems, represented a window of opportunity for social and cultural experimentation. Musicians in that period were adventurous and took risks. In light of the fact that the term "risk" is often used to valorize capitalism, especially in connection with the idea of "entrepreneurship," I would like to say something about the situation of record companies in the sixties. After all, the folks who ran these companies, and who signed artists to recording contracts, would seem to be the link between two different kinds of risk, capitalist and artistic. My aim here is to show that the two are fundamentally different, and also to give credit to some people who played an important role behind the scenes.

From the period when "record companies" first started up, until the late sixties, there were basically two kinds of company. The more established kind, such as RCA or MCA, were already a part of the set-up that has led to the emergence of global media conglomerates in the past twenty years. That is, these companies were already hooked up with film studios, radio and television networks, and companies that actually produced radios and televisions (e.g., RCA, the Radio Corporation of America). The other kind of record company was generally run by one or two key people, such as Leonard Chess, Ahmet Ertegun, or Jerry Wexler. These companies specialized in the "race music" that the establishment companies avoided. Significantly, with Ertegun and Wexler at Atlantic Records, we see a thread that runs from Little Richard and "Tutti-Frutti" to two of the most important progressive rock groups, Yes and King Crimson.

These pioneers of the small, independent labels began as record producers. "Producer" is an amorphous term today, complicated by the fact that, on the one hand, in the business of making records, there is a significant overlap with the work of the recording engineer, while, on the other hand, in the film business, the "producer" may be the person who is providing the money for the project. Chess, Ertegun, and Wexler have been producers in the sense that they both organize projects and supervise the recording. At Atlantic Records, Jerry Wexler and Ahmet Ertegun played a major role in the transformation of 1940s "blues and jazz into '50s rhythm and blues and rock 'n' roll and '60s soul," according to Ben Fisher, in a recent *Mojo* article.[17] To Wexler, there are

> [t]hree types of producer. There's the Phil Specter type, who starts with a preconceived idea of how the finished product will sound. Phil Specter is the preeminent genius of the music business. This method of recording does not usually yield outstanding artists—you think of it as a Phil Specter production. The second kind of producer is typified by Leonard Chess—the documentarian. He would go out and find, say, Muddy Waters playing in a little club on the south side of Chicago and bring him into Chess Studios, and basically just replicate the sound. The third category is the category I put myself in, along with John Hammond, Nesuhi and Ahmet Ertegun. We were basically fans, collectors of jazz and blues records, and we brought this knowledge to our productions. (p. 49)

Here is another context where it is worth mentioning that, in 1969, the Beatles produced *Abbey Road*, another great album where George Martin brought out the best from the group, while, a year later, the group released *Let it Be* (which had in fact been recorded before *Abbey Road*), which is in some sense the individual Beatles playing in a Phil Specter production.

Meanwhile, however, well-placed "fans" of rock music were in a position to allow groups such as Yes, King Crimson, Genesis, and others explore their own possibilities with labels such as Atlantic, Charisma, Harvest, and Virgin. It isn't that these producers and record-company executives were not businessmen—they certainly were, Ahmet Ertegun and Richard Branson (founder of Virgin) being among the most shrewd; however, in that period, under the social conditions that we have already discussed, these people also played the important role of patrons and impressarios.[18]

Of course money starts to play a role in the whole equation. Insomuch as this new type of impressario is part of a corporate structure that has the aim of making a profit, artistic risk is circumscribed as far as the actual making and distribution of recordings is concerned. The reasons why some record companies allowed groups to make records such as *Larks' Tongues in*

Aspic are varied and complex. There was a relatively long period, perhaps from the late sixties to the late seventies, when record companies seemed to have more money than they knew what to do with. Certainly they had more dollars than sense, when it was common for musicians—and often not the most creative of them, by any means—to go into a studio for weeks at a time, without really having completed compositions beforehand, and to "come up with something" by and by, along with ordering extravagant quantities of expensive food, drugs, and M&Ms with the brown ones removed. This extravagance was financed by a decadent capitalist society that, despite international setbacks, was still riding fairly high in the global economic order. In other words, extravagance in the West was connected, essentially, with poverty and exploitation in the Third World.

However, this situation also allowed for creative groups to more or less make the records that they wanted to make. The reason why the risks that these musicians took are not similar to the "risk" that capitalists take is that the truly creative musicians would have made creative albums whether or not there was financial success to be had from the endeavor. Capitalists can only afford to be "creative" on the condition that their "risk" leads to profit; the profit, in other words, is the aim of the process, and "creativity" only the means. A capitalist cannot say, for instance, "I am going to build this car, whether anyone buys it or not, because I believe in this car." An artist, on the other hand, can say, "I am going to write this symphony, whether or not anyone wants to hear it." At the same time, however, if no one wants to pay to hear the symphony, the artist would do well to either find a patron or to keep his or her day job. These things can and do interfere with the ability of a person to continue with artistic endeavors.

Concerning the current production and distribution of creative works, there are some important structural changes occurring in the capitalist economy even as we speak. These changes are the very sort of thing that would make it difficult for there to be "popular avant-gardes" as there were in the time of progressive rock. One aspect of this transformed "culture industry" (as Adorno and Horkheimer called it; their analysis in *Dialectic of Enlightenment* was prescient) is that there seems no longer to be room for people such as Ertegun and Wexler to play the role of impressarios.[19]

        ◪   ◪   ◪

The time of experimental rock was also a time of groups and group composition. In the "general avant-garde," group composition was the norm in rock and jazz, but even in the offshoots of the European classical tradition there was more room for members of groups to make decisions that affected the overall shape of compositions. For instance, many of John Cage's works consisted not in traditional musical notation, but instead in a set of instructions, which in many cases the performer is given broad latitude to interpret. (I think of these as rather ingenious experiments in freedom and responsibility; as it turned out, traditionally trained classical musicians were often the least responsible with Cage's compositions.) "Composition" in rock and jazz, at least until recent years, has also been largely "thematic" in nature. Case in point: Jon Anderson composed the basic thematic material for the Yes work, "The Gates of Delirium." The work of the other musicians, however, in putting flesh on those bones was also an essential part of the composition.

The basic point is that the time of progressive rock was a time in which one of the basic credos of rock music, "the group's the thing," was true to a greater extent than it had been either before or since. What Steve Howe has called the "commune feeling," the guiding spirit of many progressive groups, was part and parcel of the general milieu of social and cultural experimentation of the sixties.

        ◪   ◪   ◪

The question of "composition" in rock music, especially from the time of George Martin's work with the Beatles forward, cannot be separated from the fact that studio technology has played an increasingly important role. This has led Theodore Gracyk, in his "aesthetics of rock," to take recording technology to be the defining feature of the music.[20] I would not go that far—in fact I worry about some of what I see as overdependence on studio technology—but it is true that the innovations of experimental rock are bound up with developments in recording technology. For example, many longer works of progressive rock—prime examples of stretching out, in other words—were never performed by bands in their entirety until they had been pieced together, bit by bit, in the studio. ("Close to the Edge" is a famous example of where, in a sense, first the group played the various parts, then they had to "learn" the whole work. My guess, though I do not know this for a fact, is that *Thick as a Brick* and *A Passion Play* are similar cases.) Furthermore, the work of engineers and producers, following in the footsteps of George Martin, became coequal with that of the "musicians" themselves. (Again, *Close to the Edge* is a famous example, where Eddie Offord is pictured on the back cover along with the other members of Yes.) One of the key threads between the time of progressive rock and more recent experimental rock music has been Brian Eno's use of the studio mixing board as a musical instrument in its own right.

◢◣ ◢◣ ◢◣

One more thing needs to be said about the actual instruments typically associated with rock music. Even from the time of Bo Diddley and Louis Jordan, but especially in the late sixties, the range of instruments that might be used is quite broad. From the beginning, all of the "jazz instruments" were to be found in rock. From the middle sixties on, it was typical of the experimental trend that many of the instruments of Western classical music, such as violins, harpsichords, glockenspiels and timpani, were employed. At this time, too, a number of non-Western instruments, such as the sitar (for which there was quite a vogue for awhile), came into play. In addition, a number of new instruments, such as the electronic synthesizer and the Mellotron,[21] as well as electronic treatments for more "traditional" instruments and voice, began to play a crucial role.

In some sense, as the compositional boundaries between experimental rock and the more general avant-garde began to blur, the presence of certain instruments is what distinguished the former as still a kind of rock music. In other words, certain works of experimental rock, if they were to be scored for instruments more typically associated with European classical music, would not necessarily be recognizable as rock music. Instead, some pieces could easily be heard as what is generally called "contemporary music," the avant-garde offshoot of the European tradition. (One of my prime candidates here, discussed in my book on Yes, is King Crimson's "Larks' Tongues in Aspic, part 1.") In other words, how do we know that some experimental rock music is indeed "rock" music? There is the lineage, you might say, that the musicians have participated in—they "come out of" a background in rock music. But this doesn't mean very much in a period when anyone can come from any background and play any kind of music. (Leonard Bernstein's *Mass* is an interesting example here.) So, the other identifying feature might be the presence of instruments typically associated with rock music: electric guitars and bass guitars, trap drums (which are typical of jazz as well, of course), and electric and electronic keyboards. But this is no more than a kind of indicator; surely a genre of music should not be identified merely by the sorts of instruments used to play it.

◢◣   ◢◣   ◢◣

Thus far, I have not made a distinction between "experimental rock" and "progressive rock." My aim now will be to make that distinction. In my view, there are three main ways in which "progressive rock" may be said to constitute an identifiable musical genre.

My first point stems from what was just said about instruments. In the earlier period of experimental rock, say around the time of *Sgt. Pepper's*, diverse instruments were used to create *exotic* effects. Such exoticism was not unlike Stravinsky's exoticism in *The Rite of Spring*. All of the "weird" stuff was supposed to stand out. When we heard, for instance, a harpsichord part followed by a sitar part in a Beatles record, we were supposed to be wowed by their presence and, even more so, by their juxtaposition. This particular synthesis, however, was incomplete and thus sounds like mere exoticism and even a bit hokey to us now. (Because of this quality, *Sgt. Pepper's* is perhaps the weakest of the

Beatles' albums from *Rubber Soul* forward, even if still historically the most significant.) In full-blown progressive rock, the
synthesis is much more complete in the following way: when we
hear the presence and juxtaposition of harpsichord and sitar or
some such in a piece by Genesis or Gentle Giant (or violin and
kalimba in "Larks' Tongues"), this sounds much more like something that has been a part of music all along. We may say "wow"
at the music, but no longer at the instruments that the music is
played on.

▟ ▟ ▟

The second distinction that I would like to draw between
experimental rock and progressive rock will quite likely be controversial. In *music of Yes*, I developed the following definition of
progressive rock: "Progressive rock is visionary and experimental
music played by virtuosos on instruments associated with rock
music" (p. 39). The distinctive term here is "virtuosos." The time
of progressive rock is a time in which "world class" musicians
were playing difficult works of rock music. Some have argued
that the idea of the "virtuoso" is essentially undefinable. In rock
music, the definition of virtuoso has tended to come down to
purely quantifiable elements, especially *speed*. This is to be
rejected for a number of reasons, not least of which is the fact
that such criteria of virtuosity feed into both purely athletic and
masculinist conceptions of instrumental skills. I hesitate to
invoke athleticism here, given that the greatest athletes, such as
Martina Navratilova, Michael Jordan, Walter Payton, Dan
Marino, or Tiger Woods, exemplify the same grace and finesse
that is desired and expected from a musical virtuoso. Qualities
such as "grace" are notoriously difficult to define—therefore, virtuosity is also undefinable on some level.

However, I think that I have found some ways around these
problems, or at least ways in which it is possible to show something distinctive about progressive rock. Although not all musicians who have played progressive rock are virtuosos, neverthe-
less, by and large, most of these musicians are *really good*, they
can *really play*—about this there is a general consensus. In most
other kinds of rock music, it is even possible to have musicians

who can *barely* play their instruments, though this is of course not the norm. I hasten to add that it is even quite possible that *good* music can be produced by such neophytes, just as it is possible to have *awful* music produced by virtuosos. Furthermore, there are virtuoso rock musicians who are not players of experimental or progressive rock; Stevie Ray Vaughn or Max Weinberg would be good examples. What is the difference between a really good musician and a virtuoso? The criterion I propose is this: a virtuoso is a musician for whom difficulty is not an issue. If a piece of music needs to be played, a virtuoso can play it, and difficulty will not stand in the way.

Obviously there are limits to this, and Edward Macan makes the interesting point that sampling and other electronic technology has made it possible for less accomplished musicians to "play" music that even the most accomplished musicians could not play. He further argues that the development of such technology has played a key role in the passing of progressive rock as a major trend (see pp. 192–93). On the other hand, when I listen to John Coltrane, I often have the feeling that he could do not only everything possible with the tenor and soprano saxophones, but even some things that seem impossible. (I have a similar feeling when I watch Michael Jordan.)

If we define virtuoso in this sense, it seems to me that the progressive rock of the late sixties and early to middle seventies saw the predominance of such musicians—and this was not true of either experimental rock or rock music more generally.

Another way of coming at this is to define the musical virtuoso as someone with not only consummate instrumental or vocal or compositional skill, but also as someone with a very large musical vocabulary. Again, this seems typical of progressive rock.

Please remember, in the overall definition that I have brought forward from my work on Yes, it is the combination of musical virtuosity with a visionary and experimental approach that is essential. Instrumental "skills" by themselves, no matter how impressive in merely quantitative terms (the sort of thing that might get into the *Guinness Book of World Records*—"the world's fastest bass player" or some such), do not good music make. However, to the extent that such skills, especially an expanded vocabulary, contribute to an enriched musical vision, I think we can make a distinction between progressive rock and other experimental forms of rock music.

This section could not be properly closed without at least a few lines being devoted to what might be called "the Pink Floyd problem."[22] Many readers have undoubtedly already wondered at the absence of Pink Floyd from my first line of progressive rock groups. The fact is, they do not appear in my second line either, though I will comment on a number of Pink Floyd albums in the next chapter. This group is probably the most significant and controversial example of just where my distinction between experimental and progressive rock cuts. The members of Pink Floyd are good musicians but, in my view, their technical proficiency is not on a level with most of the members of the groups I have placed in the first and second lines of progressive rock.

So what? After all, aren't albums such as *Atom Heart Mother* and *Wish You Were Here* musically and thematically similar to many progressive rock albums?[23] As a complete presentation (or "package," if I may be excused that obnoxious term for the moment), don't these albums look and sound very much like works of progressive rock? Why then make a distinction between, say, Pink Floyd and Soft Machine, just because Hugh Hopper is a better bass player than Roger Waters, or Robert Wyatt and John Marshall better drummers than Nick Mason? After all, Nick Mason is a very creative drummer—and isn't that what really matters? (For that matter, Roger Waters is definitely a better bass player than at least a couple of those who played with King Crimson.) But let's take another example of a very creative drummer whom I would also not call a "virtuoso," namely Ringo Starr. Yet Ringo Starr is one of the great rock drummers; if I was forced to make a list, I would certainly put him in my top five. The reason that he is a great drummer is that his playing has been a crucial part of some great music, and his playing in that music is so absolutely "right" that it is very difficult to even begin to think how any of it could be improved upon.

Something similar might be said about at least some of the playing of Nick Mason and other members of the Floyd. *Wish You Were Here* is a *great* album, and it would not in any way be improved upon or better "developed" by greater technical skill on the part of the musicians. But I would say the exact same thing about *Abbey Road*, which is one reason why I brought Ringo Starr into this discussion. Should we include this album in our pantheon of great progressive rock albums? And, if we should include the album, why not the group? But then, why not also include the Rolling Stones' *Their Satanic Majesties Request*? No one is going to argue that the Stones were or are a progressive rock group, but *Satanic Majesties* shares many of the distinguishing features of progressive rock—save one, namely virtuosic musical skills.

Just to push the point one step further, perhaps we should propose *Abraxas* (1970) and *Caravanserai* (1972), by Santana, as progressive rock albums. This is challenging music and, as for virtuosity, you're not going to find a guitarist better than Carlos Santana, or a drummer better than Michael Shrieve.

Let us, then, come to the point of this exercise. There is a great deal of excellent music that hovers somewhere in the vicinity or periphery of progressive rock, sharing many of its attributes, and yet I would still try to make a distinction between this music and progressive rock. In the final analysis, progressive rock can only be defined as a *style*. An element of the style, I would argue, is virtuosic musical skills.[24]

◼   ◼   ◼

In the time that has passed since the formulation of the definition of progressive rock that I presented in *music of Yes* (and as a result of feedback from readers of that book), I have come to think that the definition needs a bit more work. This leads me to my third point. As with many of the arguments I have already given in this chapter, my procedure once again takes the form of a *via negativa*. That is, I think that we can see better what progressive rock is by trying to understand what it is not. Actually, there is another aspect of the procedure I hope to employ here, perhaps more of a *via positiva*; that is, I think it helps to proceed by way of examples. In the spirit of the previous discussion, a name for all of this cobbled-together methodology might be, "my Frank Zappa problem."

In short, the definition of progressive rock can be sharpened by gathering together some core examples of progressive rock groups and music, and attempting to see what is different about them from other music that might, at least in a purely formal sense, fit the definition that I brought forward from *music of Yes*.

Despite all the risks involved, and not letting go of the aspects of the definition already enumerated, it seems to me that we should recognize that *progressive rock sets sail from England*.[25] Recall that, in the introductory chapter, I presented a list of groups that I take to be the "first line" in progressive rock. This is not an uncontroversial claim, and more will be said about it in the opening pages of the next chapter. For now, however, I will at least take it for granted that the groups who "made the list," so to speak, are all bona-fide important progressive rock groups. Of the thirteen groups in the list, nine are from England, and two more (Gong and the Mahavishnu Orchestra) are in part from England. Of these, a large part come from a particular region of England, namely the coastal south, and even from (or near) a particular city, Canterbury. Even of the groups that I have placed in the "second line," the much larger part are from England, and I think this is not entirely or even mainly for reasons of access (though this undoubtedly plays a role; I will speak to this issue especially in terms of the Italian scene in the next chapter). To borrow the words that Steve Howe once used when discussing Yes, "there is something very English about progressive rock."

In my view, this "Englishness" goes beyond the question of style, to historical lines of development; still, there is something to the idea that there is an English style of progressive rock, or perhaps that progressive rock itself begins as an "English" style. Of course I want to avoid chauvinism and nationalism in all of this. Perhaps a comparison could be made with opera. Obviously, a composer does not have to be Italian to write an opera, but the historical fact (and perhaps what ought to be identified as an historical contingency) is that opera developed first in Italy.[26] Other opera composers, even those who seem a million miles away from anything Italian (Wagner remaining the outstanding example), take their bearings from those roots (even in reacting against them).

What is especially "English" about progressive rock? I will deal with some of the regional qualities of the movement in the next section, in a discussion of Edward Macan's *Rocking the Classics*. However, it seems to me that the most important elements can be specified in short order; they fall into two main categories, geographical and what I will call, for want of a better term, "philosophical."

Two geographical characteristics are of prime importance: England is both an island and a crossroads. In recent centuries, England has been suspended, historically, between Europe and North America. At the same time, there has been an insularity to English culture; it is a culture preoccupied with the very idea of "Englishness." The resulting cultural cauldron has left its mark on distinctive developments in rock music, including the experimental, psychedelic, and progressive trends. In cultural shorthand, it might be said that these trends began in Liverpool, developed further in Canterbury, coalesced in London—and from there went out to the world.

The "philosophical" or ideological trends that especially went into the formation of progressive rock might be grouped under the headings of English romanticism and pastoralism, especially, but also the northern European radical reformation and religious hermeticism. Both of the latter played an important role in the formation of English romanticism. Even in the science-fiction elements of progressive rock we see this romanticism and pastoralism, either in the form of communitarian utopias or in the dystopias of American-style industrialism and "pop culture" run wild. Indeed, progressive rock's inaugural album, *In the Court of the Crimson King*, goes down all of these paths.

The interesting essay by Iain Chambers, "An Island Life," serves to show the intermotivation of these themes, as well as to set the "English" context of progressive rock. As Chambers demonstrates, the last two centuries have seen the formation of an "extensive *popular* cultural consensus," only recently under serious challenge, around the idea of a "profound sense of 'Englishness'" (pp. 16–17). The primary motivating factor in the formation of this consensus has been a fundamental ambiguity regarding political modernity, capitalism, urbanism, and industrial production. Even as this ambiguity and outright rejection of these elements of Western modernity has had its populist side,

Greater Britain's long and deeply imperfect transition to capitalism (granted, all historical transitions are imperfect) has also
depended on the benefits of empire and gross oppression and
exploitation.[27]

Perhaps this two-sidedness of the British encounter with
modernity is seen best in the figure of John Locke (1632–1704). In
his *Second Treatise of Government* (1689), Locke gives us one of
the essential formulations of the ideal of the commonwealth, as
well as of popular sovereignty, but at the same time defends slavery. Locke was no mere theorist (again, the legacy is two-sided).
On the one hand, he opposed the restoration of the monarchy in
Britain in 1660, and he was continually in trouble with that
restored monarchy. On the other hand, he was involved in the
slave trade between Africa and the Americas, and he drew up a
plan for the creation of the plantation system in the colony of
South Carolina. Not to diminish the vast historical significance of
these Atlantic crossings, but such is the setting from which rock
music would emerge.

Economically dependent upon and yet fearful of its "opening"
to the wider world, the British intelligentsia developed a cohesive
and insular sense of "Englishness." As Chambers puts it,

> In their neo-Gothic architecture, pre-Raphaelite paintings, chivalric
> poetry, fourteenth-century socialist utopias, and their insistence on
> the earlier harmonies of rural life and artisan production, Victorian
> intellectuals of the most varied political persuasions sealed a pact
> between a mythical vision of the nation and their selection and instal-
> lation of an acceptable cultural heritage. British culture, and its pro-
> found sense of "Englishness" (the narrowing of the national nomen-
> clature was not accidental) was found, in both the temporal and
> symbolic sense, to exist beyond the mechanical rhythms and com-
> mercial logic of industrial society and the modern world. It has subse-
> quently bequeathed that deep seated intellectual and moral aversion
> to modernism, mass culture, and mass democracy, and a correspond-
> ing acquiescence to the authority of tradition, that has so character-
> ized English intellectual thought and official culture in the twentieth
> century. In its unbending moral clarity and particular sense of history
> it has "given us the map of an upright and decent country." (p. 17)

Two aspects of the "aversion" and the "acquiescence" require
emphasis here. First, the pastoral heritage ("the earlier harmonies
of rural life and artisan production") was in large part an illusion:

The paradox, but well-kept secret, was that what made the earlier abandonment of both the city and much of the "modern" experience possible was the wealth and space generated by the Industrial Revolution and the Empire. The city had been forsaken for the timeless sanctuary of the country, which, if you could not actually live there could be recreated in miniature in the simulacrum of the English garden. This is the suburban solution to rural mythology, where class, gender, and domesticity entwine in a miniature Eden and discover an enduring lifestyle among the potted plants. . . . Meanwhile, the real countryside was simultaneously represented in rustic and recreational panoramas. Working figures largely disappear from view, and the meanness and misery of rural life is generally obscured by a tranquil pastoralism. Symbolically transformed into an empty landscape in the canvases of Constable and Gainsborough, the countryside provided a suitably placid metaphor, once the potential disturbance of agricultural labourers and the rural poor had been literally removed from the picture, for an abstractly conceived national culture. (pp. 32–33)

In light of these comments, it is tempting to think of progressive rock as emerging from its own "secret garden."

Second, and relatedly, even oppositional and radical politics in England tended to be expressed in terms of this consensus. Chambers presents a number of important examples:

When William Morris . . . proposed a socialist society, the model he offered was not post-capitalist, but pre-, located in the harmony of a medieval village and an artisan mode of production. (p. 33)

[T]he forms in which opposition and minority causes are articulated can turn out to be an integral and crucial part of the successful reproduction of [the "English" consensus]. For example, much of the recent story of the Labour Party, of the representations of the British working class, and such initiatives by radical intellectuals as *Charter 88* [a movement to create a written constitution for England], reflect a common refusal to cut, or at least sufficiently slacken and more openly question, the knot that continues to bind these forces to the same referents—that of "Britishness," of tradition, of the national mode and mood—that have successfully hegemonized British politics and public accounting for so long.

The solutions that oppositional forces have usually offered have characteristically been drawn from the same lexicon, even the same emotional stock pile, the same national history book, as the rhetoric and representations so gainfully employed by Mrs. Thatcher and her governments in recent years. (pp. 48–49)

We might make a distinction between a radical opposition, which a figure such as William Morris certainly represented, and a "loyal opposition," such as the British Labour Party certainly is and intends to be. In the latter case, it is no surprise that we find "faithful subjects . . . rally[ing] around the flag in times of crisis" (p. 16). However, it seems as though even the "radical" opposition has been for so long immersed in the language of Empire and the culture of imperialism and the authority of an illusory "tradition" and "community" that it cannot break out of these rather constraining habits of mind.

But this is where I would want to begin to read Chambers against the grain (and here begins a discussion that will continue when I turn to Macan's perspective on the class origins of progressive rock). Perhaps the best place to begin this challenge is with Chambers's brief discussion of William Blake. Chambers amalgamates Blake to "the mode of thought that both British intellectual life and its everyday culture share," namely, the "moral faith in empiricism" (p. 22). This empiricism, Chambers argues, avoids the construction of intellectual or theoretical totalities, and instead partakes of the "transparent factuality of the world." In this respect, the "generous synthesis" which I have argued is a basic aspect of rock music, and which is present in an especially sophisticated form in progressive rock, comes to appear more a species of imperialism. In other words, the "synthesis" is in fact a rip-off and assimilation for the greater glory of Empire. Every "Other" will, in time, come under the hegemony of "Britain," "the primitive seat of the Patriarchal Religion"; "All things begin and end in Albion's ancient Druid rocky shore" (Blake). Chambers speaks of a "complex inheritance of empiricism and imperialism [that] is deeply ingrained in the English 'structure of feeling'" (p. 24).

This characterization does speak, in my view, to the actual state of power relations in the world; Chambers is right, therefore, to emphasize this side of things. Furthermore, any thematization of some "other side of things" must work through and not in any way seek to diminish this reality. Therefore, though there is a side of Blake that is in fact set against this imperialism, empiricism, and mere facticity, and instead involved in a complex, hermetic sense of connection, and though this sense of connection is also a central part of all oppositional and romantic thought from Blake to Raymond Williams to, for that matter, Jon Anderson, yet this does not mean that we can ignore the relationship between imperialism and connectedness. After all, the connection between the culture of the British Isles and the cultures of Black Africa that was forged in the American South and that gave rise to rock and roll music was a connection forged on the basis of brutal enslavement as well as the attempt to escape brutal conditions in Europe (including the potato famine in Ireland).

Still, there is this other side, perhaps the basis of a real opposition to the underside of modernity, which Chambers turns to at the very end of his essay. The final paragraphs of the essay demonstrate precisely what might be called a "turn of thought" (or perhaps "in" thought); Chambers speaks of a "deeply 'English' sense of opposition," one that is unwilling to refuse the "repertoire" of "Britishness," "or at least subject it to scepticism and crack it apart by extending its terms and shifting its grounds of legitimation" (p. 49).

> So much, including a lot of radical criticism, cultural analysis and historiography, continues to be steeped in the sense of a national (or at least "English") tradition. It is as though the solutions can only be sought there; that it lies within us, in an alternative version of the "national" character, to find a more equitable response to modern ills. . . . A national hermeneutics is preferred in which, in the shadow of the long, uninterrupted line that descends from the Magna Carta, we "play out our old roles to the end." [The quotation is from Raymond Williams.] To dig into that particular past in the hope of re-emerging with another, more democratic, more open, sense of "Englishness" is an honourable task. (p. 50)

This last sentence is where the turn in thought is truly engaged—and now we shall see how this is extended. If this discussion has seemed too much of a diversion, my argument is that we are on the verge of seeing the very essence of progressive rock.

> The problem is that today its terms of reference seem too narrow, its appeal too exclusive. The very idea of the "English" (and the ethnic, even racial, overtones should not be underestimated) has perhaps been hegemonic for too long for any hope that it can be successfully remade

solely from within. . . . It now needs to be reappropriated within a
wider context (and not merely European), where the discourses of
democracy and differences must necessarily run freer in order to
accommodate other worlds, other vocabularies, other memories.

And yet,

> [i]t is not possible to deliberately abandon such an inheritance, to
> cancel it as though it were a page that can now be torn out of the his-
> tory book. One is forced to come to terms with such a heritage, to
> revisit it, to live in its ruins and there in the gaps, openings and frag-
> ments to grasp a wider sense of the possible. To set limits to this par-
> ticular native narrative does not foreclose the further unwinding of
> its characteristic concerns: translated across a wider dialogue into
> other languages they will continue to exist as memories, traces, inter-
> rogations. To draw a line is to indicate a distinction between an inte-
> rior, a here, and an elsewhere . . . and therefore the eventual possibil-
> ity of crossing that line. (p. 50)

Living in the gaps of the English romantic and hermetic heritage,
expanding and reinterpreting that heritage in terms of some idea
of "America," an idea somehow concentrated in rock music, and
from there going beyond European sources, this seems to me a
veritable "methodology" of progressive rock.

As a matter of fact, and not surprisingly, Chambers does see
the opening toward the wider dialogue as starting off with the
late fifties, and then the sixties (in the larger political sense).

These crossings and connections can be seen on any number
of levels; let us assemble here, with five interconnected moments,
something of a travel directory covering land and sea.

We begin with one of England's unlikely windows on the
larger world, a city both poor and yet cosmopolitan; in the words
of John Lennon:

> There was nothing big in Liverpool. It was a very poor, a very poor
> city, and tough. But people have a sense of humour because they are
> in so much pain. . . . It is cosmopolitan, and it's where the sailors
> would come home with the blues records from America on ships.
> (quoted in Kozinn, p. 15)

Another poor city, in northern England, this one with no port to
the outside world: after graduating from high school (a rarity
among boys in Accrington), Jon Anderson works as a truck driver,

"delivering bricks to exotic ports of call like Manchester and Liverpool, forty miles away" (Hedges, p. 13). Yes biographer Dan Hedges reports:

> It was during a trip through Liverpool that a passing street scene later proved to be something of a vision of the future. "I saw all these people coming out of this club called the Cavern," [Anderson] remembers. "I wondered what was going on, because it excited me— the fact that *they* were excited. I didn't know what they'd been hearing down there, though, as it turned out, the Beatles and the Mersey-beat thing was just starting out at that time. That's what all those people were excited about, and I suppose that made a pretty strong impression on me." (p. 13)

Now to the "beautiful south" of England, and to a member of King Crimson from what many consider to be its most creative period, John Wetton. Here we also see the crossroads:

> I'm basically European, and my background comes from classical music, which is itself very geometric. I think we're lucky in Britain in that we stand between the two continents: we have the sort of American R&B blues music influence and we have a couple of thousand years on the other side as well. And that's where the Beatles came in—they just melted the two into one. They took American R&B, which is very plain and simple, and put European melodies and harmonies on top of it. And it's fantastic. All the late 60s bands really came in the wake of the Beatles. They just extended what the Beatles had been doing: Pink Floyd, Yes, Genesis, you name it. They were a little bit heavier, but the taste was that of the American audience. (Macan, p. 149)

Out of this matrix we can form a double axis. Our fourth moment is that motherlode of British Isles culture that came full circle, in the form of the emigrant culture in the American southeast that developed into rock 'n' roll and then, through a circuitous route that went through Chicago, Detroit, New York, and Cleveland, arrived back in Liverpool.[28] Our fifth moment is the axis running from the north of England to the south, where what the Beatles began became first psychedelic and then progressive rock.

I want to emphasize the complex nature of this double axis. Some, notably Edward Macan, have focused on the rootedness of progressive rock in the culture of the south of England, which has typically been middle- and upper-middle-class. There are many aspects of progressive rock that have to do with the sorts of influences the more privileged sectors of society might encounter—as well as the personal "space" to make something of these influences. But the culture in the southeast United States that gave rise to rock music itself is more the product of the transplantation of northern English, Scottish, and Irish cultures to that region, and these were cultures that tended to be of working-class or peasant origin, while the philosophical and religious outlook tended to be hermetic and anabaptist. This was a culture of rebellion and dissent, of poor people, of intense spiritual experience— a culture that, when it came into contact (in reality, it was never not in contact) with the culture of the sons and daughters of Black slaves, could not help but generate new and powerful forms of expression.

When "Albion's seed" returned to Liverpool, and from there made its way south, working its way back into the more proper "English" culture of, say, Ralph Vaughan Williams[29] and the more properly English counterculture of the "summer of love" rather than the "days of rage," still, these hermetic, dissident elements remained: as "openings and fragments" for grasping "a wider sense of the possible."

◪ ◪ ◪

Before leaving the question of English romanticism, or perhaps romanticism more generally, I would like to return for a moment to the interview with Chris Cutler referred to earlier.

I have tremendous respect for Cutler and the whole Henry Cow enterprise. However, it seems to me that, despite what the writer for *The Wire* or Cutler may say about things from a perspective twenty years on, it is clear that, in its time, Henry Cow was part of a "progressive rock movement." Indeed, Mike Barnes, the interviewer, forgot to slag both Magma and Robert Wyatt, who were also a part of this movement but who are mentioned in a positive light by Cutler. Something as simple as a look at Pete Frame's "Soft Machinery" family tree[30] serves well enough to show that all of the progressive groups from the south of England were connected by shared members and shared musical affinities.

My aim at this moment, however, is to further explore what Cutler himself says regarding the "Romantic" aspects of progressive rock, and thereby extend and sharpen the analysis of this theme. At the conclusion of his discussion of the way that Henry Cow and Magma drew from the more "astringent" and contemporary European composers such as Arnold Schönberg and Carl Orff, Cutler remarks that "the idea of sound and disposition of sound changed radically in the first quarter of this century" (p. 50). Cutler continues:

> That's why dragging Romantic music into Progressive rock in the 70s was so basically reactionary, I think.
> What was more interesting from our point of view was to use the music of this century, the century of recording technology, when the sound, the elements and the basis of music changed, instead of running backwards trying to find something before all those horrible things happened—when music was really music and it sounded nice. (p. 50)

There is actually the basis here for a rather long argument: instead of entering into such a discussion, I will restrict myself to nine somewhat telegraphed and undeveloped remarks. My intention is to further demonstrate, more on the terrain of progressive rock proper, some key points about the role of English romanticism in the music.

First, romanticism in general, as a movement in philosophy and the arts, and the influence of romanticism in progressive rock, runs a substantial distance beyond just borrowings from nineteenth-century European classical music. One thing that I have emphasized here (and in *music of Yes*) is the influence of English romantic poetry—and the "sensibility of this poetry"—on progressive rock. I daresay that this influence is present even in the work of Henry Cow.

Second, Why rule out the possibility of a critical appropriation of some aspects of the best of romantic classical music, including its complex counterpoint and harmony and its conceptual density? Furthermore, there is the legacy of this music's involvement with ethical and political universalism, especially in the case of Beethoven. Some progressive rock, it seems to me, has also availed itself of this legacy, and in a way that is not just back-ward looking.

Third, taking the first and second points together, we should make a very important distinction, between a critical romanti-cism that is not pitted against the Enlightenment, on the one hand, and an anti-Enlightenment, politically reactionary romanti-cism (of the sort spouted by fascists) on the other.

Fourth, Cutler is right to argue that the "disposition of sound" changed in the first part of the twentieth century, but then, this "disposition" has significantly changed a few more times since then. So, is it all a matter of taking our cues from the latest devel-opments in the European classical tradition? Anyway, why Schönberg and Orff? They both certainly had their politically reactionary aspects. (It was purely for his innovations in form that Adorno admired Schönberg, not for his express political leanings. Meanwhile, some critics have placed Orff's medieval pageantry, as with *Carmina Burana* [1937], in the same context as the anti-Enlightenment romanticism typical of Nazi "anti-bourgeois" pronouncements.) The larger point is that all of this is quite complicated, and there is no simple way to match musical influences with political positions. Again, if we are tracking changes in the "disposition" of sound, why not Charles Ives or John Cage (or, as in the case of Keith Emerson, Aaron Copland, and Alberto Ginastera)?

Fifth, and relatedly, Isn't there some need for rock music to "catch up," through critical appropriation, with earlier develop-ments in the European classical tradition, as well as with other developments in jazz? (Some classical composers and jazz musi-cians have also been open-minded enough to start learning a thing or two from rock. I do not mean, necessarily, the more obvi-ous and trite examples of low-level understandings of rock being incorporated into these musics. Instead, I think, for example, of the way that Ronald Shannon Jackson morphs his percussion into a surprising backbeat about three-fifths of the way through Cecil Taylor's monumental *Three Phases*.) The work of synthesis, whether in music or, for example, social theory, is necessarily ori-ented toward some of the latest developments, but it also needs to be oriented toward taking account of what has come before. In social theory, for example, I might be interested in reading the work of Jacques Derrida or Michel Foucault, but this does not mean that Plato or Aristotle or Kant or Marx don't still have a thing or two to teach us. When it comes to a figure such as Beethoven or Coltrane, it seems to me that we will never entirely "catch up," that their music is in some sense "infinite."

Sixth, How much of progressive rock really fits Cutler's description, of "running backwards" to when music sounded "nice"? Of the groups that I place in the first line of progressive rock, and even most of the second line, this description does not really seem to fit—here or there, yes, but not on the whole. And even when the description does fit, it seems to me this has more to do with a continued exploration of song form, which Henry Cow generally departs from, than with the desire to just make "nice" music.

Seventh, the one group that really seems to fit the derogatory definitions given by both Cutler and Barnes is Renaissance—and I do in fact find their music very problematic. Almost as a confirmation that Renaissance's goal is "nice," "Romantic" (in the limited sense in which Cutler is using the term) music, think of the line from one of their songs, "Running hard toward what used to be." I will say more about Renaissance in the next chapter; staying with the issue at stake here, however, let us at least note that it is a complicated one. Edward Macan points out that there is an element of "medievalism" in some progressive rock. I do not know if Cutler would accept this distinction (though I suspect not), but it seems to me that "medievalism" divides into two. One side of the divide is the anti-Enlightenment romanticism which is critical of "bourgeois" society and values, but in the name of feudalism. (The term "bourgeois" is placed in scare-quotes not because there isn't such a thing, but because feudalist and fascist critique of bourgeois society both fundamentally fails to understand the character of such a society and, in the end, actually supports such a society.) Renaissance, in their songs of praise for "Mother Russia" and Alexander Solzhenitsyn, seem allied with *this* romanticism. The other side of the divide has more to do with the idea of an agrarian, pastoral society and "village life," something at odds with the contemporary city, industry, and technology (the irony of course being that progressive rock would not exist without these things, but that is not the end of the story).[31]

The two sides seem to meet, quite often, in a philosophical organicism that can indeed be a politically reactionary and dangerous force. On the other hand, the *dangers* of criticizing a dependence on a form of technology that has become an end in itself (some have used the term "technologism" as a name for the problem)[32] should not cancel the need for such a critique.

Returning to the field of music proper, perhaps I could be so bold as to propose a useful dichotomy, namely that of Henry Cow/Renaissance, which might even help to define a certain perspective on progressive rock more generally. The opposition is one between the "most astringent" and the "antiastringent." I'm definitely with Cutler on this, on the side of the astringent. However, there are also times in the history of music when dissonance is somewhat played out, when it loses its force. (This is certainly the case in much academic "avant-garde" music, which seems so affected.) Groups such as Yes and King Crimson were often effective in making astringency both more "painful" (in the affirmative sense of shattering false totalities) and more powerful by contrasting it with passages in "standard tonality," passages that could be outright tuneful. (It is more typical to think of Yes in this light, but also consider, for example, "Book of Saturdays" from *Larks' Tongues*, or "Starless" from *Red*.) At the expense of sounding like a broken record, even the case of Renaissance is a bit more complicated; yes, their music is *not* astringent, and indeed seems to strive to make nonastringency some kind of guiding principle. On the other hand, there are elements of Renaissance's music that require some stretching of the imagination—some complex counterpoint, and the very duration of some of the pieces. In the sixties spirit of "all power to the imagination," I wouldn't rule out the idea that Renaissance's music might have some possibilities.

I propose such a thing at the likely expense of being overgenerous. However, there is a fundamental principle at stake here. Henry Cow were one of the few progressive rock groups that excelled at radical negativity, as opposed to the more affirmative stance that characterized most of these groups. The main danger of radical affirmation is that it can slide over into pure otherworldliness and escapism. The main danger of radical negativity is that it can slide over into cynicism. The article from *The Wire* that I have been quoting from is exemplary (unfortunately, many similar articles or passages in books could be cited) for taking up radical negativity in the context of cynicism—an all-too-typical move. It is also a move for which no real justification could be offered, other than more of the same, more cynicism. My view is that we need all of the possibilities we can get our hands on, when we live in a time of cynicism and antipossibility, and I am willing to risk overgenerosity for the sake of the possibility of possibility.[33]

Eighth, there is a contrast to be made not only between radical affirmation and radical negation (and remember, I propose a dialectical contrast that also shows their basic affinity), but also between the utopian and the merely propagandistic. There were times when Henry Cow fell into a too-orthodox, agit-prop model of music. This tendency is directly related to what might be called Cutler's "theoreticism." Cutler holds that "it is a primary need"

> that musicians themselves develop a theory of music and culture derived from their own practice. Such a theory, accompanied by a struggle for a meaningful form, must be the starting point of our work. (p. 50)

Obviously, it would be rather hypocritical for me, involved as I am in developing a theory of progressive rock, to disagree with this statement. On the other hand, it seems clear that, even the most sophisticated theory does not necessarily or straightforwardly lead to good musical practice. The reference to Schönberg is significant here, because there was something like a pure fascination with "method" at work in his circle. For anyone who hopes to think critically about music and/or society, this is a frustrating issue: there is a gap between good theory of music and good music. I would say this is the case for two reasons. For one thing, there is a division of labor to contend with. If the goal is to create superlative works in either art or theory, then one will probably have to declare a primary loyalty to one or the other and not both at the same time. This is the present reality, even for those of us who believe that the abolition of basic divisions of labor (especially the division between mental and manual labor, as well as inherited gendered divisions) is a fundamental part of the radical transformation of society. For another, we have to come to terms with the fact that, beyond a certain point, we take away from both theory and music if we seek to reduce or even too-easily translate one into the other.

These points are raised as tangential rather than straightforward disagreements with Cutler's statement about theory. In the philosophy of art (including music), a distinction is made between "cognitivist" and "emotivist" theories. The former holds that artistic activity and the interpretation of art are a matter for the understanding; in general, cognitivism holds that understanding increases appreciation. This does not mean that the emotions play no role, but instead that the emotions themselves are a part of the activity of understanding—the ready-made example is that fear of fire is inseparable from the knowledge that it can burn you (which is a knowledge that we are not born with). Emotivism holds that, with regard to art, there is a limit to understanding such that, in the final analysis, appreciation simply comes down to either feeling edified by a work or not.[34] It is plenty clear, from the statement I quoted, that Cutler is a cognivist—and, for what it is worth, so am I.

Human understanding, however, is a variegated thing, and works on many levels. For instance, to use an example especially important in the work of Ludwig Wittgenstein and Donald Davidson, if I am a competent speaker of the English language, then in some sense it can be said of me that I "understand" the language. (Obviously, the idea of linguistic "competence" is a loaded one.) This does not mean, however, that I necessarily have any knowledge of linguistics or even grammar as separate and formal fields of study.[35] Likewise, there are competent makers of music who could not necessarily give an "explanation," much less a "theory," of what they are doing. There is a philosophical trend, of which Theodor Adorno is a part, that holds that music that "lacks" an accompanying theory is somehow "lower" than music that comes with theory in hand. This is one of the distinctions that Adorno made between Stravinsky, whom Adorno saw as engaging in a kind of mere eclecticism (and, in Marxist circles, eclecticism tends to be dismissed as "petty-bourgeois"; the thing is, sometimes this critique is right), and Schönberg, who developed a theory, methodology, and school.

A more fruitful line of inquiry might ask whether, for any good or great work of music, a "theory" might be given, regardless of whether or not it can be given by the composer or musicians involved in making the music. Even most people who are quite deeply "into music" go in for emotivism, so the question may seem inconsequential to many. If a less-threatening word might be substituted for "theory," however, the point might come through more clearly. The word I would propose is "integrity" (which is, in fact, one the three elements that Thomas Aquinas said is required for great art, the other two being harmony and clarity). To ask if a theory could be given is really the same thing as asking if the work has integrity, if it represents something like a unified perspective. (It is in this sense of theory that my earlier book could be said to offer a "theory of the music of Yes.")

This is not only a starting point for an enterprise called the "philosophy of music," it is also a key ingredient of progressive rock—namely that there is a qualitatively heightened sense, in comparison with most other forms of rock, that *ideas* play an important role in the music, and the quality of the music depends in a significant way, on the quality of the ideas involved. In other words, it makes sense to talk about Henry Cow's idea(s), Yes's idea(s), Magma's idea(s), and, yes, Pink Floyd's idea(s), in the same way as it makes sense to use this language when discussing the music of Beethoven, Mahler, Schönberg, Ives, Coltrane, and Cecil Taylor.

By contrast, I feel less secure in thinking that it helps to talk about the Rolling Stones' idea(s) (except in the case of their one album of experimental rock, *Satanic Majesties*—the one that most Stones fans dislike), which does not mean that they have not made some good music.

To return to the distinction between the utopian idea in music and the merely propagandistic, we might make an analogy to literature. There is a genre within the novel called the "novel of ideas." Thomas Mann's *Doctor Faustus* is such a novel (I choose it as my example here because it has characters based on Schönberg and Adorno—apparently the former wanted to sue because he felt that his life and compositional method had been plagiarized). The novel deals with interesting ideas, and it is a great piece of writing. At its best, progressive rock is like this. At its worst, progressive rock is like Ayn Rand—bad ideas, bad writing (any reader of this book will surely know why I chose this example). And then some progressive rock is a mixed bag (in actuality, I think the music on Rush's *2112* is often pretty good, even if most of the ideas are bad—on which, more later). My point is, however, that Henry Cow and *all* of the other progressive rock groups, *by definition*, struggled with this difficult terrain—sometimes brilliantly, sometimes less than brilliantly.

Ninth and finally, even within Marxism, which is where Cutler wants to place himself (and I want to be there too, even if in a different way), we might contrast the Brechtian, defamiliarizing approach of Henry Cow with Raymond Williams' "Blakean," green-language approach. The former specializes in the possibilities of intensifying the sense of alienation in an alienating world, while the latter attempts, against very heavy odds, to make some sense of our being here in the world and somehow belonging. There are strengths and dangers to either approach. And both approaches now have to contend with a postmodern capitalist world characterized by feelings of being alienated even from alienation and of being "comfortably numb" (to coin a phrase)—of being so far from a sense of belonging that all that seems left is cynicism, even while at the same time one is enveloped in a televisual world of sensory overload. Henry Cow has given us "rock in opposition" (Cutler's term) in pursuing the strategy of defamiliarization. A few other progressive groups have followed this path of radical negation, including, at times, King Crimson, and even Jethro Tull and Emerson, Lake, and Palmer. This is clearly the minority path, though it may also be, paradoxically, the more secure one in that it can be easier in some circumstances to rail against the existing state of things than to try to imagine a different world. The other path, radical affirmation, is less secure in that there is a danger, in such an attempt at imagination, at merely giving *solace* within the terms of the world as it is; there is also the danger of just being downright goofy or merely sentimental, and this undoubtedly happened more than a few times even with the best of the "affirmative" groups. (An obvious example would be the song "The Heaven of Animals," from Yes's *Tor-*

mato—not that the sentiments expressed aren't good in them-selves, but the song does not rise above mere sentiment.)

At least in the time of progressive rock, I would contend, all of the various forms of these approaches were expressive of a radical, prophetic sensibility. "Prophetic" is a useful term here. The Biblical prophets, those old Israelites, were best known for railing against the deep flaws of their own society. And yet they were also utopians, prophesying deliverance and redemption. (The too-common notion that the prophets were in the business of predicting events is simply bad secular thinking—I won't call it scholarship—of the *Isaac Asimov's Guide to the Bible* school.) Across a very wide range, the best groups in the progressive rock movement partake of both forms of the prophetic sensibility. I see that range as a strength. Another way of coming at this point is that, no matter how good the "theory" is (Marxist or otherwise), or, for that matter, no matter how good the theory could potentially be, no social theory or political philosophy could or should tell us the "one right way" to make music. Which is one thing to be thankful for. The range of good progressive rock is representative of many different ears listening to the future.

Taking stock of this long discussion, let us now attempt to reformulate a definition of progressive rock.

As a style of music progressive rock has five specific traits: 1) it is visionary and experimental; 2) it is played, at least in significant part, on instruments typically associated with rock music, by musicians who have a background in rock music, and with the history of rock music itself as background; 3) it is played, in significant part, by musicians who have consummate instrumental and compositional skills; 4) it is a phenomenon, in its "core," of English culture; 5) relatedly, in significant part, it is expressive of romantic and prophetic aspects of that culture.

I call this *a* definition rather than *the* definition for what I hope is the obvious reason that, of course, debate and discussion on this issue should continue. Earlier, in response to Jim DeRogatis, I made a brief comment on the term "art rock"—namely that it was not originally the intention of progressive rock musicians that they depart from rock music so as to form some new school, of rock that is "art." Instead, the combined logic of the music and the times *took* them to this new place, which turned out to be a qualitative development in rock music. The definition I have proposed will be controversial not only in its formulation but, probably even more, its application. One reason for this controversy is that, in fact, what folks such as Edward Macan, Paul Stump, and myself who have undertaken systematic study of progressive rock can mainly do is offer a *characterization* of a phenomenon from the perspective of twenty- to thirty-years hindsight.

◧   ◧   ◧

Now another bit of nastiness, "my Frank Zappa problem." This is where the rubber hits the road, as regards questions of application and characterization. To put it bluntly, the definition of progressive rock that I had formulated in *music of Yes* (which basically consisted in parts 1–3 of the new definition) would have included the music of Frank Zappa, and I have increasingly seen this as a problem.

For the record, and to state the perfectly obvious, Frank Zappa was an enormously talented musician. As a guitarist, he had tremendous skill, and many of his compositions are adventurous and innovative.

However, if Zappa indeed fits into the group of musicians, such as those I listed above, who have an "idea," still, I am not personally convinced by his idea—but this is a long discussion that we cannot get very far into here.

Significantly, not many of the more fervent fans of Zappa consider his music to be progressive rock either. The English music magazine *The Wire*, in a very cynical article, "A to Z of Prog Rock," did include Zappa in their litany of antiprogressive rock screeds, but perhaps only to fill out the alphabet:

> Z is for Frank Zappa. Frank isn't *really* Prog is he? Well, maybe not, but how else do you describe a musician who funnelled a grounding in black R&B and West Coast psychedelia through sensibilities warped by exposure to Eric Dolphy's free jazz and Edgard Varese's

classical compositions and whose whole career was one long Concept Album based on some strange notion concerning poodles? (p. 35)

The "how else," in my view, has precisely to do with the poodles.

In other words, in terms of "pure music," there are numerous affinities between Zappa's music and some progressive rock (especially early Soft Machine and Henry Cow), but *thematically* there are important disaffinities. A vast tome (nearly six hundred pages) dedicated to the elevation of Zappa in neo-Trotskyist Marxist terms has been written by Ben Watson. His title, *The Negative Dialectics of Poodle Play*, seeks to bring together a key notion from Theodor Adorno, again having to do with the shattering of false totalities of commodified culture, with Zappa's sense of humor and satire, which Watson sees as disruptive of "the smooth flow of the media charade" (p. xxix).

Returning to themes from the introduction, and with regard to the perspective of Watson's book, this is another place where I would challenge readers who entertain what I would call "clichéd" misunderstandings of Marxism to think things through a bit further. Watson's perspective is representative of a neo-Trotskyist trend led by Tony Cliff.[36] In my view, this trend is representative of what Lenin called "economism," a focus on the more narrow needs and demands of the better-off sections of the urban and mainly first-world (Western Europe, North America, Japan) working class, to the exclusion of what might be called the "real proletariat"—those who have (as Marx and Engels put it in the *Manifesto*), "nothing to lose but their chains." Accordingly, this trend tends to be Eurocentric and, concomitantly, anti-"Third Worldist" (e.g., see Watson's comment on Sartre, p. xxii); and, accordingly, this trend rejects Lenin's argument that, in the present stage of capitalism, the relationship between the bourgeoisie and the proletariat typical of individual countries in the earlier stage of industrial capitalism (late eighteenth to late nineteenth centuries) has now been duplicated on a global scale. Thus, whole countries (a minority of them) play the role of the capitalist classes on the global stage, and whole other countries (the majority) are in the position of the subordinated working class. In the dominant countries, a section of the working class is, at least for a period, bought off by the spoils of (what Lenin called) superexploitation in the Third World. Therefore, this section of the working class cannot be the firm *basis* for radical social transformation, for revolution, in these countries. Instead, Lenin argued, the revolution must continually seek to ground itself at a level "lower and deeper" among the working masses.[37] This thesis of Lenin's is an integral part of his theory of imperialism; in rejecting this thesis, Trotskyist and neo-Trotskyist trends end up rejecting the theory and idea of imperialism altogether.

In this light, the neat trick that Watson's book attempts to perform is to somehow align Frank Zappa's music with the "working class," in the first-world, economistic sense, while dismissing broader conceptions of social vision. This is also significant in contrast to Lenin's perspective; in *What Is to Be Done?*, Lenin argued that while it is always necessary to go "deeper" into the proletariat, the propaganda organs of the revolution (he was mainly talking about the need for a revolutionary proletarian newspaper) should also serve as "tribunes of the oppressed," regardless of what class they belonged to. His aim was to create a broad, anti-imperialist united front under the leadership of the proletariat—and therefore his aim was to forge a strategic unity with a complete range of anticapitalist and even "antisystem" perspectives, including those of religious visionaries and utopian dreamers. In my view, Mao Tsetung carried on this perspective, which is one reason why he is often dismissed as a *romantic* or idealist by more economistic forms of Marxism. And, indeed, Mao did endorse "revolutionary romanticism" in addition to "revolutionary realism."

On another level, the difference again might be between a more "generous" form of Marxism and one that is narrow and monological, a Marxism that has nothing to learn from outside of itself. My own experience with the trend of which Watson is a part confirms well enough that they are holders of a narrow and even "robotic" perspective; certainly, too, regarding the argument for a different kind of Marxism, one mainly hears ritual denunciations from this trend, and Watson's book is littered with these. This type of thoughtless ungenerosity is also apparent in the fact that Watson finds it necessary to be dismissive of many other musicians who, musically and/or ideologically, might be seen as having some affinity with Zappa's music. For instance, Zappa is presented as a great critic and satirist of the culture of the commodity, but Devo, the Clash, and others are dismissed.[38] Watson's opening shot against "art rock" is kind of interesting, really: "The ideology of English art rock is contradictory, antagonistic to America and capitalism, yet finding in rock 'n' roll the key term in loosening the grip of the European cultural heritage" (p. 210). Watson does not go on to explain this statement, so I can only guess at exactly what is contradictory here—and I assume that it is the fact that rock 'n' roll is an "American" phenomenon. Given that, surely, Watson hopes that Zappa's music is also antagonistic to capitalism, I don't know why the same "contradiction" wouldn't apply. But he does go on to dismiss (I keep using this word because Watson's approach to the many things he does not like is to make very short work of them) the music of ELP, Yes, and Genesis as "naive, music-college exercises." Gee, couldn't you imagine someone saying just this sort of thing about Zappa? In either case it would be thoughtless, unfair, and ungenerous. Watson does go on to offer faint praise for Henry Cow and other Canterbury bands, as practitioners of a middle-class reticence who knew their limitations and thereby "gave the lie" to the "grandiosity" of Yes and company (p. 210).

For my part, I've become very tired of the "debunking of grandiosity" and "pretentiousness."[39] At the risk of lending ammunition to Watson, I would say that attempts at deflation of the Zappa sort mostly amount to something on the order of farting in church—perhaps amusing for the moment, but hardly giving us anything to think about (that is why I am not convinced by Zappa's "idea," assuming that he has one). And this is not even always amusing, unless one thinks it is some sort of "critique" to always be farting at everything. Call me a spoilsport, but I think not everything deserves this treatment. Some progressive rock goes overboard and perhaps even deserves a bit of deflationary response—and yet I would still want to attend to the impulse, which is most often *utopian*, that led to this "grandiose" music.

Incidentally, the "make a joke out of everything" school of "radical" critique is more akin to anarchism than Marxism. In this respect, it is interesting that Watson somewhat allies his own efforts, as well as Zappa's music, with the Situationists (see, e.g., pp. xxi–xxvi). Many of the critiques of capitalist culture that came out of the French section of the Situationist International were insightful and powerful.[40] On the other hand, they too had a tendency to blast anyone with whom they disagreed, including, for example, Jean-Paul Sartre, whom they called an "imbecile."[41] Now, it is one thing to *criticize* the ideas of an important radical philosopher such as Sartre, and another thing to irresponsibly *attack* someone whose contribution to the possibilities of radical social transformation is arguably quite a bit greater than that of the Situationists. What I am driving at is that I do not see in this sort of thing the "generous synthesis" that characterizes both progressive rock and the sort of Marxism that I would argue for. (This does not mean that I take them to be the same sort of enterprise in the way that it seems Watson wants to align his version of Marxism and Zappa's music.)

In the earliest phase of his recording career, Zappa poked some fun at the emerging counterculture in the United States (especially on the west coast). Some of the material on *We're Only in It for the Money* is kind of funny, though I don't know that it bears repeated listening. But I can see why Watson would valorize this "satire"; for his kind of Marxism, the countercultural and radical movements of the sixties are ultimately not the "real deal," because they did not represent the "working class." My view, and I think it is at least compatible with a kind of Marxism (but obviously not Watson's kind), is that the world-historic struggle of the oppressed, the excluded, the marginalized, the downtrodden, and, yes, the proletariat, is expressed in all kinds of ways and on many levels—and we "educators" (theorists, that is) are continually in need of being educated by these many sources.[42]

In the end, I'm afraid that I agree with those critics of Zappa who see his humor as both cynical and juvenile. Perhaps if I thought Zappa's jokes were *funnier* I would be more convinced by some of his "critique" or the attempt to explain it in Marxist terms. *Mais non.* As for Zappologists or neo-Trotskyists who want to make something of my "defense" of the "church," hey, go to town.

Ah, well. Both Zappa's canon and Watson's book are too big to really take on here. Watson's book is exhaustive and sometimes insightful—at the expense of perhaps violating the author's sense of authenticity, it might be said that not all of his arguments fall prey to the narrow perspective out of which he works. His brief encounters with progressive rock do helpfully show the influence that some of Zappa's early work, especially *Uncle Meat*, had on some of the groups. In the end, I do not think the attempt to somehow make Zappa a champion for the working class (conceived in Watson's terms) goes quite the way Watson might hope. But obviously this is not the end of the story regarding Zappa's music, nor is he responsible for the interpretation Watson has placed upon it.

On the other hand, *The Negative Dialectics of Poodle Play* can be cited as evidence that, between Zappa and progressive rock, there is a crucial difference in sensibility. (And I would certainly be interested in knowing how Watson might finesse his way around one of Zappa's latest posthumous "gifts," the disgusting *Have I Offended Anyone?*) Thinking about this difference has led me toward my present inclination to characterize progressive rock as a "style," one that specifically includes "English," romantic, and prophetic elements as part of its definition.

◼ ◼ ◼

A related question concerns the fact that there seem to be no *great* progressive rock groups from North America, even if there are perhaps a few good ones. This is especially curious given that, as Edward Macan argues, American audiences (and their money) played the key role in turning progressive rock from a relatively local English scene to an international phenomenon—and some of the musicians into international superstars. When I argue that there is a specifically "English" aspect of progressive rock, this does not mean that this aspect or a sensibility very similar to it is not transferable to other parts of the world. Indeed, there are all sorts of hermetic, utopian, and prophetic traditions in North America, which have given rise to a poetic tradition from Walt Whitman to Allen Ginsburg (a tradition very much informed, of course, by English romantic poetry), and a set of communitarian religious social movements including the Shakers and the

Mormons.[43] On the "transferability" issue, also consider progressive rock in Italy; in terms of the sheer number of very good groups, this scene was probably the biggest.

As it turns out, the comparison of the American and the Italian experiences with progressive rock is useful. For there were, in fact, many groups in the U.S. who took inspiration from or were otherwise expressive of hermetic, romantic currents—this would include large parts of the American psychedelic scene, as well as the west coast scene (and especially the San Francisco scene). Of course, these scenes overlapped to a great degree.

Progressive rock took off in a huge way in Italy, where romantic currents run very deep. (In fact, English romantic poets, especially Byron, took inspiration from the Italian landscape in the eighteenth century.) But then, progressive rock in Italy sprang full-grown from the head of Jupiter, as it were, this being the first trend from any kind of rock music to really catch on there.

Regarding America, then, the question seems to be, Why didn't hermetic and psychedelic trends mutate into progressive rock, as they did in England? Was it something to do with an American cultural tendency to be more "direct," and less likely to risk pretentiousness? Was it a greater closeness to rhythmic inspirations (consider that the great "stretch-out" groups in the American scene have been much closer to blues, jazz, and roots-rock, e.g., Santana, the Allman Brothers Band, the Grateful Dead) than to the more melodic or harmonic inspirations of England? In an interview, Edward Macan remarks on what seems to be one of the essential connections:

> in the late '80s [and] early '90s . . . I was working on my dissertation, which happened to be on the 20th century English composers Ralph Vaughan Williams and Gustav Holst. As I listened to that music something sounded familiar here; those harmonic progressions, some of the fanfare-like passages—I heard them before somewhere.
>
> So, for the first time in almost ten years I started taking out my old Genesis, Yes, and ELP albums and playing them, and then playing some of the Holst or Williams. There basically has been a 20th century English musical style that can be traced from Holst and Williams to the rock era of the '70s. (Gunnison, p. 32)[44]

The difference, then, between the directions taken in the American and English scenes, might be chalked up to contingent cultural and historical factors, especially the closeness of the English scene to both a native classical tradition as well as to the larger European tradition.

In my view, the two groups in the American scene who at times played some pretty good, if not great, progressive rock were Kansas and the Dixie Dregs. Interestingly, neither one, to my knowledge, had much connection to the psychedelic scene. The Dregs presented an interesting combination of Southern boogie and the Mahavishnu Orchestra. Kansas, hailing from Topeka, were perhaps closer to the English groups in their style of harmonic progression (at least on their first three albums). For those who do not know the wonderful state of Kansas, and therefore have fallen for all of the usual stereotypes, I might mention that there are in fact parts of the state, not so far to the west of Topeka, that could be mistaken for the green, rolling countryside of the English midlands. (Specifically, I have in mind the Flint Hills, near Manhattan, Kansas.) Both of these groups, however, are noticably "heavier," with a stronger current of American rock 'n' roll, than most English progressive groups. (Incidentally, the two groups have in common that they both use the violin—which I have always had a liking for in this music; also, Steve Morse, one of the founders of the Dregs and certainly one of the best rock guitarists playing today, served for a stint with Kansas.)

Again, by contrast we see something definitive of progressive rock, in this case its rootedness in English music and culture.

◼ ◼ ◼

To close this lengthy excursion through the theoretical issues central to an understanding of progressive rock, I turn, finally, to a more extended discussion of a signal contribution to this understanding, namely Edward Macan's *Rocking the Classics: English Progressive Rock and the Counterculture*.

Macan's effort represents the first systematic, book-length attempt to explore what progressive rock is all about. In my view, the book represents a tremendous breakthrough in an area of music where the curtain of silence, ignorance, or inane abuse had become well-nigh impenetrable. Because of this book, a whole new discussion, one that is the negation of everything represented by the typical dismissal of progressive rock, can now begin. *Rocking the Classics* will stand as an essential reference point in this discussion; I hope that it has been clear to the reader that the book is certainly essential for the work I hope to do here.

Remarkably, *Rocking the Classics* appeared at almost exactly the same time as my own *music of Yes*, around the first week of November 1996. In fact, at a book party for *music of Yes*, at the Great Expectations Bookstore in Evanston, Illinois, my graduate assistant saw Macan's book and brought it to my attention— "Hey, have you seen this?" An amazing thing, given not only the subject matter of *Rocking the Classics*, but the fact that there is a photograph of Yes on the cover and an extensive analysis of "Close to the Edge" within. I had to wonder, are we finally starting to see a turn in the Zeitgeist? Although an exploration of the larger territory of progressive rock was not my main goal with *music of Yes*, I of course had to deal with a good many of the same issues discussed in *Rocking the Classics*. And, although our general philosophical perspectives are somewhat different—even at odds in places, or so it seems—Macan and I often came to similar conclusions.

In the "commune spirit" of progressive rock itself (as Steve Howe once put it), I do not see any serious and thoughtful discussion of the genre as any kind of "competition"; on the contrary, my hope is that this serious discussion will grow, that it will help the music, that it will help the culture and society, and that the different perspectives that will come forward around the analysis of progressive rock will enter into a productive dialogue. If I tend to emphasize some of the disagreements in perspective in what follows, then, I hope that the reader will consider these disagreements in terms of the possibility of such a dialogue.

Of the many important contributions that *Rocking the Classics* makes to this discussion, none is so significant to me as the relinkage of progressive rock with the idea of the sixties counterculture. This is a linkage that is, paradoxically, almost transparently clear, and yet *startling* and almost shocking because of the way that progressive rock has been treated by the rock-music critical establishment in the past twenty years or so.

As it turns out, I do have some disagreements with Macan's understanding of the sixties and its counterculture, and I would like to get into these. However, let us begin by recognizing Macan's accomplishment in putting this question back on the map. One of the things I find especially remarkable about Macan's book is that he has forged a new unity, at least as regards progressive rock, between the formal analysis of music, which is his area of expertise as an academically trained musicologist, and the sociology of music. As I discussed in the preface to this book, Macan's example has led me to reevaluate my own sense of what I might contribute to the analysis of music; in particular, I have now endeavored to sharpen the distinctions separating the fields of musicology, sociology of music, aesthetics, philosophy of music, and a kind of social theory that takes the aesthetic dimension seriously. Macan has a great deal to offer in the first two of these fields, while I hope that I might make a contribution with the latter three. As we both aim to give something back to the music, the hope is that there are productive areas of overlap and synergy.

Macan's work is both impressive and crucial in the way that it synthesizes what little study has previously been done on the sociology of progressive rock. He extends that work in important ways, especially with regard to the social roots of both the musicians and the audience. Although the main chapter devoted to sociological questions is found well into the book (pp. 144–66), sociological themes are pursued throughout, beginning with the very first page of the preface (or "Prelude," as Macan calls it). Macan writes of having his philosophy of music "permanently altered" by his reading of two important books, Henry Pleasant's *Serious Music: And All That Jazz* and Christopher Small's *Music of the Common Tongue: Survival and Celebration in Afro-American Music* (Macan, p. vii). Macan attests to having taken away three crucial insights from this reading: first, that no music is "timeless," whether it is that of Bach, Beethoven, Blind Lemon Jefferson, or Charlie Parker; second, that "popular music has an affective power on contemporary audiences that classical music no longer has"; third, and relatedly, that traditional musicology, which tends to operate as though purely formal, "timeless" criteria could be applied to the study of music, is no longer adequate when distinctions between "serious" and "popular" music have largely broken down and when asocial and ahistorical approaches are no longer defensible (pp. viii–xi).

Significantly, Macan argues that progressive rock might also be understood under Gunther Schuller's category of "third stream" music. One might say that such music is especially representative of the breakdown of the aforementioned distinctions and approaches.

Having set the scene for the analysis of progressive rock, particularly in terms of the sixties counterculture (and even more specifically in terms of a matrix of class, gender, geography, religion, and other factors), Macan does however offer impressive structural analyses of progressive rock masterworks. In his fifth chapter, "Four Different Progressive Rock Pieces," Macan presents detailed musicological studies of "Tarkus" (ELP), "Close to the Edge" (Yes), "Firth of Fifth" (Genesis), and "Wish You Were Here" (Pink Floyd). In each case, Macan discusses both the formal structure and the historical context and significance of the work. For instance, the analysis of "Tarkus" is especially concerned with the specter of a technology that has turned the tables on its creators (a theme that ELP returns to with "Karn Evil 9"). To *integrate* the two levels of analysis, formal and historical, that is of course the great difficulty—and I do not know that Macan has completely pulled this off. But then, the philosophical framework that might allow *anyone* to completely pull this off is quite elusive.

Macan's presentation of the Yes masterpiece, "Close to the Edge," is an important piece of analysis in its own right. Having discussed the piece at some length in my own *music of Yes*, I was fascinated with Macan's approach to the subject. Whereas my analysis tends to pursue some of the "local gestures" of the music in some detail, Macan's discussion has the virtue of showing how Yes's employment of sonata form works in the large. Another important difference is that I tend to interpret the spiritual language of the piece as also having somewhat concrete social and political import as well, while Macan stays more within the terrain of religious discourse. Our difference here is actually indicative of a larger point that I will return to in a moment. However, what struck me the most in thinking about the intense interest that both Macan and I have in this music is that progressive rock deserves serious discussion—and occasionally even receives it.

My book on Yes was meant to be an exhaustive treatment (even so, in a manuscript of close to five hundred pages, there were many aspects of the music that could have been discussed at greater length). Naturally, then, the book treats complete albums, one at a time. Macan is after something different in his chapter on four important works of progressive rock. For what he hopes to show, the analyses presented are excellent. However, we might also keep in mind the fact that progressive rock was made with the complete album as the basic unit of production. "Tarkus," the seven-part suite, can be somewhat abstracted from *Tarkus*, the album, and perhaps the same can be done with "Firth of Fifth," given that *Selling England by the Pound* is more like a collection of songs than many progressive albums are, but I prefer to hear *Close to the Edge* and *Wish You Were Here* as integrated, complete works.

Two additional terms that Macan places on the table are "medievalism" (see, e.g., pp. 37, 40) and science fiction (pp. 81–82). A great deal of progressive rock seems to want to go, in a simultaneous movement, both to the pastoral past and the chrome-plated technological future. On a more local level, the desire for this paradoxical journey is perhaps embodied in what seems to be one of progressive rock's greatest contradictions: the idea of performing works whose lyrics concern ecologism, pastoralism, and antitechnological romanticism, and whose form is inspired by traditions of, shall we say, "nonelectronic" musics, from European classical to English or Irish or American folk, even while employing the most up-to-date electronic musical gear, to say nothing of megavolts of electricity.

Seen in larger terms, the paradox embodies the kind of rejection of the historical present that more orthodox materialists or Marxists find frustrating. That is, rather than purely "taking its poetry from the future," as Marx said the proletariat must do, sci-fi medievalism wants to link a supposedly better past with a hopefully better future. (It should be noted that more than a few science-fiction writers themselves engage in forms of "medieval-ism"; the *Dune* series by Frank Herbert is perhaps the most out-standing example.) Given that Macan is critical of what he terms "neo-Marxist" critiques of progressive rock (on which more in a moment), sci-fi medievalism might have been given a stronger boost. However, it is at least my good fortune to have come along after the fact, to see some interesting connections.

First, it is undoubtedly the case that a more orthodox Marxist analysis would say that such a concatenation of past and future orientations is typical of the middle classes, which feel squeezed between the capitalists and the proletariat. This view, as rigid as it is, would actually fit in nicely with Macan's own argument that the social basis of progressive rock is the "middle- and upper-middle-class backgrounds" of the musicians (p. 13). Macan him-self seems to want to stick up for these "people in the middle" and their access to "high culture," which they assimilated into forms such as progressive rock. Indeed, his dislike of the "neo-Marxist" and "populist" music critics seems to extend, at times, to a some-what snide or condescending view of the working class. This is seen even from the first page of the book, where Macan criticizes Christopher Small for sometimes engaging in "ideological hyste-ria"—"for instance, his unfortunate suggestion that classical music is a tool by which imperialistic capitalists oppress the downtrodden masses" (p. viii). Granted, a Mozart trio isn't much compared to locking hundreds of people in factories so that they burn to death if a fire breaks out, as happened in both North Car-olina and Thailand in recent years (in the latter case the victims were two hundred young girls who worked "jobs" under condi-tions of slavery in order to escape the market in sexual exploita-tion), to say nothing of napalm, nuclear weapons, or enforced malnutrition and cholera. Yet there is more than a hint in Macan's formulation that *all* talk of imperialism and the downtrodden is "ideological hysteria." But then, one has to wonder what a con-ception of the "counterculture" might be apart from the critique of capitalism. This is a key point to which I will return.

At present, however, my point is that the sci-fi/medieval syn-thesis might be defended on other terms. Most Marxists are not only critical or condemnatory toward capitalism; they also laud capitalism as a progressive stage in history, specifically for its development of productive technology. (In the *Communist Manifesto*, which someday ought to be read by those who claim to have read it, Marx and Engels call the bourgeoisie "the most revolutionary class in history.") By the time of the late sixties, there were those among the counterculture who were beginning to doubt this assessment, including an important pair of cultural theorists in England who helped initiate the "New Left," Raymond Williams and E. P. Thompson. (In truth, their reassessment goes back to the fifties and the aftermath of the Stalin period.) *This* neo-Marxism (as opposed to the sort that Macan is justifiably critical of) questioned some of the historical teleology of the more orthodox variety, teleology that seemed to make "Marxism" just as enthusiastic about vast factories and urban concentration as capitalism is. (As Mao once put it, "with enemies like these, capitalism will last forever.") Whereas orthodox Marxism tends to see any critique of capitalism that draws on pastoral, romantic, or agrarian elements as merely sentimental and not remorseless enough about a past that should simply be kicked away, the New Left was much more broad in its conceptions. It seems to me that this is the sort of counterculture that gave rise to a progressive rock that tried to look both toward the past and the future. The cause of the downtrodden and marginalized, the critique of capitalism and imperialism, and the creative extension of Marxist thought are important parts of *this* counterculture.

As I have mentioned, in reflecting on some of Macan's arguments, I have rethought my definition of progressive rock and have come to focus more on the English core of the music. One aspect of this core that Macan develops brilliantly is the role of the Anglican church (and church music) in the formation of the musical and spiritual sensibilities of many progressive rock musicians. Not all progressive rockers were from Anglican backgrounds, of course; Jon Anderson and Rick Wakeman are important exceptions, raised Roman Catholic and Baptist, respectively. But the general point still holds in the case of persons from minority religious cultures: the music and general ambience of the Anglican church was a pervasive force to be assimilated and reacted against. In particular, Macan sees two key manifestations of this influence in progressive rock music. The first of these has to do with the role of the Hammond B-3 electronic organ (see pp. 33–36). Going right back to pieces such as "The Prophet" from Yes's second album (*Time and a Word*), the Hammond played out of, and in contrast to, the tradition of church organ music. Perhaps the greatest examples of this are ELP's rendition of the Anglican hymn, "Jerusalem," on *Brain Salad Surgery*, and Rick Wakeman's extraordinary "old church/new church" organ solo in "Close to the Edge." Of course, progressive rock took over and extended an already well-established electronic organ (though of the cheesier "combo" organs—Vox, Farfisa) tradition from psychedelic rock. The great practitioners from this tradition, especially Brian Auger and Rod Argent, copped a good many links from the great jazz B-3 organists—such as Jimmy Smith, Richard "Groove" Holmes, Shirley Scott. In other words, there was a great deal of synergy and cross-fertilization going on here, which extended still further in terms of allowing rock guitarists to break up their own chordal playing a bit, given the presence of an instrument that could sustain notes and chords indefinitely (see Macan, p. 36).

More significantly, Macan links the Anglican background with the idea of "progressive rock as liturgy." In progressive rock there is a "relative de-emphasis of the individual performer," and instead an emphasis on the idea that the performers "serve as medium[s] for the transmission of the music" (p. 67). In this, progressive rock is much closer to religious music than it is to the mainstream of rock music. Even the emphasis on instrumental virtuosity is subsumed, Macan argues, "by progressive rock's ideal of collective virtuosity" (p. 67).[45] This musical ability itself is aimed at creating an opening for transcendence. And although much progressive rock incorporates the idea of "the Artist as Prophet or Seer" (here again I would set aside the music of Frank Zappa),[46] the sense of a collective project, which in the concert situation certainly includes ritual aspects, remains in the forefront.

Though Macan does not put the matter in quite these terms, the idea of progressive rock as liturgy is clearly an expression of eighteenth-, nineteenth-, and twentieth-century attempts to substitute art for religion. Such attempts are not only a part of romantic ideologies going back to Blake, Wordsworth, Hölderlin, Schiller, or Beethoven, but also form an important part of modernist art, as with Kafka or Joyce. The aim is to express a beauty that transcends the misery of this world, or that is a utopian pre-figuration of a redeemed world.

In a jaded society, it is difficult to get the idea of art-as-transcendence off the ground. Perhaps it is inevitable that progressive rock, as one of the last major art forms to take this idea to heart, comes in for special abuse in cynical and anti-utopian times. Yet, for just this reason, I think progressive rock still has a role to play—some energy to lend—in the formation of a "postsecular" sensibility.

Although I find Macan's use of sociology insightful at times, in some ways he is a bit too willing to take sociological "data" too straightforwardly. In Macan's view, progressive rock is not only, in its core, an English phenomenon; it is even the product of a particular social strata in England, namely the middle- and upper-middle classes of the southern rim of the country (pp. 144–48). While a good many groups did come from this region, and from the aforementioned privileged classes, I would still argue for putting this in a larger frame. This frame opens in the cosmopolitan and psychedelic culture of London and its club scene (the Marquee, UFO, and smaller venues) and ultimately takes in the vibrations that were flowing globally. Those musicians who did come from privileged backgrounds brought certain cultural experiences with them, including some experience with European classical music or American jazz. On the other hand, considering the matrix of the emerging counterculture, it seems to me that many of these musicians hoped to contribute to radical and utopian ideals, including the ideal of a classless society. This is not always reflected in the express attitudes of the musicians, but it is certainly an element of music that, in its experiments with form and lyrical expression, prefigures a different world. Again, much here hinges on one's conception of the counterculture, a point to which I will return.

One of the most interesting "sociological" themes that Macan pursues concerns the audience for progressive rock in the United States (pp. 154–58). As Macan argues, the fact that at least some progressive rock groups became very popular in the U.S. transformed the whole scene. One might even wonder if this popularity, which translated into millions of dollars for groups such as

Yes and Emerson, Lake, and Palmer, might have wrecked the English scene to some extent. Some became very rich, while others just scraped by, and the quality of the music did not have any direct relation with this differentiation (those who think of capitalism as some sort of meritocracy might think on this point for a moment). This works both ways: the groups that did not become rich, such as Henry Cow or even King Crimson (as Robert Fripp writes in the liner notes to the recent *Epitaph* live set, Crimson never really made any money) were obviously no less creative than those that did; on the other hand, groups such as Yes were certainly, in my view, just as creative (if not more so).[47] All the same, the injection of not only money but also "rock star" status into the progressive scene is representative of an all-too-typical corruption of the counterculture.

Significantly, Macan shows that progressive rock has been most popular in what turn out to be the most "WASPish" parts of the U.S., especially New England and the Midwest. Macan's argument here is interesting:

> [T]here is no doubt that these are the most WASPish regions of the United States; the British legacy to the Northeast and Midwest, in particular, needs no further comment. It is not surprising, then, that the nationalist element of progressive rock was much more sympathetically received in these regions than, for instance, in the Southeast. In a sense, I suspect progressive rock's British nationalism provided a kind of surrogate ethnic identity to its young white audience at a time when (for the first time in American history) the question of what it means to be a white person in America was coming under scrutiny, just as its flights of fantasy and mysticism and its quasi-liturgical live shows provided its audiences—many of whom had lapsed from mainline Christian denominations—a surrogate religion. In turn, the nationalist elements of progressive rock probably also contributed to the lack of interest the style held for blacks, hispanics, and most of the southeastern United States, where the white population had always defined itself as a culture distinct from the WASP/northern mainstream. (p. 155)

While I find this argument insightful, again I would want to broaden the context. Of course it is very troubling to think that the interest that some Americans, mostly white, middle-class males, had in progressive rock is motivated by a need for white identity formation. All the same, Macan has raised an interesting question, one that might actually fit in better with the idea of progressive rock being more a part of "high culture" aspirations in the U.S. than in the English context.

White identity formation, in the United States and in the West more generally, has always been a reaction formation.[48] "White" means "not-Black" (or "not-Red," "-Yellow," etc.). If Macan's argument about the audience for progressive rock in the U.S. is the whole story, then, whatever the formal achievements of the music, it would be hard for me to conclude anything other than that this audience was especially interested in finding a rock music that is not-Black. Certainly this is what some have said about progressive rock, that it is the antithesis of rock music's black roots, and a negation of those roots. I do not agree with this claim, and neither does Macan (I will turn to his perceptive arguments on progressive rock, race, and "authenticity" in a moment).

However, in order to carry off our denial of this kind of claim (almost universally made by white critics who seem obsessed with their own authenticity), it seems to me that we have to once again engage with the question of the counterculture. If progressive rock was, in a real sense, one of the "alternative" musics of its heyday, then we have to understand Macan's point about "British nationalism" in a different light. People were looking for alternatives—to Western politics, economics, religion, and culture. In England, progressive rock was an alternative that built on an alternative reading of English culture—that reading which takes its bearings from English romanticism and hermetic, radical spiritual traditions. At the same time, progressive rock synthesized American rock and roll, American jazz, European harmony and advanced experiments with tonality, and sounds from around the world.

In the United States, this synthesis struck a chord with American romantic, hermetic, pastoral, and communitarian traditions—including a certain romance with the idea of the "American farmer," in which case no wonder that progressive rock was popular in New England and the Midwest.[49] (Perhaps in this respect it is also no wonder that one of the few American progressive rock groups, at least for their first two albums, was Kansas.) Whether this more "positive" construction of the alternative was more powerful than the mere reaction formation in the minds of progressive-rock listeners would be an interesting subject for further ethnographic and sociological study. My own experience, growing up in a very multicultural city (Miami, Florida), was that I and most of my fellow progressive rock fans were into digging whoever and whatever seemed to be expanding the boundaries, whether that was Miles or Magma, Coltrane or Caravan, Soft Machine or Stockhausen. Even in college—and I went to college in the Deep South (Greenville, South Carolina)—the people who were into progressive rock were into experimental music, art, culture, and politics in general. Of course, I don't want to claim any sort of larger validity for these personal experiences and, as Macan notes, it is especially difficult to pursue this subject going on twenty-five years after the high point of the progressive-rock era (see Macan, p. 151). However, even if the "positive" construction is more representative of a minority point of view, I would still see this desire for an alternative music *and* an alternative world as more in the spirit of progressive rock.[50]

In an excellent discussion of "the critical reception of progressive rock" (chap. 8, pp. 167–78), Macan meticulously dissects the race ideology of the critics who oppose progressive rock. Relying on arguments from Allan Moore's *Rock: The Primary Text*, Macan ferrets out the underlying premises behind the idea that the main problem with progressive rock is its supposed lack of "black" influence.

> [T]he basic premise behind this line of thought is the belief that black music is "authentic" and "natural" in a way that white music is not: "It [the critical stance of (Dave) Marsh and his peers] entails the assumption that blacks in the southern USA lived in a state of mindless primitivism, in which they expressed themselves through music "naturally," without the intervening of any musical "theory"; hence the black sense of rhythm being "natural" and "unmediated."[51]

As Macan concludes,

> [S]ince the critics' equation of the blues tradition and "authenticity" is inherently flawed by a series of overly simplistic assumptions, their criticism of styles such as progressive rock as "unnatural" and "inauthentic" cannot be accepted at face value. (p. 171)

Macan demonstrates a number of things here and in the further development of his argument. First, it is clear that, in their desire for "authenticity," these antiprogressive critics participate in not only a kind of essentialism, but even a kind of racism—and I do not mean so-called "antiwhite racism," but instead the kind that sees Black cultural achievements as flowing from some kind of racial essence rather than from the creative transmutation of cultural sources (i.e., hard work and hard thought, the source of great art, whatever its cultural background). Furthermore, this essentialism, like all essentialisms, attempts to take part in some sort of transcendental touchstone against which to adjudicate claims of cultural authenticity. Besides the fact that such attempts to define the "blackness" of music are highly suspect especially coming from white critics (who, for sure, want to be *down* with the Black masses), this perspective does not have anything very important to say about musical structure.

Second, then, such an approach necessarily remains purely in the realm of sociology—and therefore, again, is unable to credit the complexity of much blues-based music. Simplicity is, of course, a touchstone for essentialism, so it is best to ignore complexity. As Macan puts it, this perspective "show[s] little historical awareness of the degree to which earlier African-American styles such as ragtime and jazz resulted from a high culture/low culture fusion" (p. 172). In other words, from the "authenticity" perspective, shouldn't Scott Joplin or John Coltrane be condemned? Was Joplin inauthentic or some sort of race-traitor because he wrote an opera (*Treemonisha*)?

Third, does this critical enforcement of what I've called "blues orthodoxy" mean that there could not be a kind of rock music that took off from, for example, *Chinese* musical and cultural sources?

Ultimately, despite the intentions of the "authenticity" critics, the blues orthodoxy feeds all too easily into a rock-music industry that does little more than recycle worn-out pop clichés. To return to earlier themes: the blanket condemnation of progressive rock in the name of authentic "blackness," the idea that rock music should not attempt to become "serious" music, and the idea that "irony" should be the overriding value in rock music lyrics (Macan deals with this question on p. 170; I would argue that what the critics call "irony" is instead mostly fashionable cynicism and pessimism), in fact run against what I would call the antiessential "essence" of rock music as generous synthesis. This idea parallels Sartre's claim that the essence of humanity is to have no fixed essence; humanity, therefore, is a continuous invention and reinvention. Not to go overboard with this, but it is in this light that rock music, at its best, really is the first truly "world" music; and it is in this light that we should welcome the development of Chinese, Maori, Pakistani, or what-have-you rock music. No other kind of rock music opened the way toward such possibilities the way that progressive rock did, and it seems to me a kind of pathological blindness that keeps the authenticity critics from seeing this.

One of the difficulties that I have with Macan is that he seems to buy into an essentialism of gender and class that is of the same sort that he has so insightfully criticized on the matter of race. Perhaps on the question of gender it is simply that Macan has not developed, at least in *Rocking the Classics*, his arguments as much as he probably should have. Another difficulty concerns Macan's section on "instrumentation and tone color" (pp. 31–40), where he aligns electric and electronic instruments with the "masculine," and acoustic instruments and musical passages with the "feminine." Now, credit should be given where it is due: it is yet another achievement of *Rocking the Classics* that it has put forward for consideration the idea of "feminine" qualities in progressive rock. (I pursued this theme at some length in *music of Yes*, arguing that Yes not only demonstrated a "feminine" aspect, but, perhaps more to the point, seemed markedly antimasculinist and antimachismo throughout their career as a progressive rock group.) Furthermore, Macan does add the important disclaimer that he is using "the terms 'masculine' and 'feminine' simply as metaphors and archetypes, commonly used by musicologists"; he does "not attempt to judge whether the characteristics associated with these terms are biologically grounded or socially constructed" (p. 31–32). The reference here is in fact to what has lately been called the "new musicology."[52] Despite the disclaimer, I wish that Macan had been a bit *less* straightforward with his gender analysis, or at least had shown how the use of gender terms as metaphors and archetypes had come to be part of music theory. Pursuing this line of inquiry, Macan might have gone on to show that the "that ain't rock 'n' roll" school of criticism seems to rest on the assumption that "real" rock music has to have "balls."

However, even within the somewhat essentialistic framework that Macan sets out, he reveals an important part of the sixties counterculture, namely the idea that gender categories are malleable, reconcilable, and perhaps even transcendable. That all of this was complicated and compromised by the essentially masculinist thrust of the so-called "sexual revolution," or even just the fact that, at the end of the day, progressive rock still seemed almost entirely a male affair, does not completely obliterate the significance of the idea. There never has been or will be a counterculture or alternative movement in art or politics without contradictions.

On the question of class I find Macan's position more troubling. It seems to me that, out of the desire to both show what is wrong with the critics who oppose progressive rock, as well as to fashion a conception of the "counterculture" that downplays politics, Macan falls into what I would call a simplistic and essentialistic view of class.

Another way to put this is that Macan mirrors too much the conception of class held by the "authenticity" critics, allowing them too much credit in claiming not only the mantle of the working class, but also populism and Marxism. In particular, Macan is critical of the perspectives of Lester Bangs, Simon Frith, and Dave Marsh, perspectives Macan labels "neo-Marxist." Of the three, perhaps Frith has some interest in Marxist cultural criticism, of the sort that has informed the "Birmingham School" of cultural studies. His *Art into Pop* (coauthored with Howard Horne), makes some interesting observations regarding the way that art schools in England became Bohemian havens for postwar dropouts on their way to discovering rock music. Marsh has written good biographies of The Who and Bruce Springsteen, but does not seem much inclined toward either social or musicological theory. (Interestingly, in his biography of The Who, Marsh compares the *Who's Next?* album to "art rock" experiments such as those undertaken by King Crimson; see p. 493.) Finally, to even be a bad and very dogmatic Marxist requires a little bit of thought (you at least have to acquire a little bit of vocabulary and be able to effortlessly squirt out phrases such as the "rising organic composition of capital"), and I frankly would not credit Lester Bangs

with such neuronal capacity. His cynicism ran as deep as his stu-
pidity, and it is clear that he cared no more for the working class
than for anything else. Which leaves Frith and Marsh.

Rather than allowing that either of these critics, at least when
they were condemnatory of progressive rock (otherwise, I think
they've written some pretty good stuff; but then, I like Bruce
Springsteen, Gang of Four, and other artists who are their main
focus—and I love Pete Townshend and The Who), were expressing a "Marxist" ("neo-" or whatever) point of view, I would instead
call their "working-class" advocacy somewhat narrow and, at
times, an instance of what ought to be seen as a kind of populist
opportunism.

Of course, "Marxism" now comes in many varieties; personally, I am only interested in a Marxism that is able to embrace all
of the developments in society and culture that represent a challenge and an alternative to the "smooth functioning" of adminis-
tered unfreedom that Herbert Marcuse speaks of from the very
first sentences of *One-Dimensional Man*. Any supposedly critical
methodology that starts with the perspective itself, and then in
the name of this or that "authenticity," the working class, the
"black experience," or whatever, proceeds to set aside or condemn new cultural expressions that have not yet been investigated in their own terms—well, such a "methodology" has everything backwards.

Karl Marx had a very broad and fluid sense of the working
class and of class formation more generally. To allow this conception to settle down into a mere category or ontology or "idea," a
transcendental touchstone of authenticity, is quite at odds with
his notion of the centrality of "sensuous practice." Furthermore,
Marx argued that the historic mission of the proletariat is to "lib-
erate itself and all humankind." Lenin, in *What Is to Be Done?*,
argued that the proletariat must make itself the *tribune* of *all* who
are oppressed and marginalized. Even with these fairly programmatic statements of Marxist views, I think it is clear that a critical
and liberatory Marxism is one that is open to new, genuinely creative expressions, regardless of what sector of society gives rise to
them. And, in Lenin's view, the artists and intellectuals who may
give form to emancipatory ideas and expressions are not them-

selves most often from the most oppressed classes (Lenin's famous formulation, much disputed even among Marxists, is that "working class consciousness must come to the working class from outside of itself"). A certain material basis and sense of life chances must exist in order for a person to become an artist or intellectual, and these things are most often found among the middle classes.

In short, the question of what does and does not serve the working class, or even what does or does not "come from" the working class is not settled just by claims of authenticity. To repeat, then, my criticism of Macan here is that he seems to accept such claims on the part of those he sees as "populist" or "neo-Marxist" critics, at least when it comes to the working class. And, again, this seems odd, given that Macan sees through this ruse when it comes to claims about racial authenticity.

I should add, even if this is not a theme that I can develop here, that there is by now a long tradition of Marxist cultural criticism, involving figures such as Georg Lukács, Theodor Adorno, Walter Benjamin, Ernst Bloch, Carl Dahlhaus (who, along with Adorno, has written the most on musicological questions), Herbert Marcuse, Jean-Paul Sartre, Stuart Hall, E. P. Thompson, and Raymond Williams, that is a million miles away from crude, "authentic working class"-type arguments. And this discussion goes right back to the arguments of Marx, Engels, and Lenin on the question of "proletarian" art—not one of them was a proponent of the kind of "agit-prop" (agitation-propaganda) or "direct authentic expression" model that is put forward by some of the antiprogressive rock critics in their more populist opportunist moments. (Mao, as well, though less an influence on the European figures listed above, argued against what he called the "poster and slogan" style in art.)

The question might arise, then: Why does Macan allow this narrow opportunistic perspective to define what counts as art that will serve liberatory aims? The answer to this question, it seems to me, is that Macan is interested, because of his own perspective and interpretive matrix, in shaping a perspective on the sixties counterculture that keeps concrete political issues, trends, and movements at arm's length.

We might consider that there was something like a "counter-cultural perspective" at work in the late sixties, which had, at one end, flower power, the Summer of Love, and "dropout" culture, and at the other end, Prague, Mexico City, the Events of May 1968, the "January Storm" in Shanghai, the 1968 Democratic Convention in Chicago, and the Days of Rage. The counter-culture ran the gambit from Timothy Leary to Jean-Paul Sartre, or from Donovan to Hendrix and Grace Slick, and progressive rock, especially in its English core, seems closer to flower power than to power to the people. Macan seems somewhat at pains to keep progressive rock at the "nicer" end of the countercultural spectrum, as we see from an interview he gave to *Progression* magazine:

> Keep in mind that progressive rock came out of the English counter-culture, not the American one. The English counterculture was less politically charged. It didn't have the same pressing need to be politically charged. There was no Vietnam War to tear English society apart. The English counterculture went in a more philosophical, apolitical direction than the one in America. (Gunnison, p. 34)

This more apolitical direction seems fine with Macan; interestingly, he prefaces these remarks with a few comments concerning the so-called "neo-Marxist" critics:

> Progressive rock, far more than punk rock or disco or even new wave or any of these styles [these critics] began to champion in the latter half of the '70s, really tells us all about the counterculture.
>
> It exposed some of the dichotomies and some of the tensions inherent in some of the major beliefs of the counterculture, and this infuriated the critics to no end. By trashing progressive rock, they were much more easily able to interpret the heritage of the counter-culture in this political, neo-Marxist mode of thinking they so favored. (p. 34)

But, what does the apolitical interpretation of the counterculture really look like, if it is fleshed out in detail? Personally, I do not even see what the idea of a "counterculture" could even mean if it was not in some sense a fundamentally *political* notion, not in any narrow sense, but in the broad sense of having to do with the kind of society that human beings should live in.

It is true, of course, that the Vietnam War intensified the countercultural currents of the late sixties in the United States; the war shaped those currents in particular ways. But the late sixties was a time when the whole world was rocking, and even if there is a certain insular, middle-class perspective on what a "nicer" sixties would have been, recovered now as pure fashion and without the conflict and struggle of the period, and even if there is a peculiarly "English" gloss on this that is especially insulated (the "island life" again), this does not sever the basic connection between flower power and power to the people. (To take one group that regularly sang about flowers, trees, the oceans—namely Yes—I do not think it is stretching things to say that an incipient ecological consciousness was at work; and Emerson, Lake, and Palmer, in *Tarkus* and *Brain Salad Surgery*, had certainly already written the script for *The Terminator*, with their tales of war technology run amok—a point that Macan acknowledges repeatedly).

The alternative to this interpretation that seems to be in the back of Macan's mind, if I may be so bold, is one that sees the utopian thrust of the counterculture as only referring to some other world. I am probably overstretching my bounds here, but my reading of some of the comments that Macan makes in his preface and elsewhere lead me to believe that he is coming from some sort of religious perspective, most likely a Christian perspective (for example, the book is dedicated "to God, without whom it would never have been possible," p. xiii). In this light, it is interesting that Macan places such emphasis on the use of hallucinogenic drugs in the sixties counterculture—again, as in my earlier argument concerning psychedelic drugs and psychedelic music, it seems to me to be a question of what the counterculture was really all about. There have been drugs aplenty in other marginal scenes, as attested to by the "reefer blues" of the blues scenes in Chicago, Memphis, and elsewhere in the early decades of this century; the prevalence of heroin and other hard drugs in the New York jazz scene after the Second World War (which brought down Charlie Parker, Billie Holiday, John Coltrane, Paul Chambers, Bill Evans, and countless others); and the prevalence of marijuana and variously colored tranquilizers and uppers in the Beat scene. All of these were countercultural scenes, but none of these was a comprehensive counterculture like the one that emerged in the sixties. My conclusion, then, is that Macan seizes on this element because it fits in better with the "more apolitical direction" that he is looking for.

Incidentally, I have no qualms with a Christian perspective per se, but this again divides into two: perspectives that are fundamentally otherworldly and erect barriers to political questions, retreating into a contemplative or what Macan calls a "philosophical" mode, and perspectives that are liberatory. Moses and Isaiah and Jesus and the Apostles and the early Christian movement were not meditative figures primarily concerned with purely spiritual transformation—they were concerned with the "spirit" in the largest sense, but not in an otherworldly sense.

This spirit of the early Christian movement has been continually sought after in the modern world, this spirit of messianic and redemptive transformation of this world. And, from there, to the heavens—one of the remarkable passages of the Book of Revelation tells us that there will ultimately be not only a new Earth, but also a new Heaven, an idea that should give us pause: What's wrong with Heaven as it is? Nothing, necessarily, but everything has to grow and develop, even Heaven, even perhaps God. This kind of thinking—which is manifest in the European Radical Reformation, the hermetic, anabaptist, and communal trends that worked their way through the poetry of William Blake and Walt Whitman, and through utopian religious-social movements such as the Latter-day Saints (Mormons) and the Shakers, and more recently through liberation theology—is one crucial background for the way that progressive rock comes into and out of the sixties counterculture.

Again, I may be overstepping, but while Macan would recover the aesthetic and perhaps "philosophical" value of progressive rock, and discard the "political" aspects of this particular expression of the counterculture, I would argue that there are "political" meanings to progressive rock that have yet to be fully understood.

At the same time, I do not expect progressive rock musicians, in their music, lyrics, or even interviews, to express these sorts of ideas, and certainly not in a "theoretical" way. (On the other hand, musicians such as Jon Anderson, Robert Fripp, or Chris

Cutler have certainly shown a grasp of and affinity for ideas such as these.) It may even be that, especially in interviews, some progressive rock musicians have expressed fairly retrograde ideas, and this issue has definitely been complicated in some cases by what the punks rightly called "rock star bullshit." But the music that "came through" (to use one of Jon Anderson's favorite ideas) in the time of progressive rock was capable of expressing, through experimental form and visionary lyrics, a hope for another world, a different and fundamentally better world. Again, I do not know what this hope means purely as a matter of contemplation, and therefore I see it as essentially connected to "politics."

In other words, and to quote Orson Scott Card, there is always a need for a "Deep Story that gives meaning to suffering and makes sense of the randomness of life."[53] When this story is presented in terms of a redemptive framework, the idea is that there is work for us to do in the world to create this meaning (and, returning to the passage from Fredric Jameson that I quoted in the first chapter, to create the material social conditions in which meaning is possible)—so that the suffering of countless generations will not have been for naught. Religious narratives have made their contribution to this story, as have certain versions of Marxism; my own preference is for a moral discourse that is more akin to Judaism and early Christianity, integrated with systematic analyses of the workings of exploitation, oppression, and domination. The theoretical work that is needed does not in any way replace or eliminate the need for visions of a transfigured world.

Certainly, therefore, the recovery of the aesthetic dimension is a crucial part of understanding the possibilities for a transformed world, and of course Macan is right to reject a narrow and opportunistic conception of politics. In providing a careful, thoughtful, systematic recovery of the aesthetic power of progressive rock, Macan has done a great service to the music and, perhaps even despite himself, the redemptive politics of utopia.

4

Sent through the rhythm: A guided discography

Let us finally turn to the musicians and their music. After a few introductory remarks, I will turn to *In the Court of the Crimson King*. Then we will undertake a three-part survey of the most important groups in progressive rock, focusing primarily on their albums. The time of progressive rock will be divided into three parts: 1) Emergence, 1968–1969; 2) Apogee, 1970–1974; and 3) Trials and transformations, 1975–1978.

Certainly there are alternative valid approaches to constructing a survey such as the one that follows. Because I see progressive rock as a musical trend or even movement (the former is uncontroversial, if not the latter), it seems to me best to proceed chronologically. The one exception to this pattern will be that, before discussing a few key albums that were released in 1968, I will begin with King Crimson's first album, *In the Court of the Crimson King*, which was first released in 1969. Like many others, I see this album as marking the definitive emergence (or to use a term from the previous chapter, evolutionary divergence) of progressive rock as a full-blown trend, a "species" with a developmental path of its own. Other than this one exception, I will proceed year by year, from 1968 to 1978.

Each year will be set out in terms of three categories. First, I would like to take note of other important albums from any given

150

year that fall outside of the progressive trend proper, and yet clearly have ramifications for the development of both progressive rock and rock music more generally. Many of these albums could, arguably, fit within a perfectly valid conception of progressive rock; therefore, this category will also serve to show both the porosity of definitions and the lively debate that should take place regarding what progressive rock is. Second, I will discuss important albums by groups of lesser importance. (Included in this category are a few albums that are of a "one-off" nature, for example, the *McDonald and Giles* album, or Pete Sinfield's *Still*). Third, but most significantly, I will discuss the albums that appeared in the year in question that were by what I will call the "most important" or "front-line" groups.

Clearly, the distinction I am making between "first-line" and "second-line" groups will be the most controversial. Undoubtedly, some readers will be unhappy if, in my view, one of their favorite groups did not make my "first line." Given the fact, too, that I intend to base the analysis on albums, there might be an argument for not making this sort of distinction. My reasoning is really quite simple. Again, the idea is to bring out the trend/movement character of progressive rock. The groups that I have placed in the first line are those that, in my view, consistently made high-level contributions to the genre over the course of the period in question. It may be that, in any given year, a group that I have placed in the second line has made one of the most important albums for that year. However, my main premise in elevating a group to the first line is that such a group made a *series* of important albums. Furthermore, setting things up this way demonstrates, to some extent, the contours of the larger movement: as go King Crimson, Yes, Jethro Tull, so goes progressive rock (call them the "leading aesthetic indicators" of the trend, if you will). I've tried to be fair in my assessments; if the distinctions I'm working with here spur further discussion, and perhaps bring out some good things that I missed (and there is no doubt that I will miss more than a few good things, as every one of the groups discussed here deserves lengthier treatment, and there are a million details here to keep track of), that would be a fine outcome.

This survey will undoubtedly also spur comments of the "What about so-and-so? Why didn't you talk about them?" variety.

I could imagine a whole other approach that would have discussed, for example, Captain Beefheart. Well, I'm very fond of Mr. Van Vliet, and he has certainly been a powerful and progressive force in rock music. By the same token, we could build a bridge from Beefheart's work in the seventies, and especially *Doc at the Radar Station* (1980), toward Ornette Coleman's electric music of the late seventies (e.g., *Dancing in Your Head*, 1977). I think it is important to build these bridges, which fit nicely with the thesis that throughout the seventies, a general musical avant-garde developed. In this larger movement, traditional musical categories, such as jazz, rock, or European classical music, stopped meaning very much, at least insomuch as these terms had previously functioned as barriers. All the same, the approach here is to take our bearings from the specific sources. It seems to me that, even if we were only to plot a trajectory using three sources, namely *Sgt. Pepper's*, The Nice, and *In the Court of the Crimson King*, we would see readily enough the basic terrain of progressive rock. But here the survey will be, if not exhaustive (after all, one of the great things about progressive rock is that, if you were to really attempt to trace out *all* of the connections, the effort would have to be endless), then at least representative.

Even within the first-line I would like to make a distinction. That is, of the thirteen first line groups, I see two of them as "pillars" of progressive rock: Yes and King Crimson. This has to do with more than music, but, obviously, there are no other groups who were consistent musical contributors on as high a level over a longer period of time. The double helix of albums that runs from *The Yes Album* to *Going for the One* and *In the Court of the Crimson King* through *Red* represents the summit of progressive rock. Again, this does not mean that other eagles did not soar as high from time to time. Please keep in mind that my purpose is to celebrate all of this great music and to attempt to recapture some of its redemptive energy. The distinctions employed here are intended as guides and aids to understanding, not as a way of diminishing achievements through comparison.

The "pillar" status of Yes and King Crimson goes beyond their own musical works, to their place within the trend of progressive rock and the way that their music is a leading indicator of the

health, or lack thereof, of the trend. When you consider that, by
1978 King Crimson had packed it in and Yes released *Tormato*,
you can see what I mean. On the other hand, when you consider
that, in the space of just a few years these groups made *In the
Wake of Poseidon*, *Lizard*, *The Yes Album*, *Fragile*, *Close to the
Edge*, and *Larks' Tongues in Aspic*, you also get a sense of the pin-
nacle of what was possible within this trend.

Only in a handful of cases will live recordings be discussed,
namely, in the cases where a group seems to make special contributions or show itself at its best in that context.

◪   ◪   ◪

At the expense of mentioning something that will be all too
obvious to most readers, perhaps a thing or two needs to be said
about the format of progressive rock albums in their time,
namely the long-playing (LP) vinyl record. Even now, in the time
of compact disks, I prefer to use the term "album" to refer to the
recordings that artists issue. However, in the days of the LP, there
were two further attributes of the progressive rock album that are
crucial to their status as complete works.

First, LP records have two sides, with roughly twenty minutes
to a side, and were generally created with this fact in mind. Outstanding demonstrations of the two-sidedness of LPs are two
albums by Jethro Tull, *Thick as a Brick* and *A Passion Play*. Both
come up against the limitations of having two sides, as evidenced
by the "transitional" material at the end of side one and the
beginning of side two for each album. If the CD format were
available in the seventies, it might have been the case that some
albums, especially "double-albums," that were a bit bloated at
eighty minutes, might have been subtantially improved at a
leaner sixty or seventy minutes. On the other hand, groups often
worked creatively with the LP format, intentionally creating
works or albums of works that were meant to be conceptually
"two-sided." Often groups would explore shorter forms, songs
basically, on one side, and a side-length long form on the other;
representative examples are Caravan's *In the Land of Grey and
Pink* and Yes's *Close to the Edge*.

Although probably few of us miss the pops and crackles of the LP format, there is something to be said for the warmth and intimacy of it. And, although two-sidedness may seem an "unnatural" limitation on creating musical works, there was something to be said for the limitation itself, especially in these days of albums (CDs) that are substantially too long.

A second attribute of the LP format has been lost with the coming of the compact disk, with no concomitant gain. That is, the old albums had album covers and album cover *art*—and this played a key role in the development of progressive rock. The unifying role that the best album-cover art played in bringing a given album together, into a "totality," as a complete work, was crucial to progressive rock. Frankly, I do not know how someone could *really hear* an album such as *In the Court of the Crimson King* or *Fragile* if their first or only acquaintance with the album was through the CD format. Artists such as Roger Dean (in the view of many, including myself, the most important of the progressive-rock cover artists) played an integral and substantial role in the development of the *music*. The fact that there is no such role to be played with compact disks (or, at least, the role is greatly and qualitatively diminished), may even be one of the most significant factors set against the reemergence of progressive rock as a major trend.

I will not belabor the point further. Keep in mind, however, that the albums that will be discussed here are the ones that were originally made with vinyl and with large album covers.

◢ ◢ ◢

A word is in order concerning the progressive-rock trend as it made itself manifest in Italy. I am sure that most readers of this book are aware that nowhere was the progressive trend as strong as among the Italian groups. One reason for this is that, until progressive rock took hold, there was not much rock music in Italy. Instead, there was a strong tradition of popular song in Italy (and, of course, there was and is a tremendously popular tradition of opera, out of which comes a great many songs that any Italian person would know). Perhaps this is best known in the U.S. in terms of songs such as "Volare" (the tendency is to think of handsome men riding Vespas) or Dean Martin's "That's Amore." In other words, progressive rock was the first real trend in rock music to take off in Italy—and boy, did it take off! The reason I am raising this issue before I get into the survey is that, among the first line groups, I have included only one Italian band, namely PFM (Premiata Forneria Marconi). I have full confidence that they belong in the first rank, but this is the one place where I am very much worried about the distinctions (and, implicitly, comparisons) that are employed here. The problem is that I do not know the full scope of the work of some of the other groups, such as Acqua Fragile, Area, and Banco, to name just a few. What I do know of this work is almost uniformly brilliant (and I will discuss albums by Area and Banco). Perhaps I may be let off the hook a little bit here by the fact that there are *so many* great progressive bands from Italy. Clearly, a good book could be written on this scene alone; I hope that someone does undertake such a project, and I would be happy to play a role in seeing it come to fruition.

The question of access also bears in a larger way on some of the choices represented in this survey. With the reissue of many albums on CD and with new developments in distribution (see the resources section), this question is constantly being reconfigured. In what follows, the reader will find a good sample of some of the more obscure groups (I'm taking, for example, Jonesy to be somewhat obscure, and Public Foot the Roman to be very obscure), but there will probably be readers who know of groups that are still more obscure. So there's another book for you: "*extremely* obscure progressive rock groups." Although I find it unlikely that there are any groups among these that are above the stature of Yes, King Crimson, or Henry Cow, my disgust with the "free market" as a means of bringing forward great art and my sense of contingency are strong enough that I do not doubt there are many undiscovered gems.

▰ ▰ ▰

Our story begins in the court of the crimson king. If I may inject a biographical note here, it turns out that my own interest in rock music dates from the time King Crimson came on the scene, 1969. I was twelve, going on thirteen. Of course I was aware of rock music from before that time, and even liked a good bit of it (like everyone, I loved the Beatles; the other group that I really liked was Tommy James and the Shondells, especially "Crimson and Clover" and "Crystal Blue Persuasion"). But, as a somewhat awkward adolescent, I can't say that I was *into* it. In 1969, however, I bought my first two rock albums. The first one was *Abbey Road*, and the second one was *In the Court of the Crimson King*. For me, despite all of their musical differences, those albums remain linked.

However, I do not know if we could really make a case for some sort of "torch" being passed. *Abbey Road* represents the Beatles at their most mature; perhaps it is fair to say that *In the Court of the Crimson King* represents a new kind of rock music at its *least* mature. The monstrous, bellowing face on the cover certainly looks as if it could belong to a creature that has emerged from the bog evoked in the opening moments of the album. Are these the sounds of a primitive swamp, or of a barge out on the Thames? Neither the face nor the tugboat horn seems fitting to announce a "crimson king," but then we are in a strange realm here, a realm both medieval and futuristic. As Edward Macan argued, both medievalism and science fiction are key parts of the thematic picture of progressive rock, so perhaps it is fitting that we immediately find both in the opening statement of the genre.

Perhaps the combination in "21st Century Schizoid Man" is more one of science fiction and barbarism; significantly, the song would make an excellent soundtrack for the stories of Philip K. Dick, and it anticipates the cyberpunk fictions of William Gibson by a few years. Furthermore, "Schizoid Man" sets out one pole of progressive rock that seems quite distant from the pole represented by groups such as Yes, Genesis, and Emerson, Lake, and Palmer. Not only is the music not keyboard saturated, but it is hard as nails. When I have played "Schizoid Man" for students in recent years, some have reacted to what they see as the overbearing pyrotechnicality of the song. There is something to that interpretation, to be sure, but this overbearingness is itself contrived to hit you square in the face. In terms of the sheer difficulty of the song's starts and stops, the way that it is both very tightly controlled and yet on the verge of careening out of control, there is an undeniable force at work here. Something new and unprecedented has arrived on the scene.

It is not hard to imagine "Schizoid Man" as part of a very different sort of album, one that has more in common with certain jazz-rock groups such as The Flock than with what we more ordinarily think of as progressive rock. For example, Ian McDonald is capable of bringing forth mellifluous tones from the saxophone, but there aren't any to be found here. Instead, he leans into his horn, overblowing in a cross between Coltrane's "power tenor" and some of the earlier "rock 'n' roll" and soul music sax players (e.g., the late, great Junior Walker), cranking out lines that are at times indistinguishable from Fripp's distorted electric guitar. Perhaps the fundamental combination in the song is heard best in Michael Giles's drumming, which is by turns heavy-handed, in the manner of a "hard rock" drummer, and jazzy, in the manner of drummers who stress buzz rolls on the snare and delicate cymbal work. In fact, though there were some great drummers in rock music emerging at the end of the sixties, from Ginger Baker and Mitch Mitchell to Carmine Appice, it seems to me that Giles's work was on a whole other level of sophistication. In addition to the sheer musicality of his playing, Giles also exhibits a dynamic range that is perhaps only previously heard in music by the Beatles. He really did set the bar rather high, thereby creating a standard for a series of remarkable King Crimson percussionists.

Even Greg Lake, usually the clearest of singers, adopts a harsh sound for "Schizoid Man," and Peter Sinfield's lyrics, of course, are gruesome. Someone who only heard this song might expect the whole album to consist in this hybrid "heavy metal." (I seem to recall Fripp somewhere referring to King Crimson as a "heavy-metal" group, but I tend to take everything he says with at least one grain of salt. Incidentally, one group that is more often thought of in terms of heavy metal that clearly builds on the "Schizoid Man" legacy is Voivod, especially their album *Nothing-face*.) And yet, the pure chaos that is finally unleashed at the very end settles down into a song that is actually "pretty," "I Talk to the Wind." Indeed, the song is almost the sonic and lyrical opposite of "Schizoid Man," except that it also concerns deep feelings of alienation. In other words, none of the works from *In the Court of the Crimson King* should be heard entirely in isolation from one another, as there is a thematic development and unity to both its music and lyrics.

Starting in the torture chamber, the album then turns to existential dread. Even if its vision is couched in dulcet tones, "I Talk to the Wind" is only a little less ominous than "Schizoid Man." And yet, speaking of sweet sounds, we find playing here that has once again taken a new and remarkable turn for rock music—a song that is led by the flute, for one thing, and electric guitar that is the subtle mirror image of the harshness of the album's opener. Indeed, though Fripp is certainly one of the great guitarists of our age, part of his genius, certainly on display here, is in playing music first, guitar second. And though stylistically the two are quite different, Fripp shows here that he has something in common with Steve Howe, namely that both of them compose guitar *parts*; that is, they orchestrate with the guitar, setting aside distinctions such as "lead" or "rhythm." In rock, the precedent for this would be some of the great work of George Harrison. In all three cases, when you turn your attention to this question, you can certainly hear that some excellent guitar work is being produced. But, first of all, you hear music.

And, whereas the closest that "Schizoid Man" comes to subtlety is perhaps in some of its intricate soft runs, "I Talk to the Wind" is subtle on various levels. There is an autumnal cast to what seemed to be its multitracked flutes, a quality that compares nicely to The Mamas and the Papas' "California Dreaming," as well as to Yes's version of Stephen Stills's "Everydays" (from *Time and a Word*). But whereas these songs speak of the more "ordinary" alienation of urban life, a walk in the park that turns out to have a lonely and gloomy side, "I Talk to the Wind" is part of a larger cosmic, or at least science-fiction, story, where there are ominous, much larger-than-life forces at work. Actually, the song's greatest subtlety is that it can be heard both on the level of everyday personal melancholy and as a herald that something in the world is seriously out of joint.

This feeling is confirmed, of course, with the final piece on side one, "Epitaph." Here the Mellotron, used with the string setting, makes its first major appearance—creating a link, in fact, with the closing work on the album, "The Court of the Crimson King." Whereas other groups used the Mellotron primarily to create the sound of a string orchestra, King Crimson tended to employ the keyboard as though it were an instrument in its own right. However, "Epitaph" does open with a majestic, symphonic sound, filled out by Giles's timpani, as well as one of Fripp's more haunting melodies. Indeed, the latter significantly foreshadows the haunting guitar line from "Starless." Strange to think that only five years or so passed between *In the Court of the Crimson King* and *Red*, for, in terms of everything that happened in society and music and King Crimson's music in particular, the work would appear to be that of a much longer period. Everything about "Epitaph" is an extraordinary downer, and yet the feeling is one of the vacuum of space rather than some maudlin bluesiness. By this point, the otherworldliness and sci-fi vibe of the album is firmly established. There is something like a testament to a new kind of alienation here, and though I hesitate to introduce this term at this point in the narrative, I cannot help but think of analyses such as Fredric Jameson's that point to transformations of capitalist society in the direction of the *postmodern*.

"Moonchild," which takes the late sixties idea of a "space jam" to new lengths, and which is perhaps not altogether satisfactory as a musical work, anticipates some of Henry Cow's music of just a few years later, where fairly long sections are dominated by "small sounds." Fripp again extends his use of a lovely pearlescent tone (quite appropriate, given the time-honored association between pearls and the moon), and Giles also demonstrates that a great deal can be done with cymbals. Here too, Peter Sinfield's lyrics are at their most playful, an approach that suits him better than when he aims to sound serious. Further examples will turn out to include the very sweet "Cadence and Cascade" and the almost bizarre "Catfood" (both from *In the Wake of Poseidon*). Greg Lake's voice seems to be running through some sort of distortion device here, giving it the hollow sound of transmission from outer space. At over twelve minutes in length, "Moonchild" is definitely middle-of-the-night stuff.

Incidentally, just as King Crimson has been capable of making music that is playful as well as dark and ominous, so too the

other pillar of progressive rock, Yes, is capable of dealing with
themes that are not all brightness and light. I mention this in part
because these two groups are often seen as forming some sort of
dichotomy (and the Crimson camp, or at least Robert Fripp and
Bill Bruford, has indeed encouraged this view), whereas things in
fact are much more complicated.

We are finally introduced into the "court" proper, with great
Mellotron and percussion fanfare. Is this a future kingdom, one
that has assimilated the rather insignificant planet Earth, or the
tale of a once great civilization from a place far away and a time
long ago? Perhaps both, for here we see the combination of
medievalism and science fiction common to many progressive-
rock scenarios. With "The Court of the Crimson King," this album
comes about as close as it ever will to a more celebratory spirit,
but even here there is rust and decay around the edges: "The gar-
dener plants an evergreen, whilst trampling on a flower." It is difficult not to think of the "fat man," Baron Harkonnen, from Frank
Herbert's *Dune*—perhaps the ultimate novel of science-fiction
medievalism. In other words, this seemingly great civilization is
in fact an authoritarian kingdom, and a decrepit one at that.
There are interludes, it's true, that feature electronic organ
(sounding a bit cheesy) and flute, respectively, where it seems a
less embattled form of life ekes out some kind of existence in the
margins. Some of it is even reminiscent of Sun Ra's intergalactic
travels ("We travel the spaceways, from planet to planet"). Soon
enough, though, the chorus of "aaahhhs" makes its reassertion,
singing to the glory of a king whose prison moons are even falling
apart. There's something here in the chorus, the strings, and the
percussion that spells, or perhaps pounds out, *doom*.

There is nothing arbitrary about taking *In the Court of the
Crimson King* to be the first full-blown album of progressive rock,
and yet it has to be acknowledged that, rather than presenting the
utopian spirit that is the ideological touchstone of the genre, we
instead find here gloom, alienation, and dystopia. For sure, such
elements, or at least more gothic expressions of them, are to be
found in the music of many progressive rock groups, with works
such as "The Knife" or "Selling England by the Pound" by Genesis serving as prime examples. Progressive rock has its dark side,

despite what is often said of the music by uninformed commentators. However, once this side is recognized, the issue of connecting progressive rock with the sixties counterculture becomes a good deal more complex. And yet, such complexification is much needed, either in analyses of progressive rock or of the sixties, and it is not hard to see why, in 1969, musicians would create works that testify to alienation and crumbling social orders.

A great progressive rock album is great as a totality, for creating a world, and not for just being a collection of good songs. I am struck by the way that *In the Court of the Crimson King* has a thematic unity that works on many levels, and, like many images of an austere, lonely world, somehow the very things that are repulsive are also strangely attractive. Perhaps the reference is too far afield of the music, but I cannot help but think that, among the ideological currents moving about in England at that time were both the humanistic and green Marxisms of Raymond Williams and E. P. Thompson, and a very cold, structuralist Marxism imported from France (from the thought of Louis Althusser). In addition, Sartre's existentialism (also mixed with Marxism, the "unsurpassable horizon of our time," as Sartre had famously put it in his *Search for a Method*) still had tremendous influence among young Europeans and perhaps a few folks in England (influence can extend quite beyond the group that had actually read the stuff); certainly hope and belief in radical social transformation continually wrestled with an essential alienation and loneliness in his work. This clash and intertwining of perspectives is captured brilliantly in E. P. Thompson's underappreciated novel, *The Sykaos Papers*; if a film is ever made of this story, music from the early King Crimson would serve well as the soundtrack.

On the other hand, I'm not much fond of the world where all artworks have to relate somehow to film (my reasoning on this is presented in the next chapter), and there is world enough to be found in King Crimson's first album. In my view, the group would go on to make better records, more mature and somewhat less bombastic works, but *In the Court of the Crimson King* will stand as a monument and inaugural moment.

And now, hang on to your hats, as the tour finally begins.

Emergence, 1968–1969

1968

1968 was not yet a huge year for progressive rock, but the first
tender shoots were starting to emerge, and the musical ground in
rock, in the years 1967 and 1968, was extraordinary. For example,
in 1967 Procol Harum released their first, self-titled, album, The
Doors released *Strange Days*, Jefferson Airplane put out *Surrealis-
tic Pillow*, the Moody Blues had the orchestrated *Days of Future
Passed*, Pink Floyd's first album, *The Piper at the Gates of Dawn*,
was making a big impression, Frank Zappa's *Absolutely Free* followed on the heels of 1966's *Freak Out*, and Cream and the Jimi
Hendrix Experience were blowing minds as well as amplifiers—in
short, the cauldron was on the point of boiling over.

1967 also saw the release of an album for the most part lost to
rock history, but perhaps still working its subterranean influence
in the rock avant-garde. Five New York musicians, under the
leadership of Joe Byrd, produced an album under the group
name of The United States of America. Perhaps most startlingly,
the group featured the complete absence of guitar, electric or otherwise. Heard for perhaps the first time on a recording of "rock"
music was the fretless bass guitar. The other instruments were
synthesizers, violin, percussion, and female vocals, all of these at
times "processed." Also folded into the mix were recordings of
"musique concrete," that is, examples of "found sounds," presented as possible music. Although the whole production was a
bit contrived, this was also music that hoped to integrate the
innovations of John Cage, Karlheinz Stockhausen, Edgard
Varese, and others into rock music. To some extent, such integration was also occurring in the music of the Beatles, Pink Floyd,
and Frank Zappa, but the United States's approach seemed both
purer and more far-reaching. In some sense, this road was not
taken by progressive rock "proper," but it makes a reappearance
in what we might call the "postprogressive" music of figures such
as Brian Eno and Bill Laswell.

The Beatles, a.k.a. the "White Album," was much anticipated.
When it appeared in 1968, the era of groups doing whatever
pleased them was opened. This did not mean that all of the music

necessarily pleased all of the audience, as demonstrated by the duds mixed in with the more transcendent songs (though, thirty years on, it is still a matter of opinion which is which). Be that as it may, the conversation between artists and their audiences seemed to somewhat exclude, at least for a brief, shining moment, more commercial kinds of calculations. Or, at least, the proverbial "record-buying public" was willing, up to a point, to follow seemingly visionary rock musicians into uncharted territory.

Some new trends emerged, and some recent trends consolidated and matured. With *We're Only in It for the Money*, Frank Zappa was already parodying a west-coast psychedelic scene that was, in fact, just getting started. Call it a Los Angeles-inflected take on San Francisco flower power, black coffee instead of LSD. His other album of the same year, *Lumpy Gravy*, was musically adventurous, especially in its integration of jazz influences. Though Zappa, in my view, sits uneasily beside progressive rock, he certainly shared the genre's propensity for synthesis, and was undoubtedly more sophisticated in its pursuit than most.

As far as jazz integration was concerned, 1968 also saw the appearance of the first albums by Blood, Sweat, and Tears, and the Chicago Transit Authority. (In a move that the ever-beleaguered CTA now probably regrets, this latter group was forced to shorten its name.) Both feature lots of horns and syncopation, and represent more a recapitulation of "big band" styles than those of jazz musicians of the middle or late sixties. Chicago, in particular, aligned themselves with the radical politics of 1968, even incorporating sounds from the demonstrations at the Democratic National Convention that had taken place earlier that summer ("the whole world's watching"). A goodly number of "horn bands" (a few employing violins or cellos as well) came to the forefront of rock around this time, including Chase, Lighthouse, Pacific Gas and Electric (continuing the public utility motif), and Rare Earth. All produced albums that feature at least one or two gems, but Chicago, at least in their first three albums, really pursued a larger conception, one with deep affinities with progressive rock. Let's not allow what the group became after that, mainly producers of pop pablum, distract us from the power of these first three efforts, each of which was a "double album" (as we used to say).

Songs such as "Does Anybody Know What Time It Is?" captured the mood of the period as well as anything, and the composition, arrangement, and playing were all on a very high level.

The generally forgotten acidic side of Chicago, lost in all the syrup of their post-*Chicago III* music, is also much in evidence in one of two Jefferson Airplane albums of that year, *Crown of Creation*. The title song is as harsh and pointed as anything from that time period. Also working at the street level, but with a funkitude that resonates to this day, were Sly and the Family Stone, with *Dance to the Music*. Along with the following year's *Stand!*, Sly and company operated on many levels, combining Black nationalism with internationalism (much as the Black Panthers were doing with activism), putting musicians both Black and white and male and female on the stage, and creating a new, sophisticated funk that had repercussions throughout rock music as well as in the music of Miles Davis and from there to what later was called "fusion." And, of course, the Family Stone gave us a bass guitarist whom practically every practitioner of the instrument either emulates or reacts against today, namely Larry Graham. His style is the heart of all hard funk.

From Larry Graham to Sartre might seem the weirdest of transitions, but there continued to be a great deal of rock music that combined militance with existentialism. The Doors' album of 1968, *Waiting for the Sun*, may have featured the somewhat goofy "Hello, I Love You," but it also gave us the haunting "Unknown Soldier." Simon and Garfunkel's *Bookends* also ran the gamut from silly to somber, but "Hazy Shade of Winter" captures well the college-campus side of the Vietnam War period, as does Bob Dylan's "All Along the Watchtower," from his *John Wesley Harding*.

Back in England, the "stretching-out" and virtuoso musicianship trends were starting in ernest. Jimi Hendrix, although from the United States (Seattle), was based in England, with a trio completed by English musicians. Though his *Electric Ladyland* was recorded in the New York studio of the same name, it also featured organ work from Steve Winwood and, more to the point, a psychedelic sensibility that owed as much to his rise to fame in the English scene as his debt to American blues and rock. Like *The Beatles*, Hendrix's third (again, a "double album") was somewhat patchy, and yet it also featured extraordinary work, such as a tour-de-force version of Dylan's aforementioned "All Along the Watchtower." Hendrix's use of different guitars here, including the acoustic steel-string with which he is rarely associated, is subtle and complex. His "solo" for "Watchtower," really a richly textured piece of string orchestration, anticipates similar efforts by guitarists such as Steve Howe (I'm thinking especially of the guitar solo from "Yours Is No Disgrace"). To be perfectly honest, in my view there are only a few songs on Hendrix's first album, *Are You Experienced*, that really endure (among them is "Third Stone From the Sun"), and yet this was the launching pad for millions of male adolescent (whatever their actual age) guitar wankers. *Axis: Bold as Love* and *Electric Ladyland* show, by contrast, that such six-string masturbation was not the essential part of Hendrix's music.

As mentioned in the previous chapter, Hendrix was an avid reader of science fiction. Whether readers of this genre or not, Pink Floyd, with their first two albums, established the possibilities of "space rock." With long, semiorganized pieces with titles such as "Interstellar Overdrive," "Astronomy Domine" (both from *Piper at the Gates of Dawn*, 1967), and "Set the Controls for the Heart of the Sun" (*A Saucerful of Secrets*, 1968), the group opened a territory at the intersection of inner and outer space. Richard Wright's organ sound from this period, with long-held, minutely modulated, and supremely lonely chords, stands as a signature of these excursions. Also heavy with death and mysticism was the Moody Blues' *In Search of the Lost Chord*. Transmogrified from a more "pop" unit (typified by the 1964 single, "Go Now!"), the group retained a certain lightness (perhaps even light-headedness!) throughout their late-sixties and seventies career. Still, they were the group that got everyone trying an orchestra (not often to good effect), and, with *In Search of the Lost Chord* they introduced some interesting Eastern sounds and chants. "Voices in the Sky" is enchanting, and the group could also pull off a powerful guitar-rocker every now and then, such as the romping "Ride My See Saw" (further efforts in this vein would include "The Story in Your Eyes" and "I'm Just a Singer in a Rock and Roll Band"). Combine the Floyd's more experimental and (shall we say) intellectual leanings with the Moodys' fine vocal abilities and knack for tunefulness, stir in some more advanced instrumental skills, and at least a large part of what would emerge as progressive rock is already set out for you.

Longer works in this period consisted in either drawn-out jams or song-suites. In the latter category, a remarkable work that appeared in 1968 was *S.F. Sorrow* by the Pretty Things. As Vernon Joynson writes, this album "is generally acknowledged to be the first rock opera[,] giving Pete Townshend the inspiration to write *Tommy*" (p. 425). One piece from the album, "Private Sorrow/Balloon Burning" can be heard on the recent *Supernatural Fairy Tales* progressive rock collection; it is sophisticated and haunting. Interestingly, the drummer on this album was a fellow named "Twink"; his "real" name is John Alder, and he had played on Tomorrow's one and only album earlier that year. Tomorrow, as many readers will know, featured the guitar work of Steve Howe. The "Twink connection," as with the Dylan and Hendrix versions of "All Along the Watchtower" in that same year, show how fast things were moving at that point, and how interconnected the whole scene was. (More on Tomorrow in a moment.)

A group that got its start much earlier, but that also put out an important album in 1968, was the Zombies. Featuring the excellent organ work of Rod Argent, as well as the original and jazzy vocal stylings of Colin Bluntstone, the Zombies formed in 1963 and had a huge hit with "She's Not There" the following year. In 1968, after four years of producing singles that did not sell very well, the group recorded an album's worth of material just before the group split up. CBS released *Odessey and Oracle* anyway (the misspelling of "odyssey" was intentional), and it is a document from that time well worth hearing. Most readers will be familiar with the great "Time of the Season," which again features Argent's fine work with the Hammond B-3, but also excellent are "Friends of Mine" and "Care of Cell 44." This is not progressive rock, in part because the album does not have the thematic (musical or lyrical) unity that would make it a complete "work," but *Odessey and Oracle* certainly contains many of the elements out of which progressive rock would be forged.

Led Zeppelin's first album also came out that year. As mentioned before, the career of this band was cotemporaneous with the time of progressive rock. If anything, influence went more from progressive rock toward Led Zeppelin than vice-versa but, again, the point here is that there was a milieu in which even very blues-oriented rock music was stretched into new territory. Indeed, groups such as Zeppelin, Jethro Tull, Steamhammer, Deep Purple, and probably dozens more were initially involved in playing what might be called "progressive blues." (Certainly the Stones could be seen in this light as well, at least for a few years.) Of these, only Tull became a "real" progressive rock group, though since the time of progressive rock they have moved somewhat back toward their blues roots. Consider for a moment, however, Yes's version of the Byrds' "I See You," from the former's first album (1969); the instrumental section features a guitar/drums interplay that comes right out of "Whole Lotta Love." And later Zeppelin epics, from "Stairway to Heaven" to what I think of as their "karmic" music, for example "Kashmir" (*Physical Graffiti*, 1975) or "Achilles' Last Stand" (*Presence*, 1976), certainly stand at the intersection of progressive blues rock and progressive rock "proper." There really was a milieu of experimentation and stretching out, in other words, and despite the qualitative developments that led to progressive rock, it is not as though this music was as disconnected from the rest of rock music as some critics and historians now seem to think.

1968 also saw the appearance of two albums by precursor groups to what I am calling the "pillars" of progressive rock, King Crimson and Yes. Steve Howe's group Tomorrow was undoubtedly the more solid of the two. Featuring a talented vocalist in Keith West, this very psychedelic album remains quite listenable today. By May of that year, Howe was already gigging with Bodast, a group that lasted until the end of 1967, when Howe joined Yes for their breakthrough third album. This trio (which took its name from the first two letters of its members' first names, and not from any form of the excellent sixties term, "bodacious") recorded an album that was not released until many years later (available on CD now as Steve Howe and Bodast, *The Early Years*). It is a very good record, on which bits of tunes that later made their way into Yes's music can be heard. Incidentally, Jon Anderson had been knocking around since about 1964, originally with a group called The Warriors. The drummer for that group was Ian Wallace, who would later turn up with King Crimson.

Giles, Giles, and Fripp was a truly screwy little project, and it is very hard to see how King Crimson came out of it—and that's what makes this music interesting, sort of like listening to the juvenalia of Mozart or Beethoven. Although their album, *The Cheerful Insanity of Giles, Giles, and Fripp* is most often assimilated to the psychedelic current nowadays, it is perhaps better heard as a prescient anticipation of the sort of revenge of the nerds that found its way into some new wave—Robert Fripp as precursor to David Byrne.

Full-blown progressive rock, then, at least according to my definition of the genre, was not yet in play in 1968. But three groups that would later come to the forefront of the music did release albums.

As mentioned, Jethro Tull's earliest work could be characterized as progressive blues, but with a twist. Ian Anderson's flute playing, though not exactly at odds with the blues, certainly expanded the range of that music. Though flutes appear here and there in the history of progressive rock, in the music of King Crimson, Genesis, PFM, and a few other groups, Anderson had a very distinctive style, largely derived from the work of jazz musician Rahsaan Roland Kirk. Like Kirk, Anderson created a rich sound by overblowing and humming through the flute (this is sometimes called "scat flute"), thereby liberating the instrument from its standard role of sweet ornamentation. Anderson's flute was capable of leading a group that did not hesitate to lay it on thick and heavy. On the first Tull album, *This Was*, Mick Abrahams contributed some knife-edged guitar work, Clive Bunker's double-bass-drum attack was powerful, while it was left to Glenn Cornick to bring a more melodic element on the bass guitar. Abrahams left after the first album, forming Blodwyn Pig, whose albums *A Head Rings Out* and *Getting to This* demonstrate what Tull might have sounded like had they continued in a more blues-oriented direction. (Strangely enough, Peter Banks spent a few months in Blodwyn upon his departure from Yes, but no recordings were released by this version of the group.) Perhaps the best track on *This Was* is "Song for Jeffrey," which showcases Anderson's flute.

Another important group that released their first album in 1968 would later become well-known for the similarly titled, "For

Richard." Caravan is a group that inspires immense devotion from their many fans—or perhaps the word is "affection." I know that I feel it; there's simply something very warm and inviting about their sound, especially the combination of Pye Hastings's voice and David Sinclair's organ work. The group's first, self-titled, album has only recently become available again, but all of the homey marks of the next several albums are already there. Indeed, the album opens with "Place of My Own," and closes with "Where but for Caravan Would I," perfect expressions of a chin-up sensibility that barely concealed an undercurrent of melancholy. *Very English!*

By including Caravan in my pantheon of great progressive rock groups, while at the same time setting Pink Floyd aside from the genre, I have undoubtedly left myself open to a serious challenge from meticulous typologists. In a purely technical sense, probably the best musicians in the group were bass guitarist Richard Sinclair (who would leave after the fourth Caravan album and later resurface in Hatfield and the North) and drummer Richard Coughlan. As compared with groups such as Yes or the Mahavishnu Orchestra, Caravan was not a band of virtuosos. In some ways, too, they stayed much closer to conventional song structure than other major progressive groups. However, the emotional sophistication of their material, at least up through their fifth album, displayed a depth that many of the other groups only played at. But there is a more important reason for including Caravan in the pantheon. Although I am perhaps less inclined to see progressive rock as somehow based in the Canterbury scene than some are, still, the south of England and Canterbury are without a doubt central to the emergence and development of the genre. Caravan is very much stitched into that scene.

If Caravan is in some sense the heart of the Canterbury scene and even of progressive rock more generally, perhaps The Soft Machine is the—albeit sometimes loopy—head. Many readers will know that Caravan and Soft Machine have a common origin in the legendary Canterbury group The Wilde Flowers. As Vernon Joynson (p. 575) reports, this group formed in 1961, coming out of the exclusive Simon Langton School (the fact is that these were rich kids, the richest of whom was probably Robert Wyatt). Although the group was together until 1967, they produced no singles or albums, and in fact mainly played material from Chuck Berry and the Beatles. Over the course of their existence, members of the Wilde Flowers included future Caravan members Richard Sinclair, Richard Coughlan, Pye Hastings, and David Sinclair, and future Soft Machine members Hugh Hopper, his brother Brian (who, while never a full member of the Softs, contributed some sax work to a couple of the group's projects), Robert Wyatt, and Kevin Ayers.

Incidentally, Daevid Allen, later the chief pothead pixie of the miraculous Gong, as well as Andy Summers, who would later gain much fame with The Police (and still later record an album with Robert Fripp of nearby Bournemouth), were members of early, nonrecording configurations of Soft Machine.

The Soft Machine is a much trippier effort than the more cerebral albums the group would later produce. Not all of this can be attributed to the influence of original member Kevin Ayers, for Robert Wyatt certainly has his whimsical side as well. One thing that united the two split-offs from the Wilde Flowers was an essential schoolboy silliness, seen on the first Soft Machine album in titles such as "Why Am I So Short?", "So Boot If At All," and "Plus Belle Qu'une Poubelle" (not exactly the academy's French, but something on the order of "More charming than an ashcan"). Even by this time, Robert Wyatt had absorbed a great deal from the American jazz records he had access to, and was developing into one of the great drummers. His voice, like Pye Hastings's, had the endearing consistency of warm butterscotch pudding, and blended nicely with Ayers's sharper edge. Though Ayers was in fact the "lead guitarist" of the group (as the album cover has it), *Soft Machine* is not a guitar heavy record. Instead, it is Mike Ratledge's organ, sometimes heavily distorted and feeding back, that defines the overall sound of the group. Significantly, the first Soft Machine album was recorded in the United States, while the group was on tour with another master of feedback, a guitarist by the name of Jimi Hendrix.

As the liner notes report, the Soft Machine in their first outing gave us a "Now sound." Unfortunately, this "Now" has not worn exceedingly well in terms of more recent days. Furthermore, the album cover demonstrates not only the more silly and juvenile side of the group, but also the undercurrent of schoolboy sexism that was also present in many of Caravan's efforts. The back cover features the group's name printed in letters that follow the curves of a nude woman, seen from behind, who in turn has a wind-up key coming out of her back—a rather one-sided utopia in other words, and one cannot help but associate this with the misogynist albeit ingenious writer from whom the group took its name (that is, William S. Burroughs, whose novel *Naked Lunch* also gave us the band names Steely Dan, the Meat Puppets, and probably numerous others).

Still, in these early days of progressive-rock-in-emergence, I would have to say that *The Soft Machine* was the genre's first "album of the year." However, in terms of the first appearances of groups that would later play a major role in the development of the music, we are still talking about seedlings. Admittedly, many of the other developments of that year in rock music were much more interesting and even experimental, and a "post-blues" rock music was still to come. For the most part, this would remain the case for 1969 as well, with the singular exception of *In the Court of the Crimson King*.

1969

Without going quite so far into the details as before, even a little name-dropping will show that 1969 was also a very exciting year for rock music, and the experimental currents that were creating a basis whereby progressive rock could take that crucial next step were much in evidence.

Abbey Road appeared, the Beatles' most mature and, as we now know, final effort. George Martin's production here set a standard that progressive rock producers, such as Eddie Offord, would strive to emulate, and Billy Preston's excellent keyboard work brought a new unity to the group. Even some of Paul McCartney's and Ringo Starr's silliness makes a good deal more sense in the extended suite that forms a large part of the album's second side. With "Something" and "Here Comes the Sun," George Harrison demonstrated that, at his best, he is a truly fine songwriter, while Lennon's "Come Together" is no less the prime example of acid-cool today than when it was first heard.

Among those who were extending blues rock were Brian Auger and the Trinity, Led Zeppelin with their second album, and Steamhammer. The latter's *Mk.II* album, which has much in common with the spacier jams of Soft Machine, Colosseum, and Pete Brown's Piblokto (on which more in a moment), is well worth a listen, especially for the wistful singing of Kieran White and the nocturnal sax work of Steve Jolliffe. Zeppelin took blues dynamics into whole new territory; their sound was, at turns, explosive and richly textured, especially in songs such as "Ramble On," which contrasts acoustic and electric guitars to great effect. Auger was showing himself to be one of the best practitioners of post-Jimmy Smith Hammond B-3 playing, and his group featured the singing of Julie Driscoll off and on. She would later marry Keith Tippett, an innovative jazz pianist who played on King Crimson's second album. An earlier, nonrecording version of Auger's group featured John McLaughlin and Rick Laird, later of the Mahavishnu Orchestra. So, at the expense of sounding like a broken record, let's once again take note of how closely connected were many of the interesting developments of that time.

In that same year, John McLaughlin did record with an extraordinary trio (sometimes a quartet with the addition of Jack Bruce), Tony Williams's Lifetime. This group featured the B-3 work of Larry Young, someone many people (myself included) consider to be the next step in jazz organ after Jimmy Smith. Young died in 1978 at the age of thirty-eight, of a combination of racism and medical malpractice. It might be convincingly argued that innovative jazz organ playing died with him. (Young's 1965 album for Blue Note, *Unity*, features Elvin Jones on drums and is perhaps his best effort.) Eerily, Tony Williams, the brilliant percussion prodigy and master of "free drums" and polyrhythms who began his career with the Miles Davis Quintet at the age of seventeen, died of similar causes earlier this year (1997). Lifetime's 1969 album, *Emergency!*, was the forerunner of much jazz-rock "fusion," with the difference that the music was more impassioned and plain far-out than much of what later came from that genre.

Williams, McLaughlin, and Young were also featured on Miles Davis's breakthrough albums of that year, *In a Silent Way* and

Bitches Brew. The latter album had a huge effect in galvanizing what was emerging as a general musical avant-garde, one that had some relation to "popular" music but that also knew no barriers of tradition, genre, or pedigree. In what remained for the moment jazz "proper," the year also saw the appearance of Pharoah Sanders's *Karma*, featuring the vocal composition "The Creator Has a Master Plan." The singing here, by Leon Thomas, certainly echoed the utopian textures that were beginning to reach a new level of expression in England. Thomas would later perform with Santana, who, extending the internationalism of the period, released their first album that year as well.

Dylan's *Nashville Skyline* further extended the possibilities of "folk." Meanwhile, there were some very important developments in folk and the emergent folk-rock in England. Sometimes, in the rush to connect progressive rock with European classical music, it is forgotten how close some progressive music is to both the traditional folk music of the British Isles as well as to the folk and folk-rock of the sixties counterculture. Certainly these connections are much in evidence in groups such as Jethro Tull (which, in recent years, has even shared a bass guitarist with Fairport Convention). (The history and development of English folk-rock is explored in *The Electric Muse: Folk into Rock*.) Among those in the realm of the non- or at least less electric variety of folk, Nick Drake, Al Stewart, and Pentangle all had important albums. Drake's first album, *Five Leaves Left*, established his haunting and delicate sound—again, it is a peculiarly English "existentialism" whose greatest documents are not (as with the French or Germans) tomes of philosophy or fiction. He was to produce only three albums in his short lifetime (Drake died in 1974, of an overdose of tranquilizers; despite the many reasons for leaning toward this interpretation, it is not altogether clear that he intended to commit suicide), including the more upbeat and relatively more thickly orchestrated *Bryter Later* (1970), and the once again sparse and gloomy *Pink Moon* (1972). The texture of his voice, on songs such as "Things Behind the Sun," is existentially dark, yet somehow warm. Al Stewart's *Love Chronicles* deserves mention here because it features an extended folk suite not unlike the works of progressive rock that were coming down the pike. (It is also quite good, I hasten to add, even if a bit of a period piece.) Stewart, though from Glasgow, lived in Bournemouth as a teenager, where he was often tortured by Robert Fripp's crusade to prove himself the best guitarist in the region!

Closer to the group aesthetic of progressive rock were The Pentangle, a nonelectric group, and Fairport Convention, who used electric guitars and had a louder and more rocking sound. Their albums for 1969, Pentangle's *Basket of Light* and Fairport's *Liege and Lief*, both feature excellent ensemble work and great singing, especially from vocalists Jacqui McShee and Sandy Denny. In English folk-rock there was generally more room for women musicians, even if they typically occupied the vocalist's position, than in perhaps any other kind of rock music. Fairport Convention, by the way, shares with King Crimson the honor of having had more musicians pass through the ranks than it takes holes to fill the Albert Hall.

Finally, when we come to the "English" rock style that was continuing to develop in the late sixties, and that provided the fertile ground for progressive rock, we find important albums from the Moodys, Procul Harum, and the Floyd, who gave us two LP records each (respectively, *On the Threshold of a Dream*, *To Our Children's Children's Children*; *Shine on Brightly*, *A Salty Dog*; and *Ummagumma*, which was a two-record album). Arguably the biggest development of the year, however, was the release of *Tommy* by The Who. While, in terms of musicianship and style, perhaps only John Entwistle had a major influence on progressive rock, surely the impact of an eighty-minute-long "rock opera," with developing, intertwining, and repeating themes throughout, was lost on no one. After all, to develop a story or theme at great length was one of the prime directives for at least some progressive rock musicians.

Once again the fertile ground was on the whole more interesting than what actually happened with progressive rock groups that year. The exception, as noted, was King Crimson's first album, which was not only a musical breakthrough but, furthermore, did have a broad impact among musicians and serious listeners to experimental rock music. As far as progressive rock goes, Yes's first album, which came out that year, is significant mainly because the group was up and running at that point. The album *Yes* is not quite progressive rock, though it is very psyche-delic and has a few good songs (the best and most promising of which, in my view, is "Survival"). *From Genesis to Revelation*, like Yes's initial offering, does not show us much about the later devel-opment of the group that we came to know and love. Still, there is a certain charm to the album, and it avoids the bombast that is too much in evidence on *Yes*. Caravan, Jethro Tull, and Soft Machine all presented albums that showed significant develop-ment from their first records, though again none of them quite had both feet on the terrain of full-blown progressive rock. Of the three, I'm most fond of Tull's *Stand Up*, though Caravan's *If I Could Do It All Over Again, I'd Do It All Over You* did feature the aforementioned "For Richard," one of the group's early epics. For all three groups there was a great deal of promise here, which would in fact come to fruition the following year.

Other groups that entered the fray about this time were Colos-seum, Renaissance, and two groups from Germany, Can and Amon Duul 2. Colosseum, who perhaps occupy the intersection of two genres that were emergent in the late sixties, progressive rock and jazz-rock, were led by the superb drummer Jon Hise-man and the slightly crazed saxophonist and sometime window-washer Dick Heckstall-Smith. The latter would sometimes play two horns at once, which was also a device earlier associated with Roland Kirk. Dave Greenslade, later of the progressive rock group named for him, was the Colosseum keyboardist. The group's two albums for the year, *We Who Are About to Die Salute You* and *Valentyne Suite* were, respectively, very good and excel-lent. The Renaissance that appeared in 1969 is not the group that most progressive-rock listeners are familiar with. The complete story is a bit complicated: Keith Relf, who was singer of the leg-endary Yardbirds, along with a number of other musicians who would resurface here and there (including John Hawken, who would later play with the Strawbs in their progressive-rock incar-nation), formed the original Renaissance. Somehow, this group transmogrified, in the course of about three years, into the Renaissance that most progressive rock fans are familiar with, featuring singer Annie Haslam and *not* featuring a single member from the original group. The later and better-known Renaissance will be discussed in due course, but we might note that the original group's first album, self-titled, is really a pretty good record. Strangely, it is this version of the group that is featured on *Supernatural Fairy Tales*.

Incidentally, Relf would later form Armageddon with Renaissance-mate Louis Cennamo, Martin Pugh from Steamhammer, and Bobby Caldwell of Captain Beyond. Their only album, self-titled, is really quite good, especially the atmospheric "Silver Tightrope." Armageddon and Captain Beyond, with their very tight ensemble work and high level of musicianship, form an important part of a musical trend that has yet to be investigated, and which is only barely perceived today. I would call it "progressive metal," adding the Black Sabbath of the Ozzy years and distinguishing this trend from much of what is called "heavy metal" nowadays (much of which I find not very heavy).

We see in 1969, too, the extension of the emergent trend to the European continent. Amon Duul 2 seems especially post-Timothy Leary (like fellow German group Ash Ra Temple, who in fact made an album with Leary), while Can is more post-Stockhausen. The former group broke off from Amon Duul, which decided to be more of a hippie communal living experiment than a rock group. I've never warmed up completely to Amon Duul 2's music, but their first album, the interestingly titled *Phallus Dei*, does contain some interesting syntheses of chant and science-fiction themes, and fits better with more recent techno and electronica than most progressive groups from the period. This might also be said of Can, whose individual members, especially Holger Czukay, remain important contributors to experimental trends in rock music. Like much German experimental rock, Can exemplifies a kind of "musical laboratory" approach. Can's first album, *Monster Movie*, was recorded live in the studio for the most part, reflecting the peculiar kind of "improvisation" the group was to develop, of a sort that only tangentially connects with jazz or blues. Both albums also have a "soundtrack" quality to them, and Can was soon to be invited into the field of film music. This also connects the group with more recent trends, where soundtrack music, real or "imagined," abounds. In this, I would distinguish

Can from much of what we more typically think of as progressive rock; in the latter, too much is going on for this music to be part of a film score.

1968 and 1969 were great years for rock music but not quite yet for progressive rock. Forces were definitely in motion, however. Obviously, *In the Court of the Crimson King* was 1969's "album of the year."

Apogee, 1970–1974

1970

1970, technically the final year of the sixties rather than the first year of the seventies, saw a qualitative leap in the number and quality of groups exploring the new possibilities of rock music. *In the Court of the Crimson King* had opened the door, and 1970 was the first year when it seemed a real trend had established itself.

Although 1970 also saw its share of excellent rock albums beyond the territory of progressive rock, the fact that the new trend was developing its own internal dynamic means that I will not devote as much attention to other groups and artists as I did before. Still, a number of significant developments deserve notice.

At the intersection of "hard rock" and progressive rock, we find Black Sabbath's first (self-titled) album, Led Zeppelin *III*, *Who's Next?* by The Who, and the first album by psychedelic metal monsters Hawkwind. A very different kind of intersection is represented by Joni Mitchell's *Ladies of the Canyon*, the beginning of her synthesis of jazz, rock, and folk. She would take this synthesis, along with a subtle critique of commodified culture, to its highest points with *The Hissing of Summer Lawns* (1975) and *Hejira* (1976), the latter featuring some brilliant work from Jaco Pastorius. If you don't think this is relevant to the subject ostensibly at hand, listen to Mitchell's vocal stylings alongside either Ian Anderson or Jon Anderson (for example, the jazzy phrases from the closing section of *Time and a Word*'s "Then").

Three groups from the United States released brilliant albums that, under an expanded definition, were not so far from progressive rock. Sweetwater, a group not remembered by so many today, put out *Just for You*, a broad synthesis of folk, jazz, Latin American percussion, and even classical influences. The epic title track is a dynamic, utopian celebration par excellence. Even more conceptually unified were *Abraxis* by Santana and *Twelve Dreams of Dr. Sardonicus* by Spirit, both of which surely stand as two of the best rock albums of 1970. After an initial album that showed great promise the previous year, the Santana group delivered a series of records that retain their power. Spirit, on the other hand, hit their peak with *Twelve Dreams*, but what a peak it was! The album is a sophisticated journey through the modern world, at turns folkish and metallic, always psychedelic. As a complete work, *Twelve Dreams* might very well be psychedelia's best album.

Another important concept album from the U.S., though patchy in places, combined psychedelic and experimental music with utopian, if occasionally nutty, social critique. This was the Paul Kantner/Jefferson Starship project, *Blows Against the Empire*. The album featured many of the important musicians from the left coast/Bay-area scenes, and perhaps serves as a useful gauge of how close the "green language" as it developed in America could come to English progressive rock—and how far away the two musics remained from one another.

In a weirder vein, Captain Beefheart released *Trout Mask Replica*. As with Frank Zappa's music, Beefheart exemplified another road that might be taken out of the mix of sources that also went into progressive rock.

Miles Davis gave us *Jack Johnson* that year, an extremely lively record that was actually recorded as the soundtrack for a film about the first Black heavyweight boxing champion (with narration by the formidible James Earl Jones). This album brought together John McLaughlin with drummer Billy Cobham, thereby setting up two further pieces of the Mahavishnu puzzle.

Finally from the States, Jim Morrison told a New York audience to shut up and listen to the music, as recorded on The Doors' *Absolutely Live*. Though it is doubtful that he was trying to prepare people for a rock music not mainly geared toward partying or dancing, still, his gesture was appreciated.

Back in England, the Moody Blues carried on with *A Question of Balance* and Pink Floyd with *Atom Heart Mother*. Traffic's superb *John Barleycorn Must Die* effected the same kind of broad musical synthesis that progressive musicians would aim for, but somehow with a quite different cast. And a somewhat out-of-place keyboardist named Rick Wakeman joined the Strawbs for *Just a Collection of Antiques and Curios*.

At both what I have tendentiously called the "first" and "second" lines of progressive rock, we see a new level of activity. We also find increasing diversity, such that it seems that rock's divergent trend may not have many unifying principles. By 1970, experimental rock music was going into a fragmentary period that recapitulates similar developments in European classical music and jazz. Perhaps the latter music makes for the more appropriate comparison; as we noted in the previous chapter, Chris Cutler pointed out that the new rock music of the late sixties and early seventies knew neither rules nor academic restrictions, and this might be said of jazz as well. With the development of "free jazz" (associated with the diverse work of figures such as Ornette Coleman, Cecil Taylor, Archie Shepp, Albert Ayler, and the Art Ensemble of Chicago) in the early sixties, there was a break with previous norms. Consider the comments of musicologist Ekkehard Jost regarding this genre:

> The conventions of harmonically and metrically confined jazz styles, up to hard bop, could be reduced to a relatively narrow and stable system of agreements; therefore, analysis of a given style could concentrate on detecting and interpreting the congruities present in individual ways of operating within that system of agreements. With the advent of free jazz, however, a large number of divergent personal styles developed. Their only point of agreement lay in a negation of traditional norms; otherwise, they exhibited such heterogenous formative principles that any reduction to a common denominator was bound to be an oversimplification. (pp. 9–10)

The diversity among the major progressive rock groups follows a similar pattern. And yet, just as Jost demonstrates for free jazz, in retrospect we can still see what was also apparent at the time, namely that progressive rock constituted a movement.

The relative unity of this movement was just as much ideological as musical, and, in either case, the "unity" was quite loose and perhaps only vaguely perceived. Musically, the guiding principle was simply to push the materials of rock music as far as they would go, and to combine these elements with musical influences from the four corners of the globe. Ideologically, progressive rock was formed specifically on the basis of the sixties counterculture and largely English cultural influences. Many of the musicians worked together and certainly respected and learned from one another. But, beyond these minimal perameters, things were pretty much wide open. As a result, just as critics aligned with the history of jazz up through hard bop called the new music "anti-jazz," so did rock music critics claim that progressive rock had severed its connection with rock 'n' roll. As I've endeavored to show, the connection was never fully severed. A more traditional jazz critic might wonder what the connection is between Ornette Coleman's quartet recordings of the late fifties and early sixties (e.g., *The Shape of Jazz to Come, Change of the Century*) and Louis Armstrong's Hot Five. Similarly, a school of rock music commentary that, strangely, had become very traditional and conventional, wondered what the connection was between Gentle Giant and Little Richard. In either case, there is a connection, even if this connection also works through leaps and discontinuities.

However, just as free-jazz musicians who wouldn't ordinarily be thought of as sounding much like one another could be heard as part of a trend when compared with other musicians who stuck more closely to "the conventions of harmonically and metrically confined jazz styles," so too progressive rock groups that appeared to have little in common are easily identifiable as a trend when compared with those who continued with rock music in more conventional terms. In the comparison, it is clear that progressive rock, at least by 1970, was going its own way.

All progressive rock, and much other postpsychedelic rock music besides, is involved in what I called "stretching out." (Though the phrase suggests longer works, the idea has more to do with stretching beyond established boundaries.) In the previous chapter, I proposed that one way of sorting out progressive groups regarding *how* they stretched out had to do with their comparative integration of "jazz" and "classical" approaches (remember, these terms are simply used as stand-ins for approaches that are more improvisational or more "composed," respectively). Although this is a useful device for comparison, progressive rock is a good deal more complicated than this dichotomy allows for. While groups such as King Crimson or Soft Machine are clearly more on the "jazz" side of things (and many Soft Machine albums, beginning with 1970's *Third*, are very close to being jazz albums through and through), a group such as Magma, which released its first album in 1970, is equal parts Coltrane and Carl Orff.

A good many groups that were perhaps not as consistent or significant as those I have placed in the first line came on board with the trend in 1970, and their numbers continued to swell all the way through this key period, up through 1975. Certainly there were some important contributions here. The first album by a keyboard-centered trio appeared with drumming by Carl Palmer. I'm speaking, of course, of the self-titled record from Atomic Rooster. Vincent Crane, yet another of the many fine practitioners of the electronic organ active at that time, had previously been with The Crazy World of Arthur Brown. Brown's well-known single, "Fire," had perhaps a toe or two in the experimental scene, and a little more than one whole foot in theatrical performance and even emergent glam. Palmer went on to join a slightly better-known trio, while a reformed Atomic Rooster went in a much heavier direction.

Another trio centered on keyboards also debuted that year, namely Egg. The group was from the south of England and their first, self-titled, album fits in well with other music from that area—it is sometimes quite tuneful, often disjointed, and perhaps works too hard at being esoteric. Dave Stewart's organ playing is impressive throughout. He had previously played with Steve Hillage in a group called Uriel—in the first song on the album, bassist Mont Campbell sings of having also been with that band, "and now we're doing this instead," which kind of sums up the sensibility of the Canterbury scene. Stewart and Hillage would again team up in the group Khan about two years later, and Stewart went on to perform with Hatfield and the North, National Health, and Bruford. Egg is a good example of a "minor"—or, at any rate, not major—group that all the same occupies a significant place in the history of progressive rock.

Even still we are not done with keyboard trios. Quatermass released their one and only (self-titled) album in 1970 as well. Obviously, influence of The Nice was far-reaching, and many were happy to get away from those pesky guitarists! Named for a character from a 1950s sci-fi movie, the group was oriented toward blues and rock 'n' roll. Though the music is, frankly, not much to my liking, the album cover is one of the all-time greats.

Featuring two keyboardists, minimal guitar, and some fine vocals from a singing drummer, Rare Bird's second album, *As Your Mind Flies By* has many good moments. Significantly, all of side two is taken up with a four-movement piece, "Flight." 1970 was also the year of Robert Wyatt's first solo effort, *The End of an Ear*. This is a record of mostly free-form jazz, with assists from members of the Softs and Caravan. A much stronger effort would come from Wyatt four years later, though, unfortunately, following personal tragedy.

From the second line in 1970 we find four records that are truly outstanding works of progressive rock. The first two of these are, in some sense, marginal to the genre, and yet they would clearly make any extensive list of important progressive albums. Many readers will know Pete Brown from his songwriting collaboration with Jack Bruce. His group, Pete Brown and Piblokto!, released the succinctly titled *Things May Come and Things May Go But the Art School Dance Goes on Forever* in 1970. From the very first song, "High Flying Electric Bird," this is an album that draws one in with its charm—the playing is very loose, very spacy, sometimes on the verge of falling apart, definitely hippie music. Brown's voice is warm and vulnerable, and the instrumental work is just the opposite of any kind of uptight musical competition.

The other "marginal" album is perhaps better known to listeners in the United States, as it was widely perceived as a King Crimson "spin-off." I'm referring to the *McDonald and Giles* album, featuring Ian McDonald and Michael Giles from the first incarnation of the Crimson King. Ian McDonald is quite the multi-instrumentalist, playing guitar, saxophones, and keyboards, while both he and Giles are very good singers. They are joined on the album by Michael's brother Peter on bass guitar, as well as Steve Winwood on organ and piano (those connections again— McDonald, incidentally, was at one time the boyfriend of Fairport Convention singer Judy Dyble, who contributed some vocals to the nutty Giles, Giles, and Fripp album). Although the album contains a song based on the same chord progressions as "Cadence and Cascade" from *In the Wake of Poseidon*, which on *McDonald and Giles* is called "Flight of the Ibis," otherwise it is not very Crimsonish. Nor is *McDonald and Giles* any kind of virtuoso vehicle; instead much of the playing is rather restrained and tasteful (not a word I like very much, to be honest, but it fits well enough here). Both in its intrumental music and its lyrics, the long final track on side one, "Tomorrow's People," and the "Birdman" suite, which fills side two, are perfect expressions of progressive rock utopianism. After more than twenty-five years, *McDonald and Giles* remains fresh and hopeful.

I expect to receive a good deal of criticism for not including at least one of the next two groups in my first line, and possibly for both of them. In the cases of both Curved Air and Van der Graaf Generator there is a question of consistency. Van der Graff, too, I am inclined to compare with Pink Floyd, in terms of the level of musicianship. Finally, VDGG is so dominated by the presence of Peter Hammill, a remarkable talent to be sure, that it is sometimes hard to think of them as a group. VDGG did in fact fall apart repeatedly, only to be reconvened by Hammill, which makes the title of their second album especially appropriate: *The Least We Can Do is Wave to Each Other* (1970). Still, all of this will undoubtedly get me in trouble. In any case, both VDGG and Curved Air produced some excellent albums, including in the year under review.

Hammill brings a gothic, arch, and sometimes rather sinister air to much of his music. Hugh Banton's organ fleshes this feeling out nicely. (Regarding all of these organ accolades, I should mention that synthesizers were not yet fully in the game yet, but they will make a grand entrance in 1971.) It is not hard to imagine Robert Fripp working well in this context, and in fact he did contribute guitar to 1970's *H to He, Who Am the Only One* as well as to what many people regard as VDGG's best album, 1971's *Pawn Hearts*. Not known especially for difficult passages, Van der Graaf were masters of texture. The group traveled the minor keys most often, staying in the land of doom and suicide more than any other music of the progressive rock period. Though many readers will blanch at the comparison, it seems to me that Hammill is one of the few lyricists on a par with Jon Anderson and Steve Howe. Indeed, Hammill is perhaps even more committed to poetry per se, wrapping, in operatic manner, the music around verses of different and irregular lengths. *H to He* established VDGG as one of the few progressive groups that could resist linearity and yet still clearly belong to the genre.

Curved Air's *Airconditioning* was a bit more conventional, but still plenty interesting, especially because of the presence of two very impressive instrumentalists, namely Francis Monkman on keyboards (and he did employ the synthesizer to good effect) and Darryl Way on violin, as well the fine voice of one of the few women in progressive rock, Sonja Kristina. Although Vernon Joynson calls "It Happened Today" one of the albums weaker cuts, I'm quite taken with it myself. The two parts of the song, one intense and nervy, the other drawn out and relaxed, make for a very dramatic contrast. Way's violin in the second part is truly beautiful; to me, the song is progressive-rock utopianism in a nutshell.

Of the first-line groups, nine of the thirteen were active with new albums in 1970. (Incidentally, 1973 was the only year that all thirteen first-line groups had albums; 1973 and 1974 were, by far, the biggest years for progressive rock.) Yes (*Time and a Word*), Gentle Giant (self-titled), and Magma (self-titled) were still getting started. Indeed, Yes was still not entirely on the terrain of progressive rock, though their second album is quite good (see *music of Yes*, pp. 20–35). When compared to the group's third effort, *The Yes Album*, it is easy to see that the real leap to another level and kind of music was still to come.

1970 gave us the first Emerson, Lake, and Palmer album (self-titled). Perhaps overindulging Keith Emerson's abilities in places, elsewhere the music is nicely leavened by the contributions of Greg Lake. *Emerson, Lake, and Palmer*'s long track, "Take a Pebble," is really unprecedented in rock. In fact, except for the sources out of which it came (including the background of the musicians), there isn't much that is "rock" about it. The integration of a very pretty song, powerfully sung by Lake, with Emerson's delicate piano and Palmer's masterful cymbals, gives rise to one of the rare moments in progressive rock that is overwhelmingly *careful*. Such moments, it turns out, were to be even rarer in the subsequent career of ELP.

Genesis planted themselves firmly in the field of the still-emerging genre with *Trespass*. Though many fans of the group prefer their next two albums, *Nursery Cryme* and *Foxtrot*, to this one, I must admit that I am more fond of *Trespass*. This is not because, as the reader might suspect, the album features the early concert favorite "The Knife," though this is certainly a powerful piece. Instead, it is the combination of (very English, to my mind) gloominess and a feeling of being looked upon by benign forces evinced in the opening track, "Stagnation," that is so appealing. Already, Peter Gabriel was developing the narrative skills, the ability to draw an audience into a story, that served him so well during the progressive rock period—and even, to some extent, to this very day. Here, too, the silliness that creeps into some of the later compositions is not yet present. It should also be noted that, although Genesis was never to be thought of (thankfully) as a guitar-heavy group, *Trespass* established their ability to develop fine string textures, often using layers of twelve-string acoustic guitars.

By Soft Machine's *Third*, Kevin Ayers was more fully out of the band's system, and his "replacement," bass guitarist Hugh Hopper, played a fundamental role in the transition to an even jazzier approach to experimental rock. Consisting in two LP records and four side-long tracks, *Third* could be criticized for being little more than a series of loosely structured jams, with a "head" arrangement here or there to be sure (and "head" is right!), except that these improvisations were awfully good. The horn arrangements, featuring Elton Dean, Lyn Spall, Nick Evans, and Jimmy Hastings (brother of Caravan's Pye; Jimmy was later to turn up on Chris Squire's solo album, *Fish Out of Water*, among many other places) owed something, in my view, to the postbop, post-"cool" groups of Horace Silver and Herbie Hancock (especially the latter's *Maiden Voyage*). But what really stands out on the album is Mike Ratledge's crazy lead lines on the organ, which would have stood him in good stead with either Miles Davis (*Bitches Brew* and after) or Jimi Hendrix.

A somewhat transformed and augmented King Crimson gave us *In the Wake of Poseidon* early in 1970, while a new group built around Fripp and Sinfield produced *Lizard* in the second half of the year.

Incidentally, the *Lizard* group is sometimes called King Crimson Mk.II, though one loses track of these designations by and by.

One could group the different Crimsons by actual group members, in which case every album from the 1969 to 1974 was made by a different group, or by some other sense of "period." In any case, 1970 saw the first of King Crimson's many transitions and regroupings.

Crimson's second album is in many ways like the first. "Pictures of a City" is quite similar to "Schizoid Man," while "In the Wake of Poseidon" is not unlike "In the Court of the Crimson King." Although *In the Court of the Crimson King* will forever remain significant as the work that initiated a musical trend, my preference is for the second album, which I find altogether less overbearing. Each has its flaws, in fact, and it is unclear whether King Crimson really came together as a "group" until the glory years of *Larks' Tongues in Aspic*. Other groups changed members now and then, that other pillar of progressive rock, Yes, among them. But King Crimson gives the impression of often being on the verge of falling apart. One cannot help but attribute this to the intensity of the music, the times, and the group's key member and convener, Robert Fripp. Strangely, *In the Wake of Poseidon* is framed by three "Peace" themes, the bookends for voice and acoustic guitar and the middle one for guitar alone. Most everything else about the album is war and alienation: souls lost in hell, a world on the scales, and a transmogrification of the "Mars, Bringer of War" movement from Gustav Holst's *The Planets*, here called "The Devil's Triangle." (In the recently released live set from King Crimson circa 1969, *Epitaph*, the track is simply called "Mars.") The truly odd track out is "Cat Food," featuring the manic piano of Keith Tippett—the Beatles meet Cecil Taylor! None of the music here is really "lighter" than what is found on the first album, it just seems that way because *In the Wake* is more mature.

Progressive rock in 1970 produced three records that I would call "albums of the year," and one of these was that year's other album by King Crimson. *Lizard* demonstrates a further maturation of Peter Sinfield's vision (though the trippy elements are still present here and there) and a carefully controlled brittleness in the group's orchestrations. New singer Gordon Haskell's voice is distinctive, often eerie. Actually, in some of the pieces, Haskell's enunciation is more akin to a poetry reading than singing, but this works well with this material. Still, the new album takes quite a different direction in the vocal department.

Unfortunately, *Lizard* marks the beginning of a two-album sequence where a singer is also employed on bass guitar without much competence with the instrument. I've always found it a weakness with King Crimson that Robert Fripp, apparently, takes the bass role to be something of an afterthought. (On *Islands*, this deficiency is somewhat compensated for by the presence of the great and, sadly, late double bassist, Harry Miller.) This is odd, given that the group has featured some of the greatest drummers in all rock music, including possibly the most creative of rock drummers, Bill Bruford. For that matter, though Crimson has had some very good singers, and even a couple (Greg Lake and, perhaps controversially, John Wetton) whom I regard as great, Fripp seems to regard this area in a similar way. (Significantly, at the point when Fripp really did seem to want a singing "frontman," he obtained the services of Adrian Belew, whose voice often grates.) In this connection, I've become very tired of hearing Bill Bruford (in numerous interviews) characterize Yes as somehow mainly a "vocal" group, while King Crimson is ostensibly the greater unit when it comes to instrumental work. To be sure, Yes does not excel in the sorts of improvisations that King Crimson carries to extraordinary heights, but the fact is that not only the "chops" but also the application of the instrumental abilities of a Steve Howe or a Chris Squire are excelled by no one and equaled by very few. In many ways I see Yes as the more "complete" *group*, while King Crimson, with Robert Fripp at the helm, has more the character of a (generally intermittent) *project*. And, on another level, this comparison comes down to apples and oranges, or perhaps a dichotomy of the basic possibilities of the genre, and I am grateful that we've been given the remarkable work of both groups.

This griping aside, which may not have much to do with the actual music as we find it on *Lizard*, the album is quite low key and contains many subtleties. Apart from the harsh Mellotron strings in the opening track, "Cirkus," and some intense, almost screaming electric guitar in "Bolero," much of *Lizard* is very quiet. As with *Islands*, *Lizard* features several horn players, sometimes forming a horn section from no jazz ever heard before, sometimes, as in "Bolero," sounding a loneliness not unlike Miles Davis's muted trumpet work from *Sketches of Spain*. Keith Tippett once again contributes on piano, this time sounding even more atomistic, and, as most readers will know, Jon Anderson sings the opening piece in side two's five-part "Lizard," "Prince Rupert Awakes." Anderson's high, clear voice might not have worked for an entire King Crimson album, but, for this one song, it's perfect. Whereas *In the Wake of Poseidon* gives us a little peace and a lot of war, *Lizard* reiterates themes of circus and play throughout, from "Cirkus" to the instrumental closer, "Big Top." The "circus" of rock music itself seems to be a theme here, with "Happy Family" almost certainly being a commentary on the breakup of the Beatles ("four went on but none came back"). Like actual circuses and carnivals, *Lizard* has a grim and creepy side. The album cover, conceived by Peter Sinfield and executed by Gini Barris, intertwines circus and medieval scenes with depictions of the Beatles (John Lennon holds a genie's bottle out of which is coming, of course, Yoko Ono), Jimi Hendrix (though playing right-handed), Ginger Baker, and a flutist who may or may not be Ian Anderson. The whole package demonstrates the important role, often overlooked, of Peter Sinfield in not only supplying lyrics but also ideas and unifying themes.

Jethro Tull's music reached a new level with *Benefit*. The blues and folk influences that were readily visible on Tull's first two albums are here subsumed into a more straightforward form of rock music. It might even be argued that *Benefit* is simply a very good album of rock music, without exactly being "progressive." Ian Anderson's songwriting shows great craft and economy, and only three of the album's ten songs are over five minutes long (and the longest of these clocks in at 6'15"). Although there is some piano and organ on the album, the thing that stands out is the rich guitar texture—provided by Anderson on acoustic, Barre on electric, and Glen Cornick on bass. One of the best examples of this consists in the articulated electric chords on "Teacher," which also features some very melodic, McCartney-like, bass lines.

Benefit opens, appropriately enough, with the welling-up of Anderson's flute, still in his distinctive style, but not so harsh as it can sometimes be. A muted, pleading voice ultimately gives way to a hard, yet full and rich, electric guitar, beginning a series of dynamic contrasts that develop to great effect throughout the album. In emotional tone, too, *Benefit* contrasts the heavy and the playful, with touches of melancholy in abundance. The blues influence of the earlier albums is somewhat superseded by the jazziness of "Inside," which also features a great, rolling chorus ("I'm sittin' on the corner feelin' glad"). What a neat idea, too, to write a song about the ultimate case of being left behind, "For Michael Collins, Jeffrey, and Me." Again there is a wonderful chorus that runs the complete emotional range, from the celebratory "I'm with You LEM" (Lunar Entry Module—the song is about the astronaut who stayed behind with the Apollo spacecraft on the first manned moon landing, not about the Irish freedom fighter), to the final words, barely audible and trailing-off. Here too is Anderson's emerging preoccupation with the term "money," as carrier of corruption—a theme that will develop on a much larger scale with *Aqualung*. The jazz-blues-folk synthesis comes entirely together with the album's closer, "Sossity, You're a Woman."

Finally, perhaps even exceeding *Benefit* in the sheer charm category, 1970 also gave us the wonderful Caravan album, *In the Land of Grey and Pink*. This is a great example of what the idea of the "concept album" meant at this point; there is no overriding concept for *Grey and Pink*—indeed, there was never really anything so philosophical as a "concept" that much troubled Caravan—but what we do find is such a sense of the *vibe*. The album begins with a horn flourish and a bit of goofiness, "Golf Girl." Obviously, and as previously mentioned, the Caravan sense of the better world is a bit too tied up with the decidedly nonconcept, "girl." However, the song certainly does not lack wit. "Winter Wine," track two, is the strongest song on the album. With an acoustic introduction and plaintive vocals, we have now entered another plane, in fact a utopian dreamscape. When the "rock" part of the song starts, a complex negotiation begins, between rural and urban possibilities of a transformed world. Unsurprisingly, the urban vision includes "naked dancers" and the like. Although I'll probably get into trouble for this bit of apologetics, in the context of the times this seems innocent enough, something like a sweet eroticism. The dancers are also a stand-in for the exoticism of the city, when seen from the countryside. As with most Caravan tunes, there is a trace of melancholy here, and the song ends with a return to its original pastoral setting. There is a great organ solo, by David Sinclair, in the midst of all this.

"Love to Love You" returns to the pop territory of "Golf Girl," and side one closes with the title track. The jumpy rhythm of "In the Land of Grey and Pink" fits nicely the "Boy Scout" expedition hinted at in the opening verse—again, the whole album is pure fantasy landscape, a bit out of Tolkein. One cannot help but keep the album cover in mind, too, a wonderful drawing by Anne Marie Anderson that is one of the great sleeves from the genre.

With the exception of "Winter Wine," side one serves as something of a "light programme," in preparation for the flip side's lengthy eight-part suite, "Nine Feet Underground." But even this nearly twenty-three minute long excursion is rarely heavy. Parts of "Nine Feet Underground" are very rocking, but never in an overbearing way, while other parts are quite contemplative. In the early seventies, this was late-night FM radio (which was a new thing then) music, and it is hard not to still think of it that way, even if there aren't many stations left that are cool enough to play Caravan. The piece is mostly instrumental, and, among the few lyrics there is a wonderful verse about the weather ("Will the day be warm and bright. . ."); nothing here seems especially grim, and much very hopeful, but there is an undercurrent of sweet sadness. Like many listeners, I often wish that I could live in this peaceable kingdom.

1971

Significantly, 1971 did not see a great increase in progressive rock activity; the real explosion was still a year or two away. One could argue, I suppose, that this indicates that more groups jumped on the progressive rock bandwagon at the point when it became clear that earlier groups had opened a pathway (or, more cynically, a market niche), and as the sixties receded into the past. However, I tend to read the situation differently. Contrary to much conventional wisdom, the sixties did not end in 1969 or even 1970; there was a spark that remained alive for some time into the chronological seventies, and the progressive rock "idea" incorporated this spark in terms of experiments with form and lyrical content.

Of course, conflicting interpretations of the period are possible, but it seems to me that progressive rock represented a root impulse of the period in its continual drive to take things further—to be "progressive." Some will call the addition of new groups to the scene a mere bandwagon effect; instead, I propose that musicians were *inspired* by the idea that rock music was becoming an expansive form in which anything seemed possible. If I could put this in personal terms, terms that I hope will resonate with readers who either remember the time of progressive rock directly, or who have subsequently been inspired by that time (and perhaps this will speak most of all to the musicians among us): I know that, when I heard albums such as *In the Court of the Crimson King* and, especially, *Fragile*, I didn't just say to myself, "Gee, here's a bandwagon I could jump on, because that's what all the cool kids are doing." As I recall, most of the "cool kids" were into Grand Funk Railroad or maybe Led Zeppelin, or probably the same mainstream rock and pop they've always been into. When I first heard *In the Court of the Crimson King*, I was knocked over, as most listeners were, by the incredible force and range of the music. I really did not know what to do with it, but, on the other hand, I couldn't get those sounds out of my head. A couple years later, when I had started playing guitar and bass guitar myself, *Fragile* came out. Hearing "Roundabout" on the radio, it seemed that a whole new world was opened for me, for everyone else, for music. The long and short of this bit of reminiscence is that the cynical interpretation of those times has to do with a more recent, and to my mind deadly, impulse to cynically dismiss everything from the sixties and its aftermath that can be put under the heading of the "all that": the idealism, the radicalism, hopefulness, utopianism, and romanticism.

Condemnation of progressive rock comes from these cynical quarters; the problem is, if one approaches the music from this perspective, I really don't know that one can actually *hear* this music.

Among the highlights of the year in rock more generally were Argent's *Ring of Hands* (featuring the great anthem, "Hold Your Head Up"); Chicago's third album; Funkadelic's *Maggot Brain*; Led

Zeppelin's fourth album; Joni Mitchell's *Blue*; the Moody Blues'
Every Good Boy Deserves Favour; Pink Floyd's *Meddle*; *From the
Witchwood* by The Strawbs (still featuring Mr. Wakeman); and
War's *All Day Music*. Though progressive rock was increasingly
going its own way, it is still possible to hear some of the major
progressive albums of that year in terms of a play list that
includes these other rock albums. Mind expansion was more the
order of the day, categories aside.

    1971 also saw the release of one of the great jam albums of all
time, The Allman Brothers Band *At Fillmore East*—hard country
blues stretched to the limit, often with great sensitivity. And, a
tune such as "Hotlanta" has clear affinities with progressive rock,
as well as the emerging jazz-rock. Another important album that
incorporated jazz, Latin, and African influences, also with affinities to progressive rock, was Traffic's *The Low Spark of High Heeled
Boys*. The title track is, somehow, both jazz and rock without
really being "jazz-rock," or what was coming to be called "fusion."
Further interplay in this vein was represented by Frank Zappa's
Grand Wazoo, as well as the first Weather Report album (self-
titled). Perhaps staying closer to the terrain of jazz were two projects from Keith Tippett, the excellent *Dedicated to You, But You
Weren't Listening* (named for a Soft Machine tune and with a cover
by Roger Dean) and the controversial *Septober Energy*. This latter
project was performed by about fifty musicians assembled by
Tippett, under the name "Centipede," and the album was produced
by Robert Fripp. Until Cecil Taylor was finally able to marshall
the resources for orchestral works (not until the later eighties),
Septober Energy was probably the largest experiment in free jazz.
It's difficult stuff, and the return rate on the album may even be up
there in Lou Reed's *Metal Machine Music* territory; in my view, this
is a significant experiment, if not always one that gives pleasure.

    A pair of albums that also sit on the edge of progressive rock
and, because of their Roger Dean cover art cannot help but be
associated with the genre, are the self-titled and *Woyaya* records
by Osibisa. This was a group of (mostly) African musicians, synthesizing both indigenous sources and musics from the West that
had been transformed in Black Africa into high life, macossa, and
juju. On the view that the "universal" must come through the par-

ticular, we see in Osibisa's albums—and in those of Fela Kuti, King Sunny Ade, Manu Dibango, Mandrill, and many others—how a whole other "progressive rock" could be formed from other cultural sources.

By the way, if any disk jockeys out there would like to use these annual surveys as play lists, *please*, be my guest! And, dear reader, let us also think for a moment on this world of music as it was emerging in the early seventies. I know that there is some very interesting music being made today, so I do not want to get into the frame of mind that says the glory days are behind us and everything now is no good, but it does seem to me that a survey such as the one just presented, along with the progressive albums that I will now turn to, represents a time when you could not help but feel that great things were happening—a feeling of great possibility, a feeling that I just do not get when I hear or think about, say, music that is made with samplers.

Of the second-line groups, Can presented what some consider to be their best work, *Tago Mago*. This double album featured one record of more structured music, and one of Can's unique improvisations, which owe virtually nothing to jazz or blues. Darryl Way and Francis Monkman divided the two sides of Curved Air's *Second Album* between them, compositionally speaking, and to good effect. Egg also presented their second effort, *The Polite Force*, continuing their work with difficult time signatures.

Van der Graaf Generator produced one of the most significant albums of the year, *Pawn Hearts*. Side two is taken up with the eight-part suite, "A Plague of Lighthouse Keepers," which many find to be the group's best work. Many of the hallmarks of progressive rock are there, especially the intricate ensemble work, the twisted church organ, and dramatic time changes; the emotional range of the work, which includes quiet passages of little more than piano and voice as well as full-scale rants and instrumental explosions, is perhaps greater than most of what has come from the genre. Certainly the macabre side of Peter Hammill and VDGG is seen in such titles as "The Clot Thickens." Side one also features two long works, including "Lemmings," with its images of technology out of control: "Young minds and bodies on steel spokes impaled." This harsh imagery recalls "21st Century

Schizoid Man," and impalement is also a theme in "The Letters" from Crimson's album for the year in question, *Islands*. The following year would see Yes singing of the "cold stainless nail" in "Siberian Khatru." What gives—is this a foreshadowing of the piercing fetish that has more recently come in vogue? But seriously, VDGG's "Lemmings" is part of their continued engagement with apocalyptic themes. Hammill may seem to strike a hopeful note, contrasting to the lemmings' death-wish the line, "What choice is there left but to live"? But, as Kafka once said, "there is plenty of hope, just not for us"—similarly, Hammill's life-wish is for the "little ones" four generations removed.

In the previous chapter, I drew a distinction between progressive rock at its most harsh and antimelodic and at its most lush and romantic (in the sense of drawing from late-romantic European classical music), using the examples of Henry Cow and Renaissance. As I mentioned, I have some serious issues, as they say, with the music of the latter. Here another distinction suggests itself, though one that I hope will not diminish either example. Van der Graaf constantly works the theme of death against life, what Freud framed in terms of thanatos and eros (the death and life "principles," respectively). I do not think I am going out on a limb in saying that thanatos seems to get the greater share of attention in VDGG's music (and in Peter Hammill's solo recordings). By contrast, although there is strife, tragedy, hardship, war, and heartbreak in the music of Yes (this despite what I call the "blissed out" interpretation of Yes, which has been offered often enough by both the band's detractors and many of its fans), one will never find *thanatos* in this music. Never is there the sense that death could somehow be its own principle or reality. Life will win through. Eros is abundant in the music of Yes, in its truest form: in the sense of a willingness to *embrace* the cosmos. (Eros is often associated with sex, of course, and this is not an inappropriate association; however, the concept is both broader and deeper.)

Between these two groups, then, there are two philosophies (or perhaps theologies). Perhaps the distinction could be further developed in terms of one group, Van der Graaf, being more "apocalyptic," while the other, Yes, might be considered more "millennial." Just as there are philosophies in the Western tradition (and, I assume, in other traditions as well, but here I am not competent to say) that represent either extreme—on the one hand, death is simply the lack of life, or, on the other hand, death is a force in its own right—as well as mediating positions in between, so VDGG and Yes might be considered to represent two opposite poles. The interesting thing would be if it turned out that fans who were more attracted to one group rather than the other were also attracted to the one philosophy more than the other. As trippy as the scene around progressive rock is at times, my guess is that listeners are probably able to line up the groups and philosophies pretty well—a sign, I think, of progressive rock as a *thoughtful* form of rock music. (Which means that, while these two sides are throwing insults at each other, those who just want to dance and party dismiss the whole lot.)

The positions just mentioned, regarding life and death, also map onto a longstanding debate regarding good and evil. Plato argued long ago that evil is simply a form of ignorance (while the good is a form of knowledge). Manichean thinkers, as well as Immanuel Kant, argue that there is such a thing as "radical evil," evil that exists in its own right. Although I am personally inclined toward Plato's position (or something like it), the Holocaust stands in its way. It is extremely difficult, and perhaps unjust, to think of the Nazi genocide in terms of what people either knew or did not know. As one philosopher of a more Aristotelian persuasion, Margaret Anscombe, put it some years ago, In what sense could it be *explained* to someone that it is wrong to take a newborn baby from its mother and throw it into an oven? What would be the *content* of this explanation?

On the other hand, one does sometimes hear of people who have gone through remarkable transformations. And, surely it is an inadequate view of the Holocaust to only focus on personal character and motivations and to ignore the (social) systemic factors. It does justice to no one, nor will it help to prevent other attempted genocides, to simply think it all comes down to the evil nature of Hitler or a handful of Nazi leaders.

In other words, this is a difficult and complex philosophical question; insomuch as the creatively expressed outlooks of different musical groups can be understood in the terms of this question, I see a range of works that can be appreciated and learned from. I want to learn from Kant as well as Plato; I want to hear (and learn from) Van der Graaf Generator as well as Yes, even if I ultimately prefer one to the other.

However, recalling the earlier discussion of cynical impulses and "all that," it is not difficult to see that, in a less hopeful time, some critics might be more drawn to the music of thanatos than that of eros (especially if the latter is not exactly dance music). And yet, everyone will continue to love Caravan—I know that I will—who were certainly at the eros end of the spectrum. Indeed, the assumption on the part of those who make a "mainstream" versus "alternative" distinction within progressive rock (as Paul Stump does; I will take this up in the afterword) is probably that the latter are more on the side of what I've called thanatos. But I doubt very seriously that this holds up.

Nine of the thirteen first-line groups released albums in 1971. Caravan's *Waterloo Lilly* is not nearly as strong as their previous effort, though "The Love in Your Eye" is a beautiful song. Dave Sinclair had left the group at this point, which perhaps goes some way in explaining the slump. With *1001° Centigrade*, Magma further developed the story of the interaction between Earth and the planet Kobaia. Led by Christian Vander, one of the great percussionists of our time, Magma employed chantlike phrase repetitions in a language of their own invention, on top of an instrumental background of equal parts Coltrane and Orff. In 1972, the Mahavishnu Orchestra would come on the scene, with a cosmic jazz-rock fusion that was to have wide influence. In many respects, however, Magma had already gone some distance down that road. Bridging to some extent the Canterbury of Caravan and Magma's Paris, Daevid Allen and Gong released *Camembert Electrique* ("electric cheese"), featuring the space whisper of Gilli Smyth (a.k.a. Shakti—and sometimes Bambaloni—Yoni), the saxophone and flute of Didier Malherbe (a.k.a. Bloomdido Bad De Grasse), and the drums of the excellent Pip Pyle. Chant is in evidence here, too, as is funky word-play and Smyth's unique vocal contribution. At times the album is a bit too obviously the product of stoned hippies on an extended space jam, but *Camembert* also has many lively moments. Although there are apparently two earlier albums from these cultural agitators—as Allen liked to think of himself and his fellow pixies—these are quite rare (I've never seen them, in fact), while *Camembert* established Gong as a musical force.

Jethro Tull increased their stateside popularity with *Aqualung*, whose title track drew in not only progressive-rock fans, but also listeners into heavy metal and hard rock. Thematically, much of the album is a meditation on the shortcomings of religion, especially of the Christian variety. Ian Anderson writes in the tone of someone who feels betrayed; indeed, the lyrics have a Kierkegaardian cast to them, in the sense of attacking Christendom for its failure to live up to the teachings of Christ: "If Jesus saves, then he'd better save himself"—from "money" and its servants, that is. The sumptuous weave of guitars from *Benefit* is generally replaced here with the much heavier and distorted sound of blockish chords and lead riffs. At points, I find this so overbearing that it is easy to forget the many dynamic contrasts of *Aqualung*. And, of course, things seem a bit out of kilter from the start, with the figure of the "aqualung" as some sort of religious icon, especially when mixed in with snot running down noses and little girls of bad intent. This was Clive Bunker's last album with the group, and undoubtedly his best performance. *Aqualung* also saw the replacement of bassist Glenn Cornick with Jeffrey Hammond-Hammond, which was a step back, I'm afraid. Indeed, this change in line-up was probably what opened the door to a greater emphasis on electric guitar riffs, which are much in abundance in Tull's next two albums. On the other hand, the "Aqualung" guitar solo, by Martin Barre, is certainly among the all-time great ones. The album cover, including its color scheme of dark greens and browns, contributes well to the project. Incidentally, Anderson's tone vis-à-vis Christianity will be somewhat echoed in parts of Emerson, Lake, and Palmer's album for 1971, *Tarkus*.

Gentle Giant's second album, the appropriately titled *Acquiring the Taste*, demonstrated that the Shulman brothers, Gary Green, and Kerry Minear were prepared to move into the first ranks of progressive rock. If eclecticism is, as Robert Fripp argues, one of the hallmarks of progressive rock, then Gentle Giant was perhaps the most eclectic of all. They would sometimes take this to the point of distraction, in my view, starting with *Three Friends*. There is an undercurrent running throughout *Acquiring the Taste*, however, that gives the album more unity than is found on later efforts. With its moon imagery and restrained dynamics, *Acquiring the Taste* actually has in abundance what few listeners would associate with the group, namely *warmth*.

If I have my nomenclature right, *Islands* is still considered a product of King Crimson "Mk.II." All the same, the group has two new members, vocalist and bass guitarist Boz (Burrell) and percussionist Ian Wallace. As with *Lizard* drummer Andy McCulloch, Wallace is loaded with both jazz and rock chops, which is indeed the way with all Crimson drummers (with the possible exception of more recent *Thrak* drummer Pat Mastelloto, who, make no mistake, is a very good rock drummer). Boz continues the "eerie" vocal stylings of Gordon Haskell, actually taking this a good deal further. Keith Tippett, three wind players (in addition to regular member Mel Collins), and double bassist Harry Miller augment the band, to especially great effect on the extended instrumental piece, "Sailor's Tale." The album also begins on a surprising note, with Miller's bowed contrabass introducing "Formentara Lady." Though Burrell's bass-playing ability was rather limited at that point (which didn't keep him from making the big bucks later with the supergroup Bad Company), his pedal point in this song is effective. "The Letters" deals with marital infidelity, while "Ladies of the Road" (two "lady" titles in one Crimson album—weird!) is in places a rather crude account of the groupie scene; I can't help but recall a statement that Robert Fripp made in *Melody Maker* back in those days, something to the effect that, "A rock star is someone who is available to young ladies, and I am." It seems that experimentation in musical form was not entirely incompatible with certain other aspects of the mainstream rock 'n' roll lifestyle at that point. The debate among Crimson fans regarding which is better, *Lizard* or *Islands*, rages on; though I prefer the former, I have to admit that *Islands* is right up there.

From the eerie back to the macabre, with Genesis's third effort, *Nursery Cryme*. The members of Genesis, well-off public-school (which in the U.S. means private-school) kids with the exception of new drummer Phil Collins, here present the underside of polite Victorian culture. The "nursery cryme" in question is narrated in the album's first and longest track, "The Musical Box." One sees Peter Gabriel becoming increasingly theatrical with each Genesis album, and here he assumes the role of a young boy who suddenly finds himself changed into an old man after being murdered by his young female croquet companion— Kafka with a strong bit of the legendary English quirkiness mixed in. Stranger still is the crossing of strange theology and lust in the song's conclusion. While *Nursery Cryme* is slightly more adventurous than the group's first two albums, it is still relatively quiet, and again employs the rich guitar textures (especially twelve-string guitar) which were becoming a Genesis trademark.

Yes and Emerson, Lake, and Palmer each released two albums in 1971. Two of these, *Tarkus* and *Fragile*, are in my view the most important progressive rock albums of that year. After *Tarkus*, ELP released a live recording of their arrangement of Mussorgsky's "Pictures at an Exhibition." To be honest, I have never been able to warm to this album—as with some of the rather bombastic treatments of classical works by The Nice, I would rather hear the original (which, in this case, means either Mussorgsky's original piano suite, or the better-known orchestration by Ravel). This isn't mere snobbism, I hope; instead, it just seems to me that some of Keith Emerson's attempts to "update" the classics work better as live showpieces (or show-off pieces, as the case may be) than as recordings that stand up to repeated listening.

On a whole other plane was Yes's third album, *The Yes Album*. With the addition of the brilliant Steve Howe, Yes underwent a remarkable transformation, from a quasi-psychedelic group whose first two albums are quite enjoyable, to an emerging progressive rock group whose albums have to reckoned with as significant contributions to music. Even though the level of musicianship went up (which is not meant as a slight on the excellent Peter Banks, who would go on to do better work with his own group, Flash, as well as with a superb solo album), in some ways the group simplified their song structures on *The Yes Album*. The pieces are less busy and cluttered—indeed, everything is so *clear* on this record, which retains its charm to this day. Lyrically, as well, the Yes vision presents itself on a new level, for instance with "Yours Is No Disgrace," a remarkable and subtle song about the Vietnam War, or "Your Move/I've Seen All Good People," which explores male/female relationships in terms of the game of chess. "Perpetual Change" is a complex meditation on the metaphysics of human action and hubris (inspired by the Apollo moon landing), as well as an anthem for the group's approach to music in the time of progressive rock. Though Tony Kaye was now the only member of the group not in possession of extraordinary instrumental skills, his contribution here is exemplary—understated and unpretentious, especially in his piano part in the closing measures of the underrated gem, "A Venture." Bruford, too, is restrained, with his subtle use of syncopation. As he would especially show on King Crimson's *Larks' Tongues* and *Red* albums, Bruford is one of the few drummers who can be just as effective and even forceful with what he doesn't play as with what he does. Indeed, Bruford and Fripp are a progressive-rock dream team when it comes to playing with listener's expectations. But let us not forget that Bruford's musicianship is also a crucial part of the very important trilogy of Yes albums that would begin with *The Yes Album*. Chris Squire, as always, is right out front with his trebly Rickenbacker, playing the dual role of providing a contrapuntal backbone to the music even while often leading. And Steve Howe brought influences that are often not heard in progressive rock, including a whole range of "American" music: country, as especially influenced by Chet Atkins, Appalachian flat-picking (heard not only on the solo guitar piece, "Clap," but also in the middle section of "Starship Trooper"), and even a bit of rock 'n' roll á la Chuck Berry. With one foot in progressive rock, and the other still in the larger experimental and psychedelic scene, Yes's third effort may not yet be a great *progressive* rock album, but it is a great *rock* album nonetheless.

Certainly the early seventies was a time of qualitative developments in rock music experimentation, and ELP made an important leap with *Tarkus*. The album is built around a seven-part suite, also called "Tarkus," lasting almost twenty-one minutes. Edward Macan has provided an extended analysis of "Tarkus" in his *Rocking the Classics* (see pp. 87–95). Claiming that "Tarkus" is in many ways "the archetypal progressive rock multimovement suite," Macan explains that the piece came out of Keith Emerson's explorations in the percussive and atonal piano music of

Bela Bartók and Alberto Ginastera. Originally, Greg Lake was skeptical of the idea, deeming the piece too avant-garde for the rock audience. However, once he worked his way into the non-standard (for rock, at any rate) time signatures and got a feel for Emerson's chords, Lake came fully onboard and even contributed the sixth part of the suite, "Battlefield" (along with lyrics for parts two and four). Thematically, the work concerns technology run amok, in a world where the killing machines have taken over. (As mentioned earlier, think of the first *Terminator* film.) Emerson builds his multiple keyboard work around the surging Hammond, using both the organ's percussion settings and springy Moog notes to create powerful rhythms. The whole work is a great study in dynamic contrast. In the middle of all this is the movement titled "Mass" (part four), which exhibits a harsh skepticism regarding religion, recalling not only Ian Anderson but also John Lennon (and, in fact, the basic tune for "Mass" is very "Beatles").

Starting with *Tarkus*, and most likely motivated by the desire to provide comic relief from the heavier works, ELP included a number of light and often silly songs on their albums. Here the offerings are "Jeremy Bender" and "Are You Ready Eddy?" (referring to recording engineer Eddie Offord). While the former is the much better of the two, in general I would have preferred that these exercises not been undertaken in the first place. On the other hand, I can easily imagine the typical antiprogressive rock critic thinking these are among the few places where the genre shows a sense of humor—but then, why give them the satisfaction?

Beyond "Tarkus," the other highlights of the album are the shorter pieces "Bitches Crystal" and "Infinite Space," the latter an instrumental work that employs alternating time signatures. Other than the occasional use of piano, *Tarkus* is a very "electric" album, with few acoustic sounds. And yet it is not a "cold" album, despite its subject matter, with warmth provided especially by Emerson's Hammond and Lake's voice.

Although *The Yes Album* and the coming of Steve Howe was the turning point for Yes (not only in musical terms; apparently the group was in danger of losing their recording contract), *Fragile* was their breakthrough effort. Three new players were involved at that point: Rick Wakeman, most obviously, but also Roger Dean and Eddie Offord. The latter had, in fact, produced

The Yes Album as well, but his considerable mixing talents were especially needed for *Fragile*, where everything was much more complex: large-scale keyboard and guitar orchestrations, complicated vocal harmonies, and even a track (Chris Squire's "The Fish") that developed a minor symphony of bass guitar sounds.

In contrast to the album's title and cover art, which depicts an Earth that is coming apart, *Fragile* is one of the most *vibrant* and inviting albums in all of progressive rock. Indeed, given the commercial success of the opening song, "Roundabout," we often forget two very important things. First, "Roundabout" literally drew *millions* into the orbit of progressive rock. Those who want to fragment the movement, in the name of the supposed superiority of one or two groups, could stand to remember this. I suppose that, as with the earlier afficionados of punk or, for that matter, Bruce Springsteen, the response will be that, at the point when this music became more popular, it somehow lost its original spirit or it was no longer as adventurous. But this brings us to the second point, namely that "Roundabout" is truly a brilliant piece of music which owes apologies to no one. From its opening classical figure in the acoustic guitar and backward piano chords, to its electric/acoustic contrasts, its bass line that is like nothing heard before from the instrument, its remarkable syncopation and weird snare *bonk*, its complex instrumental and vocal harmonies, and its poetic lyrics, "Roundabout" is one of the great achievements of progressive rock and of music more generally. And even its shortened, radio-single version, which most listeners in the United States probably first heard on AM radio, opened an incalculable number of doors.

Fragile was a record that established, more than any album had before, the hermetic sensibility in progressive rock: the notions of connectedness, of hidden meanings, of there being no strict separation between the human and the natural, or even between the organic and the inorganic. Certainly Roger Dean's cover and booklet art set the tone, and, as with King Crimson's first four albums, *Fragile* was something to be looked at while it was listened to. Indeed, a useful cultural barometer might be noted here: consider that, at least for a certain generation, there was greater satisfaction in sitting on one's bed holding an album cover such as this and listening to the music, than there is in watching the frantic jump-cut videos provided on MTV. This is just as much a comment on the time as on the media: if progressive rock is "sixties music" not so much through its more direct engagement with the times and events as with bearing within it the trace of utopian longings, then it certainly seems out of place in the time of MTV, where everything is reduced to the televisual surface. Hermeticism, to be sure, is just as out of place in the culture of depthlessness.

Fragile consists in four group pieces, three of them fairly long, and five solo works. Of the latter, the most interesting are Steve Howe's delicious acoustic guitar piece "Mood for a Day" and Chris Squire's innovative orchestration for bass guitars, percussion, and voice, "The Fish." The album might even have worked better with Howe's piece as a bridge on side one and Squire's on side two, with the other solo works left aside. Still, Jon Anderson's "We Have Heaven" does give a glimpse of what he would later achieve with his solo album, *Olias of Sunhillow*. (Significantly, Paul Stump has called *Olias* "probably the most complete manifesto to Progressive ideology"; see p. 188.)

Side one's closer, "South Side of the Sky," is a study in contrast, between harsh, jagged sections and incomparable warmth. As is often the case with Steve Howe, the electric guitar work here is frightening in its intensity and vituosity, while the piece's middle section features no guitar at all, but instead a kind of jazz trio (with Wakeman's piano, Squire, and Bruford's great cymbal work) with three- and four-part vocal harmonies on top. The song, too, is another great example of how, contrary to received opinion, Yes music is not all bliss and happiness: the song is basically about a failed arctic mission where everyone freezes to death.

In a not-dissimilar vein, side two's "Long Distance Runaround" and "Heart of the Sunrise" are about dishonesty in personal relationships and urban alienation, respectively. "Heart of the Sunrise" opens with one of Squire's amazing bass lines, stabbing, pulsing, uncoiling like a spring, with clear indebtedness to Paul McCartney and John Entwistle, but taking the instrument into completely new and uncharted territory. Apparently the opening riff was a take-off on "21st Century Schizoid Man," at least according to Howe (see Morse, *Yesstories*, p. 32). Jon Anderson takes his voice to new heights here, in the only song on the album that does not employ vocal harmonies.

On this last point, perhaps something additional needs to be said. In my experience, there are a good many people who are into progressive rock but who do not like Yes. More often than not, this hinges on the reaction to Jon Anderson's voice. This voice is certainly unique or quite close to it, in that Anderson sings in what is usually considered a female vocalist's range, namely alto. (For male singers, this range is sometimes called countertenor.) Although I would argue that the appreciation of music is not a merely subjective matter, and that there are cognitive aspects to this appreciation (in other words, greater knowledge can increase appreciation), it may be difficult to extend this argument to matters of the human voice. That is, this seems to be a case where a person could say something on the order of, "I recognize that x is a good (or competent, talented) singer, I just don't happen to like x's voice." Certainly the link between voice and subjectivity has been well-established, at least ever since Descartes heard an inner voice that said, "I think, therefore I exist." For that matter, the idea of the inner voice in Western traditions certainly goes back to Bible times.

However, although formulating the argument that could come between the voice and pure subjectivism would be no easy task, there are still things that can be said about why we respond in the ways that we do to certain kinds of voices. Progressive rock is already one of the more "feminine" kinds of rock music, or at least it seems to have more of a feminine aspect; however, perhaps a truly feminine voice, especially when it comes from a male singer, presses this point in a way that is too close for comfort in an androcentric (male-centered) society. In this respect, recall as well the discussion from the second chapter, regarding Little Richard and what might be called the deconstruction of gender categories. Yes, of course, is a very trebly band in any case, especially with Chris Squire's Rickenbacker (and Rotosound-string) bass and the way that Bill Bruford, like most jazz drummers, tends to emphasize the "top kit" (especially cymbals). Furthermore, there is rarely any kind of rock 'n' roll heaviness in Yes's "rhythm section." Indeed, the term does not really apply, as it is one of Yes's prime innovations to have distributed this function throughout the band—and *Fragile* demonstrated a new level in this approach. The music generally has a "center," to be sure, and yet this center is not to be found in the playing of any one or two musicians, even in the bass guitar and percussion. In this I find Yes virtually unique.

I mention these things in part because there has been a move on to separate Yes from some of the more innovative progressive groups. Not to be too much on the defensive, but perhaps those who are doing the separating might stop to compare some of the innovations just discussed with what other groups were doing. Finally, with *The Yes Album* and *Fragile*, it became clear that something like a "Yes vision" or even "ideology" (to mention a term that Jon Anderson uses from time to time) was emerging, and that there has been a general coherence to this vision even until more recent times. Here again one sees a reason for thinking of Yes and King Crimson as the two pillars: Yes was the most consistent in developing a musical language and lyrical vision throughout the time of progressive rock, while King Crimson continually reconfigured and reinvented itself.

1972

The activity in and around progressive rock increased in 1972; clearly, the trend was still growing. A good many interesting albums on the fringes of the movement were made in that year. (Again, as with music discussed in my "prehistory" of progressive rock, these albums have a validity of their own, regardless of how they relate to progressive, but they are mentioned here specifically because of their relationship with the progressive trend.) The progressive soul trend acquired two major documents with Stevie Wonder's *Talking Book* and War's *The World Is a Ghetto*, excellent albums that each had a huge impact. Bob Marley also became a real international force that year, with *Catch a Fire*. Santana's fourth album, *Caravanserai*, was a masterpiece of understatement. Weather Report released the visionary *I Sing the Body Electric*. Bridging the space between progressive rock and just plain good rock songwriting was the double record from that wizard and true star, Todd Rundgren, *Something/Anything*. In a heavier vein, 1972 saw the release of Hawkwind's *Doremi Fasol*

Latido, Uriah Heep's *Demons and Wizards* and *Magician's Birthday*—with Roger Dean covers, and Deep Purple's *Machine Head*. Two years later, incidentally, Chicago-based jazz saxophonist Eddie Harris would make an album in London that would bring together musicians from Yes (Chris Squire, Alan White, Tony Kaye) and Deep Purple (drummer Ian Paice), as well as Steve Winwood and guitarist Albert Lee. *E.H. in the U.K.* is some pretty weird "jazz," and I hope that Atlantic will reissue it on CD. An interesting concept album that sits between progressive and more straightahead blues-rock is *Who Will Save the World*, by the Groundhogs.

Two musicians who were to have a larger and continuing impact on the experimental and progressive scenes made important recordings in 1972. Stomu Yamash'ta is a virtuoso percussionist who, although not well known in the United States, was much admired by Karlheinz Stockhausen, John Cage, and other postclassical avant-garde composers. He released a solo recording, *Music of Henze, Takemitsu, Maxwell Davies*, and a group project, self-titled *Stomu Yamash'ta and Come to the Edge*. Yamash'ta would continue to perform in "classical" avant-garde settings, as well as with group projects that combined elements of progressive rock, jazz, and European classical music (in the group Go he recorded with the great Santana drummer Michael Shrieve). Better known to audiences worldwide is not only Roxy Music, which released their first album in 1972, but also original member Brian Eno, who has had a large impact on several musical trends.

In the second line, there were a few notable recordings; however, the brief list I will present here should suffice, I hope, to show that the first line really deserves the status I have afforded it. (Of course, this list of second-line efforts could be expanded, but I feel fairly confident that the recordings mentioned here are representative.) Among the albums that are perhaps noteworthy without actually being very good are the *666* double record by Aphrodite's Child, which introduced Vangelis to the world; *Music From MacBeth* by the Third Ear Band; and the self-titled album from the amusingly named German group, Subject, Esq. Some people do regard *666* as a very good album; I am not among them, I'm afraid, but I can see that the music shows promise. (Alright, maybe that's a cop-out, and maybe someday I will have the time and energy to really listen to the album again.) *Macbeth*, which was made as a soundtrack for Roman Polanski's film adaptation of Shakespeare, is probably the most gruesome and depressing music in all of progressive rock (though perhaps challenged by some of Van der Graaf's music). I have even seen articles claiming that it is the *worst* album from the genre. With their classical instrumentation (oboe, cello, violin, guitar, and percussion), there was little "rock" to be had from this group, but certainly the moodiness of this recording is something to experience, if but once. Subject, Esq., on the other hand, made a very listenable album, even if very much a journeyman's effort; they would later transmogrify into Sahara, a group with definite Tull overtones.

Perhaps too listenable, and entirely trippy, is *Lord of the Rings* from Swedish multi-instrumentalist Bo Hansson. As with Renaissance, who released their *Prologue* album in 1972, there is something of a guilty pleasure here. The music is very pretty, great fun to listen to, but there doesn't seem to be much substance to it. Whereas Hansson's albums (the next year he released the better, but still thoroughly lightweight, *Magician's Hat*) feature lots of pleasantly melodic noodling, sort of musical cotton candy, there is a great deal more craft to Renaissance's work. *Prologue*, though, shows the group still enduring birth pains.

Can began to develop a ritualistic, rhythmic sound with *Ege Bamyasi*, which also featured the bizarre but completely appropriate vocal phrasings of singer Damo Suzuki. Steve Hillage's group Khan also specialized in spacey improvisations, though of a slightly more conventional sort than Can's. The one (Can) was two-thirds Stockhausen to one-third Beatles, while the other (Khan) was the reverse. Also out of the Canterbury scene, Matching Mole combined jazz-oriented experimentation with the occasional pop hook—resulting in two tunes that were actually released as a single. The group featured Robert Wyatt on drums and vocals, David Sinclair on keyboards (and taking a break from Caravan), and Phil Miller (guitar) and Bill McCormick (bass), who had previously been in the fairly obscure but excellent Quiet Sun. Their first album, self-titled, is quite good, one of the noteworthy (as well as very good) records of 1972.

The other two very good albums from the second line come from Focus, a group from the Netherlands, and Flash, the post-Yes project formed by Peter Banks.

Focus's *Moving Waves* features the brilliant guitar work of Jan Akkerman, as well as excellent flute and keyboard work from Thijs Van Leer. Both musicians were skilled in classical and jazz styles, which they synthesized on top of a rock foundation. The album's second side consists in a sixteen-part suite of mostly short movements (the shortest is twenty-one seconds long, while the longest is a little over five minutes), titled "Eruption." Much of the music is quite moody, with occasional wordless vocals of stark beauty.

Flash was for the most part a guitar-led quartet, with keyboards here and there provided by either Peter Banks or bass guitarist Ray Bennett (as well as, on the first album, by fellow ex-Yes mate, Tony Kaye). The rhythm section of Bennett and Mike Hough was very good, a slightly heavier version of what Squire and Bruford had done with Yes—and this characterization describes the band as well. Colin Carter, singer and fourth member, had a voice somewhere between Jon Anderson and Roger Daltrey (though perhaps in thinking this I am influenced by the fact that Carter looked a bit like Daltrey), and, again, I think of Flash as a rockier, sometimes Who-like, version of Yes. Whether or not this seems a likely combination, I think it worked quite well. Flash's first album (self-titled) is perhaps good in the way that the first two Yes albums are: it shows a good deal of promise, and it has some nice extended pieces, of which "Small Beginnings" and "Children of the Universe" are the best.

The second album, which also appeared in 1972, is quite different, and altogether more interesting. For one thing, there are only minimal keyboards on the album, and Banks really comes into his own here as a guitarist. *In the Can* is constructed around three longer pieces, "Lifetime," "Black and White," and "There No More" (all in the ten- to twelve-minute range). Although large parts of these songs are extended guitar jams, Banks's looping, interweaving style is fascinating—he fills out the music without making any kind of "guitar god" statements (not that there is any doubt that, as Mark Knopfler says, "the boy can play"). In one of the solos from "Lifetime" there is even a quotation of the signature riff from Focus's "Hocus Pocus," a nod toward Jan Akkerman. Clearly, Banks needed to get some things off his chest; for this one time, his excess resulted in an excellent album. For the next outing, the even better *Out of Our Hands*, the group dynamic returned to the fore—but more on this later.

1972 was a stellar year for the first line, with the singular and startling exception of King Crimson. A rather dismal and badly recorded live album was released by the quartet of Fripp, Boz, Wallace, and Collins. At one point Boz intones, in a weirdly conceived moment of scat improvisation, "It makes no difference what you think about me. . . . it makes a whole lotta difference what I think about you." Hardly. I suppose the fact that *Earthbound* was released had to do with the usual record-company avariciousness (Fripp has extensively documented his troubled and litigious dealings with the EG label), but clearly all the juice had been squeezed from this lemon—which perhaps gives some clue to Crimson's perpetual re-reformations in that period. On a happier note, the next year would see Crimson at perhaps its best.

Otherwise, there was not a single dud from the first line, even if some albums were better than others. Emerson, Lake, and Palmer released the tuneful and often understated *Trilogy*, an album in which Greg Lake gained a share of equality with Keith Emerson, to good effect. Genesis's *Foxtrot* featured two excellent songs, the ominous "Watcher of the Skies," and the class-conscious "Get 'Em Out by Friday." The former contains haunting and somewhat depressing lines on the order of, "Judge not this race by empty remains/Do you judge God by his creatures when they are dead." For that matter, "Get 'Em Out by Friday" does not exactly set a happy scene, depicting as it does downward mobility. Genesis would continue their presentation of English class structure in 1973's *Selling England by the Pound*. These themes provided the impetus for the entirety of Gentle Giant's third album, *Three Friends*. Among the highlights in this story of three schoolmates and their respective destinies are "Schooldays" and "Mister Class and Quality?" Actually, the whole suite of (six) songs works quite well, my general reservations about the contrivedness of the group's approach aside.

Many readers are most likely ready to pounce on me for my exclusion of "Supper's Ready" from the *Foxtrot* highlights. For many, this side-long piece is one of the greatest of Genesis's works. My guess is that listeners for whom this is the case are also more favorably inclined toward the group's epic *Lamb* album. Despite the fact that both works have fine moments, I have two reservations. Genesis, it seems to me, does best with pieces of short or medium length; the ideas, whether musical or lyrical, that are needed to sustain longer works are just not there. There is no shame, I should add, in specializing in less than epic works. (Think, for example, of the *Lieder* composer Hugo Wolf; he wrote nothing but short songs for piano and voice, but what songs they are!) My second reservation is perhaps less well-founded and is simply that I have a hard time reconciling the Broadway show-tune style with progressive rock (it is another thing altogether to work variations on a melody from this source, as Keith Emerson did with "America").

The Italian group Premiata Forneria Marconi, henceforth PFM, came on the scene in that year. It is sometimes difficult to keep their albums separate in one's consciousness; once the group began making records for English-speaking audiences (starting with the following year's *Photos of Ghosts*), there were borrowings from the Italian-language albums (for example, a couple of the songs from 1972's *Entrata* show up on *Photos*). Be that as it may, the group's first album, *Entrata*, is a great debut. Though not sounding much like Yes, in many ways the groups were similar, in that PFM featured both great instrumentalists and great singers. As I mentioned in the opening pages of this chapter, progressive rock emerged full-grown out of the head of Jupiter in Italy. It is stunning, really, that PFM simply began its life as a mature progressive group. *Entrata* weaves classical and jazz influences together seamlessly, employing both violin and flute in addition to the standard rock instruments. At the expense of sounding dumb, provincial, or both, allow me to add that, at least in the mouths of practitioners such as PFM and Banco, Italian is a wonderful language for progressive rock.

Another sign that progressive rock was reaching new heights are the three recordings that I have selected as 1972's albums of the year.

I know that I am not alone in considering *Close to the Edge* as Yes's finest work. Every element that was essential to the Yes vision was at its peak with this album. Indeed, as a totality, *Close to the Edge* represents something as close to perfection as we are likely to find in this world. Thematically, the record's three pieces deal with struggle, growth, redemption, and transformation. There is a complex mixing of Christian and "pagan" ideas, and even something like a "theory of history" (though in no academic sense, as far as the presentation is concerned) at work. Musically, the album explores complex time signatures, poly- and atonality, and wide-ranging timbral resources. On the cultural barometer front, it may be useful to consider for a moment that this very difficult piece of music was, in its time, well-received by the record-buying and concert-going public—and yet there was not a single thing compromised or watered-down about it. Despite the fact, too, that the typically cynical critic of more recent times will claim that Yes's albums exemplify progressive rock's tendencies toward being overblown and pretentious, I defy those same critics to come down to cases with regard to a work such as *Close to the Edge*. Yes, the pieces are extended and difficult, but each works according to a careful logic and economy. (As the reader might imagine, an extended analysis of this album is presented in *music of Yes*, pp. 128–44.)

Perhaps as a nod toward listeners who wondered what happened to the group's blues roots, Jethro Tull released *Living in the Past* in 1972. A mostly backward-looking collection, of singles and previously unreleased material, there are a few gems there, especially the title track. (Incidentally, "Living in the Past," the song, was one of only two hit singles to be in 5/4 time, the other being "Money" from Pink Floyd's *The Dark Side of the Moon*.) In 1972, Tull's major contribution to progressive rock was, of course, *Thick as a Brick*.

Thematically, the album, whose title is an English colloquialism for "full of shit," would seem to be the opposite of something like the Yes vision of things. Despite the fact that the exercise does seem to slide to some extent into mere cynicism, however, the lyrics and album cover are also a great send-up of English pomposity, provinciality, and the class system. The cover (outside and inside) for *Thick as a Brick*, as most readers will know, is a

newspaper parody that goes under the name "The St. Cleve
Chronicle & Linwell Advertiser." The articles presented therein,
with headlines such as "Roller Skate Champ Passes Through" and
"Little Milton in School-Girl Pregnancy Row," are great fun, and
there is even a review of *Thick as a Brick* itself, by a Mr. Julian
Stone-Mason, B.A. As to the length and grandiosity of the project,
Mr. Stone-Mason reports that, "One doubts at times the validity
of what appears to be an expanding theme throughout the two
continuous sides of this record but the result is at worst entertaining and at least aesthetically palatable"! The "Little Milton"
referred to in the paternity flap piece is of course an eight-year-
old poet named Gerald Bostock, whose epic poem, "Thick as a
Brick," has been disqualified for the St. Cleve Society for Literary
Advancement and Gestation (SLAG). It turns out that "four leading child psychiatrists" had come to the conclusion that "the boy's
mind was seriously unbalanced and that his work was a product
of an 'extremely unwholesome attitude towards life, his God and
Country'." Now, instead, the prize will go to runner-up "Mary
Whiteyard (aged 12) for her essay on Christian ethics entitled, 'He
died to save the little Children'." However, there is some good
news, as we read on page two under the headline "Major Beat
Group Records Gerald's Poem"; it turns out that "one-legged pop
flautist Ian Anderson" has "written forty-five minutes of pop
music to go with" Gerald's epic.

Some may wonder if such whimsical lyrics could be part of a
piece of music that aspires to profundity, if indeed Ian Anderson
entertains such aspirations. Can comedy and satire ever move the
human spirit in the way that "serious" subjects, which often
involve some confrontation with mortality, do? In the case of
Thick as a Brick, I think the answer has to be "yes." For one thing,
on first reading, the lyrics come across as mainly obscure, and the
satirical element has to be ferreted out a bit. (There are a good
many English colloquialisms in the text as well; for example, it is
useful to know who "Biggles" is.) For another, the music itself is
not very whimsical or at all silly. In fact, the structure of the
album is very much in line with classical, and even baroque,
counterpoint. The music is built up from short themes and even
bits of "folk music" material, showing the connection between

dances and other folk forms and the earlier music of the Western classical tradition.

In light of what was said about *Close to the Edge* as cultural barometer, it might also be pointed out that both *Thick as a Brick* and its succesor, *A Passion Play*, were number one albums in the United States (as well as reaching the numbers five and thirteen positions, respectively, in the U.K.). Cats are on the upgrade!

Finally, the last group that I would like to discuss that made a major impact in 1972 is one that does not fit very comfortably under the heading "progressive rock." But where else to put the Mahavishnu Orchestra? Some members of this group had jazz pedigrees, especially its leader, John McLaughlin, and Mahavishnu is often placed in the same category as Weather Report, Return to Forever, and Larry Coryell's Eleventh House, namely "fusion." However, in 1972, fusion was still to emerge as a separate entity, and much of the categorization of the Mahavishnu Orchestra has been retrospective. McLaughlin had participated in rock and jazz-rock contexts for a number of years before forming this group—and the guy did play a double-necked electric guitar, for heaven's sake. Drummer Billy Cobham and violinist Jerry Goodman both came from New York-based groups that were heavier on the rock than jazz, Dreams and The Flock, respectively. Bassist and fellow Englishman Rick Laird had played with McLaughlin in one of Brian Auger's groups. Czech keyboardist Jan Hammer had a varied background that took him from the Beatles to Coltrane to classical studies at the Prague Conservatory to first prize in an international competition in Vienna and a scholarship to Berklee College of Music in Boston. The other significant point, to the extent that categories are important at all, is that the audience for the Mahavishnu Orchestra was very much in the vicinity of progressive rock, and it was among progressive rock musicians that the group had a huge influence. Certainly, for example, there is something to the idea that the new directions that King Crimson took with their 1973 group and album, *Larks' Tongues in Aspic*, are "post-Mahavishnu." Or listen to the third part of Yes's *Tales from Topographic Oceans*; this music does not sound a great deal like

Mahavishnu's, but it is clearly representative of an attempt, on the part of Steve Howe especially, to take account of McLaughlin's musical language.

Anyone who saw the Mahavishnu Orchestra back around 1972 or '73 can attest to the fact that this group was almost beyond belief. If I may inject personal experience for a moment: I can still remember well the buzz that went around among the musicians in my high school, to the effect that an incredible group of musicians, led by a guitarist of unbelievable skill, was going to be playing a free concert at the University of Miami a few nights hence. The first Mahavishnu album, *The Inner Mounting Flame*, was either not quite out or barely out at that point—in any case, not many of us had heard it yet. My friends Zane Edge and Garry Rindfuss (who were among the dedicatees of my book on Yes) and I went to that concert, and it is not an exaggeration to say that the experience was life-altering. From the very first chords of "Meeting of the Spirits," the audience was simply transfixed. Sections of extremely difficult ensemble play were alternated with wide-open improvisations. The energy and intensity of the group was even frightening—but also inspiring. This was serious, committed, transcendental music.

Quite often it is difficult for this sort of energy to manifest itself on record, but somehow the translation is accomplished with *The Inner Mounting Flame*. The intensity of the effort is even more pronounced because of the presence of several quiet pieces, including the acoustic guitar and piano duet, "A Lotus on Irish Streams." As far as musicians were concerned, the album had an effect similar to that of Yes's "Roundabout": we became more serious and disciplined—the idea that one could be a good musician who played rock was catching on. The question might be raised, then: Was this "musician's music"? Is this what progressive rock was increasingly becoming? These questions connect, obviously, with the issue of virtuosity for its own sake. Not to get too far back into this debate, but it seems that we could reasonably assume that the very large audiences who came to see groups such as the Mahavishnu Orchestra in the early seventies were not primarily made up of musicians.

1973

In terms of the sheer number of groups and musicians active, 1973 would have to be deemed the biggest year in the time of progressive rock. Unfortunately, because there is so much to talk about from this year, our guided tour will have to move at a fast pace.

On the edges of progressive rock, there were a number of albums that were very, very significant—and that have been written about at length elsewhere. 1973 was the year of both *Quadrophenia* and *Dark Side of the Moon*. My opinion is that the former has aged better than the latter. Again, not to get back into the definitional questions from the previous chapter, but we might think for a moment on the role that Pink Floyd's *Dark Side* played vis-à-vis progressive rock. In terms of building a bridge between the rest of the group's audience, a large part of whom were stoners, and progressive rock more generally, I don't see that the album played much of a role at all. Please do not get me wrong, however; *Dark Side of the Moon* has many good aspects. Thematically and musically, however, it was much surpassed by the follow-up *Wish You Were Here*. As a cultural document, by contrast, *Quadrophenia* simply has many more dimensions, dealing in a much more socially contextualized way with the identity crises of postwar English youth. And, despite some of the instrumental filler on the album, Pete Townshend once again shows his genius at unfolding minimal rock material to maximal effect.

Perhaps showing what progressive rock is to New Yorkers, Steely Dan released *Can't Buy a Thrill* and the excellent *Countdown to Ecstasy*—signalling the coming of postmodernism? Carrying on the psychedelic legacy and also foreshadowing the more recent pastiche, an obscure but interesting group called Brainticket released *Celestial Ocean*. And carrying forward the legacy of the Beatles, the Electric Light Orchestra put out *On the Third Day*—their best album, in my view. Two Hammond organ heavy albums on the periphery of progressive were *Closer to It* by Brian Auger and the Oblivion Express, and the first album by Tony Kaye's post-Yes group, Badger. This group featured David Foster, who had co-written some Yes music with Jon Anderson. *One Live Badger* was recorded—obviously—live, and sounds like a more straight-ahead rock version of early Yes. There is even a bit of "Jesus-rock" on there, and the cover, by Roger Dean, is quite nice.

Progressive soul continued to advance in 1973, with *War Live* (featuring an eerie, side-long, "Slippin' into Darkness"), the Isley Brothers' *3+3*, and Stevie Wonder's great *Innervisions*. In hard rock and heavy metal, four albums that circled around the progressive tree were Led Zeppelin's *Houses of the Holy*; Black Sabbath's charmingly titled *Sabbath Bloody Sabbath* (which featured guest keyboardist Rick Wakeman); Wishbone Ash's concept album, *Argus*; and the initial effort by newcomers Queen. Al Stewart's *Past, Present, Future* was also a concept album, featuring several longer pieces dealing with the historical predictions of Nostradamus.

Roxy Music, with Brian Eno, released its second album in 1973, *For Your Pleasure*, bridging glam and progressive; perhaps even more significantly, as far as progressive rock is concerned, Eno and Robert Fripp released their first collaborative effort, *No Pussyfooting*. Using tape loops, synthesized sounds, and "Frippertronics," this album foreshadows more recent trance music and, through its experimentation with "soundscapes," connects the King Crimsons of the seventies with those of the eighties and nineties.

In the areas of European and jazz avant-gardes, two albums that deserve mention are Stomu Yamash'ta's *Red Buddha* and the self-titled album from Ovary Lodge, Keith Tippett's trio. A good deal of Tippett's playing on this album, it might be mentioned, is done inside the piano. Bassist Roy Babbington would later join Soft Machine.

Finally, by way of moving back into the second line, and again as a cultural barometer, we should note Columbia Records' release of the double album, *The Progressives*, a compilation featuring the Mahavishnu Orchestra, Weather Report, Matching Mole, Walter (now Wendy) Carlos, Ornette Coleman, Soft Machine, Keith Jarrett, Charles Mingus, Gentle Giant, and others. At the time, it all made perfect sense—which says something good about the time, I think.

The second line expanded greatly in 1973. Banco, with their vastly talented operatic singer, Francesco Di Giacomo, released the excellent *io sono nato libero*. With titles such as "Nomad song for a political prisoner" ("Canto nomade per un prigioniero politico"), the group was very much current with the Maoist and autonomia trends in Italy—and the music is really good, too. Also in a more straightforwardly political vein is the second effort from Matching Mole, *Matching Mole's Little Red Record*. Can's *Future Days* saw the group moving in even more atmospheric directions, of the sort for which "Krautrock" is lauded today, at least by afficionados of techno and industrial. The self-titled album from a group called Public Foot the Roman is likely to be one of the more obscure records mentioned here. The suite of three songs on the second side, closing with "Decline and Fall," is really quite good; if you see this in a used record store at a reasonable price, snatch it up. Renaissance released *Ashes are Burning*, which begins a four-album sequence that sees the group at the heighth of their abilities. As I've said, I find their work a kind of guilty pleasure. It is hard to resist their tunefulness, as well as Annie Haslam's voice. However, both in the themes the group takes up, as well as their general approach to melody, this music seems deeply reactionary—Renaissance seems to take the medievalism of some progressive rock all the way into feudal absolutism (there's no science fiction here, either).

German keyboard-led trio Triumvirat, at least partially a Nice/ELP spin-off, released *Illusions on a Double Dimple*, a set of mostly short songs. Another interesting trio, more jazz oriented, was Sun Treader. Led by the excellent percussionist, Morris Pert, the instrumentation on *Zin-Zin* is sparse: filled out by bass guitar and electric pianos (and soprano sax on two cuts). The often effects-laden electric pianos were played by Peter Robinson, formerly of Quatermass.

Perhaps the most interesting trio of all from that period was Back Door. On their first (self-titled) album, the group used only bass guitar, drums, and saxophones. But they played rock—in fact, reviews in *Melody Maker* and elsewhere compared them to Cream. It seems Back Door was mainly known to other musicians at the time, gaining the attention of rockers from Bill Wyman of the Stones to Emerson, Lake, and Palmer (the group's final album, 1976's *Activate*, was produced by Carl Palmer). Still largely unsung, bassist Colin Hodgkinson was at least ten years ahead of his time, employing funky chords that allowed his instrument to fill up a good deal of musical space. (I see from a recent *Mojo* article that Hodgkinson is now playing with the Spencer Davis Group—from which came Steve Winwood—which has relocated to California.) Later in 1973, Back Door released a second album, *Eighth Street Blues*. It is also good, but I prefer the stripped-down sound of the initial effort.

Two post-Colosseum groups made an impact in 1973. *Greenslade*, led by Dave Greenslade, also included bassist Tony Reeves from Colosseum, second keyboardist Dave Lawson (for that double-Dave keyboard sound), and former Crimson drummer Andrew McCulloch. If progressive rock was known for its use of multiple keyboards, the appearance of this group squared that idea. Interestingly, and not unlike the keyboard-led Quatermass, Greenslade evinced both rhythm and blues and straightahead rock influences mixed in with their progressive leanings. As with Quatermass, I don't think this combination worked so well. The group released two albums in 1973, *Greenslade* and *Bedside Manners are Extra*; the Roger Dean covers for both have become classics (the six-armed figure on both covers is probably better known than the group itself). Colosseum leader Jon Hiseman also formed a new quartet, Tempest. A melding of hard rock and progressive, the album features the guitar and violin of Allan Holdsworth. He would later play with Soft Machine and Bill Bruford; Holdsworth's angular playing on the latter's first solo album, *Feels Good to Me* (1977), as well as in the later "progressive supergroup," UK, would have a huge influence on guitarists. Tempest's first album also featured excellent singing from former John Mayall vocalist Paul Williams.

For better or worse, forming a bridge between seventies progressive and late eighties and nineties new-age music was that rather grandiose project that many know as the "soundtrack" from *The Exorcist* (in reality, only a small part of the album was used), Mike Oldfield's *Tubular Bells*. The melodies are nice enough, but what distinguishes the album is the use of loads of rock instruments, especially guitars, to build up an entire orchestra.

Three 1973 albums from the second line really stand out. King Crimson lyricist and conceptual provocateur Pete Sinfield released the excellent *Still*. This is a musically diverse album, featuring everything from Vivaldi melodies (in the opening "Song of the Sea Goat") to straightahead rock 'n' roll ("Wholefood Boogie"—actually the least successful track) to intimations of glam ("Envelopes of Yesterday"), country ("Will It Be You"), and quiet poetic meditations (as in the opening section of the title track). Sinfield's voice is somewhat limited, but he clearly knows how to work with this—and, in one impressive instance, has help from Greg Lake, who takes over midverse in "Still." The album features great musicianship from a large cast, including John Wetton, Keith Tippett, Ian Wallace, and the great pedal-steel player Brian Cole.

Apparently Sinfield began work on a second solo album, two tracks for which appear on the CD re-release, *Stillusion*. According to Sinfield's notes for this album, his energies were instead taken up with producing Roxy Music and helping with the lyrics for ELP's *Brain Salad Surgery*, among other things (he also helped Chris Squire with some lyrics for *Fish Out of Water*, and his song "Heart of Stone" was covered by Cher, of all people).

Flash's third and final album, *Out of Our Hands*, is also their best. A concept album that gets a bit shaky in the idea department here and there ("a wounded crockadeercat"—what's that?), musically the group has finally created its own, integrated sound. The contributions of bass guitarist Ray Bennett are especially strong here; in fact, he also wrote about half of the album. Bennett and drummer Mike Hough are two of the excellent musicians from the time of progressive rock who are high on my "Where are they now?" list. These are people with superlative abilities who, after the high tide of the genre, have seemingly disappeared. Bennett and Banks also use minimal keyboards to good effect, and the latter has honed his expansive guitar style to a more economical and cleaner mode. This album is one of those gems that tends to fall between the cracks, so I was happy to see that it has been re-released.

Finally, from the second line, a lesser-known (especially in North America) group called Jonesy released their second album, *Keeping Up*. Among the distinctive traits of the record are some of the most brilliant Mellotron playing in progressive rock, from keyboardist Jamie Kaleth, unexpected use of the wah-wah pedal from guitarist John Evan Jones, and the Miles Davis-inflected trumpet of Alan Bown. The appearance of trumpet as a solo instrument (without any other horns in the group) is itself unique in progressive rock; Bown had previously blown his horn with a soul and blues group. Here the music is completely progressive, with hints of Crimson here and there, but largely quite original.

In 1973, all thirteen of the groups I have identified as the "first line" were active. The list of noteworthy records is full, with seven very important albums and three "albums of the year."

First, the also-rans—though I should preface this listing by emphasizing that none of these albums is below par. Assuredly, some readers will dispute these rankings; I fully admit that disputable they are (and, to quote Jerry Seinfeld, "Let's start the insanity"). Gentle Giant released two albums in 1973, *Octopus* and *In a Glass House*. The former is one of the favorites of many Gentle Giant fans. Although in some ways a masterpiece of ensemble proficiency, the group had become overwhelmingly mechanical at this point—there isn't a lot of charm there. Still, the injections of early music (medieval Western classical music) from classically trained keyboardist Kerry Minear are sometimes fascinating. (For some reason, the excellent Roger Dean cover was not featured on the U.S. release.) *Glass House*, I'm afraid, continued this trend, though the group would recover in fine style with their next two albums, wherein the human element made a welcome reappearance.

Also frighteningly mechanical was Magma's *Mekanik Destruktiw Kommandoh*, one of the group's first albums to be more widely available in North America. Here, of course, the human side was intentionally purged from the music, in the forced march rhythm of totalitarian invasion. What they were *really* up to is once again obscured by lyrics in a language that even hard-core fans were just beginning to pick up.

After being together for about five years, Henry Cow finally released their first album. The group originally formed in 1968, while the members were students at Cambridge University. Actually, though I have not placed *The Legend* among the most noteworthy albums of 1973, this is clearly an important album from one of the most important progressive rock groups. The music is very avant, especially because of the angular, jagged, and often grating guitar work of Fred Frith. The group plays with nonsense and other silliness, poking fun at commercial undertakings (as in "Teenbeat") and bourgeois society more generally. They also begin their engagement with toy instruments and "small sounds" that would grow into a musical language in its own right, especially with 1976's *Concerts*.

Finally, among the honorable mentions is another album that is also excellent in many respects, Soft Machine's *Six*. Since their *Third* album, Soft Machine had been in transition, with Robert Wyatt leaving after *Fourth* (1971). By *Six*, and the addition of drummer John Marshall and saxophonist/keyboardist Karl Jenkins, Soft Machine had transmogrified into a pure jazz outfit. Original member Mike Ratledge still retained some of his psychedelic and post-Hendrix flair, but basically the group now occupied a place between the later Coltrane and free jazz. The first of this album's two disks was recorded live, and it is very good stuff. And, what is demonstrated here, again, is the porosity of categories in that time; audiences that already followed this music felt in no way betrayed by Soft Machine's new directions, as it was a logical extension of the possibilities of the genre.

A pair of the most noteworthy albums of 1973 came from Gong, which issued the first two parts of its "Radio Gnome Invisible" trilogy in 1973, *The Flying Teapot* and *Angel's Egg*. The albums are of a piece, not only of the pothead pixie programme, but also with the French tradition of surrealism. Bits of narrative arise from hallucinations, dreams, and the unconscious, interspersed with quasi-conventional songs and space jams, all held together by Shakti Yoni's space whisper. Her "Prostitute Song" is one of the highlights, as is Daevid Allen's hilarious chant of "Have a cup of tea/have another one/have a cup o' tea!" At times, saxophonist Didier Malherbe effects a middle-eastern vibe, and Steve Hillage's guitar is nicely understated throughout. On a par with the space whisper is Tim Blake's contribution on synthesizer, which focuses more on atmospherics than melody. The trilogy would be completed by the equally cosmic *You* the following year, where Pierre Moerlen's masterful drumming especially comes to the fore. At the intersection of psychedelic and progressive, the "Radio Gnome" trilogy is *the* masterwork—even if that is a very strange term to use in the presence of music that is the very opposite of anything having to do with authority.

Though reviews of this album are mixed, in my view Caravan created one of their best albums in 1973, with *For Girls Who Grow Plump in the Night*. The crisp opening guitar chords, the chugging bass and drums, and the ethereal viola introduce an album of great wit and charm. Indeed, despite all of the usual funny stuff (is there a line in there about "a piece of gum will come tomorrow"?), this is perhaps the most dramatic work from Caravan, especially the second side, which even features an instrumental piece from Soft Machine keyboardist Mike Ratledge. Sections of the album are orchestrated, to very good effect, with arrangements by Jimmy Hastings, Martyn Ford, and John Bell. Less successfully, the group attempted to extend this orchestral experiment a couple years later, with *Caravan and the New Symphonia*. Any group that has lost a talent of the order of Richard Sinclair has obviously suffered a major loss; what makes *For Girls Who Grow Plump* especially significant, then, is the fact that it actually represents a new peak in Caravan's Canterbury tales.

Jethro Tull's follow-up to *Thick as a Brick* was musically in a similar vein, but lyrically quite different. While *A Passion Play* might seem, on the surface, to continue the verbal silliness of its predecessor, it is clear that Anderson is attempting to make an extended statement regarding one of the subjects that is obviously most dear to him, namely Christianity and its seeming betrayal of its original promise. Musically, *Passion Play* is every bit as sophisticated, perhaps even more so, than *Thick as a Brick*; the album is only less significant in that it covers some of the same musical ground. When first performed live, apparently without adequate preparation (Yes would make a similar mistake with *Topographic Oceans*), the work was not well-received. A shell-shocked Ian Anderson announced that he would retire from live performance. Were progressive rock groups overreaching their bounds? I think not; after additional rehearsal, the subsequent performances of *A Passion Play* were stunning.

Also continuing in a similar vein to their initial effort, the Mahavishnu Orchestra released *Birds of Fire*. More tuneful than its predecessor, there was still plenty of intensity to go around. With its surging violin, offbeat rhythm, and crisscrossing, searing guitar, the opening track is a classic. The group also covered Miles Davis, as well as provided more acoustic relief with "Open Country Joy."

With the help of Pete Sinfield, Emerson, Lake, and Palmer, and the latter's Manticore record lable, PFM released their first English-language record, the outstanding *Photos of Ghosts*. Although this group could play with overwhelming force, they also excelled at passages of almost unequaled delicacy. Their synthesis of jazz and classical influences is so complete that it is often impossible to tell where the music is coming from. One of their greatest effects is to have sections of intricate counterpoint, where each of six or seven instruments is playing a different line, issue in a kind of unified voice, with the drive of an anthem. Just as one is caught up in this moment, however, the group employs what I like to call a "suspension effect"—one feels as if on a high-wire without a net. The bottom has fallen out, but this nothingness retains the presence that had been established by the full vocal and instrumental ensemble.

Finally, in the list of major but not quite very major albums for 1973 is Yes's *Tales from Topographic Oceans*. Given that this is progressive rock's longest sustained work, with a single four-part symphony-like piece taking up over eighty minutes, there is no doubt that the album is highly significant. Among those who dislike the genre, *Topographic* is often the butt of anti-progressive-rock screeds. In reality, the album does not entirely come off—Jon Anderson called it "a meeting point of high ideals and low energy"—but it is also daring and adventurous at many points, and the group should receive accolades for simply attempting such an ambitious project. The third part of the piece, "The Ancient," is as far-out as anything produced by any progressive group, and, with the fourth part, "Ritual," the group finally comes fully together. Apart from hardcore fans who wouldn't change a note, there is debate as to whether the two-record album is too long by one side or two. I go with one, and my hope is that, someday, a somewhat edited version of the work might appear. If so, a near-masterpiece would surely become a masterpiece.

Now the three albums of the year. Returning to themes that propelled their other truly great album, *Tarkus*, Emerson, Lake, and Palmer released *Brain Salad Surgery*. Opening with the

Blake/Parry hymn, "Jerusalem," as clear a statement of English romanticism as ever will be found, the group ultimately arrives at the ultimate technological nightmare, a not-too-distant future when arrogant and conscious computers will no longer have any use for their human creators. Keyboard-wise, the album is roughly divided between pieces that take the organ as their bedrock, and those that feature the piano. "Jerusalem," of course, features the organ, but also soaring synthesizers. Greg Lake's voice here is magnificent, and Carl Palmer begins an album-long demonstration of what it means to orchestrate with percussion. Aside from another one of the group's silly songs ("Benny the Bouncer"), which disrupts the flow in my view, there is great pacing to *Brain Salad*. "Toccata," an adaptation of the first movement of Alberto Ginastera's First Piano Concerto, is a showpiece for Keith Emerson's percussive piano chops, as is the second movement (or "impression," as the actual title has it) of the album's epic "Karn Evil 9." The former is a bit over the top, if impressive; the latter is an important piece of music. Lake continues his series of thoughtful ballads with "Still . . . You Turn Me On."

With the well-known lines from "Karn Evil 9," the famous "Welcome back my friends to the show that never ends," one gets the impression that the computers that eventually take over had their origin in rock-music pyrotechnics. Listening to recent techno and industrial music, where there aren't many people playing what used to be quaintly called "musical instruments," this suspicion seems to be confirmed. In the third and final part of "Karn Evil 9," there is a great deal of back and fourth between humanity and the upstart computer. This dialectic leads to some great passages, especially the Jimmy Smith-inflected Hammond solo that seems to indicate, for a final moment, that humanity has the upper hand. And yet, this same dialectic leads the electronic computer voice to declare that "limited, primitive" humanity had no choice but to give birth to a higher, indeed "perfect," consciousness. In the end, the dialectic is overcome by the digital. H. R. Giger's creepy cover art captures this reductive assimilation perfectly.

Set next to this protocyberpunk scene, Genesis's *Selling England by the Pound* seems positively sentimental. The album is, in my view, the best recorded by the group. *Selling England* is indeed a very *English* record, where themes of class difference and social erosion are treated in a specifically British context, and where provinciality is afforded a degree of affection. Opening with Peter Gabriel's a cappella cry, "Can you tell me where my country lies?" (surely a double entendre), the entirety of the album is given over to answering this question. And although there is a good deal of dynamic contrast in the music, in many ways the band is restrained. Edward Macan even refers to the "'conservative' element of Genesis's harmony which—in its rock context—lends the band's music its distinctive sound" (p. 106). The first song, "Dancing With the Moonlit Knight" takes its time building up, with opening passages that are dramatic yet relatively quiet. When the group does finally kick in full steam ahead, the moment has been so carefully prepared that one hardly notices the transition. So many lines from this song could be chosen as indicative of the general theme of social decay; the line leading into the instrumental section at the song's middle is as good as any: "Knights of the Green Shield stamp and shout." The reference is to puffed-up "citizens of hope and glory," living on the glory days of "Rule Britannia," but who are really doing no more than counting their Green Shield Stamps. A cruel and subtle mirror! The song ends reflectively, sliding into the moonlit night with crystalline guitar textures and Gabriel's effective and whistful whistle.

What seems most cruel, but also most powerful, about *Selling England* is the way that the music parodies what might be called "small lives and small dreams" without actually being cynical. As I said, there is even a degree of affection for those who spend their time "chewing through . . . wimpey dreams": a future in the fire-escape trade, a love lost, a turf battle on the East side, a bit of a break at the grocery-store check-out. This is a portrait of an empire in decline, but one that works through the effects this decline has on the personal level.

For sheer formal inventiveness, the most important progressive rock record of 1973 was King Crimson's *Larks' Tongues in Aspic*. In fact, I would argue that, if you set *Larks' Tongues* alongside the previous year's *Close to the Edge* by Yes, you will really have an idea of what progressive rock is all about. (Or, for a broader picture, take all six of the "albums of the year" from 1972 and 1973.) Many readers will immediately zone in on the fact that these two albums share a common percussionist, namely Bill Bruford. On both *Close to the Edge* and *Larks' Tongues*, his contribution is crucial: there is no drummer in rock music who uses space and syncopation more capably than Mr. Bruford.

Larks' Tongues is an album of extremes, perhaps encapsulated by Robert Fripp's charge to Bruford to avoid playing any particular passage the same way twice. Bruford was also encouraged in his creativity here by the presence of Jamie Muir, another percussionist of great ability and inventiveness. (Incidentally, it was Jamie Muir who introduced Jon Anderson to the Shastric scriptures that became the basis for *Tales from Topographic Oceans*.) Many parts of the album are very harsh, with sharp and snarling textures that grate on the ears. Often these parts arise out of sections that are very quiet, though also pregnant with the sense that something devastating is about to happen. Just as one has gotten up to turn up the stereo in order to hear a quiet passage, where perhaps little bells, cymbals, and kalimba (also known as mbira or African thumb piano) predominate, something of great electrical force explodes from the speakers. It is doubtful that even the ordinarily extreme dymanic markings, of quadruple pianissimo and quadruple fortissimo (four degrees of quiet or loud) are enough to encompass this sound. Clearly the group aims for sheer difficulty in some passages, not only as regards the level of musicianship required to play them, but also in the shrillness of tones, especially from the electric guitar and David Cross's violin.

The album is divided between three instrumental pieces, tracks one, five, and six, and three songs, tracks two, three, and four. In John Wetton, Crimson has a fine and powerful singer. He is also a formidable bass guitarist; his work on the trilogy of albums from this version of Crimson is about the only bass playing in progressive rock that rivals Chris Squire's for creativity. Wetton sounds nothing like Squire, though, which makes the comparison all the more interesting. "Book of Saturday" is a short and very pretty song, with delicate guitar chords from Fripp, an understated violin solo, and minimal accompaniment otherwise. "Exiles" is richly textured, with long instrumental passages, and fascinating snare work from Bruford. "Easy Money" is, by contrast, a slippery, funky piece that takes syncopation to extremes.

Except for the presence of electric instruments, the instrumental pieces on the album are just as much a part of any genre of contemporary avant-garde music that one might think of as they are works of rock music. This goes especially for "Part One" of "Larks' Tongues in Aspic." Were this piece to be scored for standard orchestral instruments (in *music of Yes* I proposed a scoring for two violins, flute, cello, trombone, tuba, and two percussionists; see pp. 39–40), it would be indistinguishable from other experimental works that have come out of the post-Cage classical tradition. "Larks' Tongues" done this way wouldn't be nearly as loud, though, and loudness is definitely part of the game plan here. Despite that, the Crimson King has perfected here a kind of experimental "chamber rock," of the sort that Henry Cow would also excel at, and which constitutes a *somewhat* divergent path within the larger field of progressive rock. Whereas "Larks' Tongues" Part One is an exercise in maximalism, with huge and stunning contrasts, "The Talking Drum" is just the opposite. This piece builds in a repetitive fashion for the course of its entire seven-and-a-half minutes. Although there is something like soloing occurring, from the guitar and violin, throughout the piece, in fact these extended lines are more like steel cables that skim the surface of a thick and bubbling soup. Finally, "Larks' Tongues" Part Two is a big red fire truck speeding through city streets, with a final blow-out that sounds for all the world like a line lifted from the "Star-Spangled Banner."

1974

It would be very hard for any year in the history of progressive rock to compete with 1973; instead, in 1974, we see the beginnings of a scaling back. There are still a number of very important albums to be made, and even some important groups that are just appearing on the scene. But clearly the high tide was passing.

Even the number of albums that rest on the periphery of progressive rock is in decline by this point. Groups such as Steely Dan, who, while not directly related to progressive rock could all the same could be said to be working with a "postprogressive" language, are on the rise. Their work is exceedingly clever and displays craft, but there is always an undercurrent of cynicism. In this vein, their 1976 album, *The Royal Scam*, is intended as a statement on America in the time of Watergate. The idealism of the sixties is beginning to fade, and the midseventies seem to be a time of impasse or, at best, transition. Still, there is a lingering trace of utopian energy, and this energy is manifest in a handful of recordings that maintain the high standards of the genre.

Bob Dylan released an important album in 1974, *Blood on the Tracks*. Musically, the album is as good as anything Dylan ever put out; as far as the vision thing goes, Dylan also seemed to be in a period of transition, holding briefly to a kind of existentialism on the way to his later, and nutty, engagement with Christianity and Judaism. "Bittersweet observations from the eye of an emotional hurricane" is the way Iain Smith puts it in the *Rough Guide* (p. 273). More closely related to progressive rock were Jack Bruce's excellent *In from the Storm*, Tangerine Dream's first album on the Virgin label, *Phaedra*, and the first album from Todd Rundgren's Utopia. Perhaps more significant for new directions that would ultimately lead from the time of progressive rock to the current scene, Brian Eno released a pair of albums, *Here Come the Warm Jets* and *Taking Tiger Mountain (By Strategy)*. With contributions by Robert Fripp, this was punk, glam, new wave, and progressive all rolled together. Eno also took part in the *June 1, 1974* concert with Kevin Ayers, Nico, and John Cale, which also featured guitar work from Mike Oldfield and Ollie Halsall. It seemed that two sides of experimental rock, the progressive trend and the trend represented by groups such as the Velvet Underground, were coming together. The synthesis, however, seemed to be predicated on a deemphasis of counterpoint and linearity, as well as of instrumental skills. In addition, the romanticism of progressive rock was replaced with (only occasionally gothic) gloom and cynicism.

A quick survey of the second line finds a number of good albums. French group Ange released *Au-Dela Du Delire*. Argent came close to progressive rock with *Nexus*. Composer David Bedford was commissioned by the Royal Philharmonic to write a work for orchestra and rock group; the interesting *Star's End* was the result. The "rock group" consisted in Mike Oldfield, who played both guitar and bass, and Henry Cow drummer Chris Cutler. Egg reformed briefly and cut *The Civil Surface*. A group of Royal College of Music students, friends of Rick Wakeman's, formed Gryphon. Two of the members were specialists in early music, and Gryphon's albums (*their* early music, anyway) featured recorders, crumhorns, and the like. Their third, and best, album was released in 1974, *Red Queen to Gryphon Three*. The title piece is based on a chess game. The band joined Yes on the *Relayer* tour; unfortunately, crumhorn rock does not translate well to large arenas. But the album is pretty good. At the other end of the spectrum, the keyboards/percussion-duo Seventh Wave released their first (of only two) albums, *Things to Come*. Interestingly, they claimed Van der Graaf's Hugh Banton as "fugal inspiration." Speaking of which, Peter Hammill released an album that could also be said to occupy that middle ground between the Velvets and King Crimson, *The Silent Corner and the Empty Stage*. Randy California, of Spirit, guests on guitar on one of the best tracks, "Red Shift." Also at an intersection, of progressive and hard rock, was the first Kansas album, self-titled. And *Refugee*, the album that Patrick Moraz made with former Nice members Brian Davison and Lee Jackson, also came out in 1974. There are some nice moments here, but a good deal of it is really over the top. Fortunately or unfortunately, depending on your point of view, by the time the album came out, Moraz had already moved on to replace Rick Wakeman in Yes.

Seven albums from the second line deserve special mention; one of these is one of the three albums of the year. Notably, this is a year when, in terms of sheer numbers, the second line outshone the first line.

Robert Wyatt released his best solo album to date, and possibly ever, *Rock Bottom*. Two years earlier, Wyatt had been paralyzed (from the waist down) in a fall from a window, and this tragedy is reflected in the album. The instrumentation, which includes such innovations as "Delfina's tray" and a "small battery," is austere, as befitting a very personal journey into the edges of perdition. Not quite as sparse, but nearly so, is Can's *Soon Over Babaluma*, my own favorite from the group. And also in the minimalist camp is the first Island release from Jade Warrior, *Floating World*. All three of these albums are at the opposite end of the spectrum from the more lush, to say nothing of grandiose, kinds of progressive albums. Personally, I've always liked this "chamber progressive" end of things.

More in the mainstream of the movement are the albums from Nektar, *Remember the Future*, and the Strawbs, *Hero and Heroine*. Both albums set out to tell a story. The Strawbs's effort is the more lush of the two, and also represents their emergence into full-blown progressive rock. Nektar has strong Floydish leanings, especially in the vocal department. A lesser known, but excellent, album that year was released by Tasavallan Presidenti, a group from Finland. *Milky Way Moses* (which has singing in English) has great wit and many inflections from Chuck Berry and other early rock 'n' rollers. The group used only minimal keyboards, and has a very crisp sound. Another group from Finland made a good album that year, namely Wigwam. A track from 1974's *Being* appears on the *Supernatural Fairy Tales* set.

Finally, as regards the second line, 1974 saw the appearance of the first Hatfield and the North album (self-titled). This is, in my view, one of the albums of the year. The project featured some of the best Canterbury scene musicians—Richard Sinclair, Pip Pyle, David Sinclair, Phil Miller, and guest vocalist Robert Wyatt, as well as the "Northettes"—and represented the best spirit of that scene. Although the album is very jazzy, there are "songs" interspersed, with wonderful singing from not only Richard Sinclair but also the trio of Amanda Parsons, Barbara Gaskin, and Ann Rosenthal. Geoff Lee of Henry Cow helped out on saxes and flute as well. All the playing here is superlative, but I might single out Pip Pyle for special praise. Whether with the Hatfields, National Health, or Gong, he is one of the best progressive rock drummers—and often overlooked.

As I mentioned, the first line didn't hold up their end quite as well. I've already noted a few reservations I have with Genesis's *The Lamb Lies Down on Broadway*. Some have been tempted to consider this double album in the same vein as Yes's *Topographic Oceans*, because of the length. Actually, the only thing that length gives them in common is the problem of sustaining creativity. *The Lamb* is really more akin to *Quadrophenia*, thematically at least. Gong completed their Radio Gnome trilogy with *You*, probably their jazziest and tightest album—and therefore least reflecting the influence of Daevid Allen, who left after this project. Tim Blake's synthesizer-led piece, "A Sprinkling of Clouds," is one of the highlights. Perhaps as a counterreaction to the reception of *A Passion Play*, Jethro Tull made one of two albums that I would truly call below par, *War Child* (the other one was 1976's *Too Old to Rock'n'Roll*). Christian Vander put out an interesting solo album, known variously as *Wurdah Itah* or *Tristan et Iseult* (I have a copy of the latter version, which was conceived as film music): sparse instrumentation with layers of vocal chants on top. I think it's quite good. The original Mahavishnu Orchestra had fallen apart by this point. John McLaughlin reformed the group, with violinist Jean-Luc Ponty and keyboardist/vocalist Gayle Moran. Although many fans reject this version of the group, I think that the second of the two albums they released in 1974, *Visions of the Emerald Beyond*, is pretty good. However, it is certainly the case that the heady years when the Mahavishnu Orchestra was turning the world upside-down were in the past. A musician of McLaughlin's talents is, thankfully, unstoppable, and he has continued to put together new projects, including the Indian-music group Shakti in the later seventies (featuring L. Shankar on violin and Zakir Hussein on tabla) and a more recent trio with another Indian musician, percussionist Trilok Gurtu.

Two of the more noteworthy albums from the first line are Gentle Giant's *The Power and the Glory* and Henry Cow's *Unrest*. The Giant, perhaps spurred on by the political inspirations referred to in the album's title, backed up a bit from the more mechanical sound of the previous two albums. Even their more contrived devices were starting to congeal into a singular musical language that Gentle Giant could call their own. Henry Cow also developed in more coherent directions, with their radical politics coming to the fore.

Finally, the two other albums of the year belong to the pillars. King Crimson released two albums in 1974, the very good *Starless and Bible Black*, and the excellent *Red*. For the former album, the group was a quartet at this point, following the departure of Jamie Muir. The improvisational directions opened up with *Larks' Tongues* were even more in evidence at this point, and *Starless and Bible Black* was especially influenced by the open-ended improvisations that the group increasingly experimented with in live performance. In fact, Bill Bruford reports that parts of *Starless* are actually taken from live shows, with the audience noise edited out (*When in Doubt, Roll!*, p. 18). Apart from the actual "songs" (with vocals, that is), there is a general looseness to the album. Also, as with *Larks' Tongues*, acoustic textures have mostly disappeared from the Crimson repertoire (only to make the briefest return with "Fallen Angel" from *Red*).

The live performances from this period of the group's existence are indeed something to hear, and fortunately Robert Fripp has made these available in the box set, *Great Deceiver*. Few rock groups have been as telepathic and adventurous in live improvisation. I had the privilege of seeing the group in 1974, and, as with my previously mentioned experience with the Mahavishnu Orchestra, I was stunned. I had never seen Bill Bruford in concert before that; his performance, on a four-piece kit no less, made it clear that he was taking rock drumming into uncharted waters.

By the time *Red* came out, King Crimson was down to a trio (less David Cross, who at that point was simply one of five additional contributors), and soon not to exist at all. And yet this is a very strong album. Indeed, the long closing piece, "Starless," is considered by many, including Eric Tamm (author of *Robert Fripp: From King Crimson to Guitar Craft*), to be Crimson's finest moment. Where the group was somewhat short of material on *Starless and Bible Black* (hence the use of live recordings passed off as studio work), *Red* features three songs among its five tracks. "Starless" itself, while containing a long, improvised section, returns to the extended and developmental linearity that to me is essential to progressive rock. But the raw and harsh textures that were a trademark of Crimson in this period are also well in evidence, especially in the album's opener, "Red."

Yes also returned to fine form with *Relayer*. Two things contributed to the renewed energy demonstrated here. New keyboardist Patrick Moraz brought a wealth of ideas and enthusiasm—unlike Rick Wakeman, who had grown tired of playing with Yes and wanted to get more into a solo career, Moraz was clearly excited about playing progressive rock on such a high level. Secondly, Alan White developed his own style for playing with the group. On "Gates of Delirium" and "Sound Chaser," his playing is simply astounding.

The layout for *Relayer* is very similar to *Close to the Edge*: the first side features a single, epic work, while the second side is divided between two pieces. "The Gates of Delirium" shows Jon Anderson, who acknowledges that he has always had a bit of a chip on his shoulder, backing down not the least bit from the ambition he demonstrated with *Tales*. "Gates" was inspired by Tolstoy's *War and Peace*. As with ELP's "Karn Evil 9," Yes demonstrates that musical representations of war and struggle can generate some very interesting counterpoint. Here, however, the textures are more varied, as Yes employs a tremendous range of sounds. These include, at one point, an "electric slinky"—a Moraz invention, but also Steve Howe's beautiful steel guitar in the closing section, "Soon." "Sound Chaser" is a completely nutty work, taking every possibility of a "rock 'n' roll" song, at least one in the lineage of "Roundabout" and "Siberian Khatru," to crazy lengths. Finally, "To Be Over" is the sleeper of the album, a beautiful and subtle tune.

Significantly, by the following year King Crimson would no longer exist, and it would be two more years before another Yes album would appear. The high tide of progressive rock had passed. And yet, I might ask the reader to pause for a moment and consider the literally scores of albums from this five-year "apogee" that have been mentioned or all-too-briefly discussed; this is to say nothing of the many worthy albums that have not even been mentioned here. This is an exceptional body of work; I would be willing to wager that there is nothing that even comes close to this outpouring of creativity in any other period or genre of rock music, and perhaps not in any other kind of music period. Let's hold on to that, let's not let go of it easily.

Trials and transformations, 1975–1978

In the final years of the time of progressive rock, the notion of a coherent movement began to splinter. There were still good albums to come, but the underlying ideology seemed to fade. The social dynamics behind this fragmentation are taken up in the next chapter, but let us keep in mind that, in the years covered in this section, progressive rock was living on borrowed time, so to speak. There was a need for transformation if the trend was to survive. Unfortunately, by this point a large gap had begun to open up between progressive rock's "haves" and "have-nots." The former category especially consisted in groups that had become big hits in the United States. Personally, I'm not a "cultist" when it comes to these things—I'm glad that groups such as Yes, Emerson, Lake, and Palmer, and Jethro Tull became immensely popular. However, this popularity, and the concomittant financial rewards, did inject serious problems into the idea of a progressive rock movement. Record companies adjusted their expectations to suit the big sellers; therefore, groups with little or "no commercial potential" (as Frank Zappa once put it—or it was put to him) were increasingly marginalized by that great arbiter of the good, the true, and beautiful, the market. Significantly, this dynamic has ended up hurting the "haves" as much as the "have-nots"—perhaps even more, as the "have-nots" have had less temptation to sell their souls for a mess of pottage. Again, more on this next chapter; for now, let us take a brief tour of the few highlights of progressive rock's denouement—if not entirely of all the music itself, at least of "the time."

1975

Among the interesting and varied albums that came from outside of progressive rock for 1975 were Bob Dylan's *Desire*, Led Zeppelin's *Physical Graffiti*, *Natty Dread* by Bob Marley and the Wailers, Joni Mitchell's *The Hissing of Summer Lawns*, and The Who's *The Who by Numbers* (which in my view is an underrated record). Closer to the periphery of progressive rock were Parliament's *Mothership Connection*; Queen's *A Night at the Opera*; Steely Dan's *Katy Lied*; two albums from Tangerine Dream, *Rubycon* and *Ricochet*; and Frank Zappa's *One Size Fits All*. Pink Floyd released what many, myself included, hold to be one of their strongest albums that year, *Wish You Were Here*. (Edward Macan provides a careful analysis of the "Wish You Were Here" suite in *Rocking the Classics* [pp. 112–24]). Significantly, Macan sees the album as a bellwether not only for Pink Floyd but also "in the progress of progressive rock" (p. 124). In Macan's view, the whole hermetic approach which had marked *Tarkus, Close to the Edge*, and [Genesis's] "Firth of Frith" (not to mention Pink Floyd's earlier music) was clearly on the wane. The psychedelic era's conviction that music should contain hidden layers of meaning that a group of illuminati could search out was rapidly being replaced by the belief that the lyrics should relay a comprehensible message that would be readily apparent even to the casual listener, without the interference of a dense maze of verbal images and visual symbols. (p. 124)

My only possible dissension from this view is that, in the heyday of progressive rock, there was a democratic sensibility about the hermeneutic enterprise: the "illuminati" was not just a small in-group that sought to keep others out (on the contrary). Otherwise, Macan's analysis fits in well with the idea that, by the later seventies, a new time was upon us: a time when meaning is flattened and affect is lost—what Fredric Jameson calls "the postmodern." As Macan writes, the "spiritual urgency" of the sixties increasingly gave way to complacency and accommodation with the establishment (p. 125). What I will refer to as the highlights of the remaining years of the time of progressive rock, then, will be those groups and albums that resisted this complacency.

Three other groups or figures deserve mention here. Patti Smith created an early punk masterpiece with her first album, *Horses*. This might also be taken as a bellwether. One hundred and eighty degrees away from *Horses* was Santana's three-record live set, *Lotus*, recorded in Japan. For those musicians who heard this (import, at least in the U.S.) album, the impact was often great. Carlos Santana, though seemingly having little in common with progressive rock, is one of the great practitioners of the "long line," á la John Coltrane and few others. There is a logic to his soloing that, in this postinferential age of music that goes nowhere, also bears emphasis. Finally, three Eno projects deserve our attention. *Evening Star* extended Eno's collaboration with Robert Fripp. *Another Green World* is, arguably, the best of Eno's "rock" albums (featuring razor-edged guitar textures from Robert Fripp on the opening track, "Sky Saw"). And *Discreet Music* begins Eno's development of "ambient" music (on which more in the next chapter). Between Patti Smith and Brian Eno, then, the time of punk and timbre was already upon us.

Now a quick tour of the second line, with discussion of the four most notable albums at the end. It has been said that Can's *Landed* was the last very good album by the group, as well as the first to utilize sixteen-track technology. Gilgamesh, featuring the talents of the late keyboardist Alan Gowan (and, on their second album, from 1978, Hugh Hopper), was one of the new line of British fusion groups that were springing up at that point, especially around the Canterbury scene. In a similar vein, Hatfield and the North released their second album, *The Rotters Club*. Jade Warrior released *Waves*, which consists in a single, two-part suite. Steve Winwood guests on piano and Moog synthesizer, and the album is dedicated to "the last whale." Mike Oldfield finally moved on from his *Tubular Bells* success with what seems to me a much stronger album, *Ommadawn*. German jazz saxophonist/ keyboardist Klaus Doldinger released an excellent album that bridged fusion and progressive, *Looking Thru*, under the heading of his group, Passport. Also in the Canterbury fusion category was the first and only album by Quiet Sun, *Mainstream*. The group featured Roxy Music guitarist Phil Manzanera, who had originally formed the group in 1970. Robert Wyatt released another deeply oddball album, *Ruth is Stranger than Richard*. It seems that, as progressive rock became less of a movement, at least the Canterbury musicians were able to quietly continue putting out albums of high quality.

In the more lush and romantic category, Renaissance released two of their better albums, *Turn of the Cards* and *Scheherazade and Other Stories*. Again, it is tuneful and well-crafted stuff that seems to me to be deeply problematic. The Strawbs released *Ghosts*, in many ways a trimmer, and therefore better, album than *Hero and Heroine*. Van der Graaf released an album that is, if not great, still pretty good—*God Bluff*. And Seventh Wave released their second and final album, *Psi-Fi*; it isn't bad, if you can get past goofy song titles such as "Star Palace of the Sombre Warrior." Incidentally, even though Yes has never had a title even remotely resembling this one, they manage to get blamed for this sort of thing anyway.

Camel, a group hitherto not mentioned here, released the very good instrumental suite, *The Snow Goose*. The group featured veteran R&B keyboardist Pete Bardens, who had played with Them

(Van Morrison's group), and excellent guitar from Andy Latimer. "Fusion with a classical sensibility" is an expression I might coin regarding this album.

Again with the help of ELP and their Manticore label, another excellent Italian group produced an English-language record that received wide distribution, namely Banco. Their self-titled album, which features pictures of their rather large and obviously operatically trained singer, reveals traces of early Genesis, especially in the longer piece, "Nothing's the Same," and in the shorter, "Leave Me Alone." The latter is a wonderful depiction of what morning is like for someone sleeping off a rough night on a park bench. Banco features two keyboardists, one specializing on piano, the other on organ, and not too much synthesizer.

Finally, among the best second-line albums is Steve Hillage's *Fish Rising*. Featuring many of his Gong-mates, as well as Henry Cow's Lindsay Cooper on bassoon (one of the few prominent female instrumentalists in progressive rock), this superb album is by turns trippy space jam and carefully scripted ensemble work, with hermetic and wacky lyrics that make Jon Anderson look positively straightforward.

Almost unbelievably, two years after the peak of first-line activity, in 1975 there are albums from only five groups in this category. Caravan's *Cunning Stunts* shows the group starting to get very stale with their sexism, which they should have long since outgrown. By far the best song on the album is "The Show of Our Lives." The rest is merely passable. Jethro Tull came back from the not-very-good *War Child* to make a much more folk-inflected album, *Minstrel in the Gallery*. Surprisingly, the group even ventured back into near-epic territory with the quite good "Baker St. Muse."

Gentle Giant recorded their last very good album, *Free Hand*, which musicologist John Covach has called "perhaps the most thoroughly contrapuntal album in all of progressive rock" (Covach, p. 60).

Magma released the two-record *Magma Live*, in my view one of their best albums. This is a group that excelled at live performance, opening with a Mahavishnu-like fanfare, and then building layer upon layer of thick texture, where improvisation and precomposed parts intersect. Christian Vander demonstrates abundantly why he is justifiably regarded as one of the world's great percussionists, and the performances by bassist Bernard Paganotti and violinist Didier Lockwood also stand out.

The most important record of 1975, in my opinion, was the Henry Cow/Slapp Happy collaboration, *In Praise of Learning*. The group's radical politics come to the fore, and yet this is not a mere exercise in socialist realism. By turns harsh and grating, and then jazzy in an almost bebop vein, the lyrical vision is informed by Bertolt Brecht. Structurally, the influence of Brecht's collaborator, Kurt Weil, is also in evidence. The heart of the album is a four-part suite, beginning with "War" and concluding with "Beautiful as the Moon—Terrible as an Army with Banners." As these titles suggest, there is a martial air about much of the music, very insistent without being in any sense marching music. Dagmar Krause's voice, capable of ordinary beauty but staying mostly on the side of a well-crafted jaggedness, really makes the album. After the decoupling of Slapp Happy from Henry Cow, Krause stayed with the latter for their subsequent album, *Concerts*; she would also continue working with Fred Frith and Chris Cutler in the post-Henry Cow group, Art Bears.

Significantly, as the sixties spirit was fading from the rest of progressive rock, and as the genre was mainly in decline, Henry Cow made their best albums and created a situation in which most of its members would continue to be creative participants in rock music's avant-garde. As one of the groups less inclined toward the romantic and utopian side of the sixties, and more toward straightforwardly Marxist views, the longevity of Henry Cow and its offshoots becomes even more interesting. Even as someone who is inclined toward systematic radical social theory, it is not my view that having a "systematic" analysis necessarily leads to better music making. (An interesting parallel case could be set up regarding science-fiction writers.) On the other hand, if one's inspiration is mainly drawn from what is "in the air," so to speak, then clearly it will be easy to lose one's bearings when the "air" changes significantly. In other words, this is where having some developed understanding, of, say, what 1968 was all about, as opposed to simply a "positive hit," may enable an artist or musical group to take that inspiration further, especially when this inspiration is no longer right in front of you.

1976

As the reader will readily see, things really start to thin out even more at this point. Among the nonprogressive rock albums that might be mentioned are Patti Smith's *Radio Ethiopia*, which I regard as her best album, and Joni Mitchell's *Hejira*, which features fascinating interplay with the great Jaco Pastorius. His bass guitar innovations, which were turning lots of heads at that point (and not only those of other bass players, although a rather large school of imitators did indeed begin to spring up), are also heard on Weather Report's *Heavy Weather* from that year. Stevie Wonder completed his trilogy of progressive soul albums with *Songs in the Key of Life*, a double album that perhaps should have been a single, but which contains some great work nonetheless. Another excellent progressive soul album that year was the Isley Brothers' *Harvest for the World*. Led Zeppelin's *Presence* was the last real album from that group, whose trajectory followed somewhat the fortunes of progressive rock.

Slim pickings from the second line, and almost as slim from the first line. Van der Graaf made one of their better albums, and indeed their last good one, *Still Life*. Jade Warrior's *Kites* is an austere Zen tone poem, a meeting place of abstraction and subtraction. An interesting album that is more in the spirit of progressive rock's early days, especially in the vein of Genesis's *Trespass* or *The Yes Album*, is the record by the group Tai Phong, *Windows*. The group was made up of Chinese and French members.

Two of the more significant second-line albums for 1976 demonstrated future directions. I will probably be excoriated by some for mentioning this group or album (though perhaps loved by others), but the Canadian group Rush put out their first album that came quite close to progressive rock, *2112*. Despite all the things that people generally say about this group or some of its albums, and despite the ideological inspiration for *2112* in particular, I think the album is basically good. A few more comments on Rush will be found in the next chapter.

I have argued that progressive rock, or at least much of it, was already what has more recently been called "world music." An album that makes this abundantly clear, and that comes closer to the sound that people more typically associate with world music in recent years, is Patrick Moraz's *i*. The album tells the story of a hierarchical society in which everyone must engage in a pointless struggle to get to the top—at which point there is nothing left to do but to jump off into nothingness. Sounds familiar. Moraz has always had some interesting things to say on the synthesizer—he is an especially provocative note bender, as he demonstrated on Yes's *Relayer*. Here he is backed by a large group of Brazilian percussionists, as well as the great drumming of Alphonse Mouzon. This is one of the two or three best albums of 1976.

We usually think of post-Peter Gabriel Genesis in terms of the pretty awful, syrupy pop songs of the Phil Collins-fronted version. However, in 1976, Genesis made two good albums without Gabriel, *A Trick of the Tail* and *Wind and Wuthering*. The music alternates between moments that are charmingly delicate, if at times overly precious, and fusion passages that presage Collins's later involvement with Brand X. Collins is a capable singer, as demonstrated on previous Genesis albums, and an excellent drummer as well. After these albums it was not performative skills that were lacking, however, but decent material. Then, again, Genesis were not unlike most progressive rock groups, who didn't know what to do with their skills as the culture around them changed. Gentle Giant attempted the "lighten-up" option with *Interview*, while Jethro Tull took the heavy handed approach with *Too Old to Rock 'n' Roll, Too Young to Die*. Neither served as (good) answers to the question, What do progressive rockers do after their time? But Tull's album title summed up the problem well enough.

Two groups unburdened themselves of a few members, presenting themselves in stripped-down form. The streamlined Magma of *Udu Wudu* is somehow even more ominous than the full-force version. Gong, with the departure of Daevid Allen, Gilli Smyth, and Tim Blake, became a more straightforward jazz-rock affair. *Shamal* has some moments, but it is difficult to hear it as a *Gong* album.

Which leaves Henry Cow, whose *Concerts* was the best first-line album of 1976. The group used to play seated in comfortably padded chairs, in a parody of the Victorian parlor, with lamps, end tables, and other accoutrements of bourgeois civility. The music, by contrast, was anything but civil, at least in bourgeois terms. Large sections of *Concerts* are dominated by small sounds, which Henry Cow, in a manner not unlike Pharoah Sanders's work with saxophone effects, developed into a musical language of its own. To be honest, I find some of this more irritating than musically effective, but then, it becomes more and more difficult to listen to small sounds in the time of fast capitalism.

1977

For the first time, even from the perspective of progressive rock, it seems the "outside developments" have become more interesting. Readers of this book who are committed to the progressive-rock aesthetic (I assume this is the majority, to say the least) may prefer not to hear about some of these developments, or to pretend that they do not exist. But exist they do, and their appearance and the waning of the time of progressive rock are clearly connected—even if not necessarily in the way that some readers might think. There is a tendency among progressive-rock fans to think that punk and new wave came on the scene partly as a revolt of barely capable musicians against the virtuosos, and that record companies seized upon this new fad and concomitantly put progressive rock on the back burner (or back in the refrigerator). This scenario, though it may be a part of the truth, is really only a small part. Punk rock may have seemed a dominant cultural phenomenon, partly because *Time* or *Newsweek* or "Sixty Minutes" were busy fretting over it, but, in reality, the actual punk counterculture was never even as large as the progressive-rock counterculture. The fact is that, as the youth culture changed from one that, to some extent, celebrated utopian visions, to one that wanted and needed to respond to rumblings of global conflict, superpower tensions, and arms buildups, progressive rock did not *progress* along with this change. More on these themes in the next chapter.

Three good albums that were on the periphery of progressive rock were Bill Bruford's first solo album, *Feels Good to Me*, Pink Floyd's *Animals*, and Steely Dan's *Aja*. Bruford's album featured clever, often very angular, compositions, and excellent contributions from Dave Stewart, Allan Holdsworth, bassist Jeff Berlin, and vocalist Annette Peacocke. The title song for Steely Dan's *Aja* is one of their most postmodern songs, with its "angular banjos" and dude ranches by the sea. It's a great send-up of emerging new-age and yuppie culture, with great drumming from Steve Gadd.

The four other albums that I will mention here are more indicative of the emerging punk counterculture, even if two of them are not, strictly speaking, albums of "punk" music. In my view, it is no exaggeration to say that the appearance of the Sex Pistols' *Never Mind the Bollocks* changed everything—like it or not, ready or not. Recall that the middle seventies were not only a time of progressive rock; mainstream radio gave most of its airtime to what might be called "low-energy" music—such as the Eagles and Linda Ronstadt. When the Sex Pistols messed up this low-key affair, it made even "high-energy" groups of the time, such as Led Zeppelin, look like they were moving in slow motion. You can say what you want about the Pistols as "musicians," but, the fact is, if you actually listen to *Never Mind the Bollocks*, you'll hear sounds—hellacious, raucous, painful, militant sounds—that have not been heard before. And that is what music is supposed to be about. (I put the word "musicians" in scare-quotes not as a way of saying that the Sex Pistols are not musicians, but instead as a way of problematizing the term, and of showing its irrelevance to the issue at hand.)

Bob Marley and the Wailers recorded one of their most powerful albums, *Exodus*. The Clash released their first (self-titled) album, and the Talking Heads also came on the scene with *Talking Heads: 77*.

Perhaps significantly, Brian Eno put out his last "rock" album that year, *Before and After Science*. Hereafter, it's all timbre and texture, perfume and wallpaper.

Even apart from these other developments, the fact is that, in 1977, there was no more activity among first-line groups than there had been in 1968. One of these three had been active in 1968, namely Jethro Tull. After the misstep of *Too Old to Rock 'n'*

Roll, the group recovered nicely with *Songs from the Wood*. The album set the direction that Tull has followed up until this day, going back into their folk and blues roots, with admixtures of hard rock and progressive. Gentle Giant continued the effort to lighten their sound, with *The Missing Piece*. In some ways, as one of the more "technical" of progressive rock groups, Gentle Giant was the least prepared to turn any cultural corners.

Finally, after a couple of years of group inactivity, Yes released what I think of as the last "album of the year" of the time of progressive rock, *Going for the One*. The group had spent the previous two years making solo albums, the best of which are Chris Squire's *Fish Out of Water* and Jon Anderson's *Olias of Sunhillow*. In retrospect, *Going for the One* shows the group in transition to its later incarnations, and yet playing full-blown progressive rock for the most part. The title track is as good a synthesis of Chuck Berry-ish rock 'n' roll and progressive as anything you might find, though it does go on a bit too long at the end. The song features Steve Howe exclusively on steel guitar, on which instrument he burns intensely. Chris Squire's "Parallels," which obviously comes out of the same songwriting frame as did the pieces for his solo album, is the flip side of the title track, in that it is organ driven in a grand style. The church organ here is played by Rick Wakeman, who had returned to the fold. "Turn of the Century" and "Wondrous Stories" provide yet more contrast, in that both feature acoustic instruments almost exclusively. The former also shows the compositional contributions of Alan White. Finally, "Awaken" is another of the great Yes epics, perhaps their most "cosmic" piece of music—and yet it ends with a warm, almost R&B-ish guitar figure and the homely line, "Like the time I ran away—turned around and you were standing close to me."

1978

Strangely enough, this final year of what I have defined as the "time" of progressive rock sees slightly more activity than the previous year. However, though a few of the albums from the first and second lines are well worth having, at this point there is little new ground being broken: progressive rock has almost entirely ceased being progressive, and it can no longer be called a trend, much less a movement.

The Clash and Talking Heads each released a second album in 1978. Significantly, both were struggling with the problem of musical development beyond basic structures. Soon enough, beginning with the Clash's third album, punk purists would be crying "sell-out." But, what's a young punk to do—if you've mastered the one chord, doesn't it make sense to go on to another one? The Who, following the death of Keith Moon, released the synthesizer-heavy *Who Are You*. Owing a good deal more to progressive rock than most critics are willing to admit, as well as progressive soul, Hendrix, and Sly Stone, Funkadelic released *One Nation under a Groove*. Even further into the "willing to admit" category are 1978's two albums from the Cleveland group Pere Ubu, which especially bear traces of Canterbury wackitude.

Rush continued their progressive explorations, with *Hemispheres* (the previous year they had released *A Farewell to Kings*). An Italian group that demonstrated strong borrowings from the European avant-garde was Area; their *gli dei se ne vanno, gli arrabbiati restano!* is quite good. And Canterbury fusion was gearing up at that point, with the second album from Gilgamesh (*Another Fine Tune You've Gotten Me Into*), the first album from National Health (self-titled), and the quasi-Canterbury (in spirit, anyway, geography somewhat aside) first album from U.K., featuring Bill Bruford, Allan Holdsworth, John Wetton, and former Roxy keyboardist Eddie Jobson. The interplay between Bruford and Wetton is the highlight of the album, without which the song structures on top would not be that interesting.

Of the five first-line bands still active, Gentle Giant (*Giant for a Day*) and Jethro Tull (*Heavy Horses*) were moving away from progressive rock. Magma continued the streamlined approach with *Attahk*. Yes was quite evidently in the midst of a painful transition, releasing the overly produced and busy *Tormato*. There is some good music in there, somewhere, but the album has an unfinished quality about it. The horrible album cover, and title for that matter, just about summed things up. Which leaves Henry Cow; the group released a final album under the Cow name, *Western Culture*, and it is quite good. Perhaps their album cover sums things up as well.

Although some of the first-line groups would make interesting—as opposed to not interesting—transitions to the time after the time of progressive rock, perhaps it is significant that Henry Cow made one of the last really good progressive rock albums. Throughout the time of progressive rock, they were among the groups most closely connected to a larger musical avant-garde, and they maintained this connection both in the later years of the group and in the post-Henry Cow projects that individual members would undertake. Interestingly, they were arguably the group least connected to the more romantic aspects of progressive rock. I will return to these issues in the afterword.

Rather than leave the time of progressive rock with the feeling that everything went downhill toward the end, let us reflect on the many great albums that have filled these many pages. Here, then, another gathering of the "albums of the year" and some other essential records that would form the core of a good collection:

1968 Soft Machine, *Soft Machine*
1969 King Crimson, *In the Court of the Crimson King*
1970 Caravan, *In the Land of Grey and Pink*
      Emerson, Lake, and Palmer, *Emerson, Lake and Palmer*
      Genesis, *Trespass*
      Jethro Tull, *Benefit*
      King Crimson, *In the Wake of Poseidon, Lizard*
      Soft Machine, *Third*
      Curved Air, *Airconditioning*
      McDonald and Giles, *McDonald and Giles*
      Van der Graaf Generator, *H to He, Who Am the Only One*
1971 Emerson, Lake, and Palmer, *Tarkus*
      Gentle Giant, *Acquiring the Taste*
      Yes, *The Yes Album, Fragile*
      Egg, *The Polite Force*
      Van der Graaf Generator, *Pawn Hearts*
1972 Jethro Tull, *Thick as a Brick*
      Mahavishnu Orchestra, *Inner Mounting Flame*
      PFM, *Entrata*
      Yes, *Close to the Edge*
      Flash, *Flash in the Can*
      Focus, *Moving Waves*
      Matching Mole, *Matching Mole*
1973 Caravan, *For Girls Who Grow Plump in the Night*
      Emerson, Lake, and Palmer, *Brain Salad Surgery*

Gong, *The Flying Teapot*, *Angel's Egg*
Jethro Tull, *A Passion Play*
King Crimson, *Larks' Tongues in Aspic*
Magma, *Mekanik Destruktiw Kommandoh*
Mahavishnu Orchestra, *Birds of Fire*
PFM, *Photos of Ghosts*
Soft Machine, *Six*
Back Door, *Back Door*
Flash, *Out of Our Hands*
Jonesy, *Keeping Up*
Pete Sinfield, *Still*
1974 Gentle Giant, *The Power and the Glory*
King Crimson, *Red*
Yes, *Relayer*
Can, *Soon Over Babaluma*
Hatfield and the North, *Hatfield and the North*
Jade Warrior, *Floating World*
Nektar, *Remember the Future*
Strawbs, *Hero and Heroine*
Tasavallan Presidenti, *Milky Way Moses*
Robert Wyatt, *Rock Bottom*
1975 Gentle Giant, *Free Hand*
Henry Cow, *In Praise of Learning*
Magma, *Live*
Banco, *Banco*
Camel, *The Snow Goose*
Steve Hillage, *Fish Rising*
Mike Oldfield, *Ommadawn*
Renaissance, *Turn of the Cards*
1976 Henry Cow, *Concerts*
Patrick Moraz, *i*
1977 Yes, *Going for the One*
Bill Bruford, *Feels Good to Me*
1978 Henry Cow, *Western Culture*

5

After the time of progressive rock, 1977–1997

In the fall of 1996, Yes released a new album featuring the classic midseventies line-up of Jon Anderson, Chris Squire, Steve Howe, Rick Wakeman, and Alan White. *Keys to Ascension* contains both the old and the new, a set of recent performances of Yes classics, from "Starship Trooper" to "Awaken," and two new works, "Be the One" and "That, That Is." The last of these is a piece of full-blown progressive rock, quite possibly able to stand with the group's best work from the seventies. Nostalgia or rebirth? What light is cast on this question by the developments in the two decades from 1977 to 1997?

In 1977, the Sex Pistols released *Never Mind the Bollocks.* Jethro Tull gave us some *Songs from the Wood*, Yes presented *Going for the One*, Emerson, Lake, and Palmer were busy not being a band (that is, making their largely solo *Works*) and heading for the awful shores of *Love Beach*; the Crimson King had already been on open-ended sabbatical for a few years. The wood was much preferable to the beach, in my view, but had both become mere retreats from anarchy in the U.K.? Meanwhile, it at least appeared that Yes had gone even more cosmic, into a pure exploration of (what Heidegger called) fundamental ontology.

Come 1995, Ian Anderson and Tull continued to exhibit their affection for the woods and trees, with an album titled *Roots and Branches*. A fine effort, with a charm and economy not unlike that of *Benefit*, but now interpolated with an interesting Middle Eastern influence. King Crimson geared up for an extended "Thrakattak," reforming with the quartet from the eighties, and adding an additional drummer and Chapman Stick player for a "double trio" effect. I had the good fortune to hear both groups within a couple weeks of one another in the fall of 1995. Ian Anderson is on the verge of losing his voice altogether (too many years of smoking and playing in smoke-filled auditoriums), which is a very sad thing. However, his flute-playing has gained proportionately, and his compositional skills have remained on a high level ever since the few bad years of the late seventies. Martin Barre has become a more multidimensional guitarist in recent years, and the group also seems to have a solid core with the continued participation of drummer Doane Perry. The latter's style is both virtuosic and understated, not unlike an orchestral percussionist, and is emblematic of Tull's recent material.

Emerson, Lake, and Palmer, though their two albums since their reformation in the nineties are quite spotty (especially 1994's *In the Hot Seat*), have given some masterful performances as the opening act on tour with Jethro Tull. I heard them in the summer of 1996, and none of the three were playing as if they didn't really want to or know how to anymore—quite the contrary, their love for the performance of challenging music was abundantly clear. Keith Emerson seems to have figured out how to manage the problems he has had with carpal tunnel syndrome. Carl Palmer was simply astounding, his drumming as precise and difficult as any I have ever heard; indeed, in my view Palmer's musicianship was much improved from when I heard him in 1973, on the *Brain Salad Surgery* tour—which is the way it's supposed to be.

If I may stay with that August 1996 Tull/ELP concert at the World Music Theatre (near Chicago) for a moment, it does perhaps serve as something of a barometer. The music was there, at least for the most part. The occasion of Tull's tour was the twenty-fifth anniversary of *Aqualung*, so obviously there was a harkening back to the heyday of progressive rock. That particular album, which to be honest is not one of my favorites, has a following that goes beyond the usual fans of progressive, appealing to fans of heavy metal or what we used to call "hard rock" as well. The group played material from every phase of their existence, going back to *Stand Up*. This could be interpreted as a mere nostalgia trip (or money-maker), except that the band had toured the previous year with their then-new album, *Roots to Branches*, and they also played recent material on the *Aqualung* anniversary tour. Emerson, Lake, and Palmer, on the other hand, did not have much new to show for themselves, and mainly played material from *Tarkus* and *Brain Salad Surgery*. They also performed "America," with Emerson doing his thing with the Hammond. That I definitely could have done without, but this unfortunately leads to the other side of the equation at that concert. That is, the music was mostly there, but the people mostly were not. As much as I dislike going to large rock concerts in general, because of the inattentive audiences, I disliked that particular concert that much more. There were some devoted listeners in the area just in front of the stage (which is not where I, along with philosopher and Tullologist David Detmer and my Open Court editor Kerri Mommer, were sitting, unfortunately), but for the most part the audience treated the music as an afterthought—they were there to party, and the music was merely background for that. There were many people at the concert who did not stop talking—and I mean yacking, really—for the entire performance, except for one short period, namely when Emerson was tossing his organ about. That got some people's attention, at least momentarily.

In other words, what's up with progressive rock? What are groups such as King Crimson, Yes, Jethro Tull, and Emerson, Lake, and Palmer even doing *existing* in the waning years of the twentieth century? Clearly, there cannot be a progressive-rock *trend* that consists in having the old bands play mostly their old music for arena-sized audiences that aren't really listening to it. Well, so what? My point is that a music that has roots in a counterculture becomes something quite different when there is no longer a countercultural background and it is now just one of many kinds of music that a few people happen to like. But we haven't gone far enough to fill out this picture.

I should mention that, like many who will read this book, I feel very much *personally* involved in these issues, and personally *concerned* regarding the outcome of the questions that will be raised here. Although I hope to offer some useful, and I hope accurate, descriptions as well as some analytical tools here, I cannot claim that my analysis is dispassionate.

▗ ▗ ▗

No sooner had punk emerged, as a seeming negation of progressive rock, than another new development in music appeared as well, namely new wave. The progressive/punk dichotomy is in fact an oversimplification, given that both musics had roots in the idea of a cultural alternative. Certainly, punk seemed absolutely artless in contrast with *Lizard* or *In Praise of Learning*, but, as with other "raw" musics, for example the Velvet Underground or John Lennon's first solo album (*Plastic Ono Band*, 1970), there is an art to creating this effect. Contrary to popular opinion, and the opinion of many progressive-rock fans, finding a sound like that of the most powerful punk groups, such as the Pistols, the Dead Kennedys, the Circle Jerks, or Hüsker Dü, is not something just anybody can do by banging on some drums and wires. (When I say "just anybody," I'm including musicians who may be quite accomplished on their instruments.) But punk did face a quandary of sorts, namely that it had to develop musically if it was going to be anything more than a very loud roar streaming through the mosh pit. Thus, most of the major punk groups either packed it in after making their definitive statement, or in any case only put out one album with a signature sound that was worth hearing, or they developed in terms of their formal experimentation and songwriting abilities. Soon enough, Hüsker Dü released what I think of as punk's "Quadrophenia," the double-LP concept album, *Zen Arcade*. Then the Minutemen followed with *Double Nickels on the Dime*. The Clash put out *London Calling* (two records), *Sandinista* (a triple), and *Combat Rock*. By the mideighties, punk was either a "hard-core" taste for a few people with leather jackets, seemingly permanent sneers (often no longer with much social content), and mohawks, or it had merged into the larger new-wave scene.

And new wave itself both developed and carried forward and recapitulated a good deal of the material from earlier periods of rock music. The career of Talking Heads is as good an example of this as any. They began with a very streamlined sound, more artsy-alienated than angry. However, by their second album, 1978's *More Songs About Buildings and Food*, they were produced by Brian Eno. By 1980 and their fourth album, *Remain in Light* (also produced by Eno), it seemed as though the Heads created a kind of new-wave music that was the perfect synthesis of punk urgency and attitude and progressive-rock sophistication and creativity. A good deal of the more interesting rock since that time is clearly "post-Talking Heads" music, but this means that it is post-progressive rock as well.

There are numerous persons who could be named as "bridge" or transitional figures in all of this, including Bill Laswell, Peter Gabriel, and even Robert Fripp to some extent. But clearly the person who has served as the most important catalyst for post-progressive rock is Brian Eno. Consider his four solo albums of "rock" music ("rock" as compared to his work in ambient and other genres that is): *Here Come the Warm Jets* (1973), *Taking Tiger Mountain (By Strategy)* (1974), *Another Green World* (1975), and *Before and After Science* (1977). Are these albums a weird warping of some aspects of progressive rock, a strange premonition of punk, or the first approximations of the new wave? (The first two albums by Roxy Music, which also featured Eno's contributions, can be added to this list.) The answer is "all three," of course. As much as Eno and some others might want to distance themselves from the phenomena of progressive rock, however, clearly the musical language of Eno's rock albums, and his "postrock" experiments, for that matter, owe a great deal to progressive rock.

What I find interesting is that some of the distancing that has occurred—Robert Fripp being the other person I am worried about here—has been done in the name of experimentalism, while fitting in too well with other sorts of imperatives, especially the imperative to avoid the pariah status that too close an association with progressive rock can confer upon bands that hope to have large audiences. Obviously, neither Eno nor Fripp are pure seekers after commercial success; on the other hand, I personally do not see anything so experimental about working with David

Bowie or U2. Furthermore, both have wrapped themselves in the garb of being among the "deep thinkers" of experimental rock music, in supposed contrast to the continuing flower-power obsessions of those old "prog" musicians. Eno does have *some* interesting thoughts, as well as some that are not especially well-grounded—as seen in his recently published diary, *A Year with Swollen Appendices*. If he hopes to be something like the John Cage of rock, fine; if he hopes to take up where Cage left off, I think he has some way to go. (But that's o.k.—we all do.) From Cage to Eno is, in philosophical terms, something like the shift from Emerson (Ralph Waldo, that is) to Richard Rorty.[1] Fripp's pronouncements, on the other hand, are often somewhere between simply goofy and quite authoritarian. Among other things, and as with someone else in his group, namely Bill Bruford, he has not thought through the class biases of his position.

This I find interesting in the light of the way that Bruford tends to distance himself from Yes. For instance, in Tim Morse's book, *Yesstories: Yes in Their Own Words*, Bruford makes a strange comment to the effect that he once visited Jon Anderson's hometown (Accrington, an industrial town in the north of England) and parents and found the whole thing distasteful. Unlike Anderson, Bruford comes from a solid middle-class background. Clearly, having such a background gives one certain expectations and a sense of entitlement. Perhaps it is a very presumptuous thing to say, but there seems to be an ongoing struggle within the psyche of Bill Bruford regarding these expectations. Robert Fripp lately seems to be inclined to distance King Crimson, more or less for the entire course of its history, from progressive rock (see, for example, his comments in the *Epitaph* album liner notes, or even in the notes to the *Great Deceiver* set, where Fripp calls King Crimson a "heavy-metal" group). Bruford goes even further: he always seems at pains to somehow identify himself as either a "jazz" musician or as someone whose playing is more akin to that of European classical percussionists (see, for example, some of his comments in his book, *When in Doubt, Roll!*). Well, of course one theme of this book has been that categories such as "jazz," "classical," and "rock" became very malleable in the sixties. Bruford has played some music that is in the vicinity of jazz, so to speak, but I wouldn't really call him a "jazz" drummer, if only in the sense that, when

I think of who the great and near-great jazz drummers are, from Max Roach or Art Blakey or Elvin Jones or, more recently, Tony Williams or even Ronald Shannon Jackson (who has certainly played a good deal of music somewhere in the vicinity of rock), Bruford's name just doesn't seem to suggest itself. But this does not mean that he is not a great drummer—please understand, as far as I am concerned, he is as creative and technically proficient as anyone who has played the drums. The point, instead, is that Bill Bruford is one of the great rock drummers and one of the great drummers. What I wonder about is why he is not satisfied with that, and I have to wonder if it has to do with the idea that rock music is somehow not "high class" enough.

Why is any of this either here or there? True, it is strange to place the pieces on King Crimson's *Thrak* next to "That, that is" from Yes's *Keys to Ascension*. In the former case, the longest piece, "Dinosaur," clocks in at 6'35", whereas "That, that is" is nearly twenty minutes long. The lineage of the Yes piece is clear—it is a work of "full-blown" progressive rock, and makes no bones about it. But *Thrak* too has its progressive background, all denials aside. Part of what is at work here, too, is a recent tendency to somehow separate some *one group* from the rest of progressive rock. As I noted in chapter 3, Mike Barnes of *The Wire* tried to do this with Henry Cow; then he went on, in a later issue of the magazine, to do the same thing with King Crimson—which kind of complicates the issue, doesn't it? (This is a common thing in newspapers in the U.S. when King Crimson comes to town; the first sentence of the concert review is always already written, something to the effect that King Crimson seems to have "escaped the taint of those other progressive-rock dinosaurs.") Well, what artists think they are doing and what they are actually doing are sometimes two different things. It seems to me that, if you take the thirteen groups that I identified as progressive rock's first line, you will see a well-articulated range of progressive-rock possibilities. And King Crimson fits into that range, even if often, *along with Yes*, at the forefront of those possibilities.

Still, what King Crimson (or Robert Fripp or Bill Bruford) *think* they are doing, vis-à-vis progressive rock, and what Eno thinks he is doing, for that matter, does bear on the status, if you will, of progressive rock at the fin-de-siècle. In other words, just as the work (or hiatuses) of the "pillars" of progressive rock serves as a barometer of the genre in its heyday, so too can it tell us something about present possibilities.

There are good signs and bad signs, as regards these present possibilities of progressive rock. I will take account of both; rather than simply offer a diagnosis of the situation—though I will do that, to some extent—my ultimate goal is to point to ways that the "good signs" might be built upon. But, regarding the diagnosis, there is no denying that the times are against us and that the better possibilities of progressive rock require swimming against the tide.

The later seventies were obviously not the best of times for progressive rock. Critics and fans tend to focus on the actions of individual bands or musicians, asking questions of the, "Why didn't they do . . . ?" variety. In my view, this approach is wrong-headed. The reason for this is not that hard to see. If art and thought are always a part of their time, then, if "their time" passes, there has to be a change. Everyone recognizes that there was a sea-change in music in the late seventies, and that the time of progressive rock—its "heyday," as I've been calling it—came to a close. What has not been recognized so well is the larger cultural and social contexts of this change. However, I suspect that, when I lay out the terms of this cultural shift, readers will not be completely surprised.

One very straightforward way to express what happened is that, by 1977 or 1978, the sixties (as a political and cultural phenomenon, not simply as the chronological description of a decade) were mostly played out.

Now, let's not be too quick to accept this idea. In my view, the great liberatory themes and movements of that time will never be played out, at least not until humanity lives in a radically transformed and redeemed world. Looked at purely in terms of philosophy and social theory, the critique of capitalism, patriarchy, and racist social structures, offered by figures such as Herbert Marcuse, Jean-Paul Sartre, Simone de Beauvoir, Shulamith Firestone, Franz Fanon, Malcolm X, and many, many other "sixties" thinkers and activists, is still quite relevant today. Certainly there are some "bad new things" (as Bertolt Brecht put it) that also require our attention, and that require transformations of theoretical frameworks, but this does not cancel the need to make what use we can of the earlier analyses. Again, in my view, there is a great deal that we can continue to learn.[2]

Significantly, something quite similar could be said about rock music, and it is clear that the lesson has not been lost. The sixties continue to be a gold mine for those looking for musical inspiration (in a sense, *Mojo* magazine bases its entire existence on this fact), and not only from a "retro" perspective. In fact, because there are many creative musicians and groups that do not want to simply retrofit the music of the sixties, but also to make their own contributions, some recent rock music stands at the very precipice of progressive rock. This is seen in a number of trends, including a more recent version of "stretching out" (as I called it in chapter 3). Among the interesting groups that might be included here are Phish and the Dave Matthews Band.

Phish is very much in the American grain, so to speak; even though the group is from Vermont, they are frequently associated with the Bay Area scene, in particular with the Grateful Dead. Although the more psychedelic and "loose" aspects of their music are reminiscent of the Dead and other San Francisco groups, they are also capable of intricate and inventive ensemble work. Combine this with their wonderful wit and the group reminds me just as much of Caravan or the Hatfields as it does the Dead. Perhaps this should not be surprising, given that Vermont lies somewhere between Canterbury and the left coast.

The Dave Matthews Band is also possessed of great wit and a sense of irony, as especially demonstrated in a song such as "Typical Situation" from *Under the Table and Dreaming* (1994). I saw the group on television a few times when this album was released, and not only was the music interesting, but I could not help but think, "this music has a lot of affinities with progressive rock." Listening to the whole album and holding the cover in my hand further confirmed this impression. Indeed, the album cover is representative of the music contained therein, in that both work on many levels. The cover photograph, of a carnival ride (some sort of whirl-around contraption, with people hanging from cables), can also be seen as a luminescent sea creature or as a flying saucer. By the same token, the music demonstrates that peculiar combination of existentialism and transcendent vision that typifies much progressive rock. The group uses an interesting combination of instruments. Dave Matthews plays acoustic guitar exclusively, and there is no electric guitar used in the group. His exceedingly angular style is well-matched by the Billy Cobham-like percussion of ambidextrous drummer Carter Beauford. The group is completed by bass guitarist Stefan Lessard, saxophonist and flutist Leroi Moore, and violinist Boyd Tinsley.

Both Phish and the Dave Matthews Band are not unlike the best of progressive rock in that they build on the best of what has already been done in rock and yet they clearly have their own contributions to make. Both groups also seem to be making more or less the records that they want to make, and it would be worth-while to inquire as to what conditions in the music business allow this to happen.[3]

For the moment, however, let us reconnect with the earlier thought, that the sixties are played out. The two groups I have just discussed are clear examples of the fact that there is still a sixties vibe that continues to be felt. But we are also looking at this from the perspective, not of 1978, but the late nineties, when at least certain aspects of the sixties are allowable as long as they stay purely in the realm of fashion. We've gone, that is, from the time of Thatcher and Reagan, openly reactionary haters of every-thing the sixties stood for, to the time of Bill Clinton and Tony Blair, figures with a certain amount of sixties credibility (or at least some of the outer trappings). Clinton, anyway, has been able to do things that Reagan or Bush could never have gotten away with, precisely because of his sixties psychobabble schtick ("I feel your pain") (As of this writing, Blair has just come into office; one of his first acts was to place English currency more fully into the global market.)

In 1978, it seemed that one thing lacking from progressive rock was *urgency*. For all of the music's power, at its best, to speak in complex ways and on many levels, the new aggressivity of the social systems in the United States and Western Europe seemed to demand a more "in your face" response. The time of capital-ism's ideological retreat, which allowed for much creative social and artistic expression, was over. Because, contrary to the dominant ideology, money does not by itself create more money, capital cannot stand still for long. Capital, of necessity, must circulate, and carve out new territories for itself. But capitalism is forever divided against itself, and sometimes its internal tensions play themselves out on a global scale. In the late seventies, tensions between the two superpowers (one openly capitalist, the other claiming to be socialist, but in fact capitalist in all significant respects) were fostering the rhetoric of world war. Beginning in 1980, and carrying forward programs already set in place by Jimmy Carter, Ronald Reagan began a military rearmament program of utterly unprecedented proportions—the ultimate price tag topping one trillion dollars. Some analysts see this rearmament (which had wide-ranging consequences in terms of the economy, to be sure, and which ran circuits through Iran, the Contras, and the savings and loans failures) purely as "military Keynesianism," as a perverse scheme to get the American economy going. This was part of it, to be sure, but the main thrust of Reagan's militarism was to challenge the Soviet Union for global domination. Against the crazy jingoism of that time, it seemed that those who were in a position to make a public statement, including musicians, had to find a more forceful way of saying, "What kind of social system is it that, in order to sustain itself, has to risk destroying all of humanity?"

Significantly, then, the more experimental expressions of the sixties got it from both sides. The establishment declared that playtime was over, while the punks refused affirmative visions.

The much-vaunted dichotomy of progressive and punk was never as simple as some critics or fans (on either side) took it to be. In the best of cases, both sides were serious about philosophical and social themes, and about the power of music. It is commonly assumed that the latter cannot really be the case, given that many punks seemed to have meagre instrumental skills. Actually, many punk rockers are better musicians than people give them credit for being, and the style (or styles) of punk musical practice is not as easily acquired as some who are skilled at playing some instrument might think it is. (And, by the way—switching terrain for a moment, but the point still applies—who really wants to discuss Bob Dylan's music in terms of his skills as a guitarist or harmonica player?) In any case, punk (and again, I mean the best of it—why think about anything else?) shared with progressive the idea that important things could be said with and through music.

Progressive rock in the last years of the seventies did not seem up to speed for saying things that desperately needed to be said. Indeed, desperation and urgency seem qualities quite lacking from progressive rock, just as multidimensionality and introspection seem no part of punk. In the *worst* cases, punk becomes unidimensional in a way that could hardly challenge a "one-dimensional" social system, while progressive rock becomes merely ponderous. Returning to themes presented in the introductory chapter, radical negativity can give way to cynicism, while radical affirmation can become mere pie-in-the-sky "utopianism," too much flower and not enough sense of the actual workings of power. In the best of cases, however, there is not a dichotomy or opposition here, but a productive, radical dialectic. Given that the progressive-rock sixties (which occurred mostly in the chronological seventies) and the punk eighties are both declared "played out," there is a work of radical retrieval and extension to be done here.

Progressive-rock musicians in the late seventies were stymied. For a few years, some limped along, in configurations that carried on with some aspects of progressive rock, but that also seemed a faint echo of the glory days. A significant segment turned from jazz-inflected progressive rock toward more outright jazz-rock. Others took part in music that was more in the mainstream of rock.

I've focused, for the past few pages, on social and political factors in the transformations of music in the late seventies. Are there, however, factors deserving of attention that have to do more specifically with the music itself? From a dialectical perspective, there is the matter of looking at not only "external" conditions, but also the "internal" constitution of the phenomenon that is undergoing transformation. Perhaps the paradigm of progressive rock had been exhausted. Perhaps *this* configuration of avant-gardism, virtuoso skills, and English romanticism had given all that it had to give. It has to be said that it was not only rock music's avant-gardes that seemed exhausted. The whole idea of an avant-garde also seemed played out; to some extent, even the mixing of musical genres that went into full swing in the late sixties began to slow down.

As it turns out, it is almost impossible to deal with the question of "exhaustion" in its own right. Of course, no one can predict precisely what languages and discourses of the past might continue to say to us, but it is hard for me to imagine that there is nothing more to be heard from, for instance, musical experimentation, romanticism, or musicians who work hard to perfect their skills. Some combinations of these elements may seem to be not very relevant at any particular time. But perhaps something is deeply out of joint with the time itself! Perhaps the music is good, but the times are bad for hearing it. This is not to say that great music is timeless; on the contrary, great music takes time to listen to and appreciate, but such time is not always available. In this light, we might notice that progressive rock has taken it on the chin twice.

Perhaps the first time was a "fair punch," in that a good argument could be made for thinking the Reagan/Thatcher era was more a time for militant protests against the possibility of nuclear war than it was for beautiful hymns to the cosmos (in *music of Yes* I contrast the Sex Pistols' "Pretty Vacant" to Yes's "Awaken"; see p. 186). But then, when even punk musicians recognized that, after the first great albums that consisted in concentrated bursts of negativity (*Never Mind the Bollocks* remaining at the fore of this effort), they had to deepen and develop the music (in which case they generally ran up against the limitations of their basic musical material, and rarely transcended those limitations), the sort of dynamic opens up that leads, eventually, to the idea that music needs to be experimental and go somewhere—the idea that music needs to be "progressive"!

Then comes the second punch, however: now we do not have time for progressive rock because the general culture of distraction does not allow for the mental activity requisite for appreciating it. I cannot help but recall my earlier remarks regarding the fact that some critics have attacked progressive-rock pieces purely because of their length. Whether any particular piece is the appropriate length for its material is one question, but the idea that a piece of rock music should not be twenty or forty-five or eighty minutes long is preposterous. I feel sure that such critics find the time to watch television shows and movies that last longer than forty-five minutes, and I'm tempted to ask them if they've read any good books lately.

In any case, on the other side of punk—which was also only embraced, as was progressive rock, by an alternative culture—progressive rock had a hard time recovering. It has not recovered. The attention span in the time of MTV does not have enough room for progressive rock, but this is hardly an accident. One almost wants to see a conspiracy at work here, so well-designed are the cultural mechanisms that seem to specifically exclude progressive rock. Instead, what we find are the workings of capitalism in the time when an imperialist global divide (with affluence on one side and crushing poverty on the other, the one side sick from too much to eat, the other dying of malnutrition and starvation) is integrated with what Theodor Adorno and Max Horkheimer called the "culture industry."[4] I call this configuration, which caps a world where the majority lives in conditions of destitution with a glitzy, hyperreal culture of distraction, "postmodern capitalism."

One of the more mundane features of this social order is that the music business has become, in the last two decades, much less about music and much more about business. What used to be called, quaintly, "record companies," became a part of gigantic media conglomerates. These corporations began to exercise a great deal more control over their "product." Pure hype began to play a major role. There was a great deal of homogenization that had little room for artists to experiment and let the chips fall where they may. This homogenization drive did not mean that all artists started to sound the same; instead, there has been "diversity" of sorts, but in almost every case geared toward this or that particular *niche*. (Cruise the radio dial and this becomes readily apparent.) The aim is to be able to market entertainment product in a relatively predictable way. One of the ironies of capitalist ideology is that it continually protests against "centralized planning," and yet capitalism does plan, in a centralized and very far-reaching way. It has to: you can't run a company such as General Motors by just having a lot of people show up and chat about what they'd like to do on any given day! And the standard come-back, that this is a corporation, not a state, doesn't get very far when, for one thing, the largest corporations have economies that are bigger than all but the largest countries, and, for another, the interlocking web of corporations and financial institutions does indeed *rule* society, determining what people can do with their lives, which wars will be fought, what kind of air we will breathe. Music that aims to be unpredictable or is otherwise not readily niched does not have much place in this scheme.

🔳 🔳 🔳

In terms of the barriers to progressive rock that began to be erected in the late seventies, it might be informative to look at the work of four bands: Jethro Tull, Yes, King Crimson, and Rush.

Jethro Tull in some sense always worked by "extension." The differences between their earlier albums, the best of which is *Benefit*, and their more fully progressive albums, *Thick as a Brick* and *A Passion Play*, is that the latter pair connected song fragment to song fragment at some length, bringing about a transformation of quantity to quality. Indeed, keeping with their blues and folk roots, these album-length works could be understood as the orchestrated and embellished riffs and lines of a balladeer. For Tull, the solution to the "problem of progressive rock" in the late seventies was practically ready-made: what had been extended could be retracted. As with the other progressive groups that attempted to find a solution, Tull's transformation took place in fits and starts—but they were closer to a solution that made sense in terms of Tull's trajectory than the other groups were in working out their own transformations.

In other words, Tull from the later seventies on has been more recognizably Tull, while Yes has been a bit less recognizably Yes, and King Crimson is nearly unrecognizable in the terms it had set down in its earlier albums and incarnations.

Jethro Tull's first and foremost orientation was toward good songwriting; whether the pursuit of this goal shaded over into progressive rock was a secondary consideration. Another way to put this is that the group had the skills necessary for doing what-ever they wanted to do, but what they wanted to do did not always require all of their skills. Jethro Tull would go on to make a number of solid rock albums, all featuring good songwriting and playing, some venturing closer to the blues and others closer to folk music, all of them "postprogressive" in the sense of having come through that time and musical passage.

I've used the word "they" rather freely here, when in fact everything in Tull happens under the direction of Ian Anderson. The same can be said of King Crimson, which exists or does not exist according to the remote sensings of Robert Fripp. Having a key personality, so to speak, has arguably made the postprogressive passage less complicated for both Tull and Crimson. Although both groups have had more stability in the personnel departments in recent years, still, having a single convener fits better with a time when experimental rock has a more episodic character. By contrast, Yes has had a much harder time of it.

After their final album of "full-blown" progressive rock, *Going for the One*, Yes remade itself in a series of stages that were neither planned nor pretty. The 1978 release of *Tormato* is a case in point, a largely directionless album some of whose parts are greater than the whole. By 1980 Jon Anderson and Rick Wakeman had left the group, but somehow Yes carried on by an unlikely union with the Buggles. The album they made, *Drama*, was really quite good, combining some classical Yesisms with interesting borrowings from hard rock, punk, and new wave. Though it is doubtful that this group could have carried on as Yes for more than one album, still they were at least halfway to the Yes of the eighties.

Significantly, at this point, Jon Anderson came back into the group, while at the same time Steve Howe (the coauthor, with Anderson, of much of Yes's greatest music) went with a group that represents, to my mind, the aforementioned "faint echo" direction. (The reference, of course, is to Asia, which also featured John Wetton, Carl Palmer, and Geoff Downes—former members, in other words, of Yes, King Crimson, and ELP.) Even more important, Yes did find itself a strong personality around which to rebuild the group, but this was not Jon Anderson. Anderson has, as many readers will know, a very strong personality—he is well-known for the demands that he makes on his bandmates. However, one of his great strengths is that he goes to his fellow musicians and draws creative responses out of them. (Bill Bruford has remarked, for instance, that it was Anderson's demands that brought him—a drummer of all people—to the point of composing music.) In some sense Anderson embodies the paradox of participation in a passive society—he wants all of his bandmates to participate in making music, and he is willing to be a bit domineering in demanding this participation.

However, Jon Anderson linked up with the new Yes project somewhat late in its formation, by which time the central role had been taken by someone of a more standard "strong personality" type, namely Trevor Rabin. (Indeed, the original plan was for this new group—with the core of Rabin, Chris Squire, and Alan White, with Tony Kaye coming in at first as somewhat of an adjunct, and a singer to be named later—to be named not Yes but instead "Cinema." Though in some respects this is a good name, it is interesting that it is also representative of larger cultural shifts—and ones that are not much to my liking, on which more in a moment. It was only with the addition of Anderson to the group that they decided to take up the mantle of Yes once more.) Unlike others who had been in Yes over the years, who would come to the group with thematic material and other bits and pieces, Rabin brought finished songs to the band. Although changes were made here and there, the first album by the new group, *90125*, very much represents Rabin's musical vision. Yet, somehow, it is still recognizably Yes, even if a transformed Yes. At times, it is true, this version of the band sounds like a watered-down version of its former self. At worst, there is the aroma of "arena rock," and this is bad, very bad—I don't think there has ever been a more awful form of rock music. But, at its best, the "Trevor Yes" sounds like a *streamlined* version of progressive rock. What had been "maximal" was now presented in miniature, and yet the contrapuntal lines and linear development were still there.

And the whole thing happened in southern California, of all places.

The *90125* period saw Yes gain a new popularity, but the problem of what to do in the postprogressive era was not by any means solved. Although I know that some (perhaps most) readers will balk at this, the episodic existence of Yes in the eighties and nineties has produced some very good music. *Big Generator* (1987) represents a consolidation of the group's new approach, and songs such as "I'm Running" carry forward everything that is basic to Yes. However, the group was not entirely unified at this point, and Jon Anderson left once again, forming a quartet with Steve Howe, Bill Bruford, and Rick Wakeman (with Tony Levin supplying some excellent bass work). The resulting album was named for these musicians, pointedly refusing to take some group name other than Yes. *Anderson, Bruford, Wakeman, and Howe* (1989), apart from a pair of Jon Anderson's new-age tunes, returns to the large structures of progressive rock, presenting several near-epic works that stand with some of the best music of the seventies.

There was more craziness to come, however, as music-business types came up with the idea of welding Yes-London and Yes-West together into one of those "supergroups" that almost never works. As Bill Bruford said about the ABWH project (in his *When in Doubt, Roll!*), it would have been one thing if these eight musicians had been given the time and space and resources to feel each other out a bit, and to let the music develop. As a matter of fact, the two groups do not actually play together; instead, Jon Anderson sings on the Yes West material (but Trevor Rabin also provides a good deal of the lead vocals), while Chris Squire added back-up and harmony vocals (but not bass guitar) to the ABWH songs. Somehow, too, a ton of studio musicians were also injected into the process. The resulting double-length album is a mess, despised by the musicians themselves; *Union* (1991) stands as perhaps the single most representative sample of the quandaries faced by progressive rock in the postprogressive period. Apart from all of the other nonmusical factors that hover so menacingly in the background of the album, there is the overwhelming feeling that the very spirit of Yes is buried in *Union*, here and there struggling to get free, even poking its head above ground now and then, but mostly smothered by all that is set against the possibility of progressive rock.

After a financially successful tour that pit guitarist against guitarist and drummer against drummer (though my impression is that Wakeman and Kaye got along well enough), this "union" cracked apart. Surprisingly, then, Jon Anderson and Trevor Rabin teamed up to co-write a new album from Yes-West, 1994's *Talk*. Despite a lapse or two, this is a very good album. Like *Big Generator*, though perhaps with greater polish and integration, *Talk* carries forward the spirit of Yes in a postprogressive period. The spirit of Yes is not an entity in and of itself, however, but is instead a particular concentration of the elements that went into making progressive rock in the late sixties. Since *Going for the One*, Yes has preserved, in some sense, this spirit, but in an episodic way. There is a great difference between musicians coming together every few years to create a *project* that may to some degree sustain something great from the past, and musicians who are part of an ongoing *group* that is itself a nodal point within a larger *movement*. Unfortunately, the musicians from this movement cannot simply call forth a new movement at will. Yes, being quintessentially a group, and not just an episodic project wrapped around a strong personality, has suffered the most in the absence of a movement.

King Crimson, by contrast, and especially in the person of Robert Fripp (and, to a lesser but still significant extent, Bill Bruford), has been much more comfortable with the *project* orientation. Indeed—and, again, this makes me a bit angry—Fripp has rewritten history somewhat to suit this orientation, claiming that the pre-*Discipline* versions of the group were somehow unrelated to the larger progressive-rock trend. Two passages from Fripp's notes for the *Epitaph* booklet demonstrate this point. First, Fripp undermines much of the music's raison d'être:

> In 1969 rock musicians enjoyed a particularly privileged role: they were taken seriously as mouthpieces for the culture. This was probably the last year in which they were. A main concern of the young generation, particularly in America, was the Vietnam conflict. As a young musician and "hairy" travelling across America in 1969 the connection was unmistakably clear between the peace movement and rock music as an instrument of political expression and the voice of a generation. The demarcation between "straights" and "hairies" equally so. The Hairies believed that rock music could change the world. I have less hair now. I believe music can help to change our world, and now I appreciate that the action of music is more subtle than a young man knows. . . . But whatever spirit there was in the air of 1969, it never got as far as 1970. The impulse of which Crimson was a part didn't carry over into the 1970s. By 1974 the musical

"movement" had been corrupted, diverted, and gone irretrievably off-course. (p. 18)

Obviously, Fripp is offering some far-reaching theses here; more discussion is needed, but, just as obviously, the thrust of this book has been contrary to Fripp's claims. And, as we have seen, from 1969 to 1974 was a very long time, in which a great deal happened. It seems likely that Fripp's choice of 1974, which also happens to be the year that King Crimson shut down for an extended sabbatical, is no coincidence.

The second passage comes from a section of the booklet amusingly titled, "Prog Rock and Its Criminals." Fripp provides six "common Prog generalisations," numbers one through four of which seem intended to mock critics of the genre. The fifth and sixth, taken together, claim that "The most successful Progressive bands" and "[t]he main culprits of Progressive music in its Golden Age were Yes, Genesis, ELP, and King Crimson" (p. 43). (Fripp adds to the sixth generalization, "But everyone else was terrible too.")

But now things take a twist, whereby Fripp aligns himself with the critics of progressive rock—to whom he attributes all the standard views, that the music is "characterised by bombast, exaggeration, excess, self-indulgence, pretension"; furthermore, "All Prog is appalling" (p. 43). This goes on in a similar vein, until Fripp presents his coup de grace:

> The only part of this to which I take exception is to have Crimson since 1970 regularly placed alongside Yes and Genesis, and frequently ELP. We may have shared the same part of the planet and space in time, and even a musician or two, but our aims, way of doing things, history and (even) music, are very different.

Fripp then goes on to distinguish King Crimson from what he calls "mainstream" progressive rock:

> One simple reason Crimson is a bad example of mainstream Progressive rock is that Crimson changed its direction and/or personnel whenever a particular musical approach had run its course. A primary rule of commercial success is to repeat yourself. Clearly commercial success was not the priority for Crimson and in this we succeeded, which is the second simple reason that Crimson is a bad example of mainstream progressive rock. (p. 43)

Fripp plays rather fast and loose with the word "we" here, as though some "we" was making these decisions about musical direction or personnel changes. Furthermore, it seems to me that there is a difference between developing a musical language, as for example Yes did in the period from *The Yes Album* to *Going for the One*, and simply repeating what had already been accomplished. In some sense, Fripp's remarks about these musical and personnel changes are simply a cover for the fact that, unlike the other bands he mentions, King Crimson did not function according to the group concept. The claim about popularity (or commercial success, as Fripp puts it), too, has to be understood in light of the fact that the early seventies were a period when many experimental approaches to music were embraced by large numbers of people. But, of course, Fripp has already hedged this claim with the idea that, by 1970, the spirit that animated musicians and listeners in 1969, was gone.

I hope that the reader will take me at my word when I say that I have tremendous respect for what Robert Fripp has accomplished in music, and that my differences with him regarding interpretations of the time and the movement have no bearing on this respect. Of course, on some level, Fripp's arguments are undermined by the idea of calling very different groups in which he is the key and convening figure by a common name. Although he also takes pains to deny that King Crimson is "his" band, the fact is that he plays the leading role in convening musicians to form a group that will be called King Crimson (and he also has played a leading role in dispersing these groups, except in cases where band members have left the group). There isn't necessarily anything wrong with this, but let's not be disingenuous about it. If there is some sense in which each of these groups is an incarnation of the "King Crimson idea," then let's not deny the central place of Robert Fripp in formulating that idea, and let's not deny all of the other continuities that are out there as well.

In 1981, Fripp reconstituted King Crimson with Bill Bruford and, significantly, two American musicians, bass guitarist and Chapman Stick player Tony Levin, and guitarist and singer Adrian Belew. Where the King Crimson of the *Larks' Tongues* era excelled in avoiding repetition, generating powerful silences as well as tremendous dynamic contrasts, and above all in creating a sense of an open-ended future, the eighties Crimson embraced repetition, focusing on textures and minute variations. There were even affinities between this new music and, horror of horrors, disco. On the other hand, not much disco was in 17/8 time, and there was a depth to these rhythms and timbres that went beyond their surface appeal. In his lyrics, as well as his vocal and guitar phrasings, Adrian Belew injected an element of humor, even outright silliness, that had never been a part of King Crimson before. The Mellotron of the old days was gone, replaced by Fripp's evolving electronic modifications of the electric guitar (with Frippertronics and Soundscapes). In addition, acoustic sounds (except in the case of a few, but not all, of the pieces in Bruford's "mutant" drum kit) were largely absent from this group.

Instead, the central tension or contrast in the group was between Fripp's pointillistic constructions, which generated large swaths of musical fabric, and Belew's more "poppish" inclinations. The group made three albums. For the first two of these, *Discipline* (1981) and *Beat* (1982), the gamelan orchestra approach of Bruford, Levin, and Fripp, and the more "pop" approach of Belew, remained more or less in balance, creating an interesting and original new form of rock music. With the last of these albums, *Three of a Perfect Pair* (1984), things perhaps tipped too much toward the pop side. Belew is a talented musician, to be sure, but there are certain things that he does with his voice, lyrics, and guitar playing that can be very annoying. As many readers will know, much of his guitar playing consists in a series of gimmicks; some of these are interesting, but they wear thin after awhile.

I will say more about the Javanese gamelan orchestra in a moment, but let us note here that the eighties Crimson was also part of a musical movement that focused much more on creating textures than linear development. One of the leaders of this movement, at least as far as rock music is concerned, has been Brian Eno, in whose company Robert Fripp recorded two initial albums of Frippertronics, *No Pussyfooting* (1972) and *Evening Star* (1975). Critical as I may be of some of Belew's contributions to King Crimson, I would also like to recognize that the songs he situates in the midst of these textures are often the only nod toward linearity in the eighties and nineties music.

With the addition of drummer Pat Mastelotto and Chapman Stick player Trey Gunn to the previous quartet, King Crimson reincarnated sometime around 1992. After a fairly protracted period of exploration, the group finally released a full-length album in 1995, *Thrak*. The music fleshes out, often in a more harsh and heavy way, some of the possibilities of the eighties incarnation, as well as rearticulates some of the music from the *Larks' Tongues* period (in concert the group often plays "Red" and "Larks' Tongues in Aspic, Part Two"). When I saw this group in concert in the fall of 1995, there was one piece from the *Thrak* album where, at the end, I would swear that I heard the "everybody ha-ha" conclusion of the Beatles' "I Am the Walrus" welling up from the dense textures.

It appears that this version of King Crimson is set to keep working for some time, and Fripp's genius as convener and organizer here is much in evidence. Something that has played a major role in creating favorable conditions for this group, as well as some important releases from previous incarnations of King Crimson, is Robert Fripp's record company, Discipline Global Mobile. Many of the people with whom I have discussed the fate of groups such as Yes have commented that progressive rock needs more "small, mobile, and independent" record companies such as DGM. The business goals of the company, as stated by Fripp in the *Epitaph* booklet, are exemplary, especially the first aim: "to help bring music into the world which would otherwise be unlikely to do so, or under conditions prejudicial to the music and/or musicians" (p. 60). Fripp even quotes from a business-ethics text regarding matters of distributive justice (p. 61). Discussions of the relationship between the terms "business" and "ethics" will undoubtedly continue, but the point is that Fripp has done something very important for the possibilities of experimental music. That is, he has recognized that these possibilities require more of a material scaffolding than just the will or ability to play music—and he has done something about this. The set-up for something like DGM comes up against questions about the group concept and the possibility of doing more than simply creating episodic projects; however, we seem to live in a time where it may be that such projects are the best that can be achieved, and they are certainly preferable to group situations where there is a constant struggle over different managements and publishing agreements, and where music must submit at every level to the music business and its lawyers.

Completing this minor survey of the postseventies trajectories of major progressive rock groups, I would be remiss if I did not say something about Rush. Having written a book on the music of Yes, and while writing on the larger field of progressive rock, many people have asked me what I think of this group. Significantly, my interlocutors are almost always folks who were not really around for the "first generation" of progressive groups. For those of us who came along with groups such as Yes, Genesis, ELP, and King Crimson (hmm, I wonder why I thought of those four?), Rush doesn't quite make it. But this has as much to do with the time as with the music; for those for whom Woodstock and flower power were not really a living presence in their formative years, I can certainly see the appeal of Rush's combination of Yes-like progressive inclinations and Zeppelin-like hard-rock leanings. As other progressive-rock groups either disbanded or transformed themselves into nonprogressive groups, it seemed that Rush was at least, even if sometimes clumsily, continuing to carry the torch. As of the mid- to late-seventies, this was a band of very good and constantly improving musicians who were interested in difficult, extended compositions that were motivated by philosophical ideas.

But there's the rub, because, with their first album that perhaps had some claim on progressive rock, 1976's *2112* (the group's fourth album), Rush attempted an epic musical presentation of the ideas of Ayn Rand. This deeply incoherent philosophy, which sets itself against "collectivism," has always appealed to middle-class adolescents. While I cannot provide an extended critique of Rand here, let us at least note that there is no place for anyone who is not a fully formed adult in her world. People must come from nowhere, so that they will not in any way be in debt to other persons. Rand hated rock music, and she was repulsed by such expressions of collectivity as the Woodstock "spirit." (Weirdly, given that she referred to herself as a "romantic," she also hated Beethoven. But then, her tastes in art were a nutty hodgepodge that were dressed up, as was the chain smoking that eventually killed her, in terms of all-powerful Reason.) Claiming to build her life on egoism and the pursuit of happiness, she was a deeply miserable person who made others around her miserable as well (all of this is well-documented in the books about Rand by her former disciples the Brandens). Her novels are defenses of capitalism built around characters, such as architect Howard Roarke, who in some ways have admirable qualities but are in no way the real stuff of contemporary capitalism.[5] But it is not hard to see the appeal of these characters for young people who are attempting self-definition. Apart from the problematic ideas, the music on *2112* is actually pretty good.

Rush has been unfairly burdened by their flirtations with Ayn Rand Thought; the fact is that the group continued to grow past *2112*, and, by and by, they grew out of their fixation on Rand. (My understanding is that it was mainly drummer and lyricist Neil Peart who actually read the stuff.) It is also unfair to charge Rush, as some have (see, for example, Paul Stump, pp. 257–58, where he also makes the amusing error of referring to Rand as a "Canadian"), with representing the ideological degeneration of progressive rock in the years of Thatcher and Reagan. In reality, the "good side" of Rush's engagement with A.R.T. was that the fellows were interested in "heavy" ideas; if the ideas they latched onto at first turned out not to be that heavy or, in any case, good, let's still give them credit for their interest and for the fact that they kept on with this pursuit. They grew as musicians, too, with Geddy Lee becoming one of the best bass guitarists around, and one of the few who worked out of and developed the contrapuntal style established by Chris Squire. Lee's voice improved too; by the early eighties he finally had a good deal more control over what had earlier been a very irritating (at least to my ears) heavy metal shriek. In 1984, the group released *Grace Under Pressure*, an excellent example of a matured Rush. With one foot in hard rock and the other in progressive, the group represented as well as they ever had the spirit of the latter. *Grace* offers a viable direction for postprogressive music. In more recent years, the group has perhaps leaned more to its hard-rock side, but Rush continues to carry forward the traces of its trajectory. Though many Crimson fans will balk at the comparison, Rush has also done an exemplary job of running its own operation, so to speak, outside of the channels of radio airplay and MTV.

〽 〽 〽

Some other developments in the further trajectory of progressive rock, beyond its movement and its moment, deserve recognition. Despite everything, it has been said that there is at present a progressive rock *revival* in full swing. Not only are bands such as Tull, ELP, Yes, and Crimson active in recent years, but there are new bands, CD compilations of older material, and a new network of fan publications—and even the odd book here or there!

There are lots of new bands, as any perusal of the new fan publications, such as *Progression* or *Exposé* magazines or the *Music News Network* newsletter, will readily demonstrate. This or that band, for instance Ozric Tentacles or Porcupine Tree, will be touted from time to time as the "future of progressive rock," and it would seem as if "neoprog" groups are springing up like wildflowers. Furthermore, mail-order distribution and CD re-release has made work by groups both old and new available as never before. Greg Walker's Syn-Phonic catalogue, for example, carries more than a thousand albums by artists from Argentina to Yugoslavia. Even a quick perusal of this catalogue demonstrates the truly international scope of the progressive rock movement. (More on publications in a moment; addresses for those already mentioned and more will be found in the resources section of this book.)

Greg Walker has also played a leading role in the establishment of a yearly "Progfest" in Los Angeles. The double-CD *Progfest '95* set features some of the strongest of the neoprogressive groups, as well as a representative sample of the global scene: Ars Nova from Japan, Landberk from Sweden, Deus Ex Machina from Italy, White Willow from Norway, Spock's Beard from the United States, and Solaris from Hungary. The most recent Progfest of this writing, the May 1997 edition (this time organized by Shawn Ahearn), featured the bands Arena, The Flower Kings, Big Elf, once again Spock's Beard, and oldtimers Le Orme and John Wetton. I could not begin to list all of the progressive rock bands that are active at this time, but even a preliminary thumb-through of the publications mentioned above shows there are scores of them, if not hundreds.

Of the groups featured on *Progfest '95*, I was most impressed with Landberk and Deus Ex Machina; both groups already have five or six albums apiece, and their compositions are subtle and effective, pure progressive, with wonderful singing as well. It would be very difficult to not like Ars Nova, a keyboard-led trio of Japanese women who most resemble a purely instrumental ELP. As the rappers like to say, this group's got skills, to say the least (and I have a personal fondness for bassist Kyoto Kanazawa's injection of the Rickenbacker 4001 sound into this format).

Although I enjoyed Spock's Beard's presentation from *Progfest '95* (the sixteen-and-a-half minute "The Light"), I was completely knocked over by their subsequent album, 1996's *Beware of Darkness*. I live near and often visit a store that specializes in progressive, psychedelic, and otherwise classic rock, Evanston's Vintage Vinyl. When Steve Kaye, the proprietor, sees me coming, he has a way of putting something on the stereo that he suspects will lure me in and perhaps result in a few shekels passed in his direction. Few of these bits of prog-bait have pushed all of my buttons in the way that *Beware of Darkness* has—when the music first came blaring out of the speakers, I didn't know what it was, but something was beginning to break through. Namely, the title track on the album is indeed George Harrison's great song from *All Things Must Pass*. (Perhaps it is worth noting that one of the drummers for this album was none other than Alan White.) The treatment by Spock's Beard is truly a thing to behold; lead singer Neal Morse has a fine voice, which he thankfully does not strain into unnatural registers, bassist Dave Meros drives the song with a Squire-like contrapuntal pulse, and the Mellotron work of Ryo Okumoto transports the listener right back to the glory days of *In the Wake of Poseidon* or *Fragile*. The rest of the album is consistently inventive. The sources for Spock's Beard's music are generally quite apparent—the Beatles, Yes, Gentle Giant, a bit of Pink Floyd and King Crimson—and yet *Beware of Darkness* sounds entirely fresh, not derivative.

Is the album in any sense "avant-garde"? Realistically, one would have to answer in the negative, and the same answer would have to be given regarding most of the bands of the "neo-prog" movement. In some sense, these groups are attempting to carry on with a sound that, in itself, was quite arguably *not* played out, even if the times that engendered and sustained it perhaps were. The difficult question raised here is no different than the one we must confront regarding Yes's recent *Keys to Ascension*: are we seeing the true rebirth and extension of the progressive rock trend, or are the new groups, and even most of the old groups that are still around, just taking us on a nostalgia trip? Works such as *Beware of Darkness* or "That, That Is" have a strong claim on authenticity, at least circa 1973. But what about the need for *progressive* rock to *progress*? I will come back to this question, but for the moment let it be said that there is a key term left out of this dichotomy as conventionally presented, that term being what I would call "reconnection."

Like it or not (I'm not sure that I do), the 1996 Rhino Records release of the five-CD box set, *Supernatural Fairy Tales: The Progressive Rock Era*, seems to be a major event in the recent revival. Surprisingly, Jim DeRogatis (author of *Kaleidoscope Eyes*, discussed in chapter 3) gave the set a mostly favorable review. I found one of his concluding comments interesting and insightful:

> I can't help wondering about the intended audience: Prog devotees already own most if not all of this stuff. I suppose it's intended as a primer for the new listeners that about 65 percent of these artists deserve.[6]

DeRogatis hits it right on the head with his 65 percent evaluation; the question I have is, Why didn't the record company do a better job? There are undoubtedly some good things about the collection: a broad range of artists from the Nice to Rare Bird, Curved Air, Wigwam (from Finland, and represented by the excellent "Prophet/Marvelry Skimmer"), Supersister, Quiet Sun, and many more both famous and obscure; original cover art by Roger Dean; and the fact that, at least for the new listener, all of this material is in one place. However, the scales are tipped on the other side in various crucial ways. There are a goodly number of senseless selections. If groups such as Electric Light Orchestra or Golden Earring belong here at all, why represent them with their least-progressive material, "Roll Over Beethoven" and "Radar Love"?

Why represent Focus, who certainly do belong, with their novelty hit "Hocus Pocus," which can be heard in TV commercials for heaven's sake, instead of something new listeners are not likely to have heard before? (Similarly, the PFM track is "Celebration.") The Renaissance track is from the original, Keith Relf, version of the group; that's fine, but don't you suppose that most progressive-rock listeners think of the group more in terms of the Annie Haslam version? The Banco track is an instrumental piece, an odd choice considering that the group featured an incredible singer (Francesco Di Giacomo). Some of these choices might be considered creative, for instance the inclusion of Wishbone Ash's "Warrior" (or even Relf's Renaissance rather than Haslam's) except for the fact that the whole package has a very careless, thrown-together feel to it. Nowhere is this more readily apparent than with the lead-off "essay" for the album booklet, the execrable "I Was a Teenage Prog Rock Geek" by Steve Hochman. I found the list of credits for this "writer" (including *Spin* and *Melody Maker*) frightening; maybe his other work is better, but what he writes here is poorly written, appalling, and shameful garbage— and it is appalling that the album compilers included it.

Significantly, there are no tracks in the set by Pink Floyd, Soft Machine, Camel, Jethro Tull, or King Crimson. Ostensibly this was because of licensing difficulties. (Actually, they don't even mention Tull in the disclaimer, so who knows what the deal was here.) I have to wonder, however, if these difficulties were compounded by the obvious rush to get the set out on the market. Consider that the track listing includes Yes's "Siberian Khatru," except that what shows up on the CD is "And You and I," and that the little coda at the end of the piece that comes after a brief silence has been left off (because, obviously, the people involved in remastering the song didn't know there was more to it), and you see what kind of care was taken with this project.

Now, as with a project such as the book you have before you, there are a million loose ends to keep track of; it's natural that there will be mistakes here and there. However, *Supernatural Fairy Tales* feels like a rush job, and one has to wonder if it does more harm than good. Even the 65 percent grade that DeRogatis gives it (which, not to be too academic about it, might translate into a "D" if the teacher is feeling generous—but perhaps the compilers of this project were hoping for a good curve) must be predicated upon the idea that it is better to have the set than not to have it. The problem is that, because *Supernatural Fairy Tales* exists, there is less likelihood that a better, more carefully prepared progressive rock set will be produced. Such is the wisdom of the market![7]

Of course it would be interesting to know if the set has attracted new listeners, and it would be interesting to know who these people are. There are "new people" coming to progressive rock, many of whom have discovered the music in the record collections of their older siblings or even their parents. From purely informal "surveys" of these listeners, I glean that they are interested in music that is more challenging than that offered by the mainstream rock groups. They are also inclined toward the whole "vibe" of the music, though perhaps more on a "cosmic" rather than a specifically countercultural level.

As I mentioned, there are numerous publications for such listeners. The quarterly magazines *Progression* and *Exposé* offer indepth articles, interviews, and album reviews on progressive groups from the sixties and seventies, as well as the neoprogressive groups. *Progression* features insightful commentary on classic progressive albums by University of North Carolina at Chapel Hill musicology professor John Covach. *Music News Network*, edited by Lisa Mikita and Christine Holz, is a monthly publication, featuring concert and album release schedules as well as interviews. Anyone who reads these publications will see that there is certainly a progressive-rock *scene* that, even if perhaps not very much in the public view, is vibrant and perhaps even growing. (Obviously, these publications are playing an important role in sustaining and developing this scene.) The other impression that one has is that progressive rock is in some respects not unlike the punk scene of the last twenty years: the better part of the progressive rock scene is marginal, "underground," and DIY ("do it yourself"). There are some important differences, however, and these go beyond the music itself. More on this in a moment.

Let the record show, as well, that the punk-initiated 'zine movement of the last twenty years has found its way to progressive rock as well. For every better-known group there is at least one fan publication, and often two or three, and there are zines for many of the lesser-known groups as well. (Some of these are listed under "Resources.") And, no surprise to anyone, there are web pages galore on the internet, as well as discussion groups and bulletin boards. There are general progressive-rock bulletin boards with thousands of postings, on almost every conceivable subject and angle. To be honest, and I apologize if I hurt someone's feelings here, I cannot read much of this stuff without having something of a "get a life" reaction—a lot of it is not unlike a game of Star Trek trivial pursuit. I am not a big fan of internet "discussion" in general, because I find that ideas tend not to be developed very much or well, and sometimes I cannot help but think of what Clint Eastwood once said about "opinions" (actually it was his film character, Dirty Harry). However, as raw evidence of interest, it is undeniable that something is going on. One can find on the net, too, a good sense of the international dimensions of progressive rock. For instance, there is a very impressive progressive-rock scene in Argentina, with several regular radio shows devoted to the music each week, discussion groups and publications, many local neoprog groups, and many major groups coming through. King Crimson recorded their "live official bootleg," *B'Boom* in Buenos Aires. Another important site is the "Italian Progressive Rock Page"; not only can you find a general history of the music in Italy, but you can go from this page to pages for many of the Italian groups, from Acqua Fragile and Area to Zauber.

I have always found that people who are into progressive rock are elated when they hear about or meet other people who are into this music. In my travels around Chicago and the surrounding area, sometimes riding the elevated train (the "el" as it's called here) or sitting in a coffeehouse, if I happen to be wearing one of my King Crimson or Gong tee-shirts (for instance), it is not uncommon that I will soon find myself in a friendly conversation. As I've said before, I have not done any statistical sociological work on any of these questions, so everything that I will say now is little more than a hunch—but it is a strong hunch.

It has been argued that, since the heyday of progressive rock, and since the playing out of the sixties, this music has gone from being a counterculture, or at least a significant branch of a counterculture, to what sociologists call a "taste public." This point bears on what was said before about certain recent similarities between punk and progressive, regarding the institutional frameworks on the basis of which these musics operate. Most of what is happening in both punk and progressive nowadays is done apart from mainstream institutions and on a somewhat cobbled-together, marginal, and DIY basis. I doubt very seriously that John Collinge, editor of *Progression*, is expecting a call from Rupert Murdoch to discuss merger and funding possibilities—thank heaven! And, by design, Robert Fripp has set up an alternative institution (Discipline Global Mobile) that treasures its independence. But, to put the question provocatively, Are progressive rock and its alternative institutions more akin to the larger culture of punk, or do they serve a mere taste public that just happens to have its own marketing strategies? If you read a central organ of punk culture such as *Maximum Rock 'n' Roll* magazine (which is really a zine, produced quite inexpensively on newsprint), you will encounter issues that go quite beyond the music. Some readers will no doubt respond that this music cannot bear much analysis, and its point is not first of all to be music. Let us set that issue aside for the moment, and rephrase the question. Again, to put it provocatively, Is progressive rock less like punk and its culture and political discourse (such as it is) and perhaps more like, say, the scene around model railroads or some other hobby-type pursuit that does not require much in common among the participants other than that they are "into" that particular pursuit?[8]

On the rare occasions when I get involved in on-line discussions regarding progressive rock, or when I otherwise encounter other people who are interested in this music, I often find myself making new friends (or at least finding new people with whom I stay in friendly contact). In November 1994, I published an article on Chris Squire in *Bass Player* magazine. I had been working on *music of Yes* on and off for a few years at that point, but the book was several months from being finished. I wanted to do something to mark the twenty-five years that had passed since Yes made its first appearance on long-playing record. After that article came out, not a day passed for the next six months or so when I did not hear from someone somewhere in the world (mostly in the U.S., but also from Australia, Holland, and elsewhere) who wanted to express appreciation for the article and to offer help with the book (which had been announced in the writer's credit). Many people sent articles, audio and video tapes, and thoughts and reminiscences regarding not only Chris Squire or Yes, but progressive rock more generally. A number of these people have looked me up when coming through Chicago. Three of these people, Glen Di Crocco in Staten Island, David Orsini in Toronto, and Nick Kokoshis in the D.C. area, were very helpful where both factual and interpretive matters were concerned.

In February 1996 I attended a philosophy conference in Toronto. I called David Orsini to let him know I would be in town. He arranged for an excellent vegetarian dinner at the home of two other progressive rock afficionados, Brenda MacDonald and Stephen Gardner. After dinner, Stephen and Brenda, a pianist and vocalist respectively, played an impromtu recital of Yes and Emerson, Lake and Palmer music for David and me. The arrangements of "Perpetual Change," "Long Distance Runaround," "Lucky Man," and "Tarkus" were extraordinary; David held up a cigarette lighter, and we both shouted, "c'est bon!" Later, back at the hotel, David and I talked about music, culture, landscape architecture (David's profession), and philosophy well into the night.

This was a magical night, for which I will always remain grateful to David, Brenda, and Stephen. Now, maybe the scene around model trains produces something similar from time to time, though I really doubt this.[9] Everything in that night was clearly enabled by a certain vibration, something that still spoke to us in the sounds of Yes and progressive rock. Steve Howe has called this the "commune feeling." Not that it is always, or even that often, so magical—I've certainly encountered my share of people who definitely want progressive rock listeners to be nothing more than a taste culture, who would much prefer that everything utopian and redemptive about the genre completely remain in airy-fairy land, as well as people who are only into the music because you find some of the more technically proficient rock musicians there (paradiddles per second or whatnot). But I also encounter many people, and I would venture that it is the majority, who are attracted to the vibration.

Taken altogether, the musicians, those who put out the fan publications and web material, the other writers and others who in some way materially enable the music, *the listeners*, all of these people constitute something more than just a scene or a taste public. As difuse as the whole phenomenon is, there is something like an alternative or sub- culture of progressive rock here. But, in the absence of a counterculture, this subculture lacks cohesiveness and direction. Just as no one, no "strong personality," can simply stand on a hill and call forth a new progressive rock *movement*, so also can no one or even lots of no ones simply bring together a new counterculture. Without such a counterculture, progressive rock will remain a difuse subculture which, in some respects, resembles little more than a taste public when push comes to shove—that is, when people are challenged to connect their abiding interest in this music to something larger.

I put it this way because we live in a time when, for example, frat boys or skinheads can dig music about peace and love and equality (by U2 or Bob Marley) one minute, and the next minute engage in violent racist or misogynist assaults. In our postmodern time and general culture of distraction, there is seemingly no connection between one thing and another. Progressive rock is in many ways part of the *modernist* movement in music; in postmodern times, it tends to lose its way. This is another reason why, it seems to me, in order to navigate better in these times, figures such as Robert Fripp and Brian Eno have attempted to sever their connections to progressive rock. But perhaps there is an alternative. E.M. Forster said, famously, "only connect"; in a similar spirit, perhaps this formula should be extended slightly: "only reconnect." This formulation cannot be the whole picture—if it were, then progressive rock groups working today, whether they be Yes, Spock's Beard, or whomever, would indeed only be offering the comforting backward look (to the "glory days"). However, it seems to me that we do live in a time when, without reconnection, our attempt to listen to the future collapses purely into the present. With this problem in mind, let us turn for a moment to the question of music in postmodern times.

♪   ♪   ♪

Only a few lines from Fredric Jameson's important book, *Postmodernism, or, The Cultural Logic of Late Capitalism* are devoted to discussing recent music. Other kinds of art, by contrast, are discussed at great length. Still, as with film, video art, literature, and architecture, Jameson links recent music with certain attributes of the new form of capitalism he calls "postmodern"; among these are an ahistorical and spatialized consciousness. The world is flattened out and yet unmappable; temporality, meaning, and a consciousness of historical development are progressively banished; "now," which is all we have, turns out to be a space, not a time. As Jameson writes, in the only extended passage where he discusses music,

> The most crucial relationship of music to the postmodern . . . surely passes through space itself (on my analysis, one of the distinguishing or even constitutive traits of the new "culture" or cultural dominant). MTV above all can be taken as a spatialization of music, or, if you prefer, as the telltale revelation that it had already, in our time, become profoundly spatialized in the first place. . . . You no longer offer a musical object for contemplation and gustation; you wire up the context and make space musical around the consumer. . . . What MTV does to music . . . is not some inversion of that defunct nineteenth-century form called program music but rather the nailing of sounds . . . onto visible space and spatial segments. (pp. 299–300)

This description seems apt enough, and, as Jameson says, "[t]he music is not bad to listen to" (p. 298). However, and in light of previous discussions concerning radical affirmation and radical negation, we have to ask what sort of *critical purchase*, if any at all, might this postmodern music of the sort described by Jameson gain against a time of loss of affect and the flattening of meaning. How might this music work against the grain of such a spatialized time—and what does this say in general regarding the possibilities of music in postmodernity?

In other words, this "pleasant" music is, by design, not meant to be *challenging*—in the way that, for example, the best of progressive rock or punk can be. Is it simply that such music is made for a time when, supposedly, there is nothing more to challenge, or is there something more subtle going on? On some level, the shapes of postmodern music and postmodern capitalism at least seem to come together too easily, too obviously: the central element seems to be a rejection of linearity or of the idea of thematic development. With capitalism, there is the paradox of a corporate order that continues to declare that this or that product is "new" or even "revolutionary" (e.g., the Dodge commercials that claim the automobile manufacturer has "broken all the rules" and "created new rules"), and yet, at the level of the whole, is adamant in holding that there is no longer anywhere else to go. Indeed, to raise the question of the legitimacy of such a social formation, and to propose possible alternatives to the existing society, is to get into ideological issues—and we all know that ideology is finished.

There has long been a (Western) music of stasis, which music theorist David Toop traces back to the influence of gamelan music on Claude Debussy and forward to the ambient music of Brian Eno (see *Oceans of Sound*, pp. 1–22). Though this music may transport the listener to some other place, the key term here is not heroism or tragedy (or perhaps even revolution), as it is in the tradition from Beethoven to Wagner, but instead *atmospherics*. The music itself is not the active agent in whatever flight of the imagination might take place, but instead the occasion, the "space," or even the fragrance (see Toop, pp. 8–9).

Although there is a kind of utopianism to this music, I find it difficult to identify the room wired for sound with *critical* utopianism: there is no radical negation here, neither is there a radical affirmation. (The music is "pleasant enough.") In Eno's view, "Ambient Music must be able to accommodate many levels of listening attention without enforcing one in particular: it must be as ignorable as it is interesting" (quoted in Toop, p. 9; also see Eno's ambient "manifesto" and other comments in *A Year with Swollen Appendices*, pp. 293–97). Perhaps this musical wallpaper is truly expressive of an "alternately disorienting and inspiring openness through which all that is solid melts into aether." It is entirely possible to see ambient music and other minimalist musics—La Monte Young, Terry Riley, Philip Glass, Steve Reich—in the same frame as "Mark Rothko's huge slabs of muted color and Ad Reinhardt's black canvases." Perhaps one could or even should wax *situationiste* over

> works which grasp at the transparency of water, seek to track the journeys of telematic nomads, bottle moods and atmospheres, rub out chaos and noise pollution with quiet, concentrate on sonic micro-

cosms, absorb quotations and digital snapshots of sound into themselves, avoid form in favour of impression, concoct synthetic wilder-
ness in urban laboratories, explore a restricted sound range or single
technological process over long durations, seek to effect physiological
change rather than pursue intellectual rigour, or depict impossible,
imaginary environments of beauty or terror. Music that aspires to the
condition of perfume, music that searches for new relationships
between maker and listener, maker and machine, sound and context.
Music that leads the listener into a shifting zone which Peter Lamborne Wilson has described as the "sacred drift," a mode of imaginal
travel "in which the landscape will once again be invested with meaning, or rather with a liberatory aesthetics." (Toop, pp. 21–22).

For purposes of contextualization, I should mention that Peter
Lamborne Wilson is the author, under the name Hakim Bey, of a
recently popular anarchist text titled *Temporary Autonomous
Zones* (or "TAZ" for short). The "drift" to which Wilson refers
invokes the language of Guy Debord, Raoul Vaneigem, and the
Situationists of France.[9]

Described this way, this music sounds more interesting, even
if it is difficult to place it in Adornian categories such as radical
negation or radical affirmation. I am probably unfair in lopping
together everything that reminds one of the room wired for
sound, when this covers everything from the pure pablum of most
of what is seen on MTV (where, now and then, a few music
videos are sandwiched between Cindy Crawford's "House of
Style" and "The Real World") to the more adventurous, if still
intentionally spatialized compositions of, e.g., Glenn Branca or
Krzystof Penderecki. And yet, I find little of critical inspiration
when, a few pages before the more utopian passage quoted above,
Toop seems to valorize the idea of clubs where music has a
"peripheral status" (p. 11). I wonder at the common element
across this spectrum, to be described not only as spatialization,
but also as a banishment of linearity.

Let us again take note of the role played by Brian Eno in
bridging the time of progressive rock and more recent trends (for
many of which he is either the initiator or crucial inspiration).
One of the elements of progressive rock that is taken up in these
more recent trends, from ambient to techno and beyond, is experimentation with timbre, especially as this was enabled by new

electronic instruments and recording techniques. In other words, an element of music that can be heard in a "slice," or one might even say "frame," of a work comes to the fore, while elements that require more of a temporal dimension, perhaps best summed up under the larger category of "counterpoint," either disappear or move to the background. (In extreme cases, as with some pointilistic music, counterpoint is concentrated on such a micro-scopic—or "microaural"—level that it can only be perceived as part of the background fabric, much as one does not ordinarily perceive the single threads that make up a piece of cloth. King Crimson, in its *Discipline* and *Thrak* incarnations, often plays in very creative ways with what might be called the "vanishing points" of the individual threads.) It seems to me that this devel-opment in rock music has been the paradigm in recent music more generally (as well as in the work of Eno).

Significantly, this point can be illustrated with some quite dif-ferent examples.

1. Punk music, though it avoids electronic instruments and, seemingly, adventurous experimentation with timbre, in fact depends very much on two of the elements we have been dis-cussing here. One of these elements might be called "attitude," but, in more formal language, this is very much a question of timbre or texture. Second, though, like all musical works, punk songs unfold in time, they have the same atemporal quality under discussion here in that, if one takes a slice of the song, one more or less also has its musical content.

2. Listening to some punk songs (some of the best ones, in fact) is not unlike looking at a minimalist painting—the point is to get it all in one "go," one look—and, if some sense of narrative is felt at all, it is in the form of a remainder or trace. With musical works that work developmentally, and which there-fore display (if not "represent"—I'm avoiding some difficult issues here) a narrative dimension, it is almost never satisfying to listen to just a part of the work—and it is especially not sat-isfying not to hear the end of the work. The "narratology" of timbre-based music works quite differently: in some sense, this music resists closure precisely because it isn't going any-where to begin with. Does this allow "the landscape to once

again be invested with meaning," or even a "liberatory aesthetics," as Wilson argues?

3. Or, is it simply the nonassertive background music for something else—especially a film? In the passage from *Postmodernism* where Jameson speaks of "wir[ing] up the context," he goes on to say:

> In that situation, *narrative* offers multiple and proteiform mediations between the sounds in time and the body in place, coordinating a narrativized visual fragment—an image shard marked as narrative, which does not have to come from any story you ever heard of—with an event on the sound track. (p. 300)

The idea of the "imaginary soundtrack" has become popular in just the past few years—and, of course, Eno is involved. Speaking of an album project that he did with the members of U2 (and others), *Passengers*, Eno wrote, "we came up . . . with the idea of inventing films to which these [pieces] were the soundtracks" (quoted in Young, p. 27). Rob Young, in an article titled "The Soundtrack Syndrome," writes, "Take a turn patrolling the melting edges of sampling culture, Electronica, avant-garde composition and experimental freefall: that's where you'll find the imaginary soundtrack" (p. 27). Young's explanation for the emergence of this field is informative:

> Why is the notion of the imaginary soundtrack such a seductive one to this growing stratus of musical activity? Perhaps it's to do with the fluidity of film; the transformation from the mundane flow of time to the sublime sequence of events, windowed by the rectangle of the lens and transmuted at the edit. As a synchromesh constructed from an array of digital splicers, crossfading agents, location recordings, sudden jumpcuts and zooms, electronic music's audio balance replicates the vision mix. The possibilities for soundbleed and soundfill, distortions of space and compression or elastication of time, exaggerated perspectives, disorientating angles and lurid chromatics, give it the psychotropic qualities of cinema.

On the other hand:

> Maybe also this new breed of celluloid wannabes are raising their game in contrast to the waning of the soundtrack-as-art. Today, *actual* soundtracks are humdrum affairs. What's expected, even by

"cool" films like *Trainspotting* or anything by Tarantino, is a saleable compilation of "classic," "hip," or rediscovered pop toons. (p. 27)

In my view, ironies abound here. In the first passage I quoted from the article, Young sets up an exciting bit of play between the soundtrack for the film and the film itself—except that the latter doesn't actually exist. In other words, the idea is to listen to the music as if it were the soundtrack for *a* film—but what film the listener is watching depends on her or his imagination. This is an interesting exercize, undoubtedly, and I have no qualms with the idea of artforms playing off of one another. Yet I do wonder at the choice of art form, namely film, which is now supposed to be the trace of narrative of contemporary life—and it does seem to be the form which has captured the imaginations of many intellectuals in recent years, at least if the conversations I hear at conferences or before committee meetings are any indication. Now take stock of the real exercise wherein the "imaginary soundtrack" is concerned: namely that the music remains background music for a possible narrative. This idea is interesting and probably philosophically (or perhaps sociologically) significant in itself—but it seems to me that what we are really dealing with here is a nostalgia for the possibility of narrative, and we are aiming to create a kind of music that evokes both the nostalgia and the possibility.

Yet a music that seems motivated by the desire for a "hip," "cool" film such as *Pulp Fiction* to have a creative soundtrack instead of another K-Tel sampler, and which goes on to make music for films that don't exist—can this music possibly take us into the "sacred drift," much less toward liberatory aesthetics?

From an even more skeptical perspective, one has to wonder if such musical works are not really meant to be audition tapes for work in the Hollywood film industry. Notice that no one is talking about musical settings for *poems* or *novels* that do not yet exist. Even if I've gone too far in imputing pecuniary motives to the imaginary soundtrack composers, it seems to me quite legitimate to worry about not only the incorporation of all art forms into a culture industry that finds its greatest point of concentration and most representative aspect in the film business (especially Hollywood, obviously, but not only Hollywood), but, even more, a general orientation of music to film as model.[10]

Jameson has some important things to say regarding the possibility of resisting the contemporary cultural dominant, postmodernism—namely that, it is "not possible intellectually or politically simply to celebrate postmodernism or to 'disavow' it (whatever that might mean)" (p. 297). I assume that this also goes for (what he takes to be) the central aesthetic forms of postmodernism, film, video, and architecture. Therefore, I recognize that my own wish that music not follow the model of a film aesthetic is problematic.

When I mentioned Eno's involvement in the *Passengers* project, I failed to mention, but on purpose, his much earlier *Music for Films* (1978); what needs pointing out is that Eno made this album in the same time period and context as his *Music for Airports*.

4. John Cage claimed that the principle element of music is duration. His argument follows from his definition of music as the organization of sounds and silences: of the basic elements of music, only duration applies to both sounds and silences. (Duration is not the same thing as "time," beat, or rhythm. However, we might ask whether there is not a rhythm of silences—which thesis would be tested to the limit by *4'33"*. In any work other than *4'33"*, where there are at least some "sounds"—a term that is also problematized by Cage—it seems the case that the silences are marked by the trace of the larger rhythm of the work. Maybe the silence of *4'33"* is marked by some other rhythm, that of "life." This is a Cagean possibility.) The irony is that, having set duration at the center, the impulse to atemporality asserts itself right at the same moment. For Cage's "measures" now become little "time boxes" (in Cage's music, the unit of notation is often a space with a limited duration, containing an instruction of some sort—e.g., "in the next eight seconds, turn the conch shell ninety degrees"), and then we are already in the room wired for sound.

5. One of the precursors to the "imaginary soundtrack" is Cage's composition, *Imaginary Landscape n.4, for Twelve Transistor Radios*. This work is performed by twenty-four players, two for each radio; one player controls the amplitude, the other the frequency. The instructions for this work are very strict,

but, of course, each performance is made unique by its time and location. A more recent performance of *Imaginary Landscape* would be affected, as well, by the whole shift in psychology—or, as McLuhan put it, "epistemological ratios"—from the romanticism of "radio days" to the postmodern age of the film aesthetic. We might suggest a certain test for the shifts that have occurred within postmodernity itself, then: a mapping of the fate of the "image shard marked as narrative" in the transition from the imaginary radio landscape to the imaginary film soundtrack. Is the transition simply one from a succession of boxes, to one big box (from which, as Jameson says of John Portman's Bonaventure Hotel in Los Angeles, among other things, that there is no way out)? Is there a transformation from quantity to quality here, and is this transformation at the same time a fundamental interruption of any logic of development, transformation, or progress?

6. Does it not seem that, in some sense, this interruption is a recapitulation of a root ahistorical impulse that we find at the opening of the modern era? Is there not something fundamentally *Cartesian* about the armchair voyage, the room wired for sound, the circumscribed duration that becomes, in so much as this is possible for embodied creatures such as ourselves, the atemporal moment? One can sympathize with the desire to clear away the clutter, whether it is theological, metaphysical, or musical, whether it is Thomism, Wagnerianism, or even progressive rock. One can sympathize with the desire to press the reset button and find that clear, crystalline structure (even though one also risks reinventing the wheel). But there is also a side to this that seems akin to the desire of the European middle classes to secure for itself a safe haven for small-scale entrepreneurship, a desire developed over centuries—indeed, over the course of European political modernity—from Descartes to Debussy:

Claude Debussy's father had plans for his son to become a sailor but Claude, at the age of eight, was described by his sister as spending "whole days sitting on a chair thinking no one knew of what." This dedication to a life in the imagination was underlined by a letter to another French composer, Andre Messager, in which Debussy wrote,

"I have endless memories which are worth more than reality."
(Toop, p. 16)

Well, perhaps I am stretching a bit here: it is reductive to claim a simple and straightforward correlation between subjects and structures. We will need more than an opposition between "adventure" and "inwardness" to bring off this analysis, given that the former may be no more than an expression of a purely bourgeois, and most likely colonial and imperial, heroism. Still, it seems to me that there is something to this—the Cartesian and existential drive to secure a fragile individuality.

An interesting contrast might also be drawn between two minimalisms. If only for the sake of being provocative (or perhaps perverse), let us take as examples Erik Satie's *Trois Gymnopedies*, on the one hand, and James Brown's "Papa's Got a Brand New Bag," on the other. The former is more representative of an armchair, Cartesian minimalism, in its fundamentally *still*, contemplative attitude. The well known "Gymnopedie n. 1," in particular, expresses the true essence of one side of minimalism, wherein the middle voice, so valued in the tradition from the classical to the late romantic periods, and certainly in much progressive rock, seems completely absent. These more "ideological" considerations are not meant to cancel the certain beauty, and even utopian quality, of the piece in question. But neither is it inappropriate to grapple with the place from which n.1's still moment, set against the industrial noise and poverty of Satie's own situation, might be considered a utopia. This is a "minimal minimalism" of the singular quiet space. Perhaps this could also be called a "gnostic" minimalism.

By contrast is the "maximal," perhaps even "embracing," "alchemical," and "hermetic" minimalism of James Brown's subtle, insistent funk—with "Papa's Got a Brand New Bag" as my personally favorite example. The structure of this song can be heard in its melodically simple (though rhythmically complex) bass line, consisting in just four notes: an initial drop of a fifth, then an octave jump alternating with the note one step below. The backbone of this song *is* the song, but on a deeper level than is the case for many funk or hard funk (e.g., Fishbone, Chili Peppers) pieces. At one and the same moment, there is a pure simplicity—an ostinato that can fade to nothingness and yet still be there—and there is also an all-embracing openness. If "Gymnope-die n.1" is the "cogito argument" of music, "Papa's Got a Brand New Bag" is the ontological argument, a music that goes from a single thought to infinity in a continuous, uninterrupted motion, from a single voice to the embracing collective choir of heaven.

The one is Paris, the other Motown (though, in reality, Macon, Georgia). The one is Foucault's Descartes, the setting aside of noise as singular event; the other is Derrida's, the recognition that the reason/madness dichotomy structures each moment.[11]

Music for postmodern times is somewhere between trance and dance.

7. In postmodern music, the key is not linearity or the counter-point of temporal development, but instead a principle known best in terms of the metropolitan urban landscape's most rep-resentative game, "verticality."[12] Whether the music is ambi-ent, or the more recent "illbient," or somewhere in the range of musics in-between—techno, industrial, jungle, drum 'n' bass,—the key is *vertical stacking*. As with postmodern archi-tecture, the idea in this stacking is that, in principle, any sound can go with any other sound. Just as, however, even the most eclectic pastiche of a building must all the same have some sort of foundation that anchors it to the ground, verti-cally stacked music often depends on an insistent beat. There are layers of trance stacked on top of dance, often without much in the way of stylistic integration. There is something to the idea that what post-Eno postmodern music gives us is "Cage with a beat," "Cage-rock." (Eno himself, it should be added, is not so wedded to the beatbox.)

For what it is worth, I have the feeling that Cage would not have found this very interesting. There is a fundamental inversion at work here, one that yields the trance/dance com-bination. Cage's music, despite whatever some may make of his involvement with Zen, remains fundamentally a music of ideas—Cage is representative of perhaps the last period in which, for the western classical tradition at any rate, there remained a dynamic interplay among all of the arts as well as interest in large philosophical questions. After Cage, this tradition gives way almost entirely to a narrow and pedantic focus on technique (much as philosophy of the positivist sort did); it's not uncommon, therefore, to find that, with any given gathering of classical musicians, there is not a single idea to be found. (Perhaps what is even more disgraceful is that the same thing could be said for certain gatherings of philosophers.) A piece such as *Imaginary Landscape n. 4* is more the stuff of a dream, rather than a trance, with its layers of unintended meanings a ready invitation for creative psychoanalysis. In any case, one can surely say that, for Cage, the idea preceded the sound—and his arguments about bracketing intentions mainly have to do with this order of discovery, whereby it is not the case that he had a certain sound in mind that he was attempting to present.

Now, there is a sense in which this is true in post-Eno music as well. As with Cage, the approach is experimental— going in, one doesn't know what the outcome will be. But, whereas Cage approached the experiment more on the level of philosophy, or at least "intellect," wondering what would be the consequence of allowing a particular idea to express itself in music (and not knowing in advance, and creating situations where it is not possible to know or to have the music simply be the expression of the composer's intention), postmodern composition resembles more the activity of a chef experimenting with ingredients. Postmodern music is blender or mixmaster or perhaps even *bricoleur* music. One might even say that postmodern music is more purely "musical," in that it is motivated primarily by experimentation with sounds rather than ideas.

Yet, there is almost something too easy to this "experimentation," and this has everything to do with the element of technology involved. For instance, the insistent beat in much of this music is almost always generated by some sort of drum machine—and this is not an insignificant point. This technology, along with samplers and tone generators (i.e., electronic keyboards), is now widely available and relatively inexpensive. (It's the same basic transition that took us from the Univac to

personal computers and pocket calculators.) Indeed, some of
the most representative music coming out of the London
techno scene is decidedly low-tech. Whereas, with Eno, there
is a continual playing with "strategies," more akin to Cage's
experiments, techno and related musics have a more "intu-
itive, mixed-on-the-spot" feel. As Socrates (in Plato's *Gorgias*)
says of some kinds of poetry, making this music seems "a
knack, like cookery."

Significantly, one can read most of an entire issue of *The
Wire* (which covers this scene) and encounter very few "musicians" who play what used to be called "musical instruments."

8. This true musical perfume/wallpaper represents a qualitative
leap apart from (I will not say "beyond," because there
appears to be no more "beyond" in this stalled dialectic) Cage
and Eno. This is *pastoral* for the age of all-encompassing
urbanization and even cyberspace, never mind the fact that
some of the more frantic forms of techno and illbient would
drive the shepherd, along with his sheep, over the cliff. My
guess is that Jameson would say of this music what he says of
Robert Gober's "postmodern mound":

we can now . . . ask ourselves whether—far from marking the place of
Nature—it does not rather constitute something like the grave of
Nature, as the latter has systematically been eclipsed from the object
world and the social relations of a society whose tendential domination over its Other (the nonhuman or the formerly natural) is more
complete than at any other moment in human history. (p. 170)

Perhaps another way of putting it is that this music is something
like the antinomy of pastoral and English romanticism, the contradiction which has now come completely unstuck from its
dialectical "opposite."

Therefore, it now seems possible to conclude this set of ruminations with just a few brief comments.

The music of detemporalized space seems unlikely to be productive of innovation. The vertical-stacking approach implicitly
(or even explicitly) accepts the idea that music (or art more generally) is now simply a matter of trying out the combinations, fill-
ing out the grid. Instead of musicians or composers, we find

people who are clever with technology, who paste together the material generated by the "content providers" (this has become a term for actual writers, whose work is downloaded from the internet and cut up and pasted together by others). Jameson argues that postmodernism represents a new "machine age" within capitalism, the age of the computer especially—and post-modern music bears this out. When I spoke—or griped—about the absence of people who play "musical instruments," the very idea sounded quaint and old-fashioned. And perhaps it is, or per-haps we are only seeing the beginnings of something that might in fact lead to unexpected results.

This does seem to be music for a time of clever people. Jame-son remarks, interestingly, that what gives the "great" composers (or other artists) of modernity their charm is precisely the fact that they themselves are *not* modern. Instead, the charm derives from the fact that they practice "handicraft" in an age of indus-trial production. Surely this description applies to progressive rock musicians, before the age of sampling, as much as it does to any other modern artists. In Jameson's view, "postmodernism" is, in a sense, "full modernism," and thus even the handicraft of artistic production is superseded by work with/of machines (see pp. 300–304). It is difficult for me to see, therefore, how the more optimistic outcome I mentioned at the end of the previous remark might come about—unless there is a radical change of terms. For the present configuration seems set against idealism, and therefore set toward cynicism. It is a matter not simply of the figures I have discussed, especially Brian Eno (though there are others who might be seen as no more than opportunistic), but instead of the larger historical and cultural terms that are avail-able to us—the very terms that render musical idealism and attempts at profundity quaint. (Eno, significantly, worries about profundity, and even goes so far as to say that he defends "preten-tiousness"—bless his heart—in *A Year*, p. 381 and elsewhere.) Pro-gressive rock music, as created by such adventurous groups as King Crimson, Henry Cow, Soft Machine, and Yes (perhaps the most idealistic of all of them), seems to me an instructive exam-ple. The point is generally lost that progressive rock was one of the last avant-gardes to emerge from western music. Notice how quickly a commercially oriented "critical" establishment sprang up to denegrate—as pompous, pretentious, overblown—the very idea of a truly innovative rock music. This episode should be marked—and studied—as an essential cultural barometer.

I take heart in the fact that, apart from this "critical" establishment, musicians themselves seem at least implicitly aware of the importance of this popular avant-garde. (Toop, significantly, steps rather quickly around the admiring references to Yes and Rush by some of his favorite samplers.) Or perhaps the point is that people do not want to stay still, even in a space of stasis. Postmodern capitalism offers us a "dynamism" in which, despite all the buzz and bumbling confusion, nothing much really happens. How long will people run around in circles, in the room wired with the music of postmodern wallpaper? Where can we go with music that is not meant to go anywhere? You are already in the city (which no longer has any outside), and soon enough in cyberspace, so where would you *want* to go, in any case?

An appeal to the quaint, which may only take us back a few years, risks being mere nostalgia (which often brings along with it the "better times" which do not deserve even nostalgia). Even more, it appears that anything that attempts a radical romanticism will be immediately branded as such nostalgia or, perhaps even more likely, a dangerous utopianism. Such are the terms of postmodern capitalism: against utopian strivings, we are given the insistent b(l)eat of "that's the way it is." There is the danger that, in appealing to an older model of musical development against a postmodern music of impasse and stasis, we will do no more than resurrect "heroism" and individualism in a more classically bourgeois form.

What I am driving toward is the idea that this question of postmodern music will ultimately be a social question, and here let us reengage with one of the final passages in Jameson's *Postmodernism*:

> [F]or the moment, global capital seems able to follow its own nature and inclinations, without the traditional precautions. Here, then, we have yet another "definition" of postmodernism, and a useful one indeed, which only an ostrich will wish to accuse of "pessimism." The postmodern may well in that sense be little more than a transi-

tional period between two stages of capitalism, in which the earlier forms of the economic are in the process of being restructured on a global scale, including the older forms of labor and its traditional organizational institutions and concepts. That a new international proletariat (taking forms we cannot yet imagine) will reemerge from this convulsive upheaval it needs no prophet to predict: we ourselves are still in the trough, however, and no one can say how long we will stay there. (p. 417)

Still, the question might be whether it is possible in these post-modern times to create music that is something other than simply wallpaper for the trough—an *important* music that is not simply dependent on larger social dynamics but also makes a difference to these dynamics. With our ears against the wall, a double strategy recommends itself. On the one hand, we might make a slight turn on an already well-crafted formula and attempt to "only reconnect"—that is, look to models, from the romantic to the modern, that might still lend us their energy from the "front" side of the impasse. And, on the other, we are not absolved of the need to dialectically work through, in an immanent critique, the material which is presently given to us as wallpaper and perfume.

In other words, the reinvention of progressive rock in this, this "future" that is quite other than the one listened for in the early seventies, still requires listening to the future. But we must listen *from* somewhere, we must reconnect. And yet we must also attempt to find the somewhere that is buried in our present nowhere, this ahistorical space of musical wallpaper and rooms wired for sound.

Not everything in the post-Eno musical universe is techno or ambient, of course. Progressive rock and Eno together played a major role in opening up the scene that we presently call "world music." Some of the key moments in this opening include Eno's "Fourth World" series, beginning with his collaboration with trumpeter Jon Hassell, *Possible Musics*, as well as Peter Gabriel's Real World label and World Organization of Music and Dance (WOMAD), and even Jon Anderson's recent solo projects, *Deseo*, *Toltec*, and *The Promise Ring*. Some of what is presented under these headings is simply meant to introduce Western audiences to non-Western musics. But other projects are clearly undertaken in a postprogressive vein: they aim at synthesis, they often have a rock music undercurrent, with "nonrock" sounds on top (but then, what *is* "nonrock" anymore?), they generally involve musicians with a very high level of proficiency, and although they may not seem to be very directly related to English romanticism, they all the same are very clearly motivated by ideals of ethical and political universalism. Surely the idea of one, albeit diverse, human family—and the idea that certain technological, economic, and otherwise social barriers stand in the way of the achievement of this utopian goal—is not so distant from the progressive rock ideology of groups such as Yes, Emerson, Lake, and Palmer, Jethro Tull, Henry Cow, and the rest.

Although not explicitly presented as a "world music" project per se, Peter Gabriel's *Secret World* album, tour, and film surely embody the best aspects of the intersection of progressive rock and world music—and show the affinities of the two genres. Gabriel's group contains extremely capable musicians from four continents: Africa, Europe, Asia (India), and North America. The music ranges from straight-out rock and funk ("Steam," "Sledgehammer"), psychedelic ("Secret World"), Celtic ("Solsbury Hill"), Jamaican ("Don't Give Up"), to skillful incorporations of North and Central African, Middle Eastern, and Indian influences. The desire to bring all of these influences into a synthesis is rooted in an impulse that is simply *unthinkable* without the background of progressive rock. And the synthesis has been organized by one of the key figures of progressive rock in its heyday.

I cannot help but note, incidentally, that a number of recent electronica artists, including Future Sound of London, Deep Forest, Trans-Global Underground, and Global Communication, have chosen Jon Anderson's *Deseo*, an album made with Brazilian musicians, for a "remix" project.

◼ ◼ ◼

When Yes reformed in late 1995, it was with the idea of taking the group into the new millennium. Their album, *Keys to Ascension*, features a remarkable piece of new music, "That, That Is." Though clearly a piece of Yes music, this work is unlike any recorded before by the band, in that it is a six-part suite. "That, That Is" is as hermetic as anything ever produced in progressive rock, especially given that one key piece of hermetic wisdom is "as above, so below"—heaven and earth are connected, they are not completely separate realities. This theme is enacted in both the music and the lyrics. The piece begins with a short bit of heavenly keyboards, and then a very charming guitar orchestration from Steve Howe. There is a strong feeling that a narrative, told from the perspective of heaven, is about to unfold here, with Howe's orchestration moving from Spanish and Mediterranean sounds to, ultimately, the grittiness of an American inner city. "Togetherness" moves, at the end almost violently, and by way of some remarkable drum figures from Alan White, to "Crossfire." Anderson's lyrics here are exemplary of the view I have seen him express in interviews lately, where one moment he is talking about how there are eleven or thirteen dimensions of reality, and the next he is railing against corporate capitalism. In making these connections, and in his talent for expressing these things in a coherent lyrical vision, he is a William Blake of our day.

Everyone is in splendid form here, with Rick Wakeman contributing a bit less than the others. Chris Squire's bass work is everything it ever was, and more. Alan White not only shows that he is *the* Yes percussionist, with some remarkable polyrhythms as well as some straightahead rocking, but also contributes significantly to the composition. Steve Howe is a musical treasure of world-historic importance, in that he has mastered so many styles of guitar playing, and yet he makes them his own as well. He simply channels the history of the guitar. And Jon Anderson still has the voice and the vision. There are wonderful intimations of the

Beatles here, as well, for example in the "Talk is the easy send" section of "All in All" (which reminds me of "I Am the Walrus," among other things). And there is an instrumental section featuring a guitar solo that is even a bit, shall we say, Fripp-like. In terms of the linearity of progressive rock, "That, That Is" is a great place to reconnect.

But reconnect to go where? In the spring of 1997, Rick Wakeman once again left Yes, perhaps this time for good. The group has recorded an album of new material, purportedly all as good or even better than "That, That Is," apparently under the title "Know" (whether this will ultimately be the title, assuming we actually ever get to hear the album, is not known at the time of this writing). Without Wakeman, the band has to make other arrangements in order to tour; without having a tour set up, it is hard to get the album released. Perhaps all of these issues will be resolved by the time this book is published (certainly I hope this is the case), but there is a larger point here. "That, That Is" ends with a quintessential Andersonian invocation: "Just let it come through, come through." If "That, That Is" is a fine effort toward reconnecting with the time of progressive rock, still there are many things that stand in the way of allowing that time and energy and "the breaking free" (as Anderson puts it) to "come through." This has got to be the case if even a "supergroup," such as Yes, has difficulty in getting their albums released. It has been one major aim of this book to connect the time of progressive rock to larger social and philosophical questions. I conclude then, with a challenge to the reader, as well as to myself: Let us do what we can to let the time of progressive rock, and its spirit, the breaking free, to manifest itself once more, to "come through."

Afterword

Zeitgeist: sea change or heart murmur?

After a fairly long silence, there seems to be a flurry of activity around progressive rock. Not only will there be at least three book-length studies on the subject by the close of 1997, but progressive rock seems to be getting a fair amount of, if not "press" exactly, then at least notice in music magazines that have international distribution. In reviews of albums that would seem to have little or nothing to do with progressive rock, a few music critics have made a habit of mentioning that, in their youth, they were impressed with the genre, but that's all behind them now. Of course, the issue that they are skirting is that much of the newer experimental rock is very much "postprogressive."

As I mentioned in the preface, a second book devoted to progressive rock, after Edward Macan's *Rocking the Classics*, came out as I was finishing this project. I would like to devote a few comments to Paul Stump's *The Music's All that Matters: A History of Progressive Rock*, though, unfortunately, I will not be able to go very deeply into the book at this time. In general, I do think the book is a good contribution to the discussion, despite the fact that the author himself sometimes seems quite ambivalent or even cynical about his subject matter. And, perhaps out of a desire to still appear "hip" to his fellow *Wire* writers who rarely miss an opportunity to hurl abuse at the genre, Stump often affects a chatty tone that detracts from serious discussion. At times, too, the thread of the argument gets caught up in this chattiness and gives way to non sequiturs. The book is very lively and entertaining, on the other hand; Stump has a good facility with language, which I often found myself envying.

Apart from the many points where I agree with Stump (or mostly so, at any rate), with the hope of generating further discussion I would like to focus on one area where we probably have a fairly deep disagreement.

Stump makes a distinction between "mainstream" and "alternative" progressive rock:

> On the one hand, listener-friendly, Beatles-derived Progressive music, in its shotgun marriage with that ultimate symbol of Western bourgeois art music—the symphony orchestra—distanced itself from the other flank of Progressive. These were musicians—notably of the Canterbury and Notting Hill constellations—who were unwilling to divorce their music from the anti-bourgeois cultural discourses of the Underground which had kick-started their musical aspirations in the first place. (p. 82)

Stump seems to draw the distinction much as Robert Fripp or Chris Cutler does, although much to his credit (and bless his heart), he is not a Yes-basher. Stump is forthright in his admiration of albums such as *Close to the Edge*, *Relayer*, and *Olias of Sunhillow*.

Stump does in fact use the terms "bourgeois" and "bourgeois values" (and the like) throughout his book, in ways that I sometimes found perplexing. In part, it seems that Stump applies the terms whenever progressive rock musicians work hard and give great attention to craft and detail—"traditional virtues" for artists. Much progressive rock, too, is "symphonic"—not necessarily in the sense of using an actual orchestra (which, in fact, is not so common a thing in progressive rock as one might expect from reading Stump), but instead in that it employs a broad tonal palette.

But perhaps the distinction has to do with the difference between groups that are more "sharp-edged" or "astringent" (to return to the term invoked by Mike Barnes in his article on Chris Cutler, discussed in my chapter 3), and those that seem more "light weight." Is it Schönberg and Orff vs. Gershwin and Copland, or Coltrane vs. "smooth jazz"? I find the former dichotomy more problematic than the latter. Are "mainstream" progressive groups ones that tried to make their music more palatable, in terms of mainstream rock tastes?

The terms require clarification. Some "astringent" progressive rock is just as much the product of a "bourgeois" concern with craft as is the more "mainstream" variety. Conversely, although Gershwin is not as *avant* as Schönberg, he still made an original contribution; Gershwin opened fields that later generations still find fruitful for further exploration. And, at least one of the main

Canterbury bands, Caravan, was vastly less astringent than, say, ELP, Yes, or Genesis. Because I get the feeling, not necessarily from Stump, but from others who want to make the mainstream/alternative distinction, that bands such as these last three are among those the line is being drawn against (that is, they are seen as "mainstream"), I'd like to see the criteria developed further.

Surely, in other words, there are groups and albums in progressive rock that are more experimental than others. However, keeping in mind the hundreds of albums discussed in my fourth chapter and elsewhere, it seems to me that there are only a relative handful of groups and artists who might be honestly accused of attempting to make merely palatable music. Drawing the line between Henry Cow and Renaissance will probably work, but drawing it between Henry Cow and King Crimson, on the one side, and Yes, ELP, and Genesis (to name just a few), on the other, won't.

Sometimes such distinctions work according to what might be called a fetish for fragmentation, the latter being, supposedly, the sine qua non of avant-gardism. Therefore, it is assumed that groups such as Henry Cow, or perhaps even more to the point, King Crimson, are simply much "further out" because they tend to reinvent their sound more often. Indeed, the history of such groups is itself fragmented. However, all of this becomes much more problematic in a time when it is difficult to identify exactly what might really count as "avant-garde" anymore. (Indeed, if fragmentation becomes the norm in postmodernity, perhaps once again grappling with narrative becomes avant.) Certainly the combination of fragmented samples with heavy "breakbeats" (rhythm tracks generated with drum machines) is considered the latest thing in certain quarters, especially if the practitioners can also insert a line or two about Jacques Derrida or Gilles Deleuze (that rhizome stuff drives 'em wild) or Jean Baudrillard or Samuel R. Delaney into interviews—even if there is scant evidence that said practitioners have actually read—much less understood—any of this stuff.

By contrast, the work of many progressive rock artists seems "neoclassical," perhaps even in the way that Stravinsky pursued this course for close to three decades from the early forties onward. But there is also something to be said for the way that certain groups—with Yes as the key example, in terms of sustained work—developed a particular language and vision. Some of these groups were certainly no less adventurous for this fact, though some of them may indeed have fallen into various ruts.

However, there does remain the question of progressive rock's status as one of the avant-gardes of rock music. By the end of the time of progressive rock, it seemed that only Henry Cow (of the first-line groups, and perhaps a few more groups otherwise) still carried this banner forward. They called it quits, after *Western Culture*, though the members have carried on in various incarnations. These projects, such as the Art Bears, or other work by Fred Frith, Chris Cutler, Lindsay Cooper, John Greeves, Peter Blegvad, and others, have forged links with other rock avant-gardes, whether they be of continental Europe, the United States (especially the post-Velvets New York scene, as well as Pere Ubu and David Thomas), Japan, or elsewhere. Despite the fact that I have been critical of *The Wire* here, for what I regard as its all-too-hip dismissal of progressive rock, it is certainly the best source (at least in the English language) for learning about this particular postprogressive avant-garde.

King Crimson has also continued to forge new directions, even if the *Thrak*-era group is synthesizing the music of the *Larks' Tongues* and *Discipline* periods as well. In the final chapter I already discussed some reasons why it may be, shall we say, a less-complicated proposition for King Crimson and the Henry Cow musicians to remain in the forefront—the main reason being that neither camp has to deal with the constraints of working with a group. Obviously, King Crimson *is* a group, *in some sense*, but it is even more an intermittent project of Robert Fripp. This set-up allows Fripp to escape not only the expectations that a group's "fan base" might have—and this escape seems a good thing, to my mind—but also the *history* that is a part of the ongoingness (or the attempt at such, at any rate) of a group. Perhaps it is good, for the sake of musical innovation, to escape this too; without the history, however, there is a real sense in which there is no "group." King Crimson becomes something more like a "category," therefore—albeit a great one, to be sure.

The contrast with what I have called the other pillar of progressive rock, Yes, is difficult to make in recent years. Yes's existence has also been intermittent. Now, with the break-up of "Yes-West" (the eighties group with Trevor Rabin, in other words—about which I am a good deal more positive than many Yes fans; see *music of Yes*, pp. 215–19, as well as the interview with *Progression* magazine [Gunnison], p. 37), Yes is perhaps trying to be a group, but they live all over the place (Anderson and Squire in southern California, White near Seattle, Howe in England, and Rick Wakeman on the Isle of Man, although as of this writing he has left Yes once again and the group is looking for a keyboardist). Even in this cybernetic age, it is difficult to get a group dynamic going without the element of proximity. But then, relationships are hard on all levels in this time of postmodern capitalism, whether we are talking about romance or rock groups.

When Yes reformed in late 1995, there was much made about a return to the "classic" line-up. Of course, I love this line-up, in terms of the musicians involved, but what else is at stake with these ideas of "return" and "classic"? I have argued for the necessity of "reconnection," but if this imperative is pursued only under the heading of nostalgia, or, even worse, merely to make some more money from the old fan base, (which is mainly what I see, for example, Wynton Marsalis doing in jazz), then even reconnection will not be achieved. Perhaps this is where Stump's distinction does make a good deal of sense. Things either move forward or they move backwards. In this sense, music is not so much an "entity" as it is an ongoing process—and it is this sense of music that is well-exemplified by Robert Fripp and his projects. Of course, Jon Anderson knows this as well as anyone (one of his favorite words, he once said in an interview, is "movement"). Music that only aims to return to what has worked before really becomes something other than music—it congeals and reifies into a mere thing, an entity, something only to be packaged for sale to the mainstream. (This is not the same thing as recognizing that music that was innovative in 1972—or 1772, for that matter—can still speak to us and carry us forward.)

In his published diary (*A Year*), Brian Eno argues that much progressive rock (he names Yes, ELP, and Genesis, as I recall), is

more about finishing something old rather than starting something new. The something old that Eno has in mind is nineteenth-
century European classical music—which once again takes us
into the issues that Chris Cutler raised. These issues are also
raised by Stump, who puts forward and ultimately rejects the thesis that progressive rock is "the classical music of the future,"
and, obviously, Edward Macan, even in the very title of his book,
Rocking the Classics. The rejection of the "future classical" thesis
by Stump loses a good deal of its force if the proposal is not
accepted in the first place. Progressive rock is a kind of rock
music that also draws from elsewhere—as all rock music always
has—in and through a framework based in English romanticism
and advanced musical skills. Some groups have drawn a good
deal from European romantic music, some hardly at all. Unlike
Eno, I do not think that the characterization of "old" entirely captures what remains possible in the musical (and philosophical)
language of Beethoven (or in the political-poetic language of
William Blake); on the other hand, Eno certainly has something if
he is simply pointing to the way that some musicians do little
more than recycle what has already been accomplished (much
better) by artists from previous generations. Even so, we might
also notice that there is plenty of precedent for what many, shall
we say, post-Eno/postprogressive musicians are doing, much of
which, because of the wonders of sampling and other studio technology, is recycling pure and simple.

If, with his distinction, Stump is actually trying to get at something like the difference between those who still aim to experiment and those who are merely recycling, then we have a basis
for further development of the argument—which will take us
some distance beyond Canterbury and Notting Hill. Significantly,
Stump's final two chapters have to do with individuals who have
pursued postprogressive music and with the idea of the "imaginary soundtrack," respectively. This again raises the question,
What about the idea of the *group* (and group composition)? Has
the countercultural notion of collectivity been eclipsed in this
time of normalized fragmentation?

(Just as there is a technological way around the hassles of
dealing with groups, I wonder if the same impulses have made

musical instruments passé. After all, an instrument has to be treated as a musical partner. I am sure that some would say the same thing for sampling technology, but there is a difference, a *physical* difference—which again seems passé in the time of cyberspace. This physical difference—the ways of touching and feeling instruments are qualitatively different from interactions with the newer technologies—relates also to questions of collectivity, "the group," and place. But these are issues that will have to be explored at length elsewhere.)

Among those who are making similar distinctions, there has also recently been a fetishization of "Krautrock" as the real avant-garde. (Stump avoids this issue by focusing exclusively on English artists.) Recent articles in *The Wire* and *Mojo* make it appear that, to some critics, the fact that groups such as Faust are known for getting naked and smearing themselves with various substances during performances, while also using construction equipment to "deconstruct" various items on stage, is simply the height of avant-gardism. Such critics move rather quickly past the expressed desires of such artists to "reclaim" German culture—something their parents dared not openly do in the first twenty-five years after the Second World War. Perhaps some critics find this orientation a welcome alternative to strains of sentimentality and romanticism in English progressive rock. This may also be an area where my undeveloped "eros/thanatos" thesis, from chapter 4, might be pursued further. For my part, I think there is still a role to be played by a radical romanticism, beyond mere sentimentality (though, in this time of what Fredric Jameson calls the "loss of affect," I'm not sure that a little sentimentality is such a bad thing either). Furthermore, the recent interest in "Krautrock" (a term I've never been comfortable with, hence the continued use of scare-quotes) is further demonstration, it seems to me, of the coming together of certain artists from progressive rock or postprogressive music with the post-Velvet Underground (or other New York scene artists), to the exclusion of the core elements of what made progressive rock what it is. Is there a way to still work in terms of these elements and yet also to carry the music forward? Peter Gabriel's *Secret World* concert and other work, Jethro Tull's *Roots to Branches*, and Yes's "That, That Is," as well as some of the work by newer groups such as Spock's Beard and Ozric Tentacles (discussed in Stump, pp. 333–35, and Macan, pp. 217–19), is the place to begin this discussion.

The arguments I have just presented perhaps go far afield of Stump's concerns—his aim, after all, is to present a "history" of progressive rock. However, he does devote a good deal of attention to what he calls progressive rock's "ideology" (he even refers to an ideology for rock music more generally, which he charmingly calls "rockism"). This "ideology" has in many ways been the prime concern of my book, and I think it is a strength of Stump's book to have underlined the notion. A less-loaded notion of "ideology" has to do with the ideas that are possible within a philosophy, ontology, or belief system. Some critics are not enthusiastic about the ideology of progressive rock. Is this because, in their view, the ideas that are embodied in progressive rock are not good ones to begin with, or because these ideas have played themselves out or can no longer address these times? Stump shows well enough that there is at least a prima facie case for not dismissing the ideology of progressive rock out of hand, as many critics are recently wont to do; on the latter question he seems ambivalent. For my part, and perhaps having been influenced by the challenge of Brian Eno and others, I think there is a good discussion to be had regarding the place of progressive rock's ideas in postmodern times. So, let us have it, but in a forward-looking spirit.

Resources

For the person who wants to pursue the study of progressive rock beyond simply listening to the music—which, however, should remain the core of the endeavor—there are an increasing number of publications and internet resources. Accessing the latter simply requires some sort of search engine; a great deal can be found simply under headings such as "progressive rock" or some particular band name. Of course, with names such as Yes or Genesis, you are likely also to call up pages on affirmative attitudes in general ("Yes, I am a model train hobbyist") or the first book of the Bible (it's a pretty good story, by the way), so it helps to append "progressive rock" to your search category. Many of the newer groups, such as Japan's Ars Nova, have very impressive web pages. As for internet bulletin boards and chat groups, as well as for fan publications in general, I think it is good to approach with a healthy skepticism. Gossip, much of it not very constructive, abounds in these media, and tends to encourage cynicism and narrowness. As always, I urge readers to take the largest view of the progressive rock movement, and to build on the best and most advanced aspects of this movement—and let the devil take the hindmost.

Personally, I'm oriented towards books. Although I enjoy magazine and journal articles, I am most interested in seeing how a topic can be explored systematically and at length—assuming the topic will sustain such exploration, of course. Therefore, I again urge readers to check out the books by Edward Macan and Paul Stump, as well as my own earlier book on Yes (publication data for all books mentioned will be found in the bibliography). The books by Eric Tamm, on Robert Fripp (and King Crimson) and Brian Eno, are also valuable. In addition, see Thomas Mosbo's *Yes, But What Does It Mean? Exploring the Music of Yes* (write to Wyndstar, 824 Neumann Court, Milton, WI 53563), for a somewhat different approach to the group than I provided in *music of Yes*.

May the number of such books, systematic investigations of either progressive rock as a whole, or of particular groups, increase.

In terms of pure "data," there are two books that I found essential in writing this study, and that were never far from my side these past few months. Above all, it would have been close to impossible to write this book without the help of Vernon Joynson's *The Tapestry of Delights*. The sheer amount of information Joynson has uncovered is staggering. Although the book covers a much broader field than just progressive rock, and while it is restricted to British music, there is plenty here to keep the progressive-rock listener occupied for many days on end. The publisher, Borderline Productions, also publishes a number of other guidebooks to psychedelic rock (including two by Joynson), as well as a comprehensive guide to "Krautrock" (*Cosmic Dreams at Play*, by Dag Erik Asbjornsen). The address for Borderline is P.O. Box 93, Telford TF1 1UF, England.

The other major guide that I found invaluable, even if progressive rock is only a small part of it, is *Rock: The Rough Guide*. Of the first-line groups dealt with here, there are entries for all but PFM (in other words, Henry Cow is in there, as well as Soft Machine, Magma, and Robert Wyatt). Because the book was written by fans, none of the entries have the usual anti-progressive-rock snideness of most guides (i.e., *Rolling Stone, Harmony*). My understanding is that the *Rough Guide* will be updated periodically, so any enterprising readers who want to send in entries for, say, Flash, Banco, or Public Foot the Roman, ought to give it a shot. (Incidentally, the *Rough Guide* for jazz is quite good, too.)

As I mentioned in the afterword, although I am quite at odds with the British magazine *The Wire* when it comes to their view toward progressive rock, I do think that it is otherwise quite a good source on where "postrock" is going. The other general rock music magazine that I would recommend is *Mojo*; their approach is avowedly retrospective (for example, each issue features a section on the rock music scene as it was thirty years before). However, I find the magazine a very useful source in my own attempt to "reconnect." Furthermore, their in-depth articles about the history of such artists as the Byrds, Nick Drake, or Fairport Convention serve to remind me that the "rock" in progressive rock has much in common with other innovative rock trends from the sixties and early seventies.

Moving now to magazines that cover progressive rock, two in particular are excellent for keeping up on scenes both past and present (prices change, of course):

Progression: The Journal of Progressive Music, edited by John Collinge. Quarterly/$18 for four issues. Call (800) 545-7371, or write John Collinge, Publisher, *Progression*, P.O. Box 7164, Lowell, MA 08152 (United States).

Exposé ("Your central source of information for Progressive, Symphonic, Fusion and Electronic Rock"), edited by Peter Thelen. $4.50/issue, $18/four-issue subscription. Write *Exposé*, 6167 Jarvis Avenue, #150, Newark, CA 94560.

These magazines will lead you to even more sources, such as the English magazine *Audion* (address: Ultima Thule, 1 Conduit St., Leicester, LE2 OJN, England), as well as to numerous distributors of progressive rock LPs and CDs.

I do not wish to slight any of the very good distributors out there, but one that I have found dependable and, to say the least, extensive in its CD catalogue, is Greg Walker's Syn-Phonic. Write for a catalogue at Syn-Phonic, P.O. Box 2034, La Habra, CA 90631. If you are after LPs, two very good sources are Aeon Music, P.O. Box 421544, Los Angeles, CA, 90042, and ZNR, c/o S. Roberts, P.O. Box 58040, Louisville, KY 40268-0040.

A very important source for keeping up with events in the present life of progressive rock (album releases, concerts, current interviews) is *Music News Network: International Monthly Progressive Rock Newsletter*, edited by Lisa Mikita and Christine Holz. I generally find myself reading this informative publication cover-to-cover as soon as it arrives. Subscriptions are $18/year; write *Music News Network*, P.O. Box 21531, Tampa, FL 33622-1531 (checks or money orders payable to Lisa Mikita).

Finally, a few other useful addresses (some pinched from the backmatter of Paul Stump's book):

For all things Canterbury: *Facelift* fanzine, c/o Phil Howitt, 39 Nicolas Road, Manchester M21 9LG, England.

For post-Henry Cow projects: ReR Megacorp, 79 Beulah Road, Thornton Heath, Surrey DR7 8JG, England.

Gong Appreciation Society (GAS), P.O. Box 871, Glastonbury, Somerset, BA6 9FE England.

Pilgrims: The Peter Hammill/VDGG Fanzine, c/o Fred Tomsett, P.O. Box 86, Sheffield, South Yorkshire S11 8XN England.

For Jethro Tull: *A New Day* fanzine, 75 Wren Way, Farnborough, Hampshire GU14 8TA England.

Yes Music Circle: 44 Oswald Close, Leatherhead, Surrey KT22 9UG England.

Notes From the Edge, the internet Yes source, edited by Jeff Hunnicutt and Mike Tiano. Address: http://www.nfte.org

King Crimson and Robert Fripp: Discipline Global Mobile, P.O. Box 5282, Beverly Hills, CA 90209-5282 (United States).

Finally, if any readers would care to correspond with me, write to: Bill Martin, Department of Philosophy, DePaul University, 1150 W. Fullerton Avenue, Chicago, IL 60614-2204.

Notes

Chapter 1. Seize again the day

1. Following Plato, Aristotle does not allow that mere giddiness or fulfillment of purely bodily desires could lead to the deeper happiness that he associates with flourishing. This distinction has a complex legacy in Western philosophy. Perhaps the greatest difficulty with the question of happiness is seen in the philosophy of Immanuel Kant. The distinction between "surface" and "deep" happiness makes trouble for the utilitarian theories of Jeremy Bentham and John Stuart Mill as well.

2. See Mike Riesco, "Thoughts on Bill Martin's *music of Yes*, *Notes From the Edge*, p. 167 (December 30, 1996), pp. 4–5. *Notes From the Edge* is an internet journal (see the resources section for more information).

Chapter 2. The prehistory of progressive rock

1. This orthodoxy does not necessarily have much to do with blues music itself—within the realm of the blues, there is another orthodoxy, but there are also experimental trends.

2. See David Roediger's work on the making of the white working class in the United States.

3. Certain "Marxist," especially Trotskyist, trends do prefer to proceed as if these issues, of class in imperialist countries and a global imperialist system, are separable; this gives rise to a diseased "left," but perhaps this also helps explain why utopian-romantic currents in music do not have much use for the official left, even if practitioners of these currents may be hard-pressed to explain their thinking here.

311

4. Perhaps I should add that, when it comes to the contemporary use of the term "Luddite" for anyone who does not immediately jump on the bandwagon of some new technology, in this case I am certainly on the side of King Ludd. It should be noted, too, that the original Luddites were not "antitechnology" pure and simple, but were rebelling against the displacement of human labor and forms of life, and the endangerment of life and limb, by technologies that were not geared toward the benefit of working people.

5. An approach that focuses on social structures is not necessarily the same thing as what sometimes goes under the heading of a "structuralist" approach (as with Louis Althusser and others).

6. See Gracyk, pp. 149–73, as well as Lambert Zuidevaart, *Adorno's Aesthetic Theory*, pp. 230–41.

7. Judith Butler argues that sexuality *is* performance (or, at least, "performative"); see *Gender Trouble*, pp. 24–25, 33, 115, 134–41.

8. One of the most telling episodes in the time of the general suspicion of weirdness was the interest that *Mad* magazine attracted on the part of Senator Joseph McCarthy and his minions. See Maria Reidelbach, *Completely Mad: A History of the Comic Book and Magazine* (Boston: Little, Brown, and Company, 1991), pp. 26, 30, 40.

9. In this connection, see Houston Baker on the question of "conjuring"; *Workings of the Spirit: The Poetics of Afro-American Women's Writing* (Chicago: University of Chicago Press, 1991), esp. pp. 69–101.

10. See Jonathan Buckley's *Rock: The Rough Guide*, p. 244.

11. In fact, Rick Wakeman, who is committed to the Christian faith, has recently said that he now realizes that the "pagan" elements of *Tales from Topographic Oceans* are a part of what made him uncomfortable with the album; interview in *Notes From the Edge* (listed in "Resources"), p. 171.

12. In the *Rock: The Rough Guide* entry for War, Neil Nixon writes that *All Day Music* was "[p]art of a series of soul/funk records at the beginning of the seventies whose deep introspection still stands as some of the most original and disquieting music ever made" (p. 946). Not only is this absolutely true, but it seems to me that a good book could be written on this subject.

13. When I wrote my earlier book, *music of Yes*, I had the overwhelming sense that I was entering uncharted territory. There are very few books on rock "music" that actually have to do with the music itself. Although there is a good biography of The Who, Dave Marsh's *Before I Get Old*, this is a band that also deserves an extended critical analysis of their music.

14. It is also the case that ELP was preceeded by Greg Lake's tenure in The Gods—a group that also included future Uriah Heep members Ken Hensley and Lee Kerslake—as well as, of course, in King Crimson; in addition, Carl Palmer was previously a member of a keyboard-driven trio, namely Atomic Rooster.

15. Ironically, it is the sort of thing perhaps best represented in the United States by Leonard Bernstein—who apparently took umbrage at The Nice's torching of an American flag in their performances of his "America" from *West Side Story*. The double irony is that Bernstein was himself a supporter of progressive and radical causes—a great deal more so than Keith Emerson, for sure—for which he was surveilled by the FBI. See the biography of Bernstein by Humphrey Burton, pp. 392, 403.

16. There is an interesting argument to be had here regarding Kant and music and Adorno and jazz. Kant ranked music the least of the art forms; in some sense, music is too into its materials for Kant. Adorno, who certainly has a strong element of Kantianism in his work, ranks music first, but jazz and rock ("popular music") were ruled out almost altogether—perhaps also because they are too caught up in their materials. I raise this issue because it is difficult not to identify, for example, Jimi Hendrix or Carlos Santana, with the guitar—it seems their music and their instrument are practically one and the same thing. Yet, for example, you could not say this of Robert Fripp or Steve Howe. In other words, I cannot think of Hendrix or Santana without thinking of the guitar, but I can think of Fripp and Howe without first of all identifying them with their instrument; instead, I first of all identify them with music.

17. The paragraph concludes: "Lennon's song was original enough that the melodic similarities would not have been

apparent had he not retained a line of Berry's lyric. Berry's publisher sued, and in 1975, as part of the settlement, Lennon recorded "You Can't Catch Me" for his *Rock 'n' Roll* oldies collection" (p. 24).

18. We might pause here to contemplate how musical history might have been changed if Brian Wilson's mental state had allowed the completion of the follow-up to *Pet Sounds*, the aborted *Smile*. This album would have been the Beach Boys' response to *Sergeant Pepper's*. Bootlegs of the half-completed album have been in circulation for some time; even in incomplete form, this is some great stuff. The album would have included "Good Vibrations" which, thankfully, was completed and released as a single—and is an incredible song, of course. For the history of the *Smile* episode and its larger context, see Timothy White's excellent book on the Beach Boys, *The Nearest Faraway Place*, pp. 271–75.

Chapter 3. The time of progressive rock

1. Donald Davidson reformulates Kant's argument in terms of what he calls "anomalous monism"; see "Mental Events," in *Essays on Actions and Events* (Oxford: Oxford University Press, 1980), pp. 207–25.

2. A discussion of these issues is found in my *Matrix and line*, pp. 65–124.

3. See Donald Davidson, "A Nice Derangement of Epitaphs."

4. See my discussion of the notion of "project" in *Humanism and its aftermath*, pp. 20–26.

5. I have often entertained the notion that, from the standpoint of a certain kind of exploitative social system, to have large sections of the population under the sway of cynicism is in some ways preferable to too much jingoism—the person who espouses jingoism is at least committed to something, and may therefore form dangerous expectations. For further discussion of the politics of cynicism, see my "Against the strategy of cynicism," in *Politics in the impasse*, pp. 27–38.

6. An important discussion of the politics of the anti-utopian is found in the concluding chapter of Fredric Jameson's *Postmodernism*.

7. Barney Hoskyns, "Not In Bed With Madonna" (*Mojo*, March 1997, pp. 26–27). I should mention that *Mojo* is, in my view, one of the best music magazines around today—and they not only seem to avoid typical knee-jerk screeds against progressive rock, they have even managed to give the music a positive mention or two.

8. Sure enough, the fact that, by 1969, young men of all classes were being drafted to fight and possibly die in the promotion of imperial designs served as a powerful motivating factor. But this is not the whole story or the only interpretation. The argument to the effect that the antiwar movements on college campuses really only took off when the college deferment was overturned by the U.S. Supreme Court certainly has something to it. So does the argument that middle-class white kids in the U.S. were used to getting what they wanted, and they did not want to go fight and die in a war. But these arguments (or characterizations) ignore certain fundamental facts. For one thing, imperialism was, by the late sixties, militantly opposed by people all over the world—and not only U.S. imperialism, but French, German, British, Japanese, and Soviet imperialism (to name a few of the most egregious examples) as well. First and foremost, however, the point is that the Vietnam War was *wrong*, it was an immoral act of aggression and occupation against the people of Vietnam. It is interesting that some of those who make the kinds of arguments I described above want to apply something like strict Kantian requirements to the protestors. That is, they condemn the protestors for having mixed motives (for being motivated by both ethical and self-interested factors). This is an interesting and perverse way of side-stepping the actual ethical issue here, namely the morality of the war itself and the social formation that prosecuted the war.

9. Some of this analysis might be mapped onto, or at least fruitfully compared with, Derrida's discussion of the "gramme" (the hypothetical "smallest unit of meaning") in *of Grammatology*,

and perhaps this would help us with the question of comparing music to language, and with the question of the "meaning" of music.

10. Some of the themes in the following discussion have also been developed in *music of Yes*, esp. pp. 37–58. However, I have taken care here not simply to repeat what was said there. In what follows, I have used the themes of "divergence" and "convergence" to organize my thoughts, and this is a significantly different approach from that taken in the book on Yes.

11. Just to complete the picture: Jon Anderson was in a group called the Warriors, Tony Kaye was in the Federals, both more beat and R&B oriented, while Bill Bruford was in high school. Among Anderson's bandmates were drummer Ian Wallace, later of King Crimson (and who apparently played one gig with Yes in between the Bruford and Alan White eras), and bass guitarist David Foster, who later joined Tony Kaye in Badger.

12. I have altered the word order slightly for grammatical purposes.

13. I should note that, in recent conversation and correspondence, Jim DeRogatis has evinced something of a turn on the progressive-rock issue. This isn't to imply that he has come to agree with any of my arguments here, however.

14. Despite the idealizations that are often presented by folks in and around the Dead scene, the fact is that the circulation of drugs within the band partook of all the usual scamming and backstabbing that is found in the larger drug scene. Deadheads whom I've known over the years describe the wonders of being backstage before the concert, with Jerry Garcia, while he sat there like a doddering old man smoking cocaine in his pipe, as though this was simply charming. Somehow I just can't get into the spirit of that.

15. Perhaps it is worth noting that Kurt Cobain, who was a very heavy drug and alcohol user, was mainly interested in *blotting out* certain things, from the severe stomach pains that continually plagued him to, ultimately, the world. The other point that applies here, which also connects with the Grateful Dead issue, is that the idea seems to be that music can be somehow not enough, even aesthetically, on its own—in this televisual

and filmic world, we have to have something else going on besides "just" the music. Paradoxically, worshipers at the idiot box and the movie theater cannot be fulfilled by music alone, but neither can they be bothered to actually listen to music either.

16. As it turns out, one reason that I know something about this neat episode is that, when I arrived at the University of Kansas for graduate school in 1985, a group of anarchists in Lawrence were involved in a similar experiment.

17. Ben Fisher, "Jerry Wexler: The do right man" (*Mojo*, n. 40 [March 1997]: pp. 48–54).

18. See also: Dorothy Wade and Justine Picardie, *Music Man: Ahmet Ertegun, Atlantic Records, and the Triumph of Rock 'n' Roll* (New York: W.W. Norton, 1990).

19. One more thing needs to be said about the well-worn justification of capitalism in terms of "risk." What the capitalist risks, at most, is that he or she will no longer own (some part of) the means of production, and will therefore have to become a working person who is "propertyless" in the sense of not possessing the means to produce and reproduce life. In other words, the "risk" the capitalist takes is that he or she will have to share the common lot of the much greater part of humankind. Furthermore, the "risk" that the capitalist takes, in making investment decisions, is taken on behalf of those working people who have a great stake in the decision but no voice. This is why Marx argued that, in an age of fully socialized production, basic social decisions must be socialized as well, not left to a few individuals engaged in profit maximization.

20. Gracyk presses this case at some length, in the first three chapters of *Rhythm and Noise*, pp. 1–98.

21. On the workings of the Mellotron, see my *music of Yes*, p. 245, n. 26.

22. The final paragraphs of this section were written especially in response to a challenge from Edward Macan, in the form of his book as well as personal correspondence. In one of the most interesting chapters of *Rocking the Classics*, Macan presents an analysis of "Four Different Progressive Rock Pieces."

One of these four is Pink Floyd's "Wish You Were Here"
(1975). (The other three are "Tarkus" by ELP, "Close to the
Edge" by Yes, and "Firth of Fifth" by Genesis.) More will be
said about "Wish You Were Here" in the main text. In one of
our personal written exchanges, Macan writes:

I'm still not convinced by your distinction between "experimental"
and "progressive" rock. Going back to Pink Floyd, am I to say that
they're not "progressive" simply because they aren't virtuosos, even
though their music partakes in a number of other characteristics central to progressive rock, including (a) multi-movement structures, (b)
a frequent "cathedral"-like organ sound, (c) modal harmony with
similar dissonant harmonic extensions found in the music of Genesis
or Yes, and (d) emphasis on the same philosophical preoccupations
that characterize other progressive rock? Also, would an album like
Wish You Were Here really have been more fully "developed" if the
musicians were more virtuosic? And what about bands like Gentle
Giant and Van der Graaf Generator who were given to intricate
ensemble passages but not virtuosic individual solos?

Macan goes on to point out what, I take it, he considers to be
a more important distinction, between progressive groups
such as Soft Machine and the Mahavishnu Orchestra, who put
more emphasis on improvisation, and groups such as Yes,
ELP, and Genesis, who emphasize "tight ensemble arrangements of lengthy sections that are maintained note-for-note
from one performance of a given piece to the next." I take it
that I have already dealt with this distinction to some extent in
my discussion of the two different forms of "stretching out."
   Macan raises the crucial issues—these are good arguments, not to be sneezed at. Most of these issues are dealt with
in the main text (following the footnote number), but I would
like to deal with two issues here. First, regarding virtuosic
ensemble play versus individual solos, I don't see that as the
place to make the distinction. Instead, I would simply point
out that Gentle Giant's ensemble work is indeed on a virtuoso
level, in contrast to Pink Floyd's. This doesn't mean that Gentle
Giant's music is necessarily *better*. Second, I'm not entirely
sure what to do with Macan's point (b), regarding "cathedral"-
like organ sounds in progressive rock. In *Rocking the Classics*,

Macan makes an interesting argument concerning the relationship between progressive rock and English church music. I will return to this issue in the final section of the present chapter. I do not dispute the connection that Macan argues for, but I don't think I'm ready to elevate the sound of the church organ to the level of a basic component of progressive rock. On the other hand, somewhere between the church organ and Jimmy Smith is certainly where you will find at least some of the important keyboardists of progressive rock, especially Keith Emerson.

23. However, on this point I would like to return for a moment to Macan's point (c), regarding modal harmony. I would say that, while Pink Floyd's music is sometimes as harmonically complex as that of many progressive rock groups, it seems significant to me that almost nowhere is it as rhythmically complex as the music of, e.g., King Crimson, Yes, and Gentle Giant.

24. At the expense of working this issue to death, I would like to make one final comment on the "virtuoso" question. Of course it is difficult not to valorize musical works simply by using a term such as "virtuoso music." Clearly, this term complicates further the issue of the aesthetic value of rock music—the "is it art?" question. In arguing that, in the final analysis, progressive rock is a style, one of my aims is to banish the term "art rock." Certainly, *Wish You Were Here* or *Abbey Road* are every bit as much "art" as are *Close to the Edge* or *Larks' Tongues in Aspic*. But I would say the same for Elvis Costello's *Imperial Beadroom*, Talking Heads' *Remain in Light*, or Hüsker Dü's *Zen Arcade*—and anyway, why do we even have to have this conversation in the first place?

Well, there is something interesting to be said about virtuosity when it comes to at least some music that aspires to be art, namely Western classical music and jazz. That is, if a musician is not a virtuoso or close to it in the sense that I specified, namely a musician for whom the technical difficulty of music is not a barrier, then that musician is not going to be found on the concert stage with "real" classical or jazz musicians. That musician is not going to be playing with the

Chicago Symphony or the Metropolitan Opera or McCoy Tyner or Betty Carter. That musician is probably not even going to be playing with the Toledo Symphony or some locally known jazz artist—because that musician is simply not going to be able to keep up. (I don't mean to pick on Toledo or its symphony; and, the fact is, you can go to any number of blues clubs in Chicago or Memphis and hear a great many "unknown" guitarists who will knock your socks off.) But the same thing cannot be said about rock music. Not only are there rock musicians who are known globally who, "technically," are not great or even very good with their instruments; what's more is the fact that some of these musicians have created some truly excellent music. (As a bass guitarist I may have a special sensitivity to this question; people who are interested in taking up an instrument later in life often ask me if they should take up the bass, "because that looks pretty easy to get going with." The thing is, the bass guitar *is* easy to get going with, unlike, say, the violin or the trumpet. You could be a part of some great music with only minimal skill on the instrument—just ask Boz Burrell! Of course, I assume that the reader knows that really great bass guitar playing doesn't come easy.) Where to go with all of this I am not entirely sure, but I suppose that I would want to put it in the context of a general dissolution of boundaries in art, especially distinctions of "high" and "low" culture, and rock music's generally laudatory role in this.

25. In this discussion of the "Englishness" of progressive rock, I will depart somewhat from an argument that I made in *music of Yes*, or at least I will seem to. Again, I am responding to a challenge from Edward Macan. In a fascinating section, *Rocking the Classics* deals with the way that progressive rock has *regional* roots, namely in southern England. I will deal with Macan's arguments on this point in the final section of this chapter. Furthermore, in a letter to me, Macan takes me to task for having

fallen into a booby-trap inherent in Marxist analysis, which insists on analyzing a person's (or group's) actions primarily in materialistic terms. While I quite agree that there are too many people wanting to Balkanize us (*not* only according to nationality, but also according to color, ethnicity, gender, age, and every other category under the sun), I quite disagree that cultural affiliation for most people is synonymous with "the bourgeois nation-state of political modernity." Rather, for most people cultural affiliation is often a complex web of race, ethnicity, regionality, language (or perhaps regional dialect), religion, and other folk-ways. Thus while talking about "American culture" is, in my view, not terribly useful, talking about black culture and history in the southern Mississippi delta region, about Scots-Irish cultural legacies in Appalachia, about Irish Catholic culture in the Boston area, etc., could tell us quite a bit about why these particular people behave in certain ways and make certain collective choices. Likewise, talking about a vague "Englishness" in prog rock seemed useless to me, but talking about the impact of southern English culture and traditions on the development of the music (which was after all largely a phenomenon of southern England in its early stages) seemed absolutely necessary.

Macan goes on to recommend *Albion's Seed: Four British Folkways in America*, by David Hackett Fischer, which purportedly shows a basic deficiency of the "purely materialist perspective"—namely that this perspective fails to take account of cultural legacies and loyalties.

While I am not entirely sure that Macan got me entirely right in his reading of the relevant passage from *music of Yes* (the top half of p. 54), I am also ready to admit that I did not express myself very well on the question of culture and nationality. Furthermore, in response to Macan's book and correspondence, I have attempted to alter my position somewhat.

One further bit of context should be added to this discussion. As readers of *Rocking the Classics* have most likely noted, Macan is somewhat hostile to something he calls "Marxism," which he associates with certain critics of progressive rock. I will deal with this question in the main text, but I want to make a comment on it here, as well. It is no secret, of course, that I am in some sense a "Marxist," and therefore in some sense a "materialist." Without going too far into this, it is pretty clear that I am not the sort of "Marxist" that Macan (for the most part rightly) criticizes (though I have a hard time thinking of Lester Bangs as a Marxist, given that even the most unthoughtful Marxist would still be many levels of intellect above that idiot).

In the passage from *music of Yes* that Macan criticizes, I take great pains to somehow disassociate the "Englishness" of progressive rock from anything having to do with the nation-state of England, which I in turn associate with "a particular kind of class rule." Of course, these things cannot be fully disassociated. On the other hand, I misstated and overextended my point—or perhaps I wanted my cake and to eat it too—in that I somehow hoped to formulate some conception of "Englishness" that did not partake of the rise of European nation-states in the era of bourgeois revolution. What I have come to recognize now, in part thanks to Macan's helpful criticisms and in part through what I hope are developments in my own thinking (which have to do with some of my other work as a social theorist, in particular around the question of community), is the role played by a "complex network of regional/cultural influences" (Macan).

Part of my aim in criticizing the idea of a "national psyche" was to foreground the possibility of *internationalism*. The Marxism which I advocate breaks with the old-left view that internationalism is somehow built up of the various nationalisms—that the former is somehow an extention of the latter. In theory, the idea of a global community of mutual flourishing (which is what I, at any rate, mean by "communism"), a new kind of community which is historically unprecedented, is powerful both as inspiration and heuristic. However, the idea is ungrounded, undialectical, and "utopian" in a potentially bad sense of the term, if it does not also engage with the possible building blocks of this future. Furthermore, an ungrounded sense of community—which has no sense of place and therefore no respect for actual places—comes too close to the present "international" mobility of capital. Against this, it is important to understand regional histories and cultures as themselves created by the common efforts of (what I will still call) the people, even if these histories and cultures are also distorted and misappropriated by bourgeois national frameworks. There is an important strain of Marxist thought, associated with Raymond Williams, E. P. Thompson, and the "Birmingham School" of cultural studies, which pursues this "regionalist-internationalist" perspective. (Indeed, it is interesting that this perspective has developed especially in England.) I did invoke this perspective to some extent in *music of Yes*, especially as concerns Williams's idea of the "green language," but I did not develop its theoretical underpinnings. Nor will this be the place to develop those underpinnings much further. (On Williams and Thompson and the school of cultural critique of which they were a major part, see Dennis Dworkin, *Cultural Marxism in Postwar Britain*.)

Part of the upshot for progressive rock of these ruminations is that the style is both internationalist and regionalist in perspective. Progressive rock contributes to the formation of, and indeed it *already is* in important respects, "world music," *avant la lettre*. Progressive rock is "international" music, and I would even say that it is "internationalist" in its outlook, including through its utopian and communitarian aspirations (which I think—surprise!—come through most strongly in the music of Yes). At the same time, and as Macan demonstrates, progressive rock is very much a musical expression of the historical cultures of England and to some extent the southern region of the country.

This "combined" perspective is expressed with considerable power in an essay by J. B. Priestley, "Wrong Ism":

[W]e are still backing the wrong ism. Almost all our money goes on the middle one, nationalism, the rotten meat between the two healthy slices of bread. We need regionalism to give us roots and that very depth of feeling which nationalism unjustly and greedily claims for itself. We need internationalism to save the world and to broaden and heighten our civilisation. While regional man enriches the lives that international man is already working to keep secure and healthy, national man, drunk with power, demands our loyalty, money, and applause, and poisons the very air with his dangerous nonsense. (p. 257) (J. B. Priestley, *Essays of Five Decades*, edited by Susan Cooper [Boston: Little, Brown, and Company, 1949], pp. 254–57.)

Insofar as a "purely materialist perspective" cannot take account of the materiality of language, culture, and folkways, I

reject this perspective and am happy to have Macan's criticisms of it. However, I do believe there is the possibility of
(and a good part of my work as a social theorist is aimed at
working toward) a more generous historical materialism,
albeit one that must break more fully with mechanistic claims.
Ironically, mechanical materialism turns out to be a species of
philosophical idealism, in that it posits an overarchingsystem-
atic theory that cannot take account of the actual sensuous-
ness of practice. Even the most generous materialisms will
always have the tendency to fall into mechanism, given that
the aim remains systematic understanding—the sort of thing
that will allow people to be the subjects rather than the mere
objects of history. The alternative, however, is the sort of "spiritual geography" (which I appreciate as far as it goes) that we
get from Hegel; Engels said of this, rightly I think, that this
form of dialectical idealism serves fully to explain reality as it
is, but not to change that reality.

26. I'm referring to opera in the West; there is an older tradi-
    tion in China.

27. Lest there be any suspicion that such claims are exaggerated,
    the reader is directed to a recent study, Robin Blackburn's *The
    Making of New World Slavery: From the Baroque to the Mod-
    ern, 1492–1800* (London: Verso, 1997), which demonstrates
    that "[b]y 1770, profits derived from slavery furnished a third
    of Britain's capital formation, while slave-grown products had
    become ubiquitous" (quoted from the review of Blackburn by
    Eric Foner, "Plantation Profiteering," *The Nation* (March 31,
    1997): p. 25.

28. See David Hackett Fischer, *Albion's Seed: Four British Folk-
    ways in America*, esp. chap. 2, "The South of England to Vir-
    ginia;" chap. 4, "Borderlands to the Backcountry;" and the
    conclusion, "Four British Folkways in American History:
    The Origin and Persistence of Regional Cultures in the
    United States." Also see Macan's references to Fischer,
    pp. 145, 147.

29. I choose this example because of Edward Macan's interest in
    Vaughan Williams; see the interview with Macan (cited under
    Gunnison) in *Progression* magazine, as well as his article,

"'The Spirit of Albion' in 20th-century English Popular Music: Vaughan Williams, Holst, and the Progressive Rock Movement" (*Music Review* 53 [May 1992]).

30. See Pete Frame, *Rock Family Trees*, p. 16.

31. For example, is Frank Herbert's *Dune* "feudal"? On some level, yes; on the other hand, after reading it, you will think twice about just letting the water in the sink run down the drain.

32. One of the classic discussions on this subject is presented by Jürgen Habermas, "Technology and Science as 'Ideology'" (in *Toward a Rational Society*, translated by Jeremy J. Shapiro [Boston: Beacon Press, 1970], pp. 81–122). Also see Michael Zimmerman, *Heidegger's Confrontation with Modernity: Technology, Politics, Art* (Bloomington: Indiana University Press, 1990).

33. My language here is fundamentally indebted to the work of Jacques Derrida; I develop this language in a book on Derrida and social theory, *Matrix and line*, esp. the first chapter.

34. For a useful and interesting discussion of these issues in connection to music, see Peter Kivy, "It's Only Music, So What's to Understand?" in *Music Alone*, pp. 93–123. Kivy is an important analytic philosopher of music, whose work I also engaged with in *music of Yes*, pp. 87–89. His name was inadvertently left out of the index of that book, a mistake I would like to partially correct here.

35. See Donald Davidson, "Semantics for Natural Languages."

36. One of the leading intellectuals of this trend is Alex Callinicos; for a discussion of his work, see my *Humanism and its aftermath*, pp. 136–53.

37. A very important discussion of economism is found in Raymond Lotta, *America in Decline*, which contains an ongoing engagement with these themes and the terrible legacy of economism in the international communist movement.

38. As invaders into the logic of the commodity, I find the Devo albums to be serious, interesting, and extremely funny— indeed, much more durably humorous than much of Zappa's material. See Cristina Bodinger-deUriarte, "Opposition to Hegemony in the Music of Devo."

39. Also see Brian Eno's defense of "pretention" in *A Year*, p. 381.

40. The crucial compendium here is Ken Knabb, editor and translator, *Situationist International Anthology*.

41. See "Interview with an Imbecile," in Knabb, pp. 179–81.

42. On the question of the sixties and neo-Trotskyism, again see my section on Alex Callinicos in *Humanism and its aftermath*. On the idea of the "margin" and the proletariat, see my *Matrix and line*, pp. 165–70. In my essays "Going *Neuromancer*," "Conceiving postsecular socialism," and "Against the strategy of cynicism" from *Politics in the impasse*, I pursue the idea of learning from many sources within an expanded Marxist framework that is very critical of orthodox Marxism (see pp. 1–38). Finally, for some thoughts on Mao and Maoism, see "Still Maoist after all these years," also in *Politics in the impasse*, pp. 159–95.

43. See, for example, John L. Brooke, *The Refiner's Fire*.

44. Most readers of this book will recall that Holst's "Mars" movement, from *The Planets*, was performed by King Crimson (on live bootlegs, the piece is simply called "Mars"; on *In the Wake of Poseidon*, a modified version is presented under the title "The Devil's Triangle"). A perhaps less obvious connection was pointed out to me in a letter from Edward Macan, where he remarked on my analysis of Yes's "South Side of the Sky" from *Fragile* (in *music of Yes*, pp. 120–21): "For what it's worth, I always thought "South Side of the Sky" was based on Robert F. Scott's ill-fated race to the South Pole. Did you know Ralph Vaughan Williams' Seventh Symphony is also based on this event? (And like "South Side," it is a meditation on nature's vastness, power, and indifference to puny human beings.)"

45. Macan's contrast of progressive rock and heavy metal on this point is insightful; in the latter music, "the lead singer and lead guitarist are clearly predominant" (p. 67). Perhaps most gratifying, to me at any rate, is Macan's observation that "well into the 1980s heavy metal produced no virtuoso bassists." Not all *innovative* bassists are necessarily virtuosos, but Macan's point fits in well with my argument that rock music changes when the role of the bass changes.

46. I disagree with characterizations of progressive rock as simply humorless; however, perhaps there is something to the idea that, just as it is hard to imagine Frank Zappa in any kind of "prophetic" role, there is little room in progressive rock for the scatological clown—thankfully!

47. The recent attempt to divide progressive rock into "mainstream" and "alternative" sections, especially along the lines of record and concert ticket sales, is simplistic. I return to this issue in the afterword.

48. On the making of the white working class, see the books by David Roediger, Noel Ignatiev, and Cynthia Willett.

49. Some of my other work in social theory concerns the fact that Marx never really took account of this kind of agrarianism—his archetype of those living on the land was the European peasant. Also see Richard Matthews, *The Radical Politics of Thomas Jefferson*.

50. When people write me regarding my book on Yes and say that they like the analysis of the music but dislike the politics of the book, and then go on to praise capitalism, Ayn Rand, Milton Friedman, and the idea that "of course the guys in Yes are just in it for the money, since that's all that motivates anyone," then I have to think that we are simply not listening to the same music or the same band.

51. Macan is quoting from Moore, p. 65.

52. A prime example would be Susan McClary's book on music and gender.

53. Orson Scott Card, "Star Wars, Our Public Religion."

Chapter 5. After the time of progressive rock

1. To go from Cage to Eno makes me think of the trajectory in American philosophy from Ralph Waldo Emerson to Richard Rorty. The latter is a neopragmatist for whom Eno has expressed enthusiasm. For an extended discussion of Rorty, see my *Humanism and its aftermath*, pp. 72–112.

2. One very good example of learning from "sixties theory" and recontextualizing it in terms of postsixties developments is

Martin Matustik's *Specters of Liberation* (Albany, N.Y.: State
University of New York Press, 1997), which especially builds
on Herbert Marcuse's *An Essay on Liberation*, synthesizing this
work with insights from Jacques Derrida's *Specters of Marx*, as
well as deals with the so-called "death of communism."

3. Some of the ideas expressed in the next few pages are similar
   to arguments presented in *music of Yes*, pp. 185–91. Rather
   than repeat myself, I have attempted to develop the context
   presented there, and to open some other angles on these questions. Still, I have in fact nicked a line here or there.

4. I present a preliminary analysis of this social configuration in
   a section of *Politics in the impasse* titled, "Two circuits of
   thought and practice: Lenin and Adorno," pp. 168–72. I hope
   to present a more sustained analysis soon, under the title *Virtual bread and cyber-circuses*.

5. One of the incoherencies of Rand's philosophy is well-captured
   by Roarke's line, "I do not build in order to have clients, I have
   clients in order to build." No real capitalist could stand by such
   a statement; imagine the CEO of General Motors saying, "We do
   not build cars in order to have car buyers, we have car buyers in
   order to build cars." Of course this CEO could *say* this, just as
   corporations constantly flood the airwaves with advertisements
   about how much they "care"; the point is, this idealistic outlook,
   more befitting an artist, could not be the guiding philosophy of a
   capitalist, who must pursue profit first of all, and only "build"
   that which might lead to the generation of profit.

6. Review in *L.A. New Times*, n.d., e-mailed copy from author in
   my possession.

7. One reason that I perhaps feel especially cantankerous and
   stand by my right to say harsh things about *Supernatural Fairy
   Tales* is that, unlike record reviewers, I have to go out and *buy*
   the albums I want just like everyone else—and I spent sixty
   bucks on this thing.

8. Just for the record, I certainly don't have anything against
   model trains or their hobbyists. Furthermore, if interest in
   model trains can lead to socially transformative thoughts or
   actions, then more power to it. Full-sized steam trains were
   certainly a powerful metaphor for Marx.

9. Another part of the context here is that Hakim Bey has recorded a TAZ album, produced by Bill Laswell, another of the key players in this scene.

10. To be fair, it should be mentioned that Brian Eno regularly turns down offers to have his music used in films—and there is no doubt that he could make a good deal of money from this.

11. For a reading of Foucault and Derrida on the cogito argument, see my *Humanism and its aftermath*, pp. 53–57.

12. The reference here is to basketball; the "principle of verticality" has to do with the point when two players, one in possession of the ball and the other defending the basket, jump up into the air. The defender cannot violate this "principle."

Additional discography

This listing is for those recordings not mentioned in the "guided discography" of chapter 4.

Anderson, Jon. *Deseo*, 1994.

———. *Toltec*, 1996.

———. *The Promise Ring*, 1997.

Beach Boys. *Pet Sounds*, 1966.

Beatles. *Rubber Soul*, 1965.

———. *Revolver*, 1966.

———. *Sergeant Pepper's Lonely Hearts Club Band*, 1967.

———. *The Beatles* ("White Album"), 1968.

———. *Abbey Road*, 1969.

———. *Let It Be*, 1970.

Clash. *London Calling*, 1979.

———. *Sandinista*, 1980.

———. *Combat Rock*, 1982.

Coltrane, John. *Concert in Japan*, 1966.

Davis, Miles. *Sketches of Spain*, 1959.

———. *Bitches Brew*, 1969.

———. *Jack Johnson*, 1970.

———. *Miles Davis at Fillmore*, 1970.

Emerson, Lake, and Palmer. *Black Moon*, 1992.

———. *In the Hot Seat*, 1994.

Eno, Brian, and Jon Hassell. *Possible Musics* (Fourth World, Vol.1), 1980.

Future Sound of London, et. al. *The Deseo Remixes*, 1995.

Gabriel, Peter. *Secret World Live* (video, CD), 1994.

Grateful Dead. *Anthem of the Sun*, 1968.

———. *Aoxomoxoa*, 1969.

Hüsker Dü. *Zen Arcade*, 1984.

Jefferson Starship. *Blows Against the Empire*, 1970.

Jethro Tull. *Roots to Branches*, 1995.

Jordan, Louis. *Rock 'n' Roll,* 1989 (compilation of material from 1956–57).

King Crimson. *Thrak,* 1995.

———. *Epitaph,* 1997.

Lennon, John. *Plastic Ono Band,* 1970.

Minutemen. *Double Nickels on the Dime,* 1984.

Rolling Stones. *Their Satanic Majesties Request,* 1967.

Sex Pistols. *Never Mind the Bollocks,* 1977.

Shepp, Archie. *New Thing at Newport,* 1965.

Simon and Garfunkel. *Bookends,* 1968.

Spock's Beard. *Beware of Darkness,* 1996.

Talking Heads. *More Songs About Buildings and Food,* 1978.

———. *Remain in Light,* 1980.

Taylor, Cecil. *Three Phases,* 1979.

The Who. *Who's Next,* 1971.

Williams, Tony, and Lifetime. *Emergency!,* 1969.

Yes. *Keys to Ascension,* 1996.

Bibliography

"A to Z of Prog Rock." (No author given.) *The Wire*, n. 133 (pt. 1), n. 134 (pt. 2) (March–April): 1995.

Adorno, Theodor. *Ästhetische Theorie*. 2nd ed. Gretel Adorno and Rolf Tiedemann, eds. Frankfurt am Main: Suhrkamp, 1992.

———. *Introduction to the Sociology of Music*. Translated by E. B. Ashton. New York: Continuum, 1989.

———. *Philosophy of Modern Music*. Translated by Anne G. Mitchell and Wesley V. Blomster. New York: Seabury Press, 1973.

———. *Quasi una fantasia: Essays on Modern Music*. Translated by Rodney Livingstone. London: Verso, 1994.

Agger, Ben. *Fast Capitalism: A Critical Theory of Significance*. Urbana: University of Illinois Press, 1989.

Barnes, Mike. "Chris Cutler: Corporation of One." *The Wire*, n. 158 (April 1997): 49–52.

———. "Robert Fripp: Mobile Intelligent Unit." *The Wire*, n. 159 (May 1997): 30–35.

Bey, Hakim. *Temporary Autonomous Zones*. New York: Autonomedia.

Bloom, Harold. *The American Religion: The Emergence of the Post-Christian Nation*. New York: Simon and Schuster, 1992.

Bodinger-deUriarte, Cristina. "Opposition to Hegemony in the Music of Devo: A Simple Matter of Remembering." *Journal of Popular Culture* 18, n. 4 (spring 1985): pp. 57–71.

Brooke, John L. *The Refiner's Fire: The Making of Mormon Cosmology, 1644–1844*. Cambridge: Cambridge University Press, 1994.

Bruford, Bill. *When in Doubt, Roll!*. Milwaukee: Modern Drummer Publications, 1988.

Buckley, Jonathan, and Mark Ellington, eds. *Rock: The Rough Guide*. London: Rough Guides Limited, 1996.

Burton, Humphrey. *Leonard Bernstein*. New York: Doubleday, 1994.

Bussy, Pascal, and Andy Hall. *The Can Book*. Harrow, England: Serious Art Forms Books, 1989.

Butler, Judith. *Gender Trouble: Feminism and the Subversion of Identity*. New York: Routledge, 1990.

Carr, Ian, Digby Fairweather, and Brian Priestley, eds. *Jazz: The Rough Guide*. London: Rough Guides Limited, 1995.

Case, Brian, and Stan Britt. *The Illustrated Encyclopedia of Jazz*. New York: Harmony Books, 1978.

Chambers, Iain. *Border Dialogues: Journeys in Postmodernity*. London: Routledge, 1990.

Chapman, Rob. "Prog Today." *Mojo* (February 1997): 54–59.

Covach, John. "Applauding Gentle Giant's *Free Hand*. *Progression* 1, n.19 (spring 1996): 40–41.

Davidson, Donald. "A Nice Derangement of Epitaphs." In Ernest LePore, ed., *Truth and Interpretation: Perspectives on the Philosophy of Donald Davidson*, pp. 433–46. Oxford: Basil Blackwell, 1986.

———. "Semantics for Natural Languages." In *Inquiries into Truth and Interpretation*, pp. 55–64. Oxford: Oxford University Press, 1984.

DeRogatis, Jim. *Kaleidoscope Eyes: Psychedelic Rock From the '60s to the '90s*. Secaucus, N.J.: Citadel Press, 1996.

Dworkin, Dennis. *Cultural Marxism in Postwar Britain: History, the New Left, and the Origins of Cultural Studies*. Durham, N.C.: Duke University Press, 1997.

Eno, Brian. *A Year with Swollen Appendices*. London: Faber and Faber, 1996.

Fischer, David Hackett. *Albion's Seed: Four British Folkways in America*. New York: Oxford University Press, 1989.

Frame, Pete. *Rock Family Trees*. London: Omnibus, 1993.

Frith, Simon, and Howard Horne. *Art into Pop*. London: Methuen, 1987.

Gill, Andy, and Rob Chapman, "Achtung, Baby! Kraftwerk, Can and the return of the Krautrockers." *Mojo* (April 1997): 54–80.

Goodman, Nelson. *Ways of Worldmaking*. Indianapolis: Hackett, 1978.

Gracyk, Theodore. *Rhythm and Noise: An Aesthetics of Rock*. Durham, N.C., 1996.

Gunnison, Allen. "*Rocking the Classics*: Author Macan tells where it all began." *Progression* 2, n.22 (winter 1997): 32–35.

———. "Unraveling the mysteries of Yes with author Bill Martin." *Progression* 2, n. 23 (spring 1997): 35–37.

Harris, James F. *Philosophy at 33 1/3 rpm: Themes of Classic Rock Music*. Chicago: Open Court Publishing, 1993.

Ignatiev, Noel. *How the Irish Became White*. New York: Routledge, 1995.

Jameson, Fredric. *The Political Unconscious: Narrative as a Socially Symbolic Act*. Ithaca, N.Y.: Cornell University Press, 1981.

———. *Postmodernism, or, The Cultural Logic of Late Capitalism*. Durham, N.C.: Duke University Press, 1991.

———. *The Seeds of Time*. New York: Columbia University Press, 1994.

Jost, Ekkehard. *Free Jazz*. New York: Da Capo, 1994.

Joynson, Vernon. *The Tapestry of Delights: The Comprehensive Guide to British Music of the Beat, R&B, Psychedelic, and Progressive Eras, 1963–1976*. Telford, England: Borderline Productions, 1995.

Kant, Immanuel. *Critique of Judgment*. Trans. J. H. Bernard. New York: Hafner Press/Macmillan, 1951.

Kivy, Peter. *Music Alone: Philosophical Reflections on the Purely Musical Experience*. Ithaca, New York: Cornell University Press, 1991.

Knabb, Ken, ed. and trans. *Situationist International Anthology*. Berkeley: Bureau of Public Secrets, 1981.

Kozinn, Allan. *The Beatles*. London: Phaidon, 1995.

Locke, John. *Second Treatise of Government*. Ed. Richard Cox. Arlington Heights, Ill.: Harlan Davidson, 1982.

Lotta, Raymond, with Frank Shannon. *America in Decline*. Chicago: Banner Press, 1984.

Macan, Edward. *Rocking the Classics: English Progressive Rock and the Counterculture*. Oxford: Oxford University Press, 1997.

Marcuse, Herbert. *One-Dimensional Man*. Boston: Beacon Press, 1964.

Marsh, Dave. *Before I Get Old: The Story of the Who*. New York: St. Martin's, 1983.

Martin, Bill. "Chris Squire: Creating a new dimension." *Bass Player* (November 1994): 24–26, 34–35.

———. *Humanism and its aftermath: The shared fate of deconstruction and politics*. Atlantic Highlands, N.J.: Humanities Press, 1995.

———. *Matrix and line: Derrida and the possibilities of postmodern social theory*. Albany, N.Y.: State University of New York Press, 1992.

———. *music of Yes: structure and vision in progressive rock*. Chicago: Open Court Publishing, 1996.

———. *Politics in the impasse: Explorations in postsecular social theory*. Albany, N.Y.: State University of New York Press, 1996.

Matthews, Richard K. *The Radical Politics of Thomas Jefferson*. Lawrence, Kans.: University of Kansas Press, 1984.

McClary, Susan. *Feminine Endings: Music, Gender, and Sexuality*. Minneapolis: University of Minnesota Press, 1991.

McLuhan, Marshall. *Understanding Media: The Extensions of Man*. New York: McGraw Hill, 1964.

Moore, Alan. *Rock: The Primary Text; Developing a Musicology of Rock*. Buckingham, England: Open University Press, 1993.

Morse, Tim. *Yesstories: Yes in Their Own Words*. New York: St. Martin's, 1996.

Piccone, Paul. "The Changing Function of Critical Theory." *New German Critique*, n. 12 (fall 1977): 29–37.

Priestley, J. B. "Wrong Ism." In *Essays of Five Decades*, ed. Susan Cooper, pp. 254–57. Boston: Little, Brown, and Company, 1949.

Rimmer, Dave. "Hello, Atlantis! Yes Returns." *Mojo* (February 1997): pp. 60–61.

Roediger, David R. *The Wages of Whiteness: Race and the Making of the American Working Class*. London: Verso, 1991.

Stump, Paul. *The Music's All that Matters: A History of Progressive Rock*. London: Quartet Books, 1997.

Subotnik, Rose Rosengard. *Developing Variations: Style and Ideology in Western Music*. Minneapolis: University of Minnesota Press, 1991.

Tamm, Eric. *Brian Eno: His Music and the Vertical Color of Sound*. London: Faber and Faber, 1989.

————. *Robert Fripp: From King Crimson to Guitar Craft.* Boston: Faber and Faber, 1990.

Tiano, Mike. "Conversation with Rick Wakeman." Notes From the Edge, n. 171 (March 1997).

Toop, David. *Oceans of Sound: Aether Talk, Ambient Sound, and Imaginary Worlds.* London: Serpent's Tail, 1995.

Watson, Ben. *Frank Zappa: The Negative Dialectics of Poodle Play.* New York: St. Martin's, 1995.

Willett, Cynthia. *Maternal Ethics and Other Slave Moralities.* London: Routledge, 1995.

Williams, Raymond. *The Country and the City.* New York: Oxford University Press, 1973.

White, Timothy. *The Nearest Faraway Place: Brian Wilson, the Beach Boys, and the Southern California Experience.* New York: Henry Holt, 1994.

Wilmer, Valerie. *As Serious as Your Life.*

Young, Rob. "The Soundtrack Syndrome." *The Wire,* n. 153 (November 1996): 26–30.

Zuidervaart, Lambert. *Adorno's Aesthetic Theory: The Redemption of Illusion.* Cambridge, Mass.: M.I.T. Press, 1991.

Index

Abrahams, Mick, 168
Acqua Fragile, 155, 277
Ade, King Sunny, 193
Adorno, Theodore, 11, 27-30,
    35, 56, 61, 65, 74, 96,
    114, 118, 119, 123, 145,
    260, 283
aesthetic, the (as category of
    human experience), xv
aesthetics (field of philoso-
    phy), 2, 5, 131
"affirmative culture," 28, 66
Africa, 8, 37, 38, 40, 109,
    192
African-Americans, 23,
    31-32, 35, 141
Ahearn, Shawn, 272
Akkerman, Jan, 208, 209
album, the, as basic unit of
    musical production,
    41-42, 153-54
album cover art, 154, 182,
    188, 190
Allen, Daevid, 170, 196, 221,
    231, 240
Allman Brothers Band, the,
    75, 128, 192
"alternative" rock, 59, 65,
    139, 140
Althusser, Louis, 161

ambient music, 235, 290
Ames, Morgan, 4
Amon Duul 2, 175, 176
anabaptist, 112, 148
anarchism, 81, 148
Anderson, Bruford,
    Wakeman, and Howe,
    264
Anderson, Ian, 168, 177,
    188, 197, 201, 212, 222,
    248, 262
Anderson, Jon, xvi-xvii, 12,
    13, 87, 97, 109, 110-11,
    135, 148, 149, 167, 177,
    183, 188, 203, 204, 205,
    215, 223, 226, 233, 237,
    243, 247, 252, 262, 263,
    264, 296, 297, 298, 303
Anderson, Anne Marie, 190
Ange (band), 228
Anglican church, 135-36
Anscombe, Margaret, 195
anti-Black oppression, 23
Aphrodite's Child, 206
Appalachia, 32, 200
Appice, Carmen, 157
Aquinas, Thomas, 119, 288
Area (band), 155, 244, 277
Arena (band), 272
"arena rock," 263

Argent (band), 191, 228

Argent, Rod, 136, 166

Argentina, progressive rock in, 277

Aristotle, 7, 115, 195

Armageddon (band), 176

Armstrong, Louis, 180

Ars Nova, 272-73

Art Bears, the, 238, 302

Art Ensemble of Chicago, 93, 179

"art rock," 121-22, 125, 143

Ash Ra Temple, 176

Asia (band), 262

Asimov, Isaac, 121

Atkins, Chet, 88, 200

Atomic Rooster, 181

Auger, Brian, 136, 172, 213, 215

avant-garde, 6, 22, 58, 84-85, 89, 93, 99, 116, 162, 201, 216, 221, 227, 238, 258-59, 273, 285, 293, 301, 302, 305,

Ayers, Kevin, 170, 185, 228

Ayler, Albert, 179

Bad Company, 198

Bach, Johann Sebastion, 49, 131

Back Door, 217-18

Badger, 215-16

Baker, Ginger, 44, 157, 188

Banco, 155, 210, 216-17, 237, 275

Band, The, 4

Bangs, Lester, 10, 143-44

Banks, Peter, 76, 168, 199, 208, 219

Banton, Hugh, 183, 229

Bardens, Pete, 236

Barnes, Mike, 86-90, 112, 115, 253, 300

Barre, Martin, 188, 197, 248

Barrett, Syd, 86

Barris, Gini, 188

Bartók, Bela, 40, 86, 201

bass guitar, changing role of, 46-48, 226, 239

Bass Player magazine, 278

Baudrillard, Jean, 301

Beach Boys, the, 17, 39-42, 44, 47, 53, 80

Beat poetry scene, 147

Beatles, the, 17, 22, 39-44, 46-48, 51-52, 53-54, 63, 70, 71, 72, 74, 75, 76, 84, 85, 87, 88, 95, 97, 99-100, 103, 111, 152, 156, 157, 162-63, 164, 169, 171, 186, 201, 207, 213, 215, 269, 273, 298, 300

Beauvoir, Simone de, 254

Beck (Hansen), 26

Bedford, David, 228

Beethoven, Ludwig van, xiv, 113, 119, 136, 168, 270, 282, 304

Belew, Adrian, 187, 267, 268

Bell, John, 222

Benjamin, Walter, 145

Bennett, Ray, 208

Berg, Alban, 92

Berkeley, George, 63

Berlin, Jeff, 242

Bernstein, Leonard, 22, 99,
    37, 39, 52, 69, 170, 200,
    230, 243
Berry, Chuck, 5, 17, 31-32,
Berry, Wendell, 11
Bey, Hakim, 283
Big Elf, 272
"Birmingham School" of
    cultural studies, 143
Black church music, 23, 31,
    34
Black Panther Party, 164
Black Power, 3
Black Sabbath, 176, 177,
    216
Blair, Tony, 256
Blake, Tim, 221, 231, 240
Blake, William, 82, 108-109,
    120, 136, 148, 224, 297,
    304
Blakey, Art, and the Jazz
    Messengers, 88, 253
Blegvad, Peter, 302
Bloch, Ernst, 145
Blodwyn Pig, 168
Blood, Sweat, and Tears,
    163
Bloom, Harold, 79
blues, 23, 28, 31, 128, 147,
    168, 189, 211, 243,
    261-62
"blues orthodoxy," 22-23,
    51-52, 93, 141
Blunstone, Colin, 166
Bodast, 167
Boone, Pat, 34, 36
Bowie, David, 251-252
Bown, Alan, 220

Brahms, Johannes, 91
Brainticket, 215
Branca, Glenn, 283
Brand X, 240
Branson, Richard, 95
Braxton, Anthony, 3
Brecht, Bertolt, 120, 238,
    254
British Isles, 32, 109, 173
Britten, Benjamin, 22
Brown, James, 289-290
Brown, Pete, and Piblokto!,
    172, 182
Bruce, Jack, 44, 46, 172,
    182, 228
Bruckner, Anton, 91
Bruford, Bill, 79, 160, 181,
    187, 200, 204, 208, 218,
    226, 232, 242, 244,
    252-53, 263, 264, 265,
    267, 268
Bunker, Clive, 168, 197
Burrell, Boz, 198, 209
Burroughs, William S., 171
Butler, Judith, 11
Butler, Octavia, 11
Byrd, Joe, 162
Byrne, David, 168
Byron, Lord (George
    Gordon), 128
Byrds, the, 3, 53, 74, 76, 88,
    167

Cage, John, 22, 40, 70, 97,
    114, 162, 206, 252,
    287-88, 290, 292
Caldwell, Bobby, 176
Cale, John, 228

California, Randy, 229
Camel, 236-37, 275
Campbell, Mont, 181
Can, 175, 176-77, 193, 207,
    217, 229, 236
Canterbury scene, 104, 125,
    169, 181, 196, 207, 236,
    244, 255, 300, 301, 304
capitalism, 12, 25, 29, 62,
    81, 94, 96, 105-6, 126,
    134-35, 138, 256-57, 260,
    271, 281, 291, 297
capitalism, "postmodern,"
    14, 25, 27, 29, 30, 91,
    120, 159, 260, 281, 293,
    294, 303
Captain Beefheart (Don Van
    Vliet), 152, 178
Captain Beyond, 176
Caravan, 19, 60, 84, 140,
    153, 169-71, 175, 182,
    185, 189-90, 196, 207,
    222, 237,
Card, Orson Scott, 11, 149
Carlos, Walter (Wendy), 216
Carter, Colin, 208
Carter, Elliot, 22
Carter, Jimmy, 257
Cennamo, Louis, 176
Centipede, 192
Chambers, Iain, 105-9
Chambers, Paul, 147
Charles, Ray, 17, 31, 36, 39
Chase (band), 163
Cher, 219
Chess, Leonard, 94, 95
Chicago (band), 18, 163,
    164, 191

Christianity, 37, 138, 147,
    148, 149, 197, 211, 222,
    228,
Chromanticism, 92
Circle Jerks, the, 250
civil rights movement, 3
Clapton, Eric, 44
Clash, The, 125, 242, 244,
    250
class, 8, 23, 24, 36, 87, 107,
    108, 112, 123-24, 126,
    127, 132, 133-34, 137,
    142, 143-45, 209, 211-12,
    225, 252-53, 270, 288
classical music
    (Western/European), 22,
    28, 33, 49, 64, 74, 86,
    91-92, 97, 113, 114, 131,
    137, 152, 179, 180, 194,
    213, 220, 223, 252, 291,
    301, 304
Cliff, Tony, 123
Clinton, Bill, 62, 256
Cobain, Kurt, 72
Cobham, Billy, 178, 213, 256
cognitivism, 118
Cole, Brian, 219
Coleman, Ornette, 3, 86, 93,
    153, 179, 180, 216
Coleridge, Samuel Taylor, 79
Collinge, John, 278
Collins, Mel, 198, 209
Collins, Phil, 198, 240
colonialism, 24, 41, 289
Colosseum, 172, 175, 218
Coltrane, John, 2, 3, 75, 101,
    119, 140, 141, 157, 181,
    196, 213, 221, 235, 300

Colvin, Shawn, 63
commodification, culture
    of, 21, 125, 177
communism, 9, 12-13
communitarianism, 105,
    127-128, 139, 148
"concept album," 41, 189
consumerism, 15, 91
Cooper, Lindsay, 237, 302
Copland, Aaron, 114, 300
Cornick, Glenn, 48, 168,
    188, 197
Coryell, Larry, 213
Coughlan, Richard, 169, 170
counterculture, concept of,
    xiii, 15, 112, 134, 249,
    276, 277, 280
counterculture, sixties, xvi,
    14, 126, 130-31, 132,
    135, 137, 138, 143,
    145-47, 161, 173, 180
counterpoint, 91, 116, 212,
    223, 228, 233, 237, 263,
    284, 290
Covach, John, 237, 276
Crane, Vincent, 181
Crazy World of Arthur
    Brown, The, 181
Cream, 17, 44, 63, 162, 217
Cross, David, 226, 232
Crow, Sheryl, 63
culture industry, 27, 28-30,
    62, 64, 96, 260, 286
Curved Air, 19, 183, 184,
    193
Cutler, Chris, xii, 86-90,
    112-21, 149, 179, 228,
    238, 300, 302, 304

cyberpunk, 156, 224
cybersex, 8
cynicism, 6-7, 8, 9, 59,
    62-63, 66, 79, 89, 116-17,
    120, 126, 137, 141, 144,
    196, 225, 227, 228, 258,
    293, 299
Czukay, Holger, 176

Dahlhaus, Carl, 145
Daltrey, Roger, 45
dancing, music for, 32, 39,
    84, 91, 178, 290
Dave Matthews Band,
    255-56
Davis, Miles, 3-4, 140, 164,
    172-73, 178, 185, 188,
    223
Davison, Brian, 49, 229
Davidson, Donald, 56,
    118
*Day the Earth Stood Still,
    The* (film), 81
Dead Kennedys, the, 250
Dean, Elton, 185
Dean, Roger, 154, 192, 201,
    202, 206, 216, 218, 220,
    274
death, mortality, 14, 36, 212
Debussy, Claude, 40, 282,
    288
Deep Purple, 167, 206
defamiliarization, 120
Delaney, Samuel R., 301
Deleuze, Gilles, 301
Denny, Sandy, 174
Derrida, Jacques, 11, 115,
    290, 301

DeRogatis, Jim, 75-82, 85-87, 274, 275

Descartes, René, 204, 288-89, 290

Detmer, David, 249

Deus Ex Machina (band), 272-73

Devo, 125

DiCrocco, Glen, 279

Di Giacomo, Francesco, 216, 275

Dibango, Manu, 193

Dick, Philip K., 156

Diddley, Bo, 5, 17, 37-39, 40, 98

Discipline Global Mobile, 269, 278

disco music, 268

division of labor, 117

Dixie Dregs, 129

Doldinger, Klaus, 236

Donovan, 44, 146

Doors, the, 77, 82, 162, 178

Downes, Geoff, 262

Drake, Nick, 173

Dreams (band), 213

Driscoll, Julie, 172

drugs/drug culture, 43, 76-83, 147

Dyble, Judy, 182

Dylan, Bob, 49, 53, 74, 164, 165, 166, 173, 228, 234, 258

Eagles, the, 242

Eastwood, Clint, 277

eclecticism, 118, 197

ecology, 133

economism, 123-124

Eger, Joseph, 50

Edge, Zane, 214

Egg, 19, 181, 193

Electric Light Orchestra, 215, 274

electricity, 24

electronica (techno, jungle, industrial, etc.) music, 176, 217, 224, 285, 290, 292, 296

Eleventh House, 213

Ellington, Duke, 33

Emerson, Keith, 31, 49-51, 114, 184, 199, 200-1, 209, 217, 224, 248

Emerson, Lake, and Palmer, 18, 19, 49, 51, 84, 120, 125, 128, 132, 133, 138, 147, 156, 184, 197, 199, 200-1, 209, 217, 219, 223-24, 234, 235, 237, 247, 248-49, 262, 266, 270, 272, 273, 279, 296, 303-4, 306

Emerson, Ralph Waldo, 252

empiricism, 108

emotivism, 118

England, English culture, 18, 23-24, 37, 104-12, 137, 138, 139, 211, 225

"Englishness," 104-12, 127, 129, 135, 169, 180, 185, 199, 212, 225

Enlightenment, the (Western), xv, 114, 115

Eno, Brian, 20, 98, 162, 206, 216

entertainment, music as, 10, 15, 30

entertainment industry, 27, 29

Entwistle, John, 44, 45, 46, 88, 174, 203

Eros, 36, 194-96

eroticism, 34, 189

Ertegun, Ahmet, 94-95, 97

essentialism, 140-43

ethnicity, 8, 87, 109, 138

ethical-political universalism, 113

European culture, 33

Evans, Bill, 147

Evans, Nick, 185

exhaustion, cultural, 259

exoticism, 40, 99

Exposé magazine, 272, 276

facism, 114, 115

Fairport Convention, 173-74, 182

Fanon, Franz, 254

Faust (band), 305

"feminine" qualities in progressive rock, 142-43, 204

feudalism, 115

"false negativity," 27

film, 24, 67, 281, 285, 287

"film aesthetic," 288

film music, soundtracks, 176, 231, 285-86, 287

Firestone, Shulamith, 254

Flash, 199, 208-9, 219

Fleur de Lys, the, 83

Flock, The, 157, 213

flourishing (eudaimonia), 7, 9, 16, 20

Flower Kings, the, 272

Focus, 208, 209, 275

folk music, folk-rock, 23, 31, 173-74, 177

Ford, Martyn, 222

formalism, aesthetic, 10, 12, 13, 15-17, 68, 73, 131, 132

Forster, E. M., 280

Foster, David, 215

Foucault, Michel, 115, 290

fragmentation, 92, 301, 304

Frame, Pete (rock family trees by), 21, 112

Frankfurt School, 66

free jazz, 179, 192, 221

Freud, Sigmund, 27, 36, 194

Fripp, Robert, 38, 138, 148, 157, 158, 159, 160, 170, 174, 183, 185, 186, 187, 192, 197, 198, 209, 216, 226, 228, 232, 235, 251, 252, 262, 265-69, 278, 280, 298, 300, 303

Frith, Fred, 221, 238, 302

Frith, Simon, 87, 143

funk music, 164, 289

fusion music (jazz-rock), 164, 172, 192, 196, 213, 236, 240, 258

Gabriel, Peter, 40, 41, 185, 199, 225, 240, 251, 296, 305

Gadd, Steve, 242

gamelan orchestra, 268, 282

Gang of Four (band), 87, 144

Gardner, Stephen, 279

Gaskin, Barbara, 230

Gaye, Marvin, 60

gender, 8, 9, 23, 24, 35, 36, 87, 107, 117, 132, 142, 204

"general avant-garde," 70-71, 74, 93, 97, 98, 152, 173

Genesis, 19, 40, 46, 84, 95, 100, 111, 125, 128, 132, 133, 156, 160, 168, 175, 184-85, 198-99, 209-10, 224-25, 230-31, 235, 237, 239, 240, 266, 270, 301, 303

Gentle Giant, 19, 84, 100, 180, 184, 197-98, 209, 216, 220, 231, 237, 240, 243, 244, 273

Gerry and the Pacemakers, 73

Gershwin, George, 23, 31, 33, 300

Gibson, William, 156

Giger, H. R., 224

Giles, Giles, and Fripp, 49, 168, 182

Giles, Michael, 157, 159, 182

Giles, Peter, 182

Gilgamesh, 236, 244

Ginastera, Alberto, 114, 201, 224

Ginsburg, Allen, 77, 127

globalization, 8, 260

glossolalia, 35

Go (band), 206

Golden Earring, 274

Gombrich, Ernst, 57

Gong, 19, 33, 84, 104, 170, 196, 221-22, 230, 237, 240, 277

Goodman, Jerry, 213

Goodman, Nelson, 56

Gowan, Alan, 236

Gracyk, Theodore, xv, 25-26, 39, 57, 65, 97

Graham, Larry, 164

Grand Funk Railroad, 191

Grateful Dead, 43, 78-79, 129, 255

Green, Gary, 197

Green, Jerome, 38

"green language" (Raymond Williams), 178

Greenslade, 19, 218

Greenslade, Dave, 175

Greeves, John, 302

Grobschnitt, 20

Groundhogs, the, 206

"group," idea of, in rock music, 97, 187, 265, 267, 269, 302-3, 304

Gryphon, 33, 229

Gunn, Trey, 269

Gurtu, Trilok, 231

Hall, Stuart, 145

Halsall, Ollie, 228

Hammer, Jan, 213

Hammill, Pete, 183, 193, 194, 229

Hammond, John, 95

Hammond B-3 organ, 49,
    136, 166, 172, 201, 215,
    224
Hammond-Hammond,
    Jeffrey, 197
Hancock, Herbie, 185
Hansson, Bo, 207
Harris, Eddie, 206
Harris, James F., 34
Harrison, George, 72, 75,
    158, 171, 273
Haskell, Gordon, 84,
    186-187
Haslam, Annie, 175, 217,
    275
Hassell, Jon, 296
Hastings, Jimmy, 222
Hastings, Pye, 169, 170, 185
Hatfield and the North, 169,
    181, 230, 236, 255
Hawken, John, 175
Hawkwind, 85, 177, 205
Haydn, Joseph, 92
heavy metal, 157, 197, 249,
    252
Hebdige, Dick, 10
Heckstall-Smith, Dick, 175
Hedges, Dan, 111
Hegel, G. W. F., 60, 67
Heidegger, Martin, 55, 56,
    247
Hendrix, Jimi, 3, 17, 44, 75,
    78, 79, 82, 83, 146, 162,
    164-65, 166, 170, 185,
    188, 221, 244
Henry Cow, xii, 11, 19, 60,
    84, 86-90, 112, 113, 115,
    116, 117, 119, 120, 123,

125, 138, 155, 159, 194,
    220-21, 227, 228, 230,
    231, 237, 238, 240, 244,
    245, 253, 293, 296, 301,
    302
Herbert, Frank, 134, 160
hermeticism, 37, 105, 109,
    110, 112, 127-28, 139,
    148, 202, 203, 235, 289,
    297
Hillage, Steve, 181, 207,
    221, 237
Hipgnosis, 50
hippies, 75, 76, 81, 182
Hiseman, Jon, 175, 218
Hitler, Adolf, 195
Hodgkinson, Colin, 217-18
Hofman, Albert, 79-80
Holderlin, Friedrich, 136
Holdsworth, Alan, 218, 242,
    244
Holiday, Billie, 83, 147
Holly, Buddy, 23
Hollywood film industry,
    28-29, 286
Holmes, Richard "Groove,"
    136
Holocaust, the, 195
Holst, Gustav, 128, 186
Holz, Christine, 276
homogenization, cultural
    and social, 59, 260
Hopper, Brian, 170
Hopper, Hugh, 48, 102, 170,
    185, 236
Horkheimer, Max, 96
Horne, Howard, 87, 143
Hoskyns, Barney, 63-64

Hough, Mike, 208, 219
Howe, Steve, 13, 76, 79, 81, 84, 97, 104, 130, 158, 165, 166, 167, 183, 187, 199, 200, 203, 204, 214, 233, 243, 247, 262, 264, 279, 303
Hüsker Dü, 250
Hussein, Zakir, 231
Huxley, Aldous, 77, 79
"hype," 260

"imaginary soundtrack," 285-86, 304
imperialism, 24, 25, 27, 29, 66, 108, 109, 124, 134, 135, 225, 260, 289
In Crowd, the, 76
industrialism, 105-6
Internet, 277
Iron Butterfly, 75
Isley Brothers, the, 216, 239
Italy, Italian progressive rock, 104, 128, 154-55, 210, 217, 277
Ives, Charles, 114, 119

Jackson, Lee, 49, 229
Jackson, Michael, 37, 53-54
Jackson, Ronald Shannon, 114, 253
Jade Warrior, 229, 236, 239
Jameson, Fredric, 11, 14, 26, 59, 149, 159, 235, 280-81, 285, 287, 292-93, 294-95, 305
James, Tommy, and the Shondells, 44, 156

Jarrett, Keith, 216
jazz, 3-4, 23, 28, 31, 33, 49, 64, 74, 91, 92-93, 114, 128, 137, 141, 147, 152, 163, 173, 177, 180, 181, 192, 213, 223, 252
Jefferson, Blind Lemon, 131
Jefferson Airplane, 60, 162, 164
Jefferson Starship/Paul Kantner, 2, 178
Jenkins, Karl, 221
Jethro Tull, 15, 19, 41, 49, 60, 84, 120, 151, 153, 167, 168, 173, 175, 188-89, 197, 207, 211-13, 222, 231, 234, 237, 240, 242-43, 244, 247, 248-49, 261-62, 272, 275, 296, 305
Jobson, Eddie, 244
Jolliffe, Steve, 172
Jones, Elvin, 88, 253
Jones, James Earl, 178
Jones, John Evan, 220
Jones, John Paul, 46
Jonesy, 19, 155, 219-20
Joplin, Scott, 33, 70, 141
Jordan, Louis, 31, 36, 98
Jost, Ekkehard, 179
Joyce, James, 137
Joynson, Vernon, 166, 169
Judaism, 149, 228

Kafka, Franz, 137, 199
Kaleth, Jamie, 220
Kansas (band), 129, 139, 229

Kant, Immanuel, 55, 115
Kaye, Carol, 48
Kaye, Steve, 273
Kaye, Tony, 200, 206, 208,
    215, 263, 264
Khan, 181, 207
Kierkegaard, Søren, 197
King Crimson, 15, 19, 38,
    40, 41, 42, 43, 46, 49, 51,
    54, 60, 74, 75, 84, 89, 94,
    95, 99, 100, 102, 105,
    111, 116, 120, 138, 143,
    150, 151, 152-53, 154,
    155-61, 167, 168, 171,
    174, 177, 181, 182,
    185-89, 191, 194, 198,
    200, 202, 209, 213, 216,
    218, 220, 225-27, 229,
    231-32, 233, 247, 248,
    249, 252, 253, 261, 262,
    265-69, 270, 271, 272,
    273, 275, 277, 284, 293,
    301, 302
Kirk, Rahsaan Roland, 168,
    175
Knopfler, Mark, 208
Kokoshis, Nick, 279
Kozinn, Allan, 47, 52-53
Krause, Dagmar, 238
"Krautrock," 217, 305
Kristina, Sonja, 184
Kuti, Fela, 38, 193

Laird, Rick, 172, 213
Lake, Greg, 157, 159, 187,
    201, 209, 219, 224
Landberk, 272-73
Laswell, Bill, 162, 251

Latimer, Andy, 237
Lawson, Dave, 218
Leary, Timothy, 77, 146,
    176
Led Zeppelin, 17, 45,
    166-67, 172, 177, 191,
    192, 216
Lee, Albert, 206
Lee, Geddy, 271
Lee, Geoff, 230
LeGuin, Ursula, 11
Lenin, V. I., 11, 25, 32, 123,
    124, 144-45
Lennon, John, 47, 52, 53,
    69, 72, 110, 171, 188,
    201, 250
Le Orme, 272
Levin, Tony, 264, 267
Lewis, Jerry Lee, 17, 31-32,
    37, 39, 51
liberation theology, 148
life/death (eros/thanatos),
    194-96, 305
Lighthouse, 163
linear progression, linearity,
    90-91, 228, 263, 268,
    281, 283, 290, 298
Little Richard, 5, 17, 31-32,
    34-36, 37, 39, 40, 51, 70,
    94, 180, 204
Liverpool, 105, 111, 112
Locke, John, 106
Lockwood, Didier, 238
London, 105, 137
Longstaff, Gordon, 49
LSD, 76-82, 85
Luddites, 26
Lukacs, Georg, 145

Macan, Edward, xi, xii, xiii,
    xv, xvi, 6-7, 14, 26, 44,
    70, 75, 76, 101, 105, 108,
    111-12, 115, 122, 127,
    128, 129-49, 156, 200,
    225, 234-35, 299, 304,
    306
MacDonald, Brenda, 279
MacIntyre, Alasdair, 66
Madonna, 24, 59, 63
magic, 45
Magma, 19, 84, 89, 112,
    113, 119, 140, 181, 184,
    196, 220, 237-38, 240,
    244
Mahavishnu Orchestra, 19,
    40, 41, 84, 104, 129, 169,
    172, 178, 196, 213-14,
    216, 222-23, 240, 244
Mahler, Gustav, 91, 92, 119
Malcolm X, 254
Malherbe, Didier, 196, 221
Mamas and the Papas, The,
    158
Mandrill (band), 193
Manicheanism, 195
Mann, Thomas, 119
Manzanera, Phil, 236
Mao Tsetung, 11, 124, 135,
    145, 217
Marcus, Greil, 10
Marcuse, Herbert, 65-66,
    144, 145, 254,
Marley, Bob, 205, 234, 242,
    280
Marsalis, Wynton, 303
Marsh, Dave, 46, 140, 143
Marshall, John, 102, 221

Martin, George, 95, 97-98,
    171
Marx, Karl, 2, 7, 9, 11, 26,
    55-56, 115, 133, 135, 144
marxism, 6, 10, 11, 12-13,
    118, 120, 121, 123-27,
    133-34, 135, 143-46, 149,
    161, 238
Mason, Nick, 102
mass culture, 29
mass media, 24, 66
Mastelloto, Pat, 198, 269
Matching Mole, 207, 216,
    217
materialism, 133-34
Maximum Rock 'n' Roll
    magazine, 278
Mayall, John, 218
McCartney, Paul, 46-47, 53,
    72, 171, 188, 203
McCormack, Bill, 207
McCulloch, Andy, 198, 218
McDonald, Ian, 157, 182
McDonald and Giles, 151,
    182-83
McLaughlin, John, 75, 79,
    172, 178, 213, 222-23,
    231, 237
McLuhan, Marshall, 65-67,
    288
McShee, Jacqui, 174
Meat Puppets, the, 171
medievalism, 107, 115,
    133-34, 156, 217
Mellotron, 98, 158-159, 160,
    187, 219, 268, 273
Messiaen, Oliver, 40
Mikita, Lisa, 276

Miller, Harry, 187, 198
Miller, Phil, 207, 230
Minear, Kerry, 197, 220
Mingus, Charles, 216
minimalism, 289
Minutemen, the, 250
misogyny, 280
Mitchell, Joni, 177, 192, 234, 238
Mitchell, Mitch, 44, 157
mode of production, 25
modernity, 105-6
Moerlin, Pierre, 221
Mojo magazine, 63, 255, 305
Mommer, Kerri, xvi, 249
Monkman, Francis, 184, 193
Montgomery, Wes, 88
Moody Blues, 17, 44, 49, 84, 162, 165, 174, 178, 192
Moon, Keith, 45, 244
Moran, Gayle, 231
Moraz, Patrick, 229, 232, 233, 240
Mormons, 128, 148
Morris, William, 107-108
Morrisette, Alanis, 25, 63
Morrison, Jim, 178
Morrison, Van, 237
Morse, Steve, 129
Morse, Tim, 252
Mosbo, Thomas, xi
Mouzon, Alphonse, 240
Mozart, Wolfgang Amadeus, 92, 168
Muir, Jamie, 226
multiculturalism, 23

Murdoch, Rupert, 278
Murray, Charles Shaar, 82
music business, 6, 264
Music News Network, 276
music of Yes (Bill Martin), xiv, 6, 12-13, 17, 76, 99, 103, 104, 122, 130, 132-33, 142, 211, 227, 259, 278
MTV, 25, 203, 260, 272, 281, 283
musical form, analysis of, xiii-xiv
"musical ideas," xiv, 119-20, 122, 125, 290-91
musicology, xiii-xiv, 15, 93, 131, 132, 142, 145
musique concrete, 162
Mussorgsky, Modest, 199

narrative, 284-85, 286, 288, 297, 301
National Health, 181, 230, 244
Nektar, 19, 230
neo-progressive trend, 272-73, 274
New Left, the, 135
new wave music, 146, 228, 241, 250, 251
Nice, The, 17, 49-51, 152, 181, 217, 229, 274
Nico, 228
Nirvana, 59
Nixon, Richard, 58
Nugent, Ted, and the Amboy Dukes, 44

Offord, Eddie, 98, 171, 201

Oldfield, Mike, 218, 228, 236

O'List, Davey, 49

Ono, Yoko, 188

Orff, Carl, 40, 89, 113, 114, 181, 196, 300

Orsini, David, 279

Osibisa, 192-93

Ozric Tentacles, 272, 306

Pacific Gas and Electric, 163

"pagan" themes, 37, 211

Paganotti, Bernard, 238

Page, Jimmy, 44

Paice, Ian, 206

Palmer, Carl, 181, 217, 224, 248, 262

Parliament/Funkadelic, 85, 191, 234, 244

Parker, Charlie, 70-71, 131, 147

Parsons, Amanda, 230

"party scene," music and the, 78-79, 178, 249

Passport (band), 236

pastoralism, 105, 106-7, 115, 133, 135, 139, 292

Pastorius, Jaco, 177, 239

Peacocke, Annette, 242

Penderecki, Krzystof, 283

Pentangle, 173-74

Pere Ubu, 244, 302

Perry, Doane, 248

Pert, Morris, 217

Peterson, Oscar, 49

philosophy, xiii, xiv, xvi, 5, 291

Phish, 65, 255-256

Piccone, Paul, 27

Pink Floyd, 17, 44, 50, 80, 102, 111, 119, 132, 133, 162, 165, 174, 178, 183, 192, 211, 215, 234-35, 242, 273, 275

Plato, 68, 115, 195, 292

Pleasant, Henry, 131

poiesis, xv, 55, 56

Polanski, Roman, 207

Police, The (band), 170

"political" interpretations of art, 9-10

Ponty, Jean-Luc, 231

popular culture, 29

"popular music," 24, 27, 28, 39, 42, 56, 63-64, 66, 70, 131-32

"popular avant-garde," concept of, 2, 29, 96, 294

Porcupine Tree, 272

Porter, Cole, 23, 31

postmodern music, 20, 90-91, 235, 242, 280-95, 301

postmodern pastiche, 90-91, 290

Premiata Forneria Marconi (PFM), 19, 84, 155, 168, 210, 223, 275

Presley, Elvis, 36

Preston, Billy, 171

"pretentiousness," 45, 64, 73, 78, 85, 125, 128, 293, 294

Pretty Things, the, 166
Prince, 24, 37, 59
private property, 81
Procul Harem, 83, 162, 174
profundity, in music, 11, 293
Progression magazine, 272, 276, 278
Prokofiev, Sergei, 88
psychedelic rock, psyche-
    delia, 17, 37, 44, 45, 49,
    75-83, 85, 105, 128, 129,
    137, 147, 164, 167, 175,
    178, 180, 199, 200, 221,
    235, 255
Public Foot the Roman, 19, 155
Pugh, Martin, 176
punk rock, punk culture, 58,
    62, 146, 149, 202, 228,
    235, 241, 242, 244, 250,
    257-58, 260, 276, 278,
    281, 284
Pyle, Pip, 196
Pyne, Chris, 50

Quatermass, 181-82, 217, 218
Queen, 216, 234
Quiet Sun, 207, 236, 274

Rabin, Trevor, 263, 264, 303
race, 24, 35, 36, 109, 139
"race mixing," 23, 35
"race music," 24, 94
racism, 23, 35, 141, 280

radical affirmation/radical
    negation, 2, 8, 11, 30, 59,
    62, 79, 116, 117, 120,
    258, 259, 281, 282-83
radical communitarianism,
    9, 13
radical evil, 195
ragtime music, 31, 49
Rand, Ayn, 120, 270-71
Rare Bird, 182, 274
Rare Earth, 163
Ratledge, Mike, 170, 185,
    221, 222
Ravel, Maurice, 199
Reagan, Ronald, 5, 62, 63,
    256, 257, 259, 271
"reconnection," 274, 280,
    295, 298, 303
recording technology, 97-98
redemption, 38, 82, 121, 137,
    148, 149, 211, 254, 279
Reed, Lou, 192
Reeves, Tony, 218
Relf, Keith, 175-76, 275
religion, 12, 31, 132, 133,
    136, 138, 197
Renaissance (band), 115,
    116, 175-76, 194, 207,
    217, 236, 275
rhythm and blues, 23, 31,
    218
rhythm section, transforma-
    tion of, 204-5
Rindfuss, Garry, 214
Robinson, Peter, 217
"Rock & Roll" (Public
    Broadcasting System
    series), 2

rock music critics and criti-
     cism, 30, 59, 62, 63, 67,
     85, 87, 89-90, 131, 139,
     141, 167, 201, 211, 257,
     258-59, 266, 294, 306
Rockwell, John, 85
"role of music in society," xv
Rolling Stones, 43, 50, 103,
     119, 217
romanticism, 82, 88, 90, 91,
     92, 105, 110, 112-15,
     121, 124, 127-28, 133,
     135, 136, 139, 191, 224,
     228, 238, 245, 258, 259,
     270, 292, 294, 296, 304,
     305
Ronstadt, Linda, 242
Rorty, Richard, 252
Rosenthal, Ann, 230
Roxy Music, 206, 216, 219,
     236, 244, 251
Rundgren, Todd, 205, 228
Rush, 120, 239, 244, 261,
     270-72, 294

Sahara (band), 207
sampling, electronic, 26, 90,
     101, 193, 291-92, 293,
     294, 301, 304
Sanders, Pharoah, 173, 241
Santana, 18, 75, 103, 128,
     173, 178, 205, 235
Santana, Carlos, 75, 103,
     235
Sartre, Jean-Paul, 11, 61,
     65, 123, 126, 142, 145,
     146, 161, 164, 254
Satie, Erik, 289-90

Schiller, Friedrich, 136
Schönberg, Arnold, 40, 86,
     88, 92, 113, 114, 117,
     118, 119, 300
Schuller, Gunther, 33, 132
science fiction, 44, 82,
     133-35, 156, 158, 159,
     165, 176, 238
"sci-fi medievalism," 133-35,
     156, 160
Scott, Shirley, 136
Seventh Wave, 229, 236
Sex Pistols, 59, 242, 247,
     250, 259
sexuality, 24, 35
Shakers, the (religious
     community), 127, 148
Shakespeare, William, 207
Shakti (band), 231
Shankar, L., 231
Shapiro, Peter, 43
Shepp, Archie, 2, 179
Shostakovich, Dmitri, 92
Shrieve, Michael, 103, 206
Shulman, Derek, 197
Shulman, Phil, 197
Shulman, Ray, 197
Sibelius, Jean, 40, 49, 88
Silver, Horace, 185
Simon and Garfunkel, 43,
     164
Sinclair, David, 169, 170,
     190, 207, 230
Sinclair, Richard, 169, 170,
     222, 230
Sinfield, Pete, 151, 157, 159,
     185, 188
situationism, 126, 282-83

"sixties," the, 1-2, 9, 30, 34, 37, 58-62, 65, 66, 110, 126, 135, 147, 190, 228, 238, 254, 256, 257, 258, 265, 277
Skidmore, Alan, 50
Slapp Happy, 238
Slick, Grace, 146
Sly and the Family Stone, 3, 164, 244
Small, Christopher, 131, 134
Smith, Jimmy, 136, 172, 224
Smith, Patti, 235, 239
Smyth, Gilli (a.k.a. Shakti Yoni), 196, 221, 240
social theory, xiv, 2, 5, 131, 238
sociology, 13, 14, 131, 137, 141
Soft Machine, 19, 60, 84, 102, 123, 140, 169-71, 172, 181, 182, 185, 192, 216, 218, 221, 222, 275, 293
Solaris (band), 272
Solzhenitsyn, Alexander, 115
song form, 30, 71, 75, 84, 91, 115
South, the (region/culture of U.S.), 31-32, 43, 37, 38, 109, 140
Spall, Lyn, 185
Spector, Phil, 47, 95
Spencer Davis Group, 218
Spin Doctors, 63, 64
Spirit (band), 178, 229
spirituality, 6, 35, 36

Springsteen, Bruce, 24, 143-44, 202
Squire, Chris, 46, 48, 76, 87, 185, 187, 200, 202, 203, 204, 206, 208, 219, 226, 243, 247, 263, 264, 271, 273, 278, 297, 303
Stalin, Joseph, 135
Starr, Ringo, 102-3, 171
Steamhammer, 167, 172, 176
Steely Dan, 18, 171, 215, 227-28, 234, 242
Stewart, Al, 173-74, 216
Stewart, Dave, 181, 242
Stills, Stephen, 158
Stockhausen, Karlheinz, 40, 140, 162, 176, 206, 207
Stravinsky, Igor, 40, 86, 87, 88, 99, 118, 301
Strawbs, the, 175, 179, 192, 230, 236
"stretching out," 72, 74, 78, 83, 91, 98, 128, 167, 180, 255
Stump, Paul, xii, xiii, 20, 122, 196, 203, 271, 299-306
Subject, Esq., 206-7
subjectivity, 204
Summers, Andy, 170
Sun Ra, 86, 88, 90, 160
Sun Treader, 217
Supernatural Fairy Tales, 166, 176, 230, 274-76
Supersister, 274
surrealism, 221
Suzuki, Damo, 207

Sweetwater, 178
Syn, The, 76
Syndicats, The, 76
synthesizers, 26, 98, 183, 201,
    240, 244

Tai Phong, 239
Talking Heads, 242, 244, 251
Tamm, Eric, 232
Tangerine Dream, 228, 234
Tasavallan Presidenti, 230
"taste public," concept of, 14,
    277-80
Taylor, Cecil, 3, 16, 114, 119,
    179, 186, 192
technology, 116, 132, 133, 135,
    147, 201, 291, 293, 304
Tempest (band), 218
Terminator, The (film), 147, 201
Thatcher, Margaret, 5, 256,
    259, 271
Them (band), 236
Third Ear Band, 206-7
"Third Stream" music, 33, 132
Third World, the, 96, 124
Thomas, David, 302
Thomas, Leon, 173
Thompson, E. P., 135, 145, 161
timbre, 235, 242, 268, 283, 284
Tippett, Keith, 172, 186, 192,
    198, 216, 219
Tolkein, J. R., 190
Tolstoy, Leo, 233
Tomorrow, 76, 80, 81-82, 84,
    166, 167
Toop, David, 282, 283, 294
Townshend, Pete, 46, 144,
    146, 215

trance music, 290, 291
Traffic, 18, 75, 178-79, 192
Triumvirat, 217

U2, 252, 280, 285
U.K. (band), 244
"underground" music and sen-
    sibility, 34, 36, 39, 48, 58,
    276, 300
United States of America, The
    (band), 162
urban life, urbanism, 105, 115,
    158, 189, 292
Urgency, 256-57, 258
Uriah Heep, 206
Uriel, 181
utopian ideal/utopian themes,
    xvi, 8, 9, 13, 30, 40, 44,
    59, 62, 66, 79, 82, 83, 105,
    117, 119, 121, 124, 125,
    127, 137, 147, 148, 149,
    160, 171, 173, 178, 183,
    189, 191, 203, 228, 238,
    241, 258, 279, 282, 294,
    296

Van der Graaf Generator,
    183-84, 193-96, 207, 229,
    236, 239
Van Leer, Thijs, 208
Vander, Christian, 196, 231,
    237-38
Vangelis, 206
Varese, Edgard, 162
Velvet Underground, the, 77,
    229, 250, 305
verticality, in music, 90,
    290, 292

Vietnam War, 146-47, 164, 200, 265

virtuoso musicianship, 44, 87, 89, 100-3, 121, 136, 228, 241, 258, 304

Vaughan Williams, Ralph, 112, 128

Vaughn, Stevie Ray, 101

Vivaldi, Antonio, 219

Voivod, 157

Voodoo, 37

Wagner, Richard, 91, 92, 104, 282, 288

Wakeman, Rick, 135, 136, 179, 201, 216, 229, 232, 243, 247, 264, 298, 303

Walker, Greg, 272

Walker, Junior, 157

Wallace, Ian, 167, 198, 209, 219

War (band), 41, 192, 205, 216

Warriors, the, 167

Watergate scandal, 228

Waters, Muddy, 95

Watson, Ben, 123-127

Watt, James, 63

Watts, Alan, 79

Way, Daryl, 184, 193

Weather Report, 192, 205, 213, 216, 239

Webern, Anton von, 40, 92

Weil, Kurt, 238

Weinberg, Max, 101

Weinstein, Deena, 57

Welch, Chris, 45

West, Keith, 167

Wetton, John, 48, 111, 187, 219, 226, 244, 262, 272

Wexler, Jerry, 94-95, 97

Wheeler, Kenny, 50

White, Alan, 206, 233, 243, 247, 263, 273, 297, 303

White, Kieran, 172

White Willow, 272

Whitman, Walt, 127, 148

Who, The, 17, 45, 46, 48, 63, 64, 88, 143, 144, 174, 177, 215, 230, 234, 244, 250

Wigwam, 230, 274

Wilde Flowers, the, 169-70

Wilder, Webb, 32

Williams, Paul, 218

Williams, Raymond, 108-9, 120, 135, 145, 161

Williams, Tony (and Lifetime), 172

Wilson, Brian, 47, 53, 81

Winwood, Steve, 164, 182, 206, 218, 236

Wire, The (magazine), xi, 86, 89, 93, 112, 116-17, 122, 253, 292, 299, 305

Wishbone Ash, 216, 275

Wittgenstein, Ludwig, 118

Wolf, Hugo, 210

Wollheim, Richard, 57

Wonder, Stevie, 41, 205, 216, 239

Wordsworth, William, 136

world disclosure, xv, 55, 57

world music, 33, 41, 240, 295-96

Wright, Richard, 165

Wyatt, Robert, 11, 102, 112,
　169, 170, 182, 207, 221,
　229, 230, 236

Wyman, Bill, 217

Yamash'ta, Stomu, 206, 216

Yardbirds, the, 175

Yes, xi, xiv, xvi, 4, 6, 8, 18, 19,
　20, 36, 37, 40, 45, 49, 60,
　74, 76, 84, 88-89, 94, 95, 97,
　104, 111, 116, 119, 120-21,
　125, 128, 130, 132, 133,
　136, 138, 142, 147, 151,
　152-53, 155, 156, 158, 160,
　167, 169, 174-75, 184, 186,
　187, 191, 194-96, 199-200,
　201-5, 206, 208, 210, 211,

213, 214, 216, 222, 223,
225, 229, 230, 232-33, 234,
235, 236, 239, 240, 243,
244, 247, 249, 252, 253,
259, 261, 262-65, 266, 267,
269, 270, 272, 273, 274,
275, 279, 280, 293, 294,
296, 297-98, 300, 301, 302,
303, 305

"YesPistols question, the," 11

Young, Larry, 172

Young, Rob, 285-86

Zappa, Frank, 70, 86, 103,
　122-27, 136, 162, 163, 178,
　192, 234

Zauber, 277

Zombies, the, 166